Language, Symbolism, and Politics

Language, Symbolism, and Politics

EDITED BY
Richard M. Merelman

Taylor & Francis Group

LONDON AND NEW YORK

First published 1992 by Westview Press, Inc.

Published 2018 by Routledge
52 Vanderbilt Avenue, New York, NY 10017
2 Park Square, Milton Park, Abingdon, Oxon OX14 4RN

Routledge is an imprint of the Taylor & Francis Group, an informa business

Copyright © 1992 Taylor & Francis

All rights reserved. No part of this book may be reprinted or reproduced or utilised in any form or by any electronic, mechanical, or other means, now known or hereafter invented, including photocopying and recording, or in any information storage or retrieval system, without permission in writing from the publishers.

Notice:
Product or corporate names may be trademarks or registered trademarks, and are used only for identification and explanation without intent to infringe.

Library of Congress Cataloging-in-Publication Data
Merelman, Richard M., 1938–
  Language, symbolism, and politics / Richard M. Merelman.
    p. cm.
  ISBN 0-8133-8581-4
  1. Political psychology. 2. Symbolism in politics.
  3. Communication—Political aspects. 4. Rhetoric—Political aspects. I. Title.
JA74.5.M47 1992
320'.01'9—dc20   92-27242
                                                                      CIP

ISBN 13: 978-0-367-01095-9 (hbk)
ISBN 13: 978-0-367-16082-1 (pbk)

Contents

Preface vii

    Introduction, *Richard M. Merelman* 1

PART ONE
Political Interests and Political Symbolism

1   The Political Language of the Nonprofit Sector,
    Robert R. Alford 17

2   The Political Uses of Political Issues, *Benjamin Ginsberg* 51

3   Public and Private Political Realities and
    the Privatization Movement, *David J. Olson* 67

PART TWO
Elections and Symbolism

4   Constructing Explanations for Election Results:
    When 'The Voters Have Spoken,' Who Decides
    What They Said? *Marjorie Randon Hershey* 85

5   The Postmodern Election, *W. Lance Bennett* 123

PART THREE
Policy Implementation, Elite Control, and Political Symbolism

6   Law at the Margins: The Symbolic Power of
    Professional Discourse, *Kristin Bumiller* 151

7   The Neutered Mother, *Martha Albertson Fineman* 169

8   Museums, Zoos, and Ecology:
    Animal Displays on Display, *Michael Lipsky* 185

PART FOUR
Culture and Political Domination

9 False-Consciousness, or Laying It on Thick, *James Scott*   209

10 Challenge and Resistance:
Two Cases of Cultural Conflict in the United States,
Richard M. Merelman   247

PART FIVE
Symbolic Representation and Power

11 Language and Power:
The Spaces of Critical Interpretation, *Michael J. Shapiro*   269

12 Representation and the Silences of Politics, *Anne Norton*   289

Afterword, Murray Edelman   305
About the Contributors   309
About the Book   311

Preface

The papers in this volume were originally presented to a Conference on Language, Symbolism, and Politics held at the University of Wisconsin, March 30–31, 1990, in honor of Professor Murray Edelman. My thanks go to the Anonymous Fund of the University of Wisconsin for supporting the conference. I should also like to express my gratitude to Robert E. Lane, Michael Rogin, John Fiske, Joel Rogers, Diane Rubenstein, Ann Stoler, Timothy Cook, Lee Hansen, and David Trubek for their significant contributions at the conference.

Thanks also go to the Brittingham Fund of the University of Wisconsin for underwriting costs associated with the publication of this volume. Kristin Novotny of the University of Wisconsin labored heroically in the final editing of this collection. Kristin deserves much praise for her dedication, diligence, and discernment. Thanks also to Diane Morauske for efficient and careful preparation of the final copy and to Jennifer Knerr of Westview for her receptivity to the project. The unique combination of scholarship and personal example which is Murray Edelman's gift to his admirers motivated this volume; the volume merely returns the favor in a way which allows everyone interested in politics, language, and symbolism to partake generously.

Richard M. Merelman
Madison, Wisconsin

Introduction
Richard M. Merelman

The essays in this collection analyze some of the multiple roles of symbolism and language in political life. This introduction outlines a few major themes in these essays, chiefly by linking the collection as a whole to the work of Murray Edelman, the person for whom these essays, in conference form, were prepared. First, I will set forth major themes in Edelman's work that emerge in the volume. I will then briefly describe each essay, linking it to Edelman's insights. I will conclude by suggesting some unique contributions to the analysis of political language and symbolism which this volume offers.

Edelman on Symbolism, Language, and Politics

In his seminal *The Symbolic Uses of Politics* (1964) Edelman argued that political cognition is not a representation of reality, but a variable and selective construction of non-referential symbols. Edelman claimed that, "For most men most of the time politics is a series of pictures in the mind, placed there by television news, newspapers, magazines and discussions" (p. 5). Moreover, because of the absence of personal contact with political events, people see politics as "... a passing parade of abstract symbols" (p. 5). The gap between experience and perception causes the relationship between political symbolism and language, on the one hand, and political events, on the other, always to be problematic.

But the absence of personal contact with political events is not the only thing that destroys the referential qualities of political language and symbols. In fact, even political actors themselves are divorced from a stable, underlying, universally comprehensible political reality. Edelman argues that political events are so complex and ambiguous that they remain opaque even to many of those intimately involved with them. Often, too, political actors lack stable values or ideologies which would afford them a clear interpretation of events. In yet other cases political actors are *overly* committed to particular causes or interests, so much so that they engage in selective perception. For these reasons, political actors can arrive at no spontaneous consensus about the meaning of any particular political event. Whatever consensus does emerge, therefore, is artificially created, misleading, and inaccurate.

It is evident that this approach to political meaning is at variance with most rational choice and empirical social science theories. These theories assume that revealed or stated purposes, norms, preferences, and motives in politics are stable, knowable precursors to the choices political actors make. By contrast, Edelman's perspective suggests that motives, goals, purposes, and values are an often evanescent selection from an equally plausible range of unchosen alternatives. It follows that social science should attempt to understand the processes which shape perceptions, rather than simply take perceptions as a given. Indeed, Edelman contends that social scientists who concentrate on normative or empirical analyses in their conventional forms serve to perpetuate the political *status quo*, rather than to reveal "reality," much less liberate people from the tyranny of the "taken for granted."

Thus, for Edelman political language and symbolism is neither detached from, nor neutral about, political events. Instead, both language and symbolism help to *constitute* political reality. Disputing Marxist frameworks, which artificially separate material "base" from ideological "superstructure," and early logical positivist frameworks, which dismiss political language as trivial "mindstuff," Edelman views political ideologies, language and symbolism as *performatives*, that is, political actions in themselves. Thus, only a social science attuned to the analysis of language and symbolism—a social science informed by linguistics, semiotics, literary criticism, narrative theory, and social psychology—can begin to grasp political reality.

If, as Edelman argues, the language of politics is inherently ambiguous and misleading, then theories of politics which do not appreciate or capture this fact become one more aspect, not a "neutral description," of the political situation itself. Thus, for example, an untenable Marxist distinction between economic base and ideological superstructure reifies politics and deludes observers. Likewise, an untenable positivist distinction between facts and values lures observers into a fruitless search for an objective, timeless, universal "science of politics." Worse yet, these false distinctions deceive not only social scientists but also the general public, who read and believe these "experts."

The approach to language and symbolism advanced by Edelman also constitutes a significant attack on liberalism, the political philosophy which underlies American democracy. Above all, American liberalism purports to be a theory of public control over political elites. Liberals believe that elections, interest group pressure, legislative access, legal procedures, and institutional rivalries assist the public in controlling its leaders. This "bottom-up" theory of politics presupposes that the public acts on its own values; that citizens are more or less equals in their influence on elites; and that elites accept the policy consensus which the public develops.

Edelman disputes these contentions. He argues that values are not the durable intellectual "property" of individual citizens; indeed, few citizens are sufficiently and self-consciously "in touch" with political events to develop deep values. Instead, events, symbols, ambiguous language, and material interests form the public's values; values never independently influence events. Thus, the public simply cannot control its political leaders. Rather, political elites employ their power to create symbolic meanings which limit the range of political discourse, manipulate public debate, and manufacture whatever consensus ultimately emerges.

Liberalism also fails because it perceives political equality to be an objective phenomenon rather than a malleable symbol. Consider, for example, the relationship of political participation to equality. Like all political processes, participation is simultaneously an action and a symbol. As an action, widespread public participation may be more or less effective in equalizing the distribution of policy benefits. But as a symbol, widespread participation may be more or less effective in shaping perceptions, cognitions, and values. The problem is that participation is far more egalitarian in distributing symbolic benefits than in distributing material benefits. As Edelman puts it:

> Where bargaining resources are equal, participation produces real influence on who gets what. When they are strikingly unequal, as is almost always the case, participation becomes a *symbol* of influence that encourages quiescence, rather than substantive gains, for the powerless. (*Political Language: Words That Succeed and Policies That Fail*, 1977, p. 121.)

Finally, liberal political theory overestimates the extent to which the public can, through debate and pressure, control its leaders. For example, in most liberal-derived pluralist theories of politics, organization serves as the key to the political success of the public. In the form of interest groups organization affords citizens access to policy-makers; in the form of labor unions organization provides workers a stable balance against employers; in the form of political parties organization permits voters to secure the election of candidates who will respond to public demands. Most important, in all its forms organization translates the diffuse discontents of the disinherited into coherent demands to which those in power must respond appropriately.

In *Politics as Symbolic Action* (1971), Edelman disputes the pluralist conventional wisdom about organization. Indeed, he reverses the pluralist argument. To Edelman, even organizations which are intended to promote resistance to authority do not represent the achievement of success for the downtrodden, but rather the first step towards failure. Effective mass protest, Edelman argues, is almost always disorganized and leaderless; in fact, its very unpredictability is what gives mass protest its great force. As he puts it, "It is as though the absence of a well-organized resistance movement keeps the elite unaware of the seriousness of the threat it faces and also makes it impossible to negotiate a viable pattern of cooptation and concession that will maintain tensions at a non-explosive level" (29). Thus, without spontaneous explosion, protest cannot really succeed.

If *disorganization* escalates protest, leadership and organization *ritualize* and defuse protest. Leaders and organizations routinize the relationship between political elites and protestors, paving the way for negotiation, bargaining, and compromise. Although routines are psychologically reassuring and symbolize apparent success to the protestors, this perception of success is erroneous, for, like all symbols, ritualized negotiation and bargaining incorporate, yet conceal, the very conflicts of interest and inequalities which stimulated protest in the first place. Moreover, ritualization suggests there exists an "objective standard of equity rather than relative bargaining resources" (p. 22), a perception which also deescalates protest. Once leadership and organization appear, cooptation and containment of demands occurs, perpetuating inequalities of power and status. Organization thus marginalizes protest and reproduces inequalities.

Organization and leadership do not eradicate the perception of all political conflicts, however. Indeed, because elites require a pretext for retaining power, they regularly construe each other as bitter enemies in order to secure public support and to deflect critical scrutiny by constituents and followers. The resulting elite-manipulated conflict, of course, serves only to retain the existing structure of power, as widely diffused public grievances against leaders are either ignored or denounced as "subversive" to the pursuit of the "real" conflict against the external enemy.

Edelman also argues that even when policies purportedly favorable to masses do emerge from the policy-making process, they fail to be implemented. Instead bureaucracies, courts, and social service agencies employ rhetoric to protect the existing distribution of power.

Edelman analyzes the process of policy implementation most completely in *Political Language: Words That Succeed and Policies That Fail* (1977). Reflecting upon the domestic reform efforts of Democratic administrations from Kennedy to Carter, Edelman observes a massive gap between promise and performance. The promises consist of the "words that succeed;" the performance, however, lies in the "policies that fail."

Edelman pays particularly close attention not to predictably bureaucratic, ideologically conservative agencies, such as the Department of Defense or the Department of Agriculture, but to reformist agencies full of such "helping professionals" as social workers, doctors, psychiatrists, and school psychologists, who supposedly devote themselves to empowering the needy.

Edelman argues that these professional reformers actually reproduce the structures of domination they profess to transform. And since this is true for professed supporters of reform, it is true *a fortiori* for all government agencies.

The power of the helping professions to reinforce the status quo is suggested by the very term "helping profession." "Helping" construes the powerless as deeply flawed, unable to repair their lives without professional assistance. The relationship between the "helper" and the "client" is thus unequal from the outset; however, as opposed to more explicitly conflictive relationships, the weaker party in this case is assumed to be irresponsible and incapable of understanding his or her "true" interest. For example, while members of a labor union lack only power *vis a vis* employers, welfare clients are presumed incapable of discerning and articulating their own best interests. They are, therefore, rendered doubly disabled; they lack both power and self-worth.

If the term "help" is simply a symbolic reinforcement of domination, so also is the concept of "profession." Professionals enjoy a license to categorize clients in ways which buttress professional prerogatives, and disable clients. As Edelman puts it, "Categorization . . . is a political tool, establishing status and power hierarchies," (*Political Language*, p. 62). Professionals disempower clients when they categorize behavior which, in other contexts, might pass unremarked, as being somehow deficient, deviant, or dangerous. Once the professional classification takes hold, the professionals, who have, after all, identified the "deviance," become the only ones who possess the expertise to correct the problem. Thus, what might otherwise be challenged as questionable political control over ordinary behavior becomes transformed into unquestioned, legitimate "therapeutic assistance" to "cure" the "exceptional," "dangerous," and "pathological."

As we can see, Edelman argues that in the struggle over the creation of politically decisive meanings, elites generally have the advantage over the general public. He describes elite power manifesting itself through a wide array of symbol-generating mechanisms: the marginalizing of domestic dissent through the creation of external enemies; the invention and application of therapeutic language; bureaucratic and legal cooptation; the creation of myths and rituals which encourage quiescence; the manipulation of space and architectural forms in order to evoke awe for power; and the utilization of the mass media in order to disseminate elite-favoring images.

Is there no way to escape this labyrinth of language and symbolism which so often reproduces economic, social, and political inequalities? Here again Edelman's position differs from that of positivist or Marxist social science, both of which turn to science as a source of liberation. Marxists and positivists are heirs to an Enlightenment faith that a natural science of society can reveal the social laws of progress. Edelman rejects this view, claiming that logic and history demonstrate the weakness of Marxism and positivism. Though each theory has asserted its scientific superiority, neither has delivered on its promises of scientific social progress.

An alternative model must therefore be sought if social science is to aid the disadvantaged. Edelman proposes art, rather than science, as the foundation for a new, liberating political theory. As he puts it:

> Art helps counter banal political forms and so can be a liberating form of political expression. It becomes that when it estranges people from bemusement with facts, conventional assumptions, and conventional language so that they see their inherent contradictions and recognize alternative potentialities. (*Constructing the Political Spectacle*, 1988, p. 126.)

But not all forms of art do in fact draw people away from convention and cause them to see their world anew. Edelman observes that much popular culture is itself banal. Still, as at least a potentially imaginative symbolic system, art can create novel views of politics. Thus, a central issue in several of the essays to which I now turn is whether symbolism and language in their multifarious artistic manifestations can convert the political situation from one of elite control into one of group conflict, and thus liberate politics from the nether world Edelman has so powerfully analyzed.

The Essays

The first three essays in this collection explore Edelman's arguments about the relations between interests, organization, and symbolism. Of the three, Robert Alford's essay follows Edelman's argument most closely. Alford argues that the so-called "nonprofit" sector of the economy is a linguistic mystification. This is because most nonprofit organizations are in varying degrees dependent on the state and capital for support. They are, therefore, variously undemocratic and acquisitive. But as symbols, "nonprofit" organizations reduce popular discontent about persistent inequalities within the public and private sectors, while leaving the structure of interests in these governing sectors of American society undisturbed. The nonprofit symbol is "[D]emocratic rhetoric" (p. 23) which discourages citizens from effectively analyzing the material functions of nonprofits.

Alford believes that academic treatments of nonprofits have somewhat contributed to this misunderstanding. Thus, in his view of academic research he also follows Edelman. Alford ponders why it is that "comprehensive reviews of the nonprofit literature simultaneously accept the legal distinctions between 'public,' 'private,' and 'nonprofit' . . . , but question the 'independent,' 'intermediate,' 'voluntary,' and 'third sector' character of NPO's" (p. 21). Alford avoids stating an exact equivalence between organizational interest and organizational ideology, but he does demystify the argument that non-profit organizations automatically advance democracy.

David Olson also takes up the argument that symbolism obscures the institutional complexities and inequalities of power in modern polities. His target is liberalism, which, he argues, mystifies the relationship between public and private institutions. Liberalism portrays a stark separation between public and private. In reality, however, there are six dimensions which distinguish between public and private institutions; virtually all institutions are therefore part public, part private.

The symbolic over-simplification which liberalism promotes permits institutional restructuring to support persistent economic and political inequalities. For example, the move towards privatizing public services becomes a pure question of economic "efficiency," rather than a political decision. In reality, however, privatization is less an efficient means of providing services than it is a covert means of reducing public responsibilities and weakening forces of power redistribution. Privatization succeeds because liberalism paints it symbolically as being far more decisive and consequential than it actually is. While symbolism changes, the unequal distribution of power changes little, and, if at all, for the worse.

While Alford and Olson highlight the role of rhetoric in masking established economic and political interests, Benjamin Ginsberg argues that language and symbolism may also promote considerable political innovation. Ginsberg analyzes the neo-conservative ideology of the post-1980 Republican party. In terms reminiscent of Olson, he argues that, under the guise of serving the public good, this rhetoric is actually meant to "undermine the social service and regulatory agencies in which the Democrats are entrenched" (p. 52).

Ginsberg claims that the tax policies, domestic spending cuts, and deregulation sponsored by Presidents Reagan and Bush have placed severe strains upon the Democratic coalition. As a result, groups formerly in this coalition have drifted into destructive conflict against one another. For example, in newly deregulated industries labor has turned viciously against management, propelling many businesses into the Republican camp. Likewise, the low tax policies of Republicans have encouraged middle class voters to abandon the Democrats. Once, the middle class saw themselves as the beneficiaries of government programs (a self-image favorable to Democrats); now, however, the middle class sees itself as beleaguered taxpayers (a self-image which favors Republicans). "[L]abor unions, political machines and social services agencies" (p. 59) have similarly disengaged themselves from their previous adherence to the Democratic party. Finally, conservative religious and patriotic rhetoric has dislodged urban ethnics and Southerners from the Democratic coalition.

Ginsberg conceptualizes the interest-ideology connection somewhat more flexibly than does Edelman. In Ginsberg's view, politicians are relatively free to construct new policies and rhetorical appeals which disrupt longstanding interest-based coalitions. Moreover, novel symbolism, such as the "right to life," may combine with traditional symbols, such as the flag, to create new political coalitions. Finally, Ginsberg believes that symbolic appeals are never enough to entrench governing coalitions. New political elites must establish their own political institutions if they are to consolidate their power. Thus, for Ginsberg, the connections among interests, symbols, policies and political institutions are always malleable. However, Ginsberg agrees with Edelman, Alford, and Olson that policy-makers create new symbols in order to mystify and legitimize otherwise problematic political actions.

The next two essays in this collection—those by Marjorie Hershey and Lance Bennett—explore Edelman's claim that articulating public demands through elections does not insure public control over the political process. To investigate this proposition Hershey and Bennett focus upon the modern Presidential election.

Hershey demonstrates that the media quickly constructed a quite dubious explanation for the electoral "mandate" President Reagan claimed in 1984. Hershey shows that there is no evidence the voters intended such a mandate; instead, journalists selected from a host of plausible interpretations a favored few barely two weeks later. These explanations traced the election outcome to a weakened Democratic party and to the public's supposed rejection of Walter Mondale's new tax pledge.

Two aspects of Hershey's findings particularly support Edelman's argument. First, Hershey shows that the explanations the newspapers constructed derived not from an extensive analysis of voter views, but rather from the dynamics of journalistic practice. Second, once constructed, newspaper explanations created their own self-fulfilling political reality. Not only did the newspapers conclude that Reagan's no-tax pledge helped win him the election, but they also proclaimed that no sensible Presidential aspirant would propose raising taxes in the near future. Hershey suggests that this "truth" shaped Bush's "read my lips" pledge in 1988. Hershey concludes that the inherent ambiguity of election results permits political elites and the media always to construct explanations which serve their own interests, but which do not necessarily serve the general public.

Lance Bennett agrees with Hershey and Edelman that the construction of electoral reality is inherently problematic. Unlike Hershey, however, he attributes this fact less to the inherent ambiguity surrounding voter intentions than to political elites and media characteristics. He focuses on the way political elites and the media manipulate public perceptions, a basic theme in Edelman's analysis.

To Bennett the 1988 Presidential election was a watershed in American history; 1988 was the first election in which the candidates actually admitted that the campaign itself was primarily a media event. Hence, Bennett's term "the postmodern election." In 1988 politicians acknowledged that television was no longer simply an *instrument* of political communication, but was instead the prime determinant of political messages. Two conspicuous examples Bennett cites are the truncating of political messages into telegenic "sound bites" and the self-referential displacement of television coverage from actual political issues to the campaign process, including media coverage, as a media event. As he puts it, "The media reflected on their own role as never before . . . The media couldn't get out of their own loop" (p. 135).

Bennett offers several explanations for the new "telerhetoric." These include increasing candidate dependence upon small numbers of wealthy contributors; a desire on the part of campaign managers to keep inquisitive journalists at bay; and the rise of marketing experts as campaign consultants. Together these processes "impose(s) a substantial limit on what candidates say to voters, creating, in turn, important limits on the quality of our most important democratic experience" (p. 144). If Bennett is correct, it is not surprising that citizen interest in politics should be in decline, a development which helps insulate political elites from pressures to redistribute political power equitably. Thus, the rise of "telerhetoric" supports Edelman's skepticism about the limited power of citizens in liberal democracies.

In the third section of this collection, Kristin Bumiller, Martha Fineman, and Michael Lipsky ponder Edelman's analysis of legal policy, elite control, and symbolism. Significantly, the three essays focus on apparently progressive forms of public policy and innovative forms of implementation. In so doing, they explore Edelman's contention that even those public institutions supposedly most devoted to fairness, equality, enlightenment, and social change produce significant inequalities which often crowd out democratic outcomes.

Fineman and Bumiller target the legal system and the helping professions, structures *par excellence* through which liberal democracy strives towards fairness, impartiality, and redress of grievances for the disadvantaged. Bumiller's essay explores the protest/escalation/ritualization/bureaucratization policy cycle proposed by Edelman. Bumiller argues that as an insurgent social force the feminist movement created grass-roots self-help organizations, such as shelters for battered women. These shelters not only provided protection for their clients, but also raised women's consciousness about male domination. Thus, they helped to escalate protest against existing gender-based structures of power.

Bumiller contends that the shelter movement constituted a populist threat to the helping professions, especially to social workers. After all, the social work profession relies for its power upon its claimed expertise in treating victims of family violence. Social workers, therefore, could hardly welcome the non-professionals of the shelter movement, whose demonstrated success with battered women disputed these claims of expertise. To protect themselves, social service professionals created a new self-justifying organizational theory which claimed that shelters for battered women are not useful therapeutic institutions in themselves, but are only ports of entry to "social service bureaucracies," where battered women could receive superior professional help. In this way, social workers attempted to coopt the shelter movement rhetorically.

Bumiller also argues that the social work profession requires a regular supply of victims; therefore, its preferred forms of treatment place the responsibility for domestic violence upon victims—in this case, battered women—rather than upon real perpetrators, violent men. The social work bureaucracy also attempts to reconstitute the batterer's family—the crucible which spawned the violence originally. Social workers thus force battered women back into a dangerous situation, telling them to accept their traditional identities as wives and mothers, and to direct their energies towards developing a "healthy" relationship with their husbands or boyfriends. Most important, because social work professionals continue to pretend to a unique expertise about "the battered woman," the battered woman herself is silenced. Finally, the legal system endorses and enforces the social work ideology; in so doing, it helps to disempower an insurgent movement. The ultimate beneficiaries of this process are males, who retain their position of domination.

For her part, Martha Fineman considers a flawed legal reform—no-fault divorce. Fineman contends that liberal feminists—leaders in family law and no-fault divorce reform—have excluded the category "mother" from legal discourse about gender relations and the family. As a result, family law, including divorce law, now relies exclusively on the sexual bond to define the family. The unique mother-child family *relationship* thus fades from legal view. True, the law recognizes "mother-headed families," but these it sees as incomplete, undesirable, and potentially pathological.

Fineman argues that, whatever its virtues, the no-fault divorce reforms of the 1970's created an unholy alliance between liberal feminists and father's rights advocates, both of whom, for very different reasons, were united in opposition to motherhood. Under the new no-fault rhetoric mothers must now compete as legal equals *vis a vis* men in the workforce, an unreasonable expectation given the demands of motherhood, the prevalence of mother's custody of minor children, and the persistence of gender discrimination in education and employment. Thus, family legal reform penalizes mothers as a group.

The problem stems mainly from the fact that liberal feminists—the chief movers of reform—have treated all women alike. They see women as undifferentiated individuals competing for economic and political power. They have thus "neutered" mother in pursuing liberalism's ideal of gender neutrality, putting mothers in a condition of severe economic disadvantage.

It is ironic that a reform sincerely intended to liberate women should instead have created a new form of female disability. Yet, as Fineman observes, "In a world in which gender is more than semantics, feminist legal theory *cannot* be gender-neutral, nor can it have as its goal equality, in the traditional, formal legal sense of the word" (p. 180). Fineman concludes that the liberal language of equal opportunity creates legal reforms which perpetuate rather than remove gender inequalities.

Finally, Michael Lipsky argues that oft-overlooked public agencies—in this case museums and zoos—". . . affect the way people locate their place in the society and understand their relations to others..." (p. 192). Museums and zoos are complex public institutions torn between competing forces. Though meant to attract the general public, they must often charge fees to survive. Though meant to entertain, they must also instruct. And increasingly they must reach out to an ethnically and racially diverse society, although in origin museums in particular reflected the interests and tastes of the rich.

Not surprisingly, these conflicting forces influence the actual character of museum and zoo displays. On the one hand, recent display policies are clearly progressive; these policies encourage ecological awareness rather than celebrate domination of nature. On the other hand, museums have also become mechanically didactic, discouraging imagination and curiosity. In addition, zoos struggle to resolve the contradiction between holding animals captive and promoting respect for animals in their natural habitats. Therefore, even the most benign zoos and museums reinforce elite power.

The next two essays in this collection—those by James Scott, and Richard Merelman—constitute a meditation on Edelman's propositions about language, culture, art and elite domination. James Scott's analysis of Gramsci's concept of cultural hegemony disputes Edelman's arguments about symbolic domination. After laying out two versions of hegemonic theory, Scott attacks both approaches. He claims that the theory of cultural hegemony does not account for group conflict, and is also historically incomplete. Not only have subordinate groups often asserted themselves culturally, but they have also used dominant group culture to advance their own political interests.

Scott argues that subordinate groups rarely accept ideological domination by their oppressors. To the contrary, the ideological formulae dominant groups create actually permit subordinates to respond effectively in their own behalf. Subordinates also construct their own ideologies of resistance, non-cooperation, protest, and revolt. While subordinate groups rarely mount active group resistance, their quiescence may be attributed to political, economic, and strategic choices, not to ideological domination. Finally, Scott observes that, because dominant groups have written history in their own "official transcript," social scientists have given greater weight to theories of hegemony than the real historical facts warrant.

Scott explores the way some subordinate groups have used the "official transcript" to promote insurgency. Normally subordinates cunningly conceal their cynicism about and hatred of their superiors. But subordinates are occasionally able to interpret dominant group ideological formulae to their own advantage. In so doing, subordinates launch sometimes oblique, sometimes direct attacks upon the dominant ideology. Although Scott agrees that such attacks always proceed from positions of structural weakness, on balance his arguments are more optimistic about subordinate resistance than are Edelman's.

Merelman's contribution complements Scott's critique of Edelman's work. Merelman argues that American blacks—a subordinated racial group—have been able in recent years to launch a number of cultural challenges against white dominants. He analyzes two such challenges: the Martin Luther King, Jr. Holiday—a symbolic celebration of black achievements—and the early films of Spike Lee, which provide white Americans a uniquely challenging subordinate interpretation of race relations in the United States. Merelman argues that American pluralist politics in the case of the King holiday and the market-driven demand for entertainment in the case of Lee's films regularly promote subordinate cultural challenge to dominants. Thus, Merelman partly dissents from Edelman's arguments about the hegemony of dominant group culture in modern societies.

At the same time, the two cases Merelman analyzes reveal certain limitations in subordinate cultural challenge. The King celebration venerates such traditional American values as individualism, and thereby eschews group conflict as a motif. Also, Lee's films are formally quite traditional, a fact which blunts their political message. Moreover, even the films' content is sometimes double-edged and politically ambiguous, occasionally derogating subordinates. Despite these limitations, however, Merelman concludes that cultural challenges to dominant group power are widely dispersed throughout American popular culture, creating a single ensemble capable over time of assisting political change.

The final two essays in this collection—by Michael Shapiro and Anne Norton—suggest new forms of social analysis to replace the positivist and Marxist approaches Edelman attacks. Michael Shapiro turns to the work of Michel Foucault for inspiration. He argues that Foucault's genealogical approach reveals that all "systems of intelligibility" are "... false arrests ... the arbitrary fixings of the momentary results of struggles between contending forces, struggles that could have produced other possible systems of intelligibility and the orders they support" (p. 270). Genealogy reconstructs the history of institutions and social philosophies in order to reveal structures of power which obscure certain phenomena and exaggerate others.

In order to minimize these obfuscatory tendencies, Shapiro directs our attention to the spatial dimension of social institutions and philosophies. All systems of order, he argues, situate agents within specific spatial parameters. These parameters subtly constrain interpretation and reinforce inequalities. For example, after the zenith of Greek tragedy theater became increasingly private; therefore, theater is now much less capable of energizing democratic action than it was at its Greek origins. Moreover, by accepting this privatization, drama critics have enlisted in an elitist defense of the very inequalities which promote privatism. Thus, the "space" of dramatic representation has come to reproduce elite power.

Shapiro attacks both liberalism and critical theory for their attempts to construct self-contained spaces for the conduct of unrestricted political conversations. Persisting in this fruitless search prevents language and art from accomplishing the liberating project Edelman envisages. As an escape from spatial enclosures, Shapiro recommends the practice of *writing*. Writing, he claims, exposes the spatial dimension, unmasking the hidden face of power.

Anne Norton disputes Shapiro's faith in writing. Norton claims that "writing ... is cast in theory and practice, in popular culture and the academy, as the medium of external domination" (p. 297). Contrary to Shapiro, Norton argues that writing and speech subordinate the liberating possibilities of politics. To Norton, liberal political theory errs in placing so much faith in speech and the written word; both, she claims, estrange the subject from the word. Reading "the silent texts of speech," however, makes way "for those who had been silenced as well" (p. 301).

According to Norton, contemporary political theory has ignored the way written language, speech, and, especially, visual imagery actually operate. Echoing Edelman, Norton calls upon social scientists to denounce the dominating effects of the word and the image, and to abandon the pretense of ethical neutrality regarding these symbols' effects. Norton thus ends this collection on an appropriately normative note, while leaving unresolved the problem of locating the best form of representation with which to contest the systems of domination Edelman describes.

Conclusion

Though topically diverse, the essays in this collection all draw inspiration from Murray Edelman's work. But these papers are not slaves to Edelman's ideas. Instead, they debate, extend, and modify Edelman. In so doing, they draw upon structuralism, deconstruction, textual analysis, post-structuralism, critical theory, and neo-Marxism—approaches which sometimes go beyond Edelman's work. More important, they use Edelman's work to analyze major issues of political organization, political symbolism, elections, public policy, political culture, and political philosophy. That so many important political topics can be tied together with the help of Edelman's analysis of language and symbolism is not only a tribute to Edelman himself, but also amply testifies to the central place of language and symbolism in politics.

PART ONE

Political Interests and Political Symbolism

1

The Political Language of the Nonprofit Sector[1]

Robert R. Alford

Murray Edelman has pursued a single major theme through several books: the way political language is used to mystify ordinary people about the actual workings of our political economy, and how the rhetoric of political language contradicts the reality of who benefits. Edelman's writings are eloquent testimony to a continuing tradition of quiet debunking of the celebration of American democracy.[2]

My argument is based upon a pervasive perspective in Edelman's work, which is developed most explicitly in his 1988 book: *Constructing the Political Spectacle*. The basic premise is that political language constructs both political subjects (such as leaders or enemies) and political objects (such as social problems or news). But, unlike some contemporary poststructural analysts of discourse, he does not reduce all political language to text and to interpretation. Nor does he reduce language to ideology and mere rationalization of interests. As he says, "ideology and material interests are part of the same transaction."[3] What this means more concretely is that there is no such "thing" as a political subject or object. "The language that interprets objects and actions also constitutes the subject."[4] Such an argument undermines the "premise, itself constructed very largely by the term 'leader,' that identifiable officials are originators of coherent courses of action."[5] That premise is found in much discourse which blames or praises individuals such as Presidents Bush or Yeltsin for the origins or outcome of political events.

More generally, "accounts of political issues, problems, crises, threats and leaders now become devices for creating disparate assumptions and beliefs about the social and political world rather than factual statements."[6] Consequently, "the political entities that are most influential upon public consciousness and action, then, are fetishes: creations of observers that dominate and mystify their creators."[7]

This paper is a critique of the political language used to distinguish the "nonprofit" sector from the "public" and "private" sectors as a "third" or "independent" sector, or as composed of "voluntary associations."[8] The political entity which "dominates and mystifies its creators" is the "nonprofit sector." Substitution of a different language will show how the conventional categories mystify the social world, although they may have positive consequences for some economic and political interests.[9]

The Political Language of the Nonprofit Sector

The tripartite distinction between public, private and nonprofit is highly problematic, even for scholars committed to the goals identified with voluntarism and independence. Paul DiMaggio, discussing the ambiguity of the tripartite distinction, has suggested that legal incorporation as a nonprofit entity be the only criterion used for classification, leaving all issues of purposes, goals, values or intentions of the founders, participants, beneficiaries and constituents to be either independent or dependent variables. This is a legitimate procedure, if the empirical criteria are not overlaid with political symbolism.[10]

Other writers make the same point. Stuart Langton, in an essay on "developing nonprofit theory," says that there is still no commonly accepted way to refer to the types of institutions which are the foci of the field . . ." (whether the "institutional entities" are to be called voluntary, nonprofit, or third, or independent). Furthermore, "we do not have adequate language to describe the actual roles and preferred relationships between nonprofit and other institutions . . . Above all, this calls into question the most essential concept that has been used to describe and distinguish nonprofit institutions—the metaphor of sectors."[11] And Lester Salamon says in the same volume that

> our failure to perceive the reality of extensive government-nonprofit ties is . . . in substantial part a product of the limitations of the conceptual lenses through which this reality is being perceived. Both the theory of the 'welfare state' and the theory of the voluntary sector . . . have been at fault. Neither leaves much conceptual room for a flourishing public-private partnership.[12]

Robert Wuthnow's introductory essay, in yet another volume of essays on the theme of "between state and market," is a good example of how easy it is to slide from a general concern with voluntary associations as examples of non-state, non-market organizations with Tocquevillean democratic functions, to the nonprofit sector as the embodiment of all of the positive functions of voluntary associations. Wuthnow distinguishes between "state," "market" and "voluntary" sectors, but acknowledges that the line between state and voluntary sectors is often "blurred" because of "cooperative programs between the two, government chartering of voluntary associations, and governmental financing." Moreover, the "boundary between voluntary and market sectors is sometimes vague as well, especially in instances of complex organizational schemes that bring for-profit and nonprofit activities under the same administrative umbrella."[13] Similarly, "government agencies concerned with social welfare programs have sometimes taken over the activities once performed by voluntary organizations ..." and "market principles" have been extended into the "service sector."[14]

The mystification introduced by using the tripartite distinction while acknowledging overlap and "hybridization" is indicated by an observation by economist Burton Weisbrod regarding changes since 1980: "Supporters of both the nonprofits and the proprietary organizations agree that cutbacks in federal funding (beginning around 1980) have led an increasing number of nonprofits to seek new revenue by engaging in profit-making activities; as a result, the two forms of institutions have come into growing conflict."[15] If nonprofit organizations (NPOs) are "nonstate" and "nonprivate," following the image of support by voluntary activity and funding, what are they doing being funded by the state and, worse, engaged in profit-making? Surely something is wrong with these categories, if used as more than legal descriptions.

Another article by two scholars of public administration recognizes the interaction between the nonprofit sector, the state, and capital—particularly changes taking place toward "increased government dependency and commercialization. As nonprofits increasingly resort to the traditional revenue sources of the public sector (grants) and the for-profit sector (fees for services), they tend to mirror them."[16]

A recent analysis by British political scientist Alan Ware provides a comprehensive treatment of these issues.[17] The book's very title, *Between Profit and State,* and the subtitle "intermediate organizations" makes the fundamental assumption, also stated explicitly by Weisbrod, that "three major forms of institutions are available to every society: proprietary, governmental, and nonprofit."[18] Ware is concerned with the "boundaries between these organizations and the liberal democratic state, on the one hand, and the market system, on the other."[19] He acknowledges immediately that "the boundaries with the market are difficult to define, and many organizations that pass as IOs are partly or wholly, commercial enterprises ... [and] similarly, the boundaries with the state are often imprecise."[20]

For descriptive purposes it may be adequate to call such entities "hybrid" if they combine nonprofit and profit components. Ware cites the example of Roanoke Memorial Hospital in Virginia which owns a collection agency, a warehouse, a conference center, a motel, and the Roanoke Athletic Club. And Voluntary Hospitals of America is an example of such a "complex intertwining of for-profit and non-profit concerns . . . that, while the legal status of each individual organization is necessarily either for-profit or non-profit, it is much more difficult to classify the entire complex as being one or the other."[21]

Ware is finally critical of the assumption that there is in fact a relatively homogeneous "third" (or voluntary, or independent, or nonprofit) sector. Although at the "core" there may be some organizations which exhibit the prototypical qualities of responsiveness to social needs, volunteerism, and participation, "it is far from evident that the 'third sector' is not merely an amalgamation of disparate organizations."[22] But, despite this criticism of the core concept of a "third" or "independent" sector, Ware uses phrases which imply an arms-length relationship between nonprofits and the other two institutional forms. Chapter 7, for example, deals with how the "state . . . has sought to regulate the activities of these organizations."[23] He then lists "seven purposes the liberal democratic state might have when introducing and reevaluating mechanisms for regulation,"[24] as if "the state" was an entity which could have rational purposes and implement them through laws and policies. Such a usage can be subjected to the critique that Murray Edelman makes of such terms as "leadership" or "social problem."

Jon van Til's "map" of the third sector is a good example of an analysis which uses the conventional distinctions for descriptive purposes, but overlays them with the ideological categories associated with the logic of democracy. The subtitle—"voluntarism"—and the view in the introduction that the nonprofit sector is equivalent to the "independent" or "voluntary" or "third" sector indicates his position. Van Til assumes that there are "three separate institutional worlds": "business," "government," and the third (or voluntary or independent or nonprofit) sector. Van Til says that his book "aims to explore the interrelationship of the three sectors" as if they are separate institutions related to each other in various ways. This is legitimate if one is investigating the empirical correlates of legal status, but too often such statements are coupled with inferences which presume the "independence" of the "sector."[25]

The multiple and conflicting interests at stake in the formation and operation of NPOs is indicated by the extent of legal battle over their role and the accusations of "corruption" and "abuse," a sure sign of contradictory roles. For the IRS, "nonprofits are an endless source of litigation . . ."[26] In 1985, nonprofits were the subject of "six cases before the Supreme Court and sixteen before the United States Court of Appeals." And Weisbrod gives numerous examples of "the potential for utilizing nonprofits as for-profits in disguise."[27] Using economists' language, he notes that the "'currency' of nonprofit trustworthiness" is "debased." Furthermore, "the information required to detect abuses is itself costly."[28]

To summarize, comprehensive reviews of the nonprofit literature simultaneously accept the legal distinction between "public," "private," and "nonprofit" organizations as important for empirical and descriptive purposes, but question the "independent," "intermediate," "voluntary" and "third sector" character of NPOs.[29] My argument accepts both aspects of this literature as important, and asks: what are the symbolic politics associated with the multiple linguistic images of "nonprofit"?

The Institutional Logics of Capital, State and Democracy

My basic point is a simple one, but my theoretical standpoint requires brief elaboration. The societal uses of NPOs are not fully understood if only the legal status of "public," "private," and "nonprofit" is used to describe these organizations. Many *legally* NPOs are neither voluntary, independent, intermediate, nor a "third" sector, and none of these labels follow logically or inevitably from their legal status. These symbols are drawn from the logic of democracy, but conceal the links of some "nonprofits" to the state and capital.

In this paper I am dealing with institutions which function within the multiple constraints of what Cohen and Rogers call "capitalist democracy."[30] In such societies, three sets of institutional arrangements have both interdependent and contradictory relations: capitalism, the state and democracy. Each set of institutions is shaped and penetrated by the others; each is both necessary for and undermines the other's survival.[31]

Capitalism is a short-hand word for the fundamental social relations which constitute the rights of "ownership," "accumulation," "hiring of labor," "investment," "buying and selling." Those words refer to powers and privileges enforced by the state, but they exist independently of the state. The structural interests of capital are embodied in specific organizational forms—banks, firms, corporations, trusts—and have the power (under some legal and political conditions) to change those forms.[32]

If one's categories of analysis focus only on economic organizations and do not recognize the underlying structural interests which control their existence and forms, one cannot understand such innovations as junk bonds, leveraged buyouts, and the capacity of corporations to drain off the resources of others (as has recently happened with Texas Air, Eastern Air Lines, and many savings and loan associations). Such actions were neither recognized nor sanctioned by the state in advance, but became "legal" because they were not successfully challenged in the courts or the political arena. Under current political circumstances, the symbols associated with the logic of capital—privatization, competition, social choice, efficiency—enjoy considerable power.

The state is a collection of organizations—the Presidency, Congress, courts, operating agencies such as the FAA, CAA, Department of Agriculture—which operate within a framework of laws, rules and practices. The state has powers independent of both capitalism and democracy. The state establishes the conditions under which *all* types of organizations—public, nonprofit, for-profit—operate, at least if they wish to receive state subsidies or tax exemptions. Almost all formal organizations, except the most transitory, come under state purview of some kind.

Democracy is a short-hand term for a collection of practices which can permeate the institutions of every-day life, of civil society, and which enjoin or allow participation, "citizens' initiatives," and the formation of associations to serve the diverse needs of individuals and social groups. Democracy—unless backed up by mass social movements, popular organizations and a powerful cultural tradition embedded in the daily practices of much of the population—supplies the rhetoric, but not the substance, of political life. This is one of Murray Edelman's fundamental insights.

To the extent that state agencies carry out demands by popular interests or serve popular needs, they embody responses to democratic values, but they need not. There is no automatic "democratic" character to any state action. Rather, most state policies are a response to the triple vectors of the interests of state officials, the economic interests with a stake in a particular policy, and the popular interests (if any) which have become mobilized to initiate or support a policy.

It may seem strange to sharply distinguish the logic of the state from that of democracy, but the point, consistent with the critical edge of Edelman's work, is that whether the state does something or not has very little to do with democracy. Democracy stems from popular action, from civil society, from the autonomous desires and needs of individuals and social groups before, during or after exposure to bureaucratic surveillance of corporate commodification. It is important to postulate undefined needs and unsatisfied demands which are potentially mobilizable as pressures upon both capital and state. By definition, the boundaries of such needs and demands cannot be specified in advance, since they derive from the changing perceptions of social groups regarding what is possible under different historical conditions.

The remainder of this paper will be devoted to showing how NPOs are subjected to contradictory demands, depending on their relations to the institutional logics of the capitalist economy, the bureaucratic state, and a democratic culture. Democracy provides the political symbols but not the substance necessary for their survival.[33]

Nonprofit Organizations: Corporate, Public and Popular

Given this theoretical argument, I can now develop a classification of NPOs based on the assumption that many are dependent on the state and capital for funding and political support. When, as in the Reagan and Bush eras, conservative forces are dominant, they reduce public funding for non-profits, forcing them into corporate modes of marketing and fund raising, but then challenge them for "unfair competition" with private firms.

My categories assume that in capitalist democracies most NPOs can be located within the "orbit" of the structural interests associated with capital ("corporate nonprofits"), democracy ("popular nonprofits") and the state ("public nonprofits"). Those located at the intersection of more than one "orbit" are subjected to conflicting demands which lead to both external pressures and internal tensions.[34]

Democratic rhetoric creates legitimate space for the corporate and public nonprofits to operate, shielded by the notions of voluntarism and participation. What Weisbrod and van Til identify as the main characteristics of the nonprofit sector—its role in filling the gaps left by both markets and government failure; its responsiveness to the diverse demands of many groups in a democratic, pluralistic society; its voluntary, participatory character—are only the democratic *aspects* of the nonprofit sector. Rather than cloaking the entire nonprofit sector in the shimmering rhetoric of democracy, a democratic culture is only one source of the needs and demands which lead to nonprofit activity. Nonprofits are established *by* government, and *by* for-profit organizations, and an understanding of their societal role is not helped by reifying them, as if "they" or "it" assume a totally different character because of their nonprofit status.[35]

The reification of the distinctions between public, private and nonprofit ignores the dynamics of internal transformation under external pressures, as happens when a nonprofit organization which has been supported with public funds must seek to form a profit-making subsidiary in order to defend its existence. The traditional categories cannot make sense of such changes.

The language I am proposing allows recognition of the pressures upon NPOs to become commodified (to sell products and services, develop real estate, usually by fictitious subsidiaries or spin-offs), to become politicized (to seek public funding from a legislature or state agency, to seek political support), or to become democratized (to attempt to increase participation by clients, members, or constituents, to change its structure in ways which presumably will increase voluntary activity).

Popular Nonprofits

Political symbolism justifies the nonprofit sector in terms of the rhetoric of democracy. Lester Salamon cites as "one fundamental feature" of the nonprofit sector, in the eyes of some, "its availability as an agent of social and political change," or, in other words, its "advocacy role."[36] Peter Hall has recently defined an NPO as a "body of individuals who associate" together for certain purposes, including "performing public tasks ... delegated to them by the state" which neither the state nor for-profit organizations is "willing" to fulfill. Or the purpose can be to try to "influence" the policies of state or profit-making organizations.[37] This language emphasizes the voluntary actions of individuals choosing to influence each other or others, and joining together for common purposes.

However, Hall's historical sketch shows that the nonprofit sector was not seen as a pure manifestation of democratic association, but as a fragile set of institutions which needed to be protected from democracy. According to Daniel Webster, "it will be dangerous ... to hold these institutions subject to the rise and fall of popular parties, and the fluctuations of political opinions. If the franchise may be at any time taken away, or is impaired, the property may also be taken away, or its use perverted."[38]

Institutions such as philanthropic charities or colleges thus need to be insulated from democracy, in order to safeguard their special values. The vagaries of public opinion and popular support should not be allowed to undermine the goals which NPOs serve. However, they also need to be safeguarded from excessive bureaucratic control by the state and from the kinds of economic calculations and pressures typical of profit-making organizations. The basic point is that NPOs are seen as important because they seem to escape the pressures from all three societal forces: capital, state and democracy—if the latter is identified with the whims of majorities and public opinion, not to mention self-interested politicians.

However, the political language of voluntarism, of participation, of independence seems to elevate the image of pluralist democracy once again as the symbolic basis for the nonprofit sector. What is striking in recent surveys of different types of NPOs is the emphasis on what I would call the "informal popular" types, such as social movement organizations, rather than "formal popular" types such as trade unions. But the analyses of such organizations almost never locate them within the context of larger societal institutions, except within a worldview which simply takes as given a multiplicity of types of organizations, labelling them as members of the diversity called the "nonprofit sector." In order to make my alternative approach more explicit, I shall contrast three types of popular nonprofits: social movement organizations, community development organizations, and trade unions.

J. Craig Jenkins epitomizes the focus on the democratic logic which legitimizes the nonprofit sector. Jenkins summarizes the literature on social movement organizations, most of which, of course, are nonprofit. He emphasizes, as Piven and Cloward did before him, the serious, if not disastrous, impact of funding exigencies and elite patronage upon the advocacy thrust of social movements: "Patronage has tended to convert the advocacy organizations into centralized service purveyors, demobilizing masses by emphasizing services and projecting images of elite responsibility."[39] Jenkins agrees that NPOs in capitalist democracies cannot transcend the limits that these structural and historical realities impose; ". . . the nonprofits' claim that they counter the special interests by simply organizing larger numbers and securing procedural reforms is naive." In effect, the "centralized professional organizations without grass-roots bases" will always be subordinated to the power of capital. Jenkins is arguing that it takes a political environment in which militant social movements are pressing for significant and tangible reforms to restore nonprofit advocacy organizations to the missions which their rhetoric claims for them.

Because of Jenkins' tight empirical focus upon the conditions under which public advocacy organizations operate, he does not consider how the legitimating symbols of democracy are used by all NPOs, even those closely linked to the state or capital. The cultural resonance of the symbols of participation, voluntarism, or independence are important regardless of the actual practices of the organizations.

Carl Milovsky, in a related article,[40] contrasts the "bureaucratic model" with the "community" or "voluntary model" of neighborhood organization. The former is characterized by clear boundaries, definite norms, and specific uses. Voluntary associations, by contrast, are the "bedrock of democracy." They knit the community together, establish a "cohesive, moral unit which provides a sense of purpose and identity for individuals" and are "vehicles of political mobilization and political education." Here the logic of democracy is clear: those institutions of civil society which are neither controlled by nor originate in the requirements of the market or the state.

The example of community development corporations illustrates the multiple and contradictory pressures that NPOs are under, particularly those which were begun and are legitimated by the symbols of democracy.[41] The problematic character of the trichotomy public/private/nonprofit is vividly illustrated by CDCs. CDCs have usually begun either as popular nonprofits (if they originated from grass roots movements) or as public nonprofits (if started from state funds), and now are under heavy pressure to become corporate nonprofits, in the interest of survival. Which path any given CDC takes will depend on the particular community coalition supporting them and the specific fund-raising and political skills of key staff members. But they are unlikely to lose their mixed character, and therefore are permanently subject to contradictory demands.

Community development organizations arose in the 1960s, some from grass roots protest movements, some from federal War on Poverty money and/or foundation support. With the decline of protest movements, there has been little necessity to attempt to coopt potential disruption; thus little funding for community organizing is made available. The consequences for staffing have required less recruitment from the grass roots, more job searches, and hiring outside staff with high levels of training and skills in planning, finance, and law. As federal funds were cut, the CDCs faced painful choices between "soft" development, such as community organizing and advocacy, and "hard" development, such as residential or commercial development or real estate management. Critics within the "movement" argue that CDCs have become just another set of developers.

But as developers bidding for scarce resources over and beyond operating funds, CDCs often compete among a variety of private developers for city contracts. They must try to rationalize and professionalize while simultaneously networking politically, a role for which they have little time or staff. At the same time, the CDCs are being scrutinized by the foundations and by the local neighborhoods for signs of genuine community participation, ranging from boards which represent the social composition of the neighborhood to community outreach and volunteer activity. The CDCs "literally can't afford to do outreach, given their small size, limited funds, staff and volunteer labor, while also completing the many time and resource consuming steps for project development."

One example in Worcester, Massachusetts illustrates the contradictory pressures created by the mixed character of CDCs. Main South is a partnership with Clark University. Local government as well as other funders "require that Main South submit 'tight' highly professional documents. They couch their praise ... in such terms as 'knowing how to make deals' and 'acting professionally.'" This puts a premium on technically proficient leadership and/or training. At the same time, "community organizing and outreach are also necessary to maintain contact, visibility and credibility within the community on the basis of the legitimacy and the claims of the CDC in the first place." Since the substitution of local government and state funds for vanished federal funds is not secure (in this case because of the fiscal crisis in Massachusetts), the CDCs must attempt to juggle all of these funding balls, attempting to respond in some way to all the expectations. One would expect considerable instability in such nonprofits, given the contradictory demands on them.

To take another example, labor unions are a good example of formally organized popular NPOs. For the same reason that other "mutual benefit" organizations are not studied, they have not been treated in relationship to other types of NPOs in the recent literature. There are only five passing references to unions in the 1987 research handbook on the nonprofit sector,[42] and no chapter. The only substantive discussion classifies trade unions as "mutual benefit organizations" which "negotiate collectively for their members."[43] Several other recent collections of articles on the nonprofit sector have no chapters and no index references to trade unions." No does Weisbrod's *The Nonprofit Economy*, although he includes trade unions as one of the categories of NPOs which "pursue the private interests of their constituents or members and have only modest or nonexistent external benefits to outsiders," and lumps unions in with mutual insurance companies and "far more."[45]

On the other hand, Ware asserts that "of all the nineteenth century working class mutual-benefit organizations, trade unions have made the greatest impact on social and economic life..."[46] Curiously, in view of the paucity of analyses of unions as NPOs, he also argues that because "of all the mutuals they are the ones about which most has been written in relation to their impact on both the capitalist economy and their contribution to democratization in the capitalist state," he will give unions "considerably less attention" than other nonprofits.

As we have already seen, conventional treatments of the nonprofit sector restrict it to the service sector, charitable organizations, and those organizations which presumably are formed to meet needs which neither government nor markets are satisfying. Despite their nonprofit status, bureaucratically organized mutual benefit organizations such as labor unions do not fit the image of voluntarism which nevertheless legitimates the entire sector. And Ware is certainly right that extensive studies exist concerning the relations of labor unions to the state and capital. But unions have not been analyzed as part of the nonprofit sector.

A few examples will illustrate the impossibility of understanding the emergence of certain kinds of corporate nonprofits without referring to unions. A corporate nonprofit—the National Construction Employers Council—was formed in 1978 in the construction industry, designed to parallel the AFL-CIO Building and Construction Trades Department, to deal with the "thousands of collective bargaining agreements between local craft unions and employers associations." A second corporate nonprofit—the Associated Builders and Contractors—represents the nonunion contractors in 45 local or state chapters with 8000 construction firms. It was formed as a result of "anti union or open-shop activities in the construction industry."[47] But none of these analyses see unions as part of the structure of power which integrates workers into capitalist democracy, which is Edelman's position. "Major unions... serve as an integrating link, hoping to furnish political and organizational support for government, union, and business bureaucracies, and at the same time providing symbolic reassurances for the workers and the mass public. By supplying these diverse benefits... unions help to preserve the system and the established power and status relationships within it."[48]

This statement reveals once again the underlying radical implications of Edelman's argument. A major type of NPO is seen as having a mixed character. Trade unions provide necessary political support for both the state and capital, but both economic and symbolic benefits for workers are also required. "Workers are likely to acquiesce without wide or deep dissent in the continued incumbency of their union officials as long as the economic benefits of an affluent society continue to roll in and as long as the union officials present an appropriate dramaturgical performance suggesting they are furthering the interests of their followers."[49] To put it another way also consistent with Edelman's perspective, the more unions respond to corporate or political interests, the more they must use the rhetoric of democracy to conceal whose interests are being served.

Churches are another example of popular nonprofits which constitute a large fraction of the "sector" by membership, voluntary activity, and funding. Because my concern in this paper is with the symbolic politics of the nonprofit sector and the way contradictory institutional logics are concealed, I shall only mention one interesting example of an attempt to apply the logic of capital to churches, which involves an effort to challenge tax exemptions.

In 1987, the Financial Accounting Standards Board, the "chief rule-making body for accountants" (and itself probably an NPO which has been given state authority) proposed forcing churches to depreciate their "houses of worship, monuments, and historical treasures," thus reducing their income.[50] The churches argued, drawing upon the examples of pyramids, the Sphinx and the Sistine Chapel, that their buildings were irreplaceable and unique aspects of the cultural heritage of all humanity.

The logic of capital reduces them to accounting categories defined as "capital assets." The assumption is that they are equivalent to a tool or factory building, and can be assessed for the cost of replacement. An FASB project manager said that "in looking at all nonprofit assets, we had to be even-handed." The notion of "evenhandedness" is a bureaucratic one, as is the assumption that all physical objects "wear out" and therefore "have" to be depreciated. The FASB referred to the "parts" of a church, as if they were like parts of a car, which wear out, but can be "salvaged."

The state is involved indirectly, because the logic of capital is established through tax provisions which help profitable enterprises replace capital equipment through the device of depreciation. Here the state enforces the logic of capital by imposing the symbol of bureaucratic "uniformity and comparability." The categories used to classify and reduce monuments or church buildings to just another capital asset are drawn from the image of a replaceable and profitable instrument.

Classifying informal and genuinely voluntary associations with those formal organizations which claim to represent popular and community interests—such as labor unions and community development corporations—as both "popular" organizations runs the danger of ignoring the structures of power which coopt and transform human activities into their opposites. In order to make the larger comparison with corporate and public nonprofits, I shall run that risk in this argument.

In conclusion, it is indeed important to include as part of the theoretical concept of NPOs those collectively-organized human activities which are neither commodified nor politicized—the voluntary, independent, and autonomous activities which take place in families, communities, neighborhoods, small groups, churches. These activities constitute an enormous fraction of "nonprofit" human behavior in the conventional sense of "nonstate" and "nonmarket" behavior, and are nearly equivalent to what is usually called "civil society." However, the political language and symbols attached to the concept of "nonprofit sector" silently appropriates their voluntary, independent and participatory aspects and attaches those qualities to the "sector" as a whole.[51]

Public Nonprofits

With the category of public nonprofits—those which are organized by and funded by the state, and serve state interests—we come to more glaring cases of the contradiction between the rhetoric of voluntarism and independence which legitimates the nonprofit sector as a category, and the reality of subordination to the state. Few of the organizations discussed below are "charitable" organizations [IRC 501 (c)(3)] and therefore little attention is paid to them in the nonprofit literature.

All of the organizations normally classified as nonprofit are already, in a crucial sense, part of the state, since they have applied for and received a tax exemption (although, depending on their tax status, contributions to them may or may not be deductible). They are therefore subsidized by the state through public monies, and are subject to various pressures for accountability and constraints on their activities because of that dependence. Because of a turbulent environment of fiscal stress, shifting public tastes, competition for scarce funds, and vacillating political support, many nonprofits have banded together to form new nonprofits which serve as lobbying or defense organizations, such as Independent Sector. But just because all nonprofits have some interest in common (and thus can form a pressure group in the narrow sense), does not mean that with respect to larger societal roles they are similar.

As Ware points out, the state itself creates NPOs of all kinds: "... in some policy areas the state actually wanted to create groups that would be politically active, in order to carry out its own policies."[52] More than one in ten of the "citizen groups" begun in the United States between 1945 and 1980 got government funds at their founding. Ware quotes another source as concluding that "the federal government has become an important source of seed money in the formation of large-multiple-issue environmental citizens interest groups."[53] Whether those should be classified as "public" or "popular" depends on whether the state agencies had been penetrated by popular interests or whether the state was coopting those interests.

But the nonprofits cannot count on permanent state funds, since funding vacillates as the political spotlight shifts from one public policy to another. Different programs move in and out of favor, as Edelman has pointed out, in order for political elites to get the credit for something new, and as the need for symbolic response to different social problems shifts from one type of program to another. As a result there is a growing "need to generate income from fee-paying activities, and this brings some IOs into competition with for-profit enterprises."[54]

Ware's examples illustrate how the state is used by capital to challenge the nonprofit sector. "The state" thus cannot be seen as an actor with separate purposes. The case of the Small Business Administration challenging the "unfair competition" of the nonprofit sector is a case in point. Ware points out that this is a typical instance of the

> incentive for branches of the [state] administration to develop and cultivate client groups. The only unusual feature of the lobby the SBA helped to cultivate was that it was part of the for-profit economy which found itself in a relatively disadvantageous position in mobilizing against its opponents; more commonly, it is for-profit enterprises which enjoy the advantages.[55]

This example illustrates how strategically-located interests use their resources, including access to state authority.

Harassment of popular nonprofits which challenge the state itself is not unusual. In one such instance, the "IRS maintained that an organization formed to promote world peace and disarmament was not a charitable organization because it encouraged civil disobedience at protest demonstrations."[56] This is a good example of how important it is conceptually to separate the logic of democracy from that of the state. Conversely, sometimes nonprofits usurp state power, instead of the state controlling the conditions under which nonprofits operate. The NPO National Endowment for the Preservation of Liberty was Ollie North's instrument for raising more than $2 million in tax-exempt contributions to purchase illegal military aid for the Contras.

Another case illustrates how a state organization can be transformed into a combination of corporate and public nonprofits and private economic interests which defies neat classification. That complexity again exists because of the strategies of specific political and economic interests.[57]

County agricultural extension agents were established in 1914 by the Smith-Lever Act and acquired an ambiguous status through concurrent financial support from county, state, and federal governments, and from private sources.[58] Although avowedly "unpolitical," and concerned with "education," an important part of the agent's job was to form local support groups of farmers. The end result, by the 1920s, was that

> the county agents had organized with the aid of public resources and at the direction of the United States Department of Agriculture not merely an array of local organizations of farmers, but the most powerful private pressure group agriculture has ever produced, the American Farm Bureau Federation. The local groups, the county "farm bureaus," had federated into state Farm bureaus, and these in turn had formed the national Federation.[59]

The American Farm Bureau Federation was in the mid 1960s a national NPO, with 102 staff members and over 3 million members. It is an example of a "private association called into being by actions of government officials" and which "acquires the power to exert great influence over policy and administration..."[60]

McConnell notes that "recurrent demands have been made that the relationship between the county farm bureaus and the county agents be ended," and calls the situation an "anomaly: ... the constituent units were public bodies, but their state and national federations were private organizations."[61] In my terms, at the local level, the bureaus are part of the state, but at higher levels, they are corporate nonprofits.

Another revealing example drawn from McConnell is that of the creation of advisory boards to help the federal government manage the arid lands in the West and reduce "overgrazing" by cattle. This is a direct illustration of the appropriation of public power by private interests, and the strategic use of nonprofit and "advisory groups" to monopolize public authority.

As chronicled in innumerable Western movies, the cattlemen in the West at first simply enclosed vast areas of the public domain for their own use, precipitating violent battles with sheepmen and homesteaders. The Taylor Grazing Act of 1934 was an attempt to regularize the use of these lands, establishing the bodies and procedures typical of regulation: hearings, conferences, administrative bodies, state advisory committees, local committees to gain support.[62] The goal was to develop districts within which permits for cattle grazing would be issued.

One of the Federal Director of Grazing's first acts was to issue orders for a special election of district advisors, to be elected by local cattlemen. "Their function ... was no less than to be the local governing agencies regulating the districts ... the grazing districts [and thus the local advisory boards] derived no authority from the states and were not parts of local government in any formal sense. Formally, they were simply advisory." However, they became the instruments whereby local cattlemen maintained their control over the use of local public lands. By 1939, the district advisory boards were recognized by law, and in 1940 a National Advisory Board Council was created "at a meeting of representatives of various districts. Shortly thereafter state boards were created. All of these bodies were outside of government and had no official relation to it."[63] Ultimately the NABC and the state boards were given official standing in the Federal Range Code. This "was a simple recognition of reality—that the various boards were governing bodies."

The National Advisory Board Council has changed its name several times since 1976, mainly in an attempt to incorporate more than just "grazing" interest groups, and is currently the National Public Advisory Council, whose members are appointed by the Secretary of the Interior. Technically a citizens advisory council, the members do not get paid and are only reimbursed for travel expenses. According to an informant in the Bureau of Land Management, whenever a meeting of the council is needed, anybody who believes that they have a legitimate interest in the issues can apply to attend. The council has no continuing staff, but is called into existence for these meetings. It is thus technically not even an NPO, but an ad hoc committee. It is probably a case of a prevalent type: a temporary coalition of interests which, under some conditions, will become either a branch of a state agency, an NPO, or even perhaps a "private" organization. In my perhaps cumbersome terminology, it is an "informal public nonprofit."

As a result of these state actions, two parallel orders of government have been created: a public bureaucracy and a system of boards. *Both* are heavily influenced by a private economic interest group: the cattlemen. The public agency was influenced by the requirement that the officials be Westerners and that they have "practical" experience, which meant that in practice they frequently *were* cattlemen. The formally public bodies were penetrated by persons with clear private interests. In turn, the formally private bodies—the boards—were given public authority. "Although recognition of the Boards in the Federal Range Code compromises the private character of these bodies, the Boards especially at the levels of their state and federal associations are effectively private political bodies." Thus, an apparent reform—establishing a formal permit system to regulate private grazing on public lands—actually reinforced and consolidated private control by the largest private owners. The "public" agency was so thoroughly penetrated by "private" interest groups that it was impossible to tell which was which. "Decentralized administration had . . . created a strong national interest-group organization which was a public body when it was convenient and a private lobby when that was expedient."[64]

This example demonstrates, in still another context, the misleading character of the basic sectoral distinctions. One would not understand these developments if these organizations were classified according to their legal status, and their attributes were correlated with other variables.

A recent development has been the formation of "community associations" which are public nonprofits, formed to replace some functions of local government. In 1988, Houston alone had 400 such homeowner groups. One of these, the Clear Lake Community Association, established by an EXXON subsidiary which had built a development next to NASA, described itself as a "state-chartered, nonprofit, private corporation, formed primarily to provide municipal-type services." These associations are simply a competing form of local government, given certain powers to provide services which are ultimately enforceable by the state (in this case through the "deed-based private-contract agreements each member [of the Association] must sign"). The relevant point here is the political language being used: this public nonprofit was described by the author as an example of "giving power back to the people," since it manifests the "residents' power to . . . freely choose a form of governance."[65]

To conclude, I have shown the symbiotic character of the relations between private, public, and nonprofit "sectors" from another standpoint: that of the state. Once again, democratic rhetoric mystifies the political language, whatever its consequences for legitimating practices.

Corporate Nonprofits

The power of capital sometimes appears in assessments of the nonprofit sector which assume the primacy of a democratic culture, but capital is assumed to be subject to the power of the state, in turn assumed to reflect democratic values. Salamon's appeal to a public-private "partnership" recognizes that the nonprofit sector, if not disciplined and held accountable by government to serve the poor, is dominated by those who "command the greatest resources."[66] The consequence is that the "sector comes to be shaped by the preferences not of the community as a whole but of its wealthy members." Salamon assumes that government, potentially at least, is in a position to "set priorities on the basis of a democratic political process instead of the wishes of the wealthy . . ."[67] By not recognizing the ways in which the state is also shaped by the "preferences of the wealthy," the force of his argument for a partnership between the government and the nonprofit sector is weakened.

Despite the prevalence and importance of corporate nonprofits—those established by and serving the interests of capital—they are barely referred to in recent literature on the nonprofit sector, precisely because of the almost exclusive focus upon nonprofits in the legal category of "charitable" organizations. Edward Skloot, in an article entitled "Enterprise and Commerce in Nonprofit Organizations," for example, does not deal with corporate nonprofits.[68] Like most other authors, he analyzes only those nonprofits with a "charitable purpose;" those for which profit-making is a "secondary activity."[69] His case studies include Planned Parenthood (condoms), the Bank Street College of Education (word-processing software), the Film Forum (building rental), and the Children's Television Workshop (*Sesame Street* products). However, nothing is said about those nonprofits which do not make any money at all, but are organically linked to major corporations and industries.[70]

Planned Parenthood and the others mentioned are not corporate nonprofits, but "popular" ones which are forced to adopt profit-making strategies in order to survive. A better example of a corporate nonprofit which benefits from the ideology of service to needs is Blue Cross, as described by Hollingsworth and Hollingsworth.[71] Initially and for some years after, by setting rates on the basis of "community experience" (not individual) they "effectively subsidized insurance for poor and elderly persons . . ."[72] Because Blue Cross

> initially billed itself as providing a service to the community through affordable participation, it could secure special privileges from state and federal governments. In many states Blue Cross plans were exempt from various requirements imposed on commercial insurance companies and from paying property taxes as well as taxes on earned income. This preferential treatment remained long after the community service role became smaller.[73]

Although "most Blue Cross plans have eliminated the implicit subsidy to high-risk persons" and have successfully competed with commercial insurance companies because their rates have been increasingly based on the "experience of particular groups rather than community rating," they have successfully maintained the image of a community service institution. One of their main achievements for the industry was to "fuel hospital expansion and cost inflation." In effect, Blue Cross acted as an agent for capital expansion in the hospital industry, but, as a nonprofit, benefitted from the ideology of community service. Blue Cross executives made conscious attempts to minimize their similarity to commercial firms, by "referring to members instead of policyholders, rates instead of premiums, service instead of indemnity, enrolling instead of selling, and enrollment representatives instead of salesmen."[74] The ideological purpose of concealing their location within the orbit of capital is clear.

"Joint ventures" of nonprofits and for-profit firms are probably usually within the orbit of capital. In 1985, one third of the nonprofit hospitals were engaged in joint ventures, and "most of the others were considering it."[75] And "one of the largest for-profit hospital chains in the nation, Hospital Corporation of America, has formed a nonprofit foundation, the HCA

Foundation, which gives grants to other nonprofit organizations."[76] Weisbrod calls these hybrids "institutional innovations."

Since 1979, there has been no legal limit on how much profit an NPO can make, only on what they can do with it.[77] Once nonprofits are allowed to make profits, even though they allegedly do not distribute them to "owners," the way is open for many "abuses" such as "excessive" salaries.

Note that such accusations do not arise, or at least do not have serious consequences, in profit-making enterprises, no matter how outrageous the income. (Michael Milken of the recently defunct Drexel Lambert junk bond firm made $500 million in 1987, reaping only grumbling and envy. His conviction was not for extortion or theft.) But nonprofits of any stripe which enjoy profitable subsidiaries can pay handsome salaries and have the ability to shift such costs as capital equipment, office space, and salaries to their profit-making partners.[78]

An example of a corporate nonprofit within the orbit of capital is Second Harvest, which distributes "surplus" food to the needy. For-profit food processors such as Kellogg and Tropicana appointed board members, whose job was both to "prevent donated products from being resold commercially and to take advantage of corporate tax benefits."[79] Kellogg gave "107,000 cases of a cereal that was not selling well, and Tropicana gave 2.4 million quarts of grapefruit juice that was discolored but 'perfectly drinkable.'" The point is not to criticize this operation—clearly it is better to have food distributed free than destroyed—but only to point out that the nonprofit form in this case has nothing to do with voluntarism, participation, being "intermediate" or "independent" or "mediating," but instead serves a direct economic interest.

A last example is the kind of nonprofit that is never analyzed anywhere in the literature, those organizations which directly serve corporate interests and never mention voluntarism or independence. In order to defend their nonprofit status, of course, they have to define the public needs that they serve. A recent issue of the trade journal *High Technology Business* describes the formation of a corporate nonprofit.[80] The Motorola Corporation introduced a new computer chip called the 88000, utilizing the new RISC technology ("reduced instruction set"), and then formed an NPO called 88OPEN to promote sales and standardize software. By May of 1988 the NPO had 28 members, including Data General, Tektronic and Convergent Technologies.

Another NPO—a research consortium—was formed in 1972. Called Computer Aided Manufacturing International, it conducted a study for 40 corporations aimed at developing new guidelines for accounting for the actual costs of high-technology products: "Better accounting methods will help companies make better investment decisions . . . because companies will have a more reliable way to figure out whether such investments are worthwhile."[81] The sponsors of the project include such CAM-I members as Boeing, General Dynamics, General Electric, Lockheed, and Westinghouse, as well as six of the Big Eight accounting firms.

The description of the activities of the organization illustrate its "nonprofit" concerns, and, in the absence of any other information about its connection with capital, would seem like any other education or research organization serving a public need:

> CAM-I plans to promote changes in accounting practices by spreading the word about project findings. The consortium will ask academia to include CMS concepts in its classes and research, and plans to present findings at conferences. CAM-I also hopes to meet with legislative and regulatory groups to preach the importance of cost-management systems to industry and the national economy.

A direct challenge to the commercial activities of many NPOs has been mounted, mainly by those who favor the allegedly greater efficiency of private, profit-making enterprise. These analyses, unlike those in the "mainstream" nonprofit literature I have mostly cited, include details about the activities of what I am calling "corporate nonprofits" (as well as the commercial activities of other nonprofits).[82] What is relevant to my argument in this paper is that the authors make no claim about NPOs being either voluntary, independent, or participatory. Quite the opposite. They even use the term "public nonprofits" to refer to "public sector firms [that] enjoy most of the special privileges (especially tax exemptions) that benefit nonprofits."[83]

It is striking that the political language used to describe corporatist structures is sometimes that of "voluntary associations." A study of corporatism in Quebec begins: "Theoretical discussion of the corporatist structures that develop out of the exchange between *voluntary associations* [italics added] and state agencies in advanced industrial societies... differ in their assessment of the relative stability of these structures."[84] However, the corporatism literature overlaps little with the literature on the nonprofit sector, partly because the latter takes as its model the voluntary, independent association, and the former takes as its model the "compulsory, noncompetitive associations representing major socio-economic producer groups..."[85]

The NPOs which the corporatist studies deal with, usually without naming them as such, are what we would call either "corporate" or "public" nonprofits. Clearly the "peak associations" representing powerful economic interest groups are far different in almost every characteristic from the usual conception of a "voluntary association." But, as this article indicates, the political language is sometimes that of "voluntary associations." Obviously, this political language is important.

Nonprofit Organizations as Political Actors

Multiple structural logics are embedded in most if not all NPOs which rely upon contributions or public funding. They are legitimated democratically, organized bureaucratically, and funded competitively, which means that they are organized internally on contradictory principles. This inevitably leads to conflict over goals and purposes, not to mention operating procedures. No wonder that boards of directors are "frustrated." No wonder that their goals are often "vague, hard to quantify and open to multiple interpretations."[86] But Middleton, taking the standpoint of organization theory, which separates the "organizations" from its "environment," does not draw any conclusion from the observation that "nonprofits often experience conflicting claims made on them by diverse constituencies such as donors and beneficiaries."[87] This formulation reifies the concept of "organization" (in addition to the image of "nonprofit"), seeing an organization as an intact entity which "experiences" conflicting claims, rather than being constituted by contradictory institutional logics.

Additionally, those nonprofits not set up originally with corporate activities find it hard to handle them, another indication of contradictory logics. According to Skloot, "commercial activities are not easily absorbed within nonprofit organizations [with charitable purposes], at least at first. They often bring with them new legal structures, management styles, and reporting procedures that run counter to less formal, possibly less rigorous approaches."[88]

Now that the nonprofit sector is in existence as a set of tax-exempt organizations, it has become, like any other heterogeneous interest group, an active agent defending whatever common interests can be defined, and using resources—legal, political and economic (not to mention symbolic) available to them. Nonprofits will seek to maximize their support from various sources: sales, grants, donations, tax-exemptions, subsidies. Their nonprofit status gives them special access to certain kinds of resources: tax-deductible donations, tax-free income, or both. They have an advantage over strictly proprietary or commercial firms in that they have the ideological veneer of public service of "mutual benefit," but that is a fine line that they must walk with caution.[89]

The power of NPOs to control the state is illustrated by another example taken from Ware. They are not simply passive in the face of state regulation and taxation. The Reverend Jerry Falwell threatened to move his church from Lynchburg, Virginia, and the city council was forced to choose between "losing 2,000 jobs and a $32 million annual payroll or foregoing $400,000 a year in property taxes."[90] Many other examples could be given.

NPOs need to be analyzed not only in terms of their community services, but also as interest groups which have successfully carved out a niche for themselves in capitalist democracies, ideologically buttressed by the language of voluntarism, legally supported by tax-exempt status, and politically adept at defending themselves through creating lobbying organizations which seek legislative support for them.[91]

As part of the overall defense strategy, the symbolic construction of the "third sector" is proceeding apace. A refreshingly frank summary of the progress in this task is given by Michael O'Neill, who, as director of the Institute for Nonprofit Organization Management at the University of San Francisco, is certainly an actor in the scene.[92] Contrasting the "clear, strong, no-nonsense words" *business* and *commerce* with the "weak and diffuse" image of the nonprofit sector, he says that the "conceptualization and semanticization of the nonprofit sector are among its principal tasks ... perhaps one of the reasons the nonprofit sector is collectively weak is that it is all reality and no illusion."[93] O'Neill goes on to describe the burgeoning of public commissions, research centers (now seventeen), graduate programs (including his own), courses, theories, research, nonprofit coalitions of nonprofits (such as Independent Sector, formed in 1980 by John Gardner, with an initial membership of 600 large nonprofits), the Foundation Center, etc. Clearly the symbolic politics which are creating a new institutional entity are well under way. As O'Neill says, "it is much too early to tell whether this movement ... will become a significant long-term influence in American education and public perception."[94]

One critical strategic choice, affecting the survival and success of the nonprofit, will be the relative emphasis upon "bureaucratic" v. "clan" networks. Both are necessary to some degree, depending on the institutional orbit to which the nonprofit is related and the tasks that origin implies. If the bureaucratic emphasis is chosen, staff members will be chosen according to technical competence, credentials, and planning capability; these qualities of the organization will be advertised to potential givers of grants, donations, and legislative allocations. If the clan emphasis is chosen, staff members will be chosen according to their status in the community, their political ties with relevant elites, their informal contacts, and their capacity to create solidarity and a sense of community in the volunteers, staff, and various constituencies.

Networks of support must be developed regardless of whether a bureaucratic or clan emphasis is chosen, and the most successful nonprofits must try to maximize the appearance both of technical efficiency and political support in the relevant constituencies.

Given the low social power of popular organizations in capitalist democracies, one might expect variations between these types of nonprofits in both income stratification and economic competitiveness, and there is some evidence of such variation. The average wage in the "philanthropic subsector" of the economy was three quarters of the average wages for all employees, and, within the subsector, was highest in the legal and health services organizations, lowest in the social service and membership organizations. Those nonprofits connected to well-paid professions (and in turn to capital and the state) were much better paid than employees of the organizations playing "democratic" roles.[95] Nor are popular nonprofits as economically competitive as corporate ones. Skloot observes that the nonprofits least likely to be able to create commercially viable ventures are the ones which "serve the neediest . . . population": the "social service, criminal justice, environmental organizations, and advocacy groups."[96]

Corporate nonprofits—because of their service to the most powerful structural interest in capitalist democracies—probably enjoy the least public visibility (in the sense that they make the least "news"), exhibit the least vacillations of funding, the least internal conflicts, the least turnover of key staff, and are least likely to split in two or change names. Popular nonprofits are probably the most visible, conflictual, changeable, and vulnerable to attack, because they have multiple and contradictory expectations placed upon them by their various constituencies, and—if they survive—will be most likely to change their character.[97]

The resources devoted to symbolic legitimation clearly reduce those available for task achievement, thus undermining the legitimacy derived from effectiveness and efficiency. But effectiveness and efficiency cannot be demonstrated without resources devoted to public relations, fund raising, communication, mass media, networking, and lobbying. Precisely because popular nonprofits must demonstrate efficiency, accountability, and public service, they must attempt to convince a variety of constituencies of their service to conflicting goals. The resources consumed by these forms of symbolic legitimation are not available for substantive programmatic activity and thus undermine the very message they want to convey. This contradiction becomes most evident when the organization is most under fiscal pressure, most under surveillance, and most subjected to conflicting demands, because the different constituencies will demand tangible evidence of service to their particular goals.[98] These behaviors and their consequences are probably most evident in popular nonprofits, least for corporate nonprofits.

The opposite side of the coin is that NPOs may be able to take advantage of their multiple symbolic images as well. Liberal middle-class publics may be convinced because of the existence of an NPO in a given area that *something* is being done about a problem or a cause which concerns them, which they can either contribute to or participate in as a "friend," a "member," a "subscriber," a "contributor." The more they get involved, the more they become committed to the belief that the organization represents significant action on behalf of the cause or problem. If this is the case, then nonprofit legal status reaffirms the social significance of the contribution of the organization—it confirms through government endorsement that the activity is indeed "charitable." And the appearance of businesslike management confirms to the donors that their gift will be used efficiently—even high and competitive salaries can be seen as necessary to obtain the best management.

One difficulty with empirical investigation of such hypotheses is that the statements of principles issued by the NPOs themselves cannot be taken at face value, but must be treated as symbolic politics—another lesson of Edelman's work. Precisely because such fragile organizations must seek to develop multiple sources of support (political, economic, symbolic), they need to conceal increasing corporate and state dependency with the rhetoric of democratic participation, political accountability, and economic efficiency.

Conclusions

What is striking about the political language of the nonprofit literature is how critical many people are of the metaphors of "independence" and "voluntarism" and yet see no alternative to the image of a "third sector."[99] David Harrington Watt, for example, says that "independent" is a "remarkably inappropriate adjective to apply to what I am calling the third sector." He comments that Americans are reluctant to recognize the corporate character of much of America, and asserts that the image or the rhetoric of independence is a political ploy to defend the privileged tax position of NPOs.[100] More neutral observers recognize the diversity and "hybrid" character of NPOs, and try to explain it. The most recent review of the literature from a sociological standpoint uses a clever metaphor to make my basic point. DiMaggio and Anheier say that "in historical perspective, U.S. nonprofit organizations appear less a single form than a kind of cuckoo's nest occupied by different kinds of entrepreneurs for different purposes."[101]

My way of analyzing this diversity is to argue that it is important to see the complex institutional relations which constitute a whole society as the context in which legally NPOs are formed and operate. The "sector" has no autonomy, and does not mediate between "public" and "private," despite the political language used by its defenders. By the same token, "it" is not homogeneous, but has distinctively different aspects in relationship to the fundamental institutions of capitalism, state and democracy. In DiMaggio's and Anheier's words, " 'nonprofitness' has little consistent transnational or transhistorical meaning."[102]

The imprecision of boundaries between different types of NPOs, in fact their overlap, is part of the essential character of these organizations. Manipulation of their symbolic and institutional boundaries for specific political and economic interests is the best way to understand their societal character.

If alternative organizational forms are seen as strategic choices of elites weighing various economic, legal and political advantages, rather than as a problem of classification, we will better understand their formation and transformation under different historical conditions.

To the extent that the nonprofit sector has come to assume a degree of symbolic autonomy, some degree of additional legitimacy may have been won for the principle of voluntary participation in activities to meet human needs. It is difficult to complain about that achievement. But that legitimacy is highly precarious, as Peter Dobkin Hall has pointed out. From the 1980s on, Federal policy toward the nonprofit sector has exhibited a fundamental contradiction. On the one hand, the Reagan and Bush administrations since 1982 attempted to cut federal social and cultural expenditures while "rhetorically supporting voluntarism," but simultaneously favored tax plans which would eliminate the tax incentive for charitable giving. In education, the Reagan administration favored private institutions by establishing tuition tax credits, but simultaneously favored cutting direct aid to higher education and student loan programs.[103] Hall says that these are "contradictory proposals."[104] One possible explanation may be that they are only contradictory on the surface. A deeper consistency may be that the aim of all of these policies is to reduce *both* government activities and private giving to such services. Regardless of whether the consequence is intended, the result is to render the population more vulnerable to the vicissitudes of the labor market. If poor children cannot gain access to higher education, and social services—whether public or private—are less available to them, they will be forced to accept whatever employers offer them. The recent welfare "reforms" are an extension of these policies. From the standpoint of class politics, the cuts in the incentives to give indirect support for popular NPOs have clear consequences.

The symbolic politics of the nonprofit sector is probably more desperate and self-interested in the United States than in countries where social services are stably funded by the state. Where a social service or welfare system is dependent on voluntary agencies without stable and adequate funding, as in the United States, as compared to the Netherlands or Sweden, the result is that "service functions are overwhelmed by grantsmanship, budget-justification research and accountability rituals." Particularly when the agencies must in desperation seek profit-making activities,

> the new alliance between voluntarism and vendorism ... does not threaten agency autonomy or even advocacy as much as it deflects resources to the scramble for subsidies and then to rituals of reporting and accountability— the often meaningless counts of 'outputs,' such as number of interviews, hospital days, or meals served.[105]

In conclusion, my general argument does not imply that there is not something "different" or "real" about NPOs, or about the consequences of their existence. Regardless of their symbolic construction, they are *not* the same as purely profit-making organizations, and certainly not the same as governmental agencies. Popular nonprofits, in particular, have served to stimulate participation and "voice" (in Hirschman's sense) around such issues as environmentalism, safety, utility rates, the spotted owl controversy in Oregon, and educational innovation, to mention only a few obvious and recent examples.

To emphasize, as I have done, the symbolic functions of the political language which lumps together highly disparate organizational forms with quite different societal roles and links to economic and political interests does not therefore mean that I minimize the impact of NPOs on the society. Quite the contrary. Their existence and role would not be so controversial were there nothing significant at stake. But to restate my basic point—regarding the "nonprofit sector" as an undifferentiated entity, distinct from market and public, or economy and government, or capitalism and the state (whatever theoretical metaphors one accepts for this fundamental distinction) does not help understand the interests at stake and why they choose the nonprofit form.

Notes

1. I am indebted to Carroll Estes, Richard Merelman, Joel Rogers, Sam Sieber, Paul DiMaggio and Al Imershein for helpful comments on an earlier draft. Part of the argument was worked out jointly with Professor Estes, a leading scholar in this area of health and social service delivery. Professor DiMaggio and the other readers saved me from a number of over- and mis-statements, but cannot be held responsible for the remaining ones.

2. For samples of Murray Edelman's wide-ranging work, see *The Symbolic Uses of Politics* (Urbana: University of Illinois Press, 1964); *Constructing the Political Spectacle* (Chicago: University of Chicago Press, 1988); and *Politics as Symbolic Action* (Chicago: Markham, 1971).

3. Edelman, *Constructing the Political Spectacle*, p. 3.

4. Ibid, p. 9.

5. Ibid.

6. Ibid, p. 10.

7. Ibid, p. 11.

8. As far as I know, Edelman has never explicitly analyzed the nonprofit sector as such, as a symbolic creation which serves to pacify mass publics and serve elite interests—probably his most general and pervasive hypothesis. References to specific nonprofit organizations occur, of course, but the category itself is never singled out as a topic for discussion.

9. Use of the concept "nonprofit sector" or "voluntary associations" for descriptive and empirical purposes (as, for example, in studies which compare the pro-

portion of nonprofit and for-profit hospitals which accept Medicaid patients) is of course appropriate, since it uses a legal/nominal difference as a basis for empirical classification. My concern is with writings which use the category for discursive and ideological purposes, either defending or criticizing the "sector." Sometimes the two purposes get mixed up, particularly when legally nonprofit organizations are assumed to be "independent," "voluntary," or a "third" sector contrasted with the "state" and the "market," or when "it" is criticized for "competing" with profit-making organizations. The confusion of empirical and descriptive purposes with normative, policy, or ideological purposes is another illustration of my basic point about political language.

10. Paul DiMaggio, "Nonprofit Organizations in the Production and Distribution of Culture," in Walter W. Powell, editor, *The Nonprofit Sector: A Research Handbook* (New Haven: Yale University Press, 1987), pp. 196-7. See also DiMaggio and Helmut K. Anheier, "The Sociology of Nonprofit Organizations and Sectors," *Annual Review of Sociology*, 1990, Vol. 16, pp. 137-159 for a review of the literature.

11. Susan A. Ostrander, Stuart Langton, and Jon van Til, editors. *Shifting the Debate: Public/Private Sector Relations in the Modern Welfare State* (New Brunswick: Transaction Books, 1987), pp. 141-2.

12. Ibid, p. 33.

13. Robert Wuthnow, ed., *Between States and Markets: The Voluntary Sector in Comparative Perspective* (Princeton: Princeton University Press, 1991), p. 10.

14. Ibid, p. 17. Wuthnow assumes that the nonprofit sector is almost equivalent to the voluntary sector. In several places, he substitutes the term "nonprofit agencies" for that of "voluntary associations," as if they are equivalent (p. 4, 7, 11, 22).

15. Burton Weisbrod, *The Nonprofit Economy* (Cambridge: Harvard University Press, 1988), p. 108. Weisbrod uses "society" interchangeably with "we," as if "we," the society, decide on the policies to decide what nonprofits shall and shall not do, and whether or not they shall be subsidized by tax exemptions and other benefits. (See p. 117 and elsewhere.) This assumption makes it difficult to see a society as composed of strategically located interests (political, economic, cultural) possessing the power to buttress the organizations representing them with legal authority, economic resources, and political support.

16. James M. Ferris and Elizabeth Graddy, "Fading Distinctions Among the Nonprofit, Government and For-profit Sectors," in Virginia A. Hodgkinson, Richard W. Lyman and Associates, editors, *The Future of the Independent Sector* (San Francisco: Jossey Bass, 1989), p. 123. (A publication of Independent Sector). See also a review of Powell by sociologist James R. Wood. Wood says that one of the "most exciting trends in the past two decades of organization studies" has been the "increased attention to nonprofit (nonbusiness, nongovernment) organizations." (*American Journal of Sociology*, May, 1989, p. 1442). Then he goes on to say that the increased attention is to the "interrelationships" of the sector with the "business and government" sectors. This formulation begs the question, if Ferris and Graddy are correct, that nonprofit organizations are increasingly coming to "mirror" either state or corporate organizations.

17. Alan Ware, *Between Profit and State: Intermediate Organizations in Britain and the United States* (Princeton: Princeton University Press, 1989).

18. Weisbrod, p. 16.
19. Ware, p. 4.
20. Ibid.
21. Ibid, pp. 97–98.
22. Ibid, p. 173.
23. Ibid, p. 201.
24. Ibid, p. 202.
25. Jon van Til. *Mapping the Third Sector: Voluntarism in a Changing Social Economy* (New York: The Foundation Center, 1988), p. 3. Even though acceptance of the tripartite sectoral distinction is fundamental to his argument, van Til does not claim that the voluntary or third sector is autonomous. "The third sector is an interdependent, rather than an independent, arena of action. Boundaries between third sector organizations and organizations in the other sectors (government, business, household) are permeable, blurred, and laced with intersectoral connections" (p. 167).
26. Weisbrod, pp. 2–3.
27. Ibid, p. 13.
28. Ibid.
29. Even computer dictionaries legitimate the altruistic image of the concept of "nonprofit." In the Wordperfect 5.1 thesaurus, two of the main meanings of nonprofit are "charitable" and "public service," and the antonym is given as "commercial."
30. Joshua Cohen and Joel Rogers, *On Democracy: Toward a Transformation of American Society* (New York: Penguin, 1983). Democracy in their terms—entailing full civil liberties, full employment, political equality, social control of investment, and workplace democracy—does not exist yet anywhere. Cohen and Rogers make a sharp distinction between "capitalist democracy" and "democracy." What is interesting and relevant is that the institutional implementation of what they call the "principle of democratic legitimacy" (p. 149) sounds remarkably like the ideal conception of the nonprofit sector. Individuals are free and equally able to form associations, the organizations are not confined to the "formal arenas of politics" (i.e., nonstate), and "autonomy" or "self-governing capacities" involving "social cooperation" are essential. But Cohen and Rogers do not deal at all with specific organizational forms which will implement these principles. Nothing is said about the balance between public and private, let alone anything approximating a nonprofit sector. Presumably that is left for democratic debate among the citizenry.
31. See Robert R. Alford and Roger Friedland, *Powers of Theory: Capitalism, the State and Democracy* (Cambridge: Cambridge University Press, 1985), and Roger Friedland and Robert R. Alford, "Bringing Society Back In," in *The New Institutionalism in Organization Theory*, edited by W. W. Powell and P. J. DiMaggio, (Chicago: University of Chicago Press, 1991) for extensions of this theoretical argument. For an excellent brief discussion of institutional contradictions, see Claus Offe, "Legitimacy vs. Efficiency," in *Contradictions of the Welfare State* (Cambridge: The MIT Press, 1984), pp. 130–134.
It should be noted that the inconsistency between rhetoric and reality which is a central theme of Murray Edelman's work is not necessarily the same as an insti-

tutional contradiction, which forces change or creates paralysis. The rhetoric of public benefits may well allow the silent allocation of private benefits to proceed smoothly—until the inconsistency is exposed.

32. For a discussion of the concept of "structural interests," applied to the case of health care, see Robert R. Alford, *Health Care Politics* (Chicago: University of Chicago Press, 1975).

33. The notion of institutional logics is not new, although by extending it to the societal level of analysis I am certainly violating the principle of methodological individualism. For a somewhat different usage, see William G. Ouchi, "Markets, Bureaucracies and Clans," *Administrative Science Quarterly*, Vol. 25, March 1980, pp. 129–141. Befitting an argument within the "transaction costs" approach, these are seen as different modes of individual relations, although he defines them as constituting different types of organizations. An organization is "any stable pattern of transactions between individuals or aggregations of individuals" (p. 141). Markets control behavior through prices, bureaucracies through rules established by legitimate authority, and clans through traditions and socialization. Hollingsworth and Lindberg apply this scheme to the American economy, adding a fourth type: associations. See J. Rogers Hollingsworth and Leon Lindberg, "The Governance of the American Economy: the Role of Markets, Clans, Hierarchies and Associative Behavior," in Wolfgang Streeck and Philippe Schmitter, editors, *Private Interest Government: Beyond Market and State* (Beverly Hills: Sage Publications, 1985), pp. 122–267.

34. The spatial metaphor of "orbit" may or may not be clarifying, but I have found it useful as a heuristic image. "Sphere of influence," "arena" and "organizational field" are similar metaphors, each with its own connotations.

Precisely because the symbolic politics of the nonprofit sector involves conceptual sleight-of-hand, it is necessary to be very careful with terminology. I recognize that I face the same problem of arbitrarily classifying essentially complex and multifaceted entities when I distinguish between corporate, public, and popular nonprofits, but the issue is *which* abstractions can be theoretically justified. Most of the literature deals with "charitable" organizations, with a so-called 501(c)(3) designation in the Internal Revenue Code. I am adding so-called "mutual benefit" organizations, the "noncharitable nonprofits," some of which I would call "corporate" and others "popular" nonprofits. Also, I include as popular nonprofits those voluntary associations which have no legal status whatsoever.

35. A further classificatory distinction is needed between "bureaucratic" (or "formal") and "clan" ("informal") nonprofits. This distinction is necessary because sometimes loose and transitory voluntary associations which stress participation and voluntary action by individual citizens are viewed as the most "democratic." Organizations can enjoy a bureaucratic apparatus—paid and appointed staff, files, hierarchy of authority—without necessarily losing their democratic character. Too often democracy is equated with temporary and voluntary. Both formal and informal organizations exist among each of the categories of corporate, public and popular nonprofits.

36. Powell, p. 112.

37. Peter Dobkin Hall, "A Historical Overview of the Private Nonprofit Sector," in Powell, p. 3.

38. Quoted in Hall, p. 5.

39. J. Craig Jenkins, "Nonprofit Organizations and Policy Advocacy," in Powell, p. 314.

40. Carl Milovsky, "Neighborhood Organizations: A Market Analogy," in Powell, editor, pp. 277–295. Milovsky acknowledges that the analogy of the market is imperfect, and when he describes neighborhood organizations substantively, uses the language of the logic of democracy.

41. Lily M. Hoffman, *Community Revitalization Partnerships: A Midcourse Assessment of Seedco* (New York: Community Development Resource Center, Graduate School of Management and Urban Policy, New School for Social Research, 1990).

42. Powell, *The Nonprofit Sector*.

43. Douglas, p. 51.

44. Ostrander, et al.; Streeck and Schmitter; Susan Rose-Ackerman, editor, *The Economics of Nonprofit Institutions: Studies in Structure and Policy* (New York: Oxford University Press, 1986); Hodgkinson, Lyman and Associates; van Til.

45. See Weisbrod, p. 68, Figure 4.3.

46. Ware, p. 63.

47. See Hollingsworth and Lindberg, "The Governance of the American Economy," in Streeck and Schmitter, p. 252.

48. Edelman, *Politics as Symbolic Action*, p. 142.

49. Ibid, p. 144.

50. *Wall Street Journal*, Apr. 16, 1987.

51. My argument is not intended to question the core importance of what Elinor Ostrom calls "self-organized collective action," in her book *Governing the Commons: The Evolution of Institutions for Collective Action* (Cambridge: Cambridge University Press, 1990). Ostrom explicitly distinguishes situations of "common-pool resources" from purely competitive markets or situations in which state regulatory agencies or a court system are required to "monitor and enforce self-negotiated contracts" (p. 25). She never uses the term "nonprofit organization," but her work deals with "third sector" collective forms which are neither state nor market. Ostrom assumes that conditions exist under which "a self-organized group must solve the commitment problem without an external enforcer" (p. 44). Most of her cases, however, presuppose a state able to enforce compliance with the rules, even though the producers have decided upon them, and also a market for products.

52. Ware, p. 228.

53. Ibid, p. 229.

54. Ibid, p. 236.

55. Ibid, p. 223.

56. Weisbrod, p. 120.

57. The classic work by political scientist Grant McConnell, *Private Power and American Democracy* (New York: Alfred A. Knopf, 1967), contains several case studies which perfectly illustrate the symbolic character of the concept of private, public, and non-profit sectors, and therefore the profoundly misleading character of a theory based on a comparison of organizations classified as belonging to one of the sectors.

58. McConnell, p. 75.

59. Ibid, pp. 57–76.
60. Ibid, p. 147.
61. Ibid, p. 231.
62. Ibid, p. 204.
63. Ibid, p. 206.
64. Ibid.
65. See Randall Fitzgerald *When Government Goes Private: Successful Alternatives to Public Services* (New York: Universe Books, 1988), pp. 49–50.
66. In Powell, p. 112.
67. Ibid, p. 113.
68. Edward Skloot, "Enterprise and Commerce in Nonprofit Organizations," in Powell, pp. 380–393.
69. Ibid, p. 387.
70. In this section I am focusing upon "noncharitable nonprofits," in John G. Simon's phrase, which include "social clubs, veterans' organizations, labor unions, burial societies, chambers of commerce, marketing cooperatives, and other associations which may roughly be described as carrying forward the private interests of the members . . ." ("The Tax Treatment of Nonprofit Organizations," in Powell, p. 69.) Gifts to such organizations are not tax deductible, but their income is exempt from federal income tax: ". . . any profits [the organization might make] may not be distributed to owners or other private persons," the so-called "nondistribution constraint" (p. 68). It should be emphasized that the literature on nonprofits pays very little attention to corporate nonprofits, precisely because they do not conform to the image of voluntarism.
71. J. Rogers Hollingsworth and Ellen Jane Hollingsworth, *Controversy about American Hospitals: Funding, Ownership and Performance* (Washington, D.C.: American Enterprise Institute for Public Policy Research, 1987).
72. Ibid, p. 31.
73. Ibid, p. 32.
74. Ibid.
75. Ibid, p. 2.
76. Weisbrod, p. 2.
77. Ibid, p. 121.
78. Ibid, pp. 115–117. A good example of the ways in which different institutional logics create conflict between national and local levels of nonprofit organizations is the forcing out of the head of United Way of America over his allegedly "lavish" life style, including a salary of $463,000. (See the *New York Times* front page story, February 28, 1992.) William Aramony was challenged by many of the 2,100 local affiliates, as well as by other nonprofits for making the "charity resemble a corporation." In fact, the members of the board of governors of the United Way included 20 chief executives of some of the largest corporations in America. Mr. Aramony's rewards were perfectly appropriate for the private corporation the national United Way modelled itself after (to make executives "feel comfortable"), but not for nonprofit organizations legitimated at the grass roots level by a popular/democratic ideology, in this case charitable giving in the workplace to meet human needs.
79. Weisbrod, p. 12.

80. *High Technology Business*, Aug. 1988.

81. Ibid, p. 38.

82. See James T. Bennett and Thomas J. DiLorenzo, *Unfair Competition: The Profits of Nonprofits* (Lanham, Md.: Hamilton Press, 1989).

83. Ibid, p. 13. An example of an analysis by an economist who uses only a model based on the structural logic of capital focuses upon how "nonprofit firms compete with one another in the markets for donations, memberships, clients and sales," and also how the sector as a whole "competes with the for-profit and government sectors in the markets for skilled labor, sales and reduced (or zero) cost service provision." (Richard Steinberg, "Nonprofit Organizations and the Market," in Powell, pp. 118–138.) Given the strategic, financial and political interdependence of different types of nonprofits, such a formulation begs all the questions. If nonprofits can in fact make profits and be completely funded by government, (or even be in "partnership"), then the problem cannot be defined in terms of competition between sectors.

The absurd results of relying upon such models is shown by a table in which Steinberg computes "concentration ratios by industry" for museums, country clubs, aid to the poor, and health clinics. Country clubs are found to be reasonably competitive, but museums are somewhat monopolistic, as measured by their "share of total revenues in the relevant market." Steinberg comments that the concentration ratio index has "certain ambiguities," because he does not know whether or not the market for country clubs and museums includes "competing government and for-profit firms." It is hard to know what to say about such an argument.

84. William D. Coleman, "State Corporatism as a Sectoral Phenomenon: The Case of the Quebec Construction Industry" in Alan Cawson, editor, *Organized Interests and the State: Studies in Meso-Corporatism* (Beverly Hills: Sage Publications, 1985), p. 106.

85. Ibid, p. 107.

86. Melissa Middleton, "Nonprofit Boards of Directors: Beyond the Governance Function," in Powell, pp. 141–153.

87. Ibid, p. 141.

88. Skloot, p. 387.

89. "Public" television has come perilously close to the dividing line between an acknowledgement of support and a commercial ad by first allowing a corporate logo to be shown, and then a one sentence mention of a sponsor.

90. Ware, p. 101.

91. It is tempting to argue that different sources of funding are associated with each type of nonprofit organization. Public contributions are state funds allocated by statute or administrative decision to categories of organizations. Corporate contributions are those given as tax-deductible by corporations, commercial firms or individuals who are not members or participants. Popular contributions are the dollars and/or labor contributed by individuals who are the constituents, members, beneficiaries of the nonprofit organization. The balance of such contributions may be correlated with the power of life and death over the organization and many of its goals and activities, although popular contributions (such as, for example, those raised by highly centralized mass fund raising organizations) may not necessarily support the democratic character of a nonprofit organization. (I am indebted to Paul DiMaggio for this qualification.)

92. See Michael O'Neill *The Third American: The Emergence of the Nonprofit Sector in the United States* (San Francisco: Jossey Bass, 1989), O'Neill has separate chapters on religion, private education, health care, arts and culture, social services, advocacy and legal service, international assistance, foundations and corporate funders, and mutual benefit organizations. The chapter on the latter lumps together unions, the American Tobacco Institute, TIAA-CREF, Blue Cross and Blue Shield, and the "3,000 trade and professional associations in Washington DC, . . . one of [whose] chief tasks is to lobby the federal government" (p. 166). O'Neill, after raising the issue of why such groups should receive tax exemption, merely says that "these questions, however legitimate, illustrate the need for more understanding of the complexities and roles of mutual benefit organizations." His concern is to maintain the integrity of the "sector" as a whole, not to criticize one part of it.

93. Ibid, pp. 169–170.

94. Ibid, p. 171.

95. Gabriel Rudney, "The Scope and Dimensions of Nonprofit Activity," in Powell, pp. 59–60.

96. Skloot, p. 399.

97. This argument is analogous to the one made by Roger Friedland, Frances Fox Piven and the present writer concerning the consequences of different structural locations within the state. See our chapter "Political Conflict, Urban Structure, and the Fiscal Crisis," in Douglas Ashford, editor, *Comparing Public Policies: New Concepts and Methods* (Beverly Hills: Sage Publications, 1978).

98. See Sam D. Sieber, *Fatal Remedies: The Ironies of Social Intervention* (New York: Plenum Press, 1981), for a cogent theoretical argument about the unanticipated consequences of political action.

99. David Harrington Watt, "The United States: Cultural Challenges to the Voluntary," in Wuthnow, ed., p. 278.

100. Watt uses Habermas' concept of the public sphere to challenge the ideological character of the "voluntary" or "independent" sector. He argues that a "relatively small proportion of the voluntary associations in America actually offset privatization" (p. 279), acting in any way relevant to Habermas' notion of the "public sphere" as a "place where people . . . may rationally discuss questions of the common good in a manner that is not distorted by either the power of the state or that of the marketplace" (p. 244). Watt concludes that voluntary associations in America, with some exceptions, do not constitute elements of a "public sphere" in Habermas' sense. Instead, they "illustrate the pressures that eat away at the public sphere in advanced capitalist societies" (p. 279).

101. DiMaggio and Anheier, p. 141.

102. Ibid, p. 154.

103. For recent analyses of the legitimation crisis in the nonprofit sector, see Carroll L. Estes and Robert R. Alford, "Systemic Crisis and the Nonprofit Sector," *Theory and Society* Vol. 19, 1990, pp. 173–198; Carroll L. Estes, Elizabeth A. Binney and Linda A. Bergthold, "How the Legitimacy of the Sector has Eroded," in Virginia A. Hodgkinson, Richard W. Layman, and Associates, *The Future of the Nonprofit Sector* (San Francisco: Jossey-Bass, 1989), pp. 21–40; and Carroll L. Estes and Linda A. Bergthold, "The Unravelling of the Nonprofit Service Sector in the U.S.," in "The

Service Economy" special issue of *International Journal of Sociology and Social Policy*, edited by Joel I. Nelson, Vol. 9, 1989, No. 2/3, pp. 18-33.

104. Hall, p. 21.

105. See Harold Wilensky's foreword to Ralph M. Kramer's important comparative study of the United States, England, Israel and the Netherlands. (*Voluntary Agencies in the Welfare State* (Berkeley: University of California Press, 1981), p. xviii. The myths that voluntary, participatory agencies are the most innovative and the most responsive to needs, that government funding necessarily leads to government control, that voluntarism and dependence on donations leads to responsiveness to community needs are refuted by Kramer's study of voluntary agencies for the handicapped in four countries: ". . . the most innovative vanguard agencies are among the largest, most bureaucratized, and most professionalized . . ." (p. xix).

2

The Political Uses of Political Issues

Benjamin Ginsberg

Observers of American politics often take issues and policy proposals at face value and seek to assess existing or prospective government programs in terms of their consequences for the social, economic or international problems these programs' proponents claim to address. Nearly 20 years ago, however, Murray Edelman pointed out that "the significant 'outputs' of political activities are not particular public policies labeled as political goals, but rather the creation of political followings and supports."[1] In other words, political leaders often are concerned less with the social, economic or international implications of a course of action they advocate than with the program's potential for enhancing their own political standing and undermining that of their political opponents.

This political conception of public policy is the key to understanding the programs proposed and adopted by the Reagan and Bush administrations over the past ten years, as well as Democratic opposition to them. Whatever their nominal goals, the economic policies, domestic social policies and defense policies of the Reagan and Bush years have also been weapons of political struggle. They have served as instruments through which forces associated with the Republican party have been able to mobilize support for themselves while laying siege to the political bases and power of their Democratic opponents. At the same time, the political threat posed by these policies, as much as opposition to their nominal goals, has fueled Democratic efforts to block them.

In the decades following the New Deal, the Democrats established a solid political base in the social service and regulatory agencies of the domestic state. Since winning control of the presidency in 1980, the Republicans have sought to undermine these Democratic strongholds and create a constellation of institutions, policies and political forces to entrench themselves in power. The principal weapons the Republicans have deployed against their

51

opponents are domestic spending cuts, tax reductions and deregulation. These weapons have served both to weaken important institutional bastions of the Democrats and to disrupt the social groups and forces upon which that party depends for support. At the same time, through national security, monetary and fiscal policy, the Republicans have undertaken to reorganize social forces and establish mechanisms of governance to sustain their rule. Of course, these disparate strategies are not components of some master plan that the Republicans devised prior to winning control of the presidency. Rather, they emerged in the course of conflicts within the GOP and between the White House and the various institutions controlled by the Democrats.

Disrupting Democratic Institutions

Since gaining control of the White House in the 1980s, the Republicans have sought to undermine the social service and regulatory agencies in which the Democrats are entrenched. Central to this endeavor are the tax reductions, domestic spending cuts, and efforts at deregulation promoted by the Reagan and Bush administrations. These Republican policies have weakened the extractive, distributive and regulatory capabilities of institutions over which the Democrats exercise influence. In turn, this has reduced the ability of the Democrats to achieve their policy objectives, overcome divisions in their coalition, and provide benefits to groups allied with the party.

In 1981, the Reagan administration sponsored legislation which substantially cut individual and corporate income tax rates and indexed these rates to inflation. Congressional Democrats responded to the administration's bill by introducing a proposal of their own. As a result of the ensuing bidding war, a tax bill was enacted that reduced revenues more sharply than the White House had planned. Coupled with the administration's military buildup and inability to secure the drastic cuts in domestic spending it had proposed, these tax cuts produced the enormous budget deficits of the 1980s. Thus, the federal government's annual deficit increased from approximately $60 billion at the end of the Carter administration to a peak of over $200 billion during the Reagan presidency. Annual deficits began to decline from that peak in the late 1980s, though this came about largely as a result of surpluses in the Social Security trust fund.

Five years later, in the 1986 tax reform act, tax rates were further reduced and numerous loopholes—deductions, exemptions and tax preferences—were eliminated from the federal tax code. By closing the loopholes for influential groups that had made nominally high income tax rates politically feasible, the 1986 tax reform act has made it difficult for Congress to restore any of the lost revenues. Thus when seeking to reduce the budget deficit at the beginning of the Bush administration, Congress only found it possible to consider increasing taxes which produce little in the way of revenue, such as those on alcohol, gasoline and tobacco.

These restrictions on the extractive capacities of Congress have impaired that institution's distributive capabilities. Because the federal government has been strapped for revenues, funding levels for existing programs have come under pressure, and it has been all but impossible for congressional Democrats to enact new social programs despite demands that more be done to cope with such problems as the AIDS epidemic and homelessness.[2]

At the same time, Republican tax policies have exacerbated cleavages within the Democratic camp. During the New Deal and postwar decades, the claims that disparate groups made on the federal treasury were accommodated through logrolling arrangements that characteristically were negotiated by the Democratic leadership of Congress. These arrangements entailed a steady growth of the public sector through a process of budgetary "incrementalism," as Aaron Wildavsky termed it at the time.[3] This pattern of policy making depended upon a steady expansion of public revenues, which was achieved without the political conflict that would have resulted from repeated increases in nominal tax rates by allowing inflation to steadily increase real rates of federal income taxation through what came to be called "bracket creep."

By slashing federal tax rates and introducing indexation to prevent bracket creep, the Republicans have undermined the fiscal foundations of the New Deal pattern of accommodations among the beneficiaries of federal expenditure programs. The enormous deficit that was created by Republican fiscal policies exerts constant pressure upon the funding levels of domestic programs. To protect their favorite programs in this fiscal environment, lobbyists representing such groups as farmers, organized labor, senior citizens, advocates of welfare spending, and local government officials have been compelled to engage in zero-sum conflict, in contrast to the positive-sum politics of the New Deal and postwar systems. One group's gain now has become another group's loss.[4] This has placed strains on the Democratic coalition.

Finally, after gaining control of the White House in the 1980s, the Republicans undertook to restrict the regulatory capabilities of the federal government. They promoted deregulation in the transportation, energy, banking, and financial sectors of the economy, and curtailed enforcement of environmental, health, safety, consumer, and antitrust laws. Consequently, regulatory agencies are now less likely to intervene against business on behalf of groups disadvantaged by market processes. For example, financial deregulation and the relaxation of antitrust enforcement in the 1980s left labor and other Democratic constituencies with little protection against the threat to their interests posed by the largest wave of corporate reorganizations—hostile takeovers, leveraged buyouts, plant closings—since the days of J.P. Morgan. A second consequence of deregulation has been to erode the accommodations between business and labor fashioned by the Democrats. During the New Deal period the federal government established or extended a regime of regulation over numerous sectors of the American economy. Characteristically, these regulations restricted price competition among firms within the regulated industry, and in some cases erected barriers to the entry of new firms. To the extent that firms within such industries could pass added costs on to their customers without having to worry about being undersold by their competitors, they lost an incentive to control their labor costs. Consequently, union-management relations in most regulated industries were less adversarial than cooperative in character. Rather than fight one another over wages and work rules, unions and employers entered the political arena as allies to defend and extend the regulatory regime and to secure direct or indirect public subsidies for their industries.

Asserting that these business-labor accommodations served "special interests" at the expense of the "public interest," an unlikely coalition of conservatives and liberal consumer advocates secured a substantial measure of deregulation during the late 1970s.[5] Through deregulation, conservatives sought to get business to break its accommodations with organized labor. Consumer advocates, for their part, were happy to weaken the labor unions and business interests that had been their rivals for influence within the Democratic party.

In the face of the threats that Reaganism posed to them both, liberals and labor rekindled their alliance in the 1980s. Increasingly, organized labor gave its support to liberal causes it would formerly have disdained such as the nuclear freeze and comparable worth. Liberals, for their part, have begun to see merit in a number of causes supported by organized labor, such as protectionism, and have lost their enthusiasm for deregulation. The Republicans, on the other hand, have continued to press for deregulation, and with good reason. Particularly in airlines, telecommunications, and trucking, deregulation has led to the emergence of non-union firms that undersell the established giants in their respective industries. This has compelled established firms to demand give-backs from their unions to lower their own labor costs, and has disrupted alliances between business and labor.

Reorganizing Political Forces

By undermining the governing capacities of institutions over which the Democrats exercise influence, the Republicans have also weakened the Democrats' social base. They have done this by disorganizing some of the major political forces upon which the Democrats depend and reorganizing them under Republican auspices. While most observers assume that politicians must deal with whatever groups they find in society, it is important to note that political leaders are not limited to working with some predefined constellation of forces. At times, they can destroy established centers of power, reorganize interests, and even call new groups into being. There are several ways in which leaders can attempt to reorganize the constellation of interests that play a significant role in the political process. They may be able to transform the political identities of established groups, create new political forces by dividing existing groups, or construct new interests by uniting previously disparate elements. In these ways, the Republicans have sought to reshape the political attachments of businessmen, middle-class suburbanites, blue-collar ethnics, and white southerners.

Reunifying Business

Over the past fifteen years the Republicans have undertaken to unify the business community under their auspices. In the years following World War II, the Democrats had reached an accommodation with many segments of big business—internationally competitive firms that benefitted from free trade policies, firms in capital-intensive industries that found it relatively easy to make concessions to organized labor, and defense contractors that benefitted from a foreign policy of internationalism.[6] However, proprietors of smaller firms that were not involved in international markets often found Democratic labor and social programs onerous, and characteristically aligned themselves with the Republican party. This breach between Wall Street and Main Street undermined the political potency of American business.

During the 1970s, the accommodation between big business and the Democratic party was severely strained by two developments that the Republicans sought to exploit. The erosion of America's position in the world economy caused firms that previously had accepted the high labor costs and taxes associated with the Democrats to be no longer willing to do so. And Democratic support for environmental, consumer, and other new regulatory programs further alienated many of the party's allies in the business community. In his 1980 presidential campaign, Ronald Reagan appealed for the support of business by indicating that he would trim costly social programs, weaken the influence of organized labor, and relax the environmental rules and other forms of regulation that had been sponsored by Democratic politicians during the 1960s and 1970s. Moreover, Reagan offered the thousands of firms that stood to benefit from military contracts substantial increases in defense spending. Enacted into law, these policies helped to reunify American business and attach it to the Republican party.[7]

From Beneficiaries to Taxpayers

Middle-income suburbanites are a second group to which the Republicans have tried to appeal. The GOP has sought to convince these voters to regard themselves less as beneficiaries of federal expenditure programs than as taxpayers. After World War II, many suburbanites were integrated into the political process and linked to the Democratic party by federal programs that subsidized mortgages, built arterial highways, and expanded access to higher education. At the same time, by placating the poor and reducing working-class militancy, Democratic welfare and labor programs promoted social peace. In exchange for the benefits they received, members of the middle class gave their support to the various expenditure programs through which the Democratic party channeled public funds to its other constituency groups: crop subsidies for farmers, maritime subsidies for the shipping industry, and so on. This system of interest group liberalism enabled the Democrats to accommodate the claims of the host of disparate groups they sought to include in their electoral coalition.[8]

During the 1960s and 1970s, many of the benefits that middle-income Americans had come to expect from federal programs and policies were sharply curtailed. For example, rising mortgage interest rates increased housing costs, affirmative action programs seemed to threaten the middle class's privileged access to higher education, social peace was disrupted by urban violence and riots, and, above all, double-digit inflation during the late 1970s eroded the middle class's real income and standard of living. The curtailment of these benefits undermined the political basis of the loyalty that many middle-income individuals had shown to the Democrats. This provided the GOP with an opportunity to win their support.[9]

In wooing suburbanites, the GOP has chosen not to base its appeal on new federal benefits—although, to be sure, it has not sought to repeal existing middle-class benefit programs. Instead, it has sought to link these individuals to the Republican camp in their capacity as taxpayers. In 1980, Ronald Reagan declared tax relief to be a central political issue. The Republican campaign, moreover, sought to link the issues of taxation and inflation by blaming high rates of inflation on Democratic tax and spending policies. Indeed, Reagan called inflation the "cruelest tax of all."

After Reagan's election, his administration cooperated with Federal Reserve Board Chairman Paul Volcker in a relentless attack on inflation.[10] The Reagan-Volcker war on inflation was successful, albeit at the cost of a severe recession and high rates of unemployment for blue-collar workers. At the same time, the Reagan administration provided middle- and upper-income groups with a sizeable reduction in federal income tax rates. An important element in Reagan's successful 1984 campaign against Walter Mondale was his warning to middle-income voters that the Democrats wanted to take their tax cuts away. This theme was echoed by George Bush in 1988. Bush promised to oppose any efforts to raise federal income tax rates and heaped scorn on Michael Dukakis's proposal to step up collection of delinquent federal taxes. Bush derided what he characterized as a Democratic plan to put an Internal Revenue Service auditor into every taxpayer's home.

Republican efforts to convince middle-income Americans to focus on taxes have been quite successful. For example, although in 1976 only 2 percent of middle-class voters identified taxes and spending as important national problems, by 1984, 23 percent of voters with above average incomes did so. Of these voters, 67 percent cast their ballots for the Republican presidential candidate.[11]

The chief reason that the Republicans have sought to appeal to members of the middle class as taxpayers rather than as beneficiaries is that they hope to erode middle-income support for domestic expenditures in general. Transforming middle-class Americans into taxpayers not only links them to the Republican party, but also helps to undermine the entire apparatus of interest group liberalism through which the Democrats have maintained the allegiance of their various constituencies. This helps to disorganize the Democrats' political base.

Republican tax policies have also served to divide a politically important middle-class group—college educated professionals—that had given substantial support to the Democrats during the 1960s and 1970s. Socially this group is quite heterogeneous, ranging from ill-paid social workers to lavishly compensated attorneys—so much so, in fact, that sociologists have debated whether it is meaningful to speak of this "new class" as a coherent social and political force.[12] But groups are constituted in the political realm, and during the 1960s and 1970s political entrepreneurs were able to mobilize large numbers of professionals on behalf of such liberal causes as environmentalism and opposition to the Vietnam war.

The Republicans have sought to divide the new class by shifting the political debate to the issues of tax and budget cuts. The 1981 tax cut was promoted as a means of stimulating the private sector. The tax reform package that Ronald Reagan made the centerpiece of his second administration was especially beneficial to professionals with high salaries. Professionals in a position to take advantage of these new opportunities—namely, those who work in the private sector—were attracted to the Republican party.

At the same time, Republican reductions in federal domestic expenditures have restricted opportunities for professionals who work in the public and nonprofit sectors. The Republicans, however, have not been altogether unhappy to see school teachers, social workers, and university professors try to defend their interests by becoming increasingly active in Democratic party politics. The more committed the Democrats become to the cause of boosting domestic expenditures, the more likely it is that taxpayers, businessmen, and private-sector professionals will flock to the Republican party.

This Republican strategy has been quite successful. College graduates working in public sector occupations gave the Republicans only 40 percent of their votes in the 1984 presidential election. On the other hand, college graduates in the private sector supported the GOP by the overwhelming margin of 68 percent to 32 percent for the Democrats. In terms of party identification among college graduates in the public sector, Democrats outnumber Republicans 54 percent to 20 percent. By contrast, among private-sector college graduates, 40 percent identify with the Republican party and only 29 percent with the Democrats.

From Workers to Patriots

A third group to which the GOP now appeals are blue-collar ethnics. During the New Deal era, members of urban ethnic groups had been integrated into politics in their capacity as workers. This was accomplished by organizations informally affiliated with the national Democratic party—trade unions, political machines, and urban service bureaucracies. These institutions provided members of urban ethnic groups with public and private employment at relatively high wages, with social services, and with preferential access to locally administered federal programs. At the same time, trade unions, and urban machines and bureaucracies functioned as the local institutional foundations of the national Democratic party, mobilizing urban ethnics to support Democratic candidates.[13]

The Republicans have weakened the links between the Democrats and blue-collar workers by attacking these institutions. They have undermined organized labor by encouraging employers to engage in anti-union practices; indeed, the Reagan administration set an example by destroying the Professional Air Traffic Controllers Organization when the group conducted a strike in 1981.[14] In addition, Republicans have appointed commissioners hostile to organized labor to the National Labor Relations Board, an agency formerly controlled by labor sympathizers. Moreover, as discussed above, the Reagan and Bush administrations have supported policies of deregulation that provide business firms with a strong incentive to rid themselves of their unions. Finally, the Republican commitment to free trade allows foreign goods to flood American markets, increasing unemployment in heavily unionized industries and reducing labor's bargaining power. As a result of these policies, union membership dropped sharply during the 1980s.

The Republicans have attacked urban political machines and national and municipal service bureaucracies mainly through domestic spending reductions. The programs whose budgets have suffered most under Reagan and Bush are precisely those that once provided local governments with substantial funds, such as revenue-sharing and the Comprehensive Employment and Training Program (CETA). In addition, the tax reform package whose enactment was secured by the Reagan administration in 1986 reduced the deductability of local sales taxes (thereby heightening taxpayer resistance to rate increases) and restricted the ability of local governments to issue tax-free bonds. These changes in the tax code further diminished the resources available to municipal governments. The Justice Department has also attacked urban machines and bureaucracies by launching a series of investigations of corruption in municipal government whose primary targets have been large cities controlled by the Democrats.[15]

The attack on labor unions, political machines and social service agencies diminishes the ability of these institutions to provide benefits to urban ethnics, and thus undermines the institutional linkage between this group and the Democratic party. The disruption of these institutional foundations gives the Republicans an opportunity to capture the support of what formerly had been a staunch Democratic constituency.

In appealing to urban ethnics, the Republicans have been handicapped in one important way. In their capacity as workers, many of these individuals have been hurt by Republican economic and tax programs, which mainly serve the interests of the upper-middle class and segments of the business community. Instead of seeking to appeal to members of urban ethnic groups on economic grounds, however, the Republicans have attempted to secure and institutionalize their support on three other bases. First, they have sought to link urban ethnics to the GOP on the basis of their moral and religious convictions. The Republicans have undertaken to politicize these concerns by focusing on so-called family issues—above all, the issue of abortion. In this endeavor, they have sought to make use of Catholic churches, which have made it their business to rally the faithful against pro-abortion[16] candidates. The importance of this political transformation became evident during the 1984 presidential election. White working class voters who belonged to trade unions but did not regularly attend a church gave Ronald Reagan only 46 percent of their votes. By contrast, among white working class voters who attended a church regularly but did not belong to a union, the Republicans received 67 percent of the vote.

In addition to using moral appeals, the Republicans have also attempted to mobilize urban ethnics with patriotic appeals. In this effort they have at times been able to harness the national media—an institution whose editorial pages and televised commentary frequently have been hostile to their policies. Both Ronald Reagan and George Bush have created news events filled with patriotic symbols and appeals that the media could neither attack nor ignore. In addition, where the risks of failure have been low, Republican administrations have used military force abroad not only to demonstrate America's resolve to foreigners but also to reinforce national pride among Americans. The 1984 Grenada invasion and the 1986 bombing of Libya are examples, as is the 1990 invasion of Panama. These earlier uses of military force helped to create a climate of public opinion which made it possible for the Bush administration in 1991 to undertake a major military offensive against Iraq. During the 1988 presidential campaign, George Bush sought to make political use of patriotic sentiments by charging that his Democratic rival, Massachusetts Governor Michael Dukakis, had demonstrated a lack of respect for the American flag when he vetoed a Massachusetts bill that mandated the daily recitation of the pledge of allegiance in public schools.

Finally, the Republicans have made use of race-related issues to seek support among white ethnic voters. The Reagan and Bush administrations have opposed affirmative action and school busing plans and have supported efforts to narrow the rights that the liberal Warren Court had granted to persons accused of crimes. In his 1988 presidential campaign, George Bush made a major issue of the Willie Horton case. Horton, a black man, had been convicted of murder and sentenced to life imprisonment without parole. However, under a program supported by Governor Michael Dukakis, Massachusetts prison authorities granted him a weekend furlough. While on furlough, Horton fled the state and raped a white woman in Maryland. Groups supporting the Bush campaign repeatedly broadcast television ads displaying a picture of Horton and asserting that Dukakis was soft on crime.

From Southerners to Evangelicals

Finally, the Republicans have sought to add southern whites to their camp. For a century after the Civil War, white southerners had participated in politics through the Democratic party, which had defended the southern caste system. These voters were linked to the Democrats not simply by their racial attitudes, but also by local political institutions that were connected with the party—county commissions, sheriffs, judges, voting registrars—and that guaranteed white political power by excluding blacks from participation in government and politics.[17]

The civil rights revolution and, in particular, the Voting Rights Act of 1965 destroyed the institutional foundations of the traditional southern Democratic regime by preventing local governmental institutions from being used to maintain white privilege at the expense of black political subordination. The disruption of this system gave Republicans an opportunity to win the support of southern whites. As noted above, Republicans have been willing to appeal to voters on the basis of race-related issues; this has helped them to win support among white southerners as well as blue collar urbanites. At the same time, the GOP has also appealed to southerners on the basis of their religious orientations. By focusing on such issues as abortion, school prayer and pornography, Republicans have sought to politicize the moral concerns of white southerners. Moreover, they have made use of evangelical churches, which are such a prominent feature of the southern landscape, to forge institutional links between southern whites and the Republican party. Republicans have made evangelical churches, in effect, organizational components of their party. For example, funds and technical support are provided to these churches for voter registration activities.

As a result of these efforts, southern whites increasingly have been integrated into politics through their evangelical religious affiliations. This has helped to give the Republicans a firm social base in the white South for the first time in the party's 130-year history. In 1984, for example, Ronald Reagan received the votes of 78 percent of white fundamentalist and evangelical Christian voters. In 1988 an even larger proportion of these voters—81 per cent—supported George Bush.[18]

As was true in the case of urban ethnics, who are mainly Catholic, the most important moral issue that Republicans have used to appeal to white southerners is the issue of abortion. Indeed, Republicans have used the question of abortion to promote an alliance between evangelical southern Protestants and conservative Catholics and to attach both to the Republican party. Organization around the right-to-life issue was initiated for this purpose by Richard Viguerie, Paul Weyrich, Howard Phillips and other conservative Republican activists. Seeking to take advantage of the furor caused by the Supreme Court's pro-choice decision in *Roe v. Wade*, these politicians convinced Catholic political activists and evangelical Protestant leaders that they had common interests and worked with these leaders to arouse public opposition to abortion. Thus the right-to-life issue helped to bring about the political unification, under Republican auspices, of two religious groups that had been bitter opponents through much of American history.[19]

The Republicans also have sought to use foreign policy and military issues to mobilize support among southerners. Military bases and defense plants play a major role in the economy of many southern states. Republican support and Democratic opposition to a military buildup during the 1980s tied many southern workers, businessmen, and local communities ever more closely to the GOP. This serves as the material foundation for the patriotic appeals that the Republicans use so successfully to woo support in the white South. Significantly, almost none of the several dozen military installations closed as a cost-cutting measure in 1989 were located in the South; hence, that region's stake in defense spending will continue.[20]

Constructing Mechanisms of Governance

In contrast to the Democrats, who have entrenched themselves primarily in the social service and regulatory agencies of the domestic state, the Republicans have relied more heavily upon two alternative mechanisms of governance. These are the military and national security apparatus, and monetary and fiscal policy.

The National Security Apparatus

Since the 1980s, the Republicans have undertaken to enhance the size and power of America's military and national security apparatus and to use it as an instrument for governing and perpetuating the power of the GOP. Toward this end, the Reagan administration sponsored the largest peacetime military buildup in the nation's history. Military expenditures in constant dollars increased from $171 billion per year at the end of the Carter administration to $242 billion by the middle of President Reagan's second term. Subsequently, congressional opposition limited further increases in military spending to the annual rate of inflation. But, the enormous military buildup of the first Reagan administration has enlarged the base upon which changes in military spending are now calculated.

When they controlled the White House, Democratic administrations had initiated domestic spending programs to solidify the party's ties to its numerous constituency groups. At the same time, such expenditures stimulated economic growth and employment, thereby identifying the Democrats as the party of prosperity. Thus, even many interests that were not direct recipients of federal spending were given reason to support the Democrats. While professing to reject the economic theory associated with Democratic spending programs, the Republicans have adopted a program of military Keynesianism. Republican military programs have directly benefitted segments of the business community, regions of the country, and elements of the electorate whose fortunes are tied to the military sector. But at the same time, the Republicans expect that the economic growth, high levels of employment, and healthy corporate profits promoted by these programs will provide Americans more generally with reasons to support the GOP.

In addition to this program of military Keynesianism, the Republicans have sought to develop a military version of the industrial policy often espoused by the Democrats. Under Democratic variants of industrial policy, decisions regarding the allocation of capital and the organization of production that now are the prerogative of businessmen would involve union and public influence as well. The Republicans, by contrast, have sought to enhance the competitiveness of American industry through means that reinforce rather than limit the prerogatives of corporate management. The Reagan/Bush military buildup has been central to this endeavor.

Republican military programs have emphasized the production and procurement of new weapons systems rather than bolstering personnel or enhancing readiness and maintenance. The purchase of new weapons provides subsidies to business and promotes the development of new technologies that may increase the strength and competitiveness of American industry. The Strategic Defense Initiative (SDI) or, "Star Wars," was the most ambitious effort in this regard. The impressive performance of complex weapons systems during the Persian Gulf war should bolster Republican efforts in this area.

The Republicans have also undertaken to use military programs as a form of social policy. While seeking to drastically slash domestic social spending, they have largely defended the health care, educational and income maintenance programs administered by the Veterans Administration (VA). Indeed, during Ronald Reagan's last year in office the VA was elevated to a cabinet-level department. The programs administered by this department are identical to domestic welfare programs in all respects but one—historically they have been linked to conservative veterans' organizations rather than to liberal political forces. Thus, under the rubric of putting an end to waste, fraud and abuse, the Republicans have slashed the welfare programs that were politically beneficial to their opponents. At the same time, however, they have been happy to continue funding programs that serve their political friends. Conservative veterans' groups, for their part, have been more than willing to endorse Republican military ventures and lobby on behalf of GOP foreign policies.

Obviously, the continuing capacity of Republicans to make use of military and defense programs was predicated on the outcome of the Persian Gulf war. A relatively rapid American military victory that produced few casualties served to publicly validate Republican policies. A protracted and bloody struggle leading to an unsuccessful conclusion, on the other hand, would have destroyed popular support for national security programs and made it very difficult for the Bush or subsequent administrations to justify heavy military outlays in the future.

Monetary and Fiscal Policy

The complex of Republican policies described above is sustained by a fiscal regime that is one of the most notable features of the contemporary American political economy.[21] Central to this regime are the enormous budget and trade deficits of the Reagan-Bush years. The budget deficit resulted from the tax reductions and military spending increases of the first Reagan administration coupled with Congress's opposition to further domestic spending cuts. In conjunction with the restrictive monetary policies the Federal Reserve pursued in its fight against inflation, the budget deficit led to sharp increases in real interest rates and the value of the American dollar in the early 1980s. This, in turn, greatly reduced American exports and encouraged a flood of foreign imports into the U.S. During the second Reagan administration, coordinated central bank intervention led the dollar to fall, but by this time foreign manufacturers had established such a solid position in the American market that the nation's trade deficit continued to grow. Thus, the U.S. balance of trade, which had been positive from the second world war through the 1960s, reached a deficit of approximately $170 billion in 1987 before declining somewhat to roughly $140 billion in 1988.

Despite the economic risks they pose, however, these deficits provide the Republicans with important political benefits and opportunities. First, by making it difficult for politicians to appeal for votes with new public expenditure programs, the budget deficit impedes efforts by the Democrats to reconstruct their political base. More important, the twin deficits function as a novel revenue-collection apparatus that, at least in the short run, enable the Republicans to finance government expenditures without raising taxes and alienating their political constituency.

This apparatus works as follows. The Reagan administration's fiscal policies encouraged Americans to purchase foreign, especially Japanese and German, goods. At the same time, America's high interest rates and political stability have encouraged foreign bankers—most notably the Japanese—to purchase U.S. Treasury securities with the profits their nation's manufacturers make in the United States. Thus, during the 1980s, what might be called "autodollars" came to be recycled by Japanese banks, much as "petrodollars" were recycled by American banks in the 1970s. These autodollars, invested in U.S. government securities, have been used to help finance the American budget deficit.[22] In essence, Japanese industrialists and bankers have served as tax collectors for the Republican administration. Although Americans, in their capacity as voters, demonstrated in 1980, 1984 and again in 1988 that they opposed increased taxation, as consumers they willingly—indeed, enthusiastically—hand over billions of dollars for this purpose whenever they purchase Japanese and other foreign-made goods.

The costs of this revenue system are borne by unemployed workers in the manufacturing sector, and by employers who fail to restructure their firms to meet foreign competition. The benefits, however, flow to groups with which the Republicans are allied. Military spending benefits the defense industry and its thousands of subcontractors. The fiscal stimulus of the deficit boosts corporate profits. High income professionals have received substantial tax cuts, access to foreign goods at low prices, and high rates of return on the federal securities they purchase.

This fiscal regime came under attack during the late 1980s and, again, during the "budget crisis" of 1990, and the White House has been compelled to accept some adjustments to it. Nevertheless, it remains central to the structure of extraction and distribution prevailing in the United States today, accounting for perhaps one-third of the federal government's discretionary spending. In this way, it is a key component of the political and governmental system that the Republicans constructed in the 1980s.

Taken together, the fiscal, monetary and national security policies of the Reagan and Bush administrations strengthened the institutional bastions and governing capacities of the Republicans while threatening those of the Democrats. This Republican offensive and the Democrats' subsequent response initiated the institutional conflicts that are at the heart of American politics today. To take any of these programs at face value, and debate their consequences for the economic, social and international problems they nominally address is to misunderstand their true political significance which, as Edelman might have predicted, is to be seen precisely in terms of the "creation of political followings and supports." Republican presidents have sought to use domestic and international programs to expand their own base of support, divide the Democratic coalition, and energize and mobilize their core supporters. Democrats have opposed many Republican initiatives primarily in order to prevent the Republicans from achieving their political—as opposed to nominal—objectives. For better or worse, the world of American politics over the past decade has been precisely the type of political world described by Edelman.

Notes

1. Murray Edelman, *Politics as Symbolic Action* (New York: Academic Press, 1971), p. 4.

2. William Schneider, "The Political Legacy of the Reagan Years," in Sidney Blumenthal and Thomas Edsall, eds., *The Reagan Legacy* (New York: Pantheon, 1988), pp. 51–98.

3. Aaron Wildvasky, *The Politics of the Budgetary Process*, (Boston: Little, Brown, 1964).

4. John Ferejohn, "Congress and Redistribution," in *Making Economic Policy in Congress*, ed. Allen Schick (Washington, D.C.: American Enterprise Institute, 1983).

5. Martha Derthick and Paul Quirk, *The Politics of Deregulation* (Washington, D.C.: The Brookings Institution, 1985).

6. Peter Gourevitch, *Politics in Hard Times* (Ithaca, N.Y.: Cornell University Press, 1986), chap. 4.

7. Thomas Edsall, *The New Politics of Inequality* (New York: W.W. Norton, 1985), chap. 3; see also Thomas Ferguson and Joel Rogers, *Right Turn* (New York: Hill and Wang, 1986).

8. Theodore J. Lowi, *The End of Liberalism* (New York: W.W. Norton, 1979).

9. Mike Davis, *Prisoners of the American Dream* (London: Verso, 1986), chaps. 4 and 5.

10. William Greider, *Secrets of the Temple* (New York: Simon and Schuster, 1987).

11. 1984 election data are drawn from the National Election Survey of the University of Michigan's Center for Political Studies. 1988 data are from the New York Times/CBS News exit poll.

12. Steven Brint, "New Class and Cumulative Trend Explanations of the Liberal Political Attitudes of Professionals," *American Journal of Sociology* 90 (July, 1984): 30–71.

13. John Mollenkopf, *The Contested City* (Princeton: Princeton University Press, 1983), chap. 3.

14. Michael Goldfield, *The Decline of Organized Labor in the United States* (Chicago: University of Chicago Press, 1987).

15. Martin Shefter, *Political Crisis/Fiscal Crisis* (New York: Basic Books, 1987), pp. xi–xx.

16. Connie Paige, *The Right to Lifers* (New York: Summit, 1983).

17. V. O. Key, Jr., *Southern Politics* (New York: Random House, 1949). Also, J. Morgan Kousser, *The Shaping of Southern Politics* (New Haven: Yale University Press, 1974).

18. *New York Times*, 10 Nov. 10, 1988, sect. B, p. 6. On the role of evangelicalism in the Republican coalition, see Gillian Peele, *Revival and Reaction* (New York: Oxford University Press, 1985).

19. Benjamin Ginsberg, *The Captive Public* (New York: Basic Books, 1986), chap. 4.

20. See Mike Mills, "Base Closings: The Political Pain is Limited," *Congressional Quarterly Weekly Report*, Vol. 26, no. 53 (December 31, 1988): 3625–3629.

21. Cf. Paul Peterson, "The New Politics of Deficits," in *The New Direction in American Politics*, eds. John Chubb and Paul Peterson (Washington, D.C.: The Brookings Institution, 1985), chap. 13. On the political uses of macroeconomic policy in the pre-Reagan era, see Edward Tufte, *Political Control of the Economy* (Princeton: Princeton University Press, 1978).

22. Robert Gilpin, *The Political Economy of International Relations* (Princeton: Princeton University Press, 1987), chap. 8.

3

Public and Private Political Realities and the Privatization Movement

David J. Olson

Public and Private Political Realities

Western democracies in the last quarter of the twentieth century are marked by the decline of public life, even while opposite forces appear in Eastern Europe, the former Soviet Union, and even South Africa. People and governments in the West increasingly turn away from public participation and public institutions, embracing instead private life and private institutions. Nowhere are such developments more pronounced than in the U.S.

The retreat from public life is manifested in reduced citizen participation in conventional political processes. Even in landslide elections, recent presidents command support from barely a quarter of the electorate. Political parties see their sway over voters replaced by mass media, management consultants, PACs, and entrepreneurial candidates. Nonconventional participation similarly ebbs, where protest and resistance politics yield to the hope and promise of security and shelter in private life. Shrinking state activity parallels participation declines, as diminished tax revenues accompany reduced public service provision, and the state withdraws from its accustomed regulatory, subsidy, ownership and monitoring roles. Writ large, private life eclipses public life.

This chapter inquires into the varied and conflicting meanings associated with public and private life, in order to chronicle the multiple public and private political realities involved in contemporary politics. The chapter proceeds by introducing classic liberalism's sharp separation of the private from the public, where the two are conceptualized as dichotomous and as autonomous within their respective spheres. In contrast, the public and private are here viewed as differing across a half dozen not necessarily co-varying dimensions, the specification of which suggests the multiple realities of public and private life. These, in turn, create a continuous rather than dichotomous relationship between the two arenas, and suggest interconnections between them. The complexity in relations between public and private life, and the multi-dimensional characteristics which differentiate the two spheres, create opportunities for elites to manipulate the symbols of publicness and privateness to advance their own ends and to construct language which evokes simplifications among mass publics consistent with the inheritance from classic liberalism. Finally, the complex conceptualization of public and private life is then applied to the movement toward privatization by recent conservative governments.

Public and Private as Simple Dichotomy

There remains a continuing inclination to speak, write, and think about the separate and distinct spheres occupied by the dualities of public as against private life, as if the two realms are uniformly distinguished as opposites. This practice is neither new nor surprising. It has informed political discourse from the nation's beginning and is the continuing legacy of a tradition inherited from classic liberalism, which remains the dominant ideology at mass and elite levels of society.

Conventional discussions tend to dichotomize the relationship between public and private, characterizing each as separate and distinct from the other, with each possessing an autonomous existence. Popular and scholarly language thus refers to public and private *spheres* in social relations, as if geometrically differentiated; public and private *realms* or *domains* in political relations, as if defining a kingdom; and public and private *sectors* in economic relations, as if pieces of a whole. By this construction all arenas of life become separable into dualities of existence. Social, political and economic activities are assigned to separate spaces, lacking interrelationships. They are also hierarchically ordered, with preference given the private over the public in the liberal calculus. Whether employed as analytic categories or purported statements of reality, the simple dichotomy between public and private confuses more than it clarifies, yet remains the currency of contemporary discourse.

Dividing social, political, and economic life into simple categories of public and private derives from the received tradition of classic liberalism. It is classic liberalism which conceptualizes society as divided into two distinct spheres, the civil (or private) and the political (or public).[1] These are sharply differentiated both with respect to form and function. The civil sphere is given primacy because within it individuals and groups aspire to self-fulfillment by pursuing their individually-defined interests. Most social activities among individuals and groups occur within the civil sphere. The political sphere in the classic construction is the bastard agency, a necessary evil, instituted to secure and protect individual liberties, rights to private action, and the common defense.

Two sources of threat preoccupy advocates of the dichotomous view of public and private life. The first and greatest concern involves the tendency of the former to encroach upon the latter, where the political penetrates guaranteed liberties and individual freedoms in civil society.[2] This preoccupation recommends the setting of bounds, barriers and barricades against inappropriate migration of the political into the private.[3] The opposite tendency, involving inappropriate migration of private concerns into the public arena, provides a second type of threat to the separate existence of the public and private, and increasingly troubles modern observers. Here the problem occurs when private interests engage political processes, essentially capturing public life and using it to serve private ends. Bachrach and Botwinick pose the liberal paradox thus created: "The concept of the public is a formal necessity in liberal theory that has institutionally been susceptible to privatization from within."[4]

Antiseptically separated private and public spheres provide the framework for Arendt's[5] argument about the baneful effects of modernism. To Arendt, the rise of the social, where private interests assume political significance, largely blurs the private-public distinction by interjecting economic concerns into the latter—thereby trivializing the citizen role and overpowering the public realm within which citizens act. Arendt argues that the public realm, particularly its political forms, requires protection from private questions which are not appropriate for public discussion or decision, because in the end such questions destroy the public realm.

Regardless of how widely it continues to be affirmed, or how appealing its simplicity, the conventional dichotomy between public and private lacks conceptual utility in a world where many, if not most, issues are neither wholly private nor wholly public. Instead, modernity forces complexity and multi-dimensionality upon such issues, creating attributes which simultaneously are partly public and partly private. Some social issues (e.g., abortion, school prayer, gay and lesbian rights) combine questions of public policy with the most private, even intimate, human activities. Other economic issues (e.g., privatized service provision, government service provision) involve complex relationships between public and private goods production which link the private firm and the government agency, particularly as public policy choices are made. The complex interconnections between public and private involved in such questions are hardly exceptional in current experience. What this suggests is that alternative conceptualizations may be required to avoid confusion over what distinguishes the public from the private. A more complex conceptualization of the public and private should itself reflect the multiple realities which distinguish the public from the private, and give form and substance to the interwoven relationships between them. Clearer specification of the several dimensions across which the public and private range, in a continuous rather than dichotomous relationship, requires recognition that social, economic, and political issues may vary between the public and the private simultaneously, and even in contradictory directions.

Dimensions of Publicness and Privateness

A first approximation toward a better understanding of what distinguishes public from private life can be made by inquiring more deeply into the meaning of privateness and publicness. Pitkin solicits this kind of inquiry by asking "When we talk of public and private, do we know what we are talking about?"[6]

Publicness and privateness are complex, multi-faceted concepts. The different meanings of the public and the private may be discerned by inquiring into the several dimensions across which the two vary. A result of their complex multi-dimensionality is that the concepts of public and private create various opportunities for elites to manipulate symbolic meaning systems between public and private, and to use these meanings to advance their own ends.

Two initial dimensions distinguishing the public from the private are drawn from rational choice theory:[7] the criteria of exclusion and consumption. All goods, by the rational choice account, possess basic or intrinsic characteristics that are defined by the special attributes attaching to the goods or services. Understanding the basic characteristics allows distinctions to be made between what are private goods and what are public goods.[8]

The first criterion is *exclusion*. People who have not contributed to the production of a good or service can realistically be excluded from enjoying some goods, where exclusion is feasible, but not other goods, where exclusion is infeasible. Thus goods such as a loaf of bread or an automobile are private because exclusion from their use is highly feasible, while public goods like lighthouses or national defense are less subject to the exclusion of potential users. The feasibility or infeasibility of exclusion turns on the costs to suppliers of monitoring and enforcing exclusion. Beyond goods and services, the principle of exclusion may be applied to places and things, some of which are normally open or available to all, such as parks and clean air. For other places and things, such as movie theaters or personal residences, access is limited or prohibited.

The second criterion is *consumption*. Some goods and services are nonsubtractable, and can be used or consumed simultaneously by many users without being diminished in quality or quantity, e.g. commercial television channels or toll roads. Other subtractable goods are diminished in quality and/or quantity in the act of consumption, e.g. grocery products. The latter tend to be private goods, the former public goods. When combined, the criteria of exclusion and consumption yield a four cell matrix[9] where private goods are contrasted with public, or collective goods, but where the intermediary types of toll goods and common pool goods also appear.

A third dimension differentiating the public from the private is the assignment of *property rights*, which vary between individual and collective. In part, the property rights dimension is forwarded as a corrective to the more limited focus on the nature of goods and services in the rational choice account.[10] For the latter, exclusion and consumption criteria are viewed as intrinsic characteristics of goods and services and sufficient to distinguish public from private goods. Property rights theorists counter that it is meaningless to talk about intrinsic characteristics prior to the establishment of property rights for goods and services. Property rights are said to have the capacity to alter the character of goods and services, and thus become interrelated with exclusion and consumption. A riverfront lot owned as individual property, for example, may be a private good, but it becomes a public good when the state creates a national park and assigns collective or public property rights to it. Property rights thus need not be assumed, and goods and services lack intrinsic qualities prior to and separable from the assignment of property rights.

Visibility provides a fourth dimension along which the public may be distinguished from the private. Some activities are public by virtue of their high visibility, or by their status for most people as matters of public knowledge. They are by their nature observable, and thus attract publicity and become the focus of public attention. Thus factory smokestacks belching pollutants arouse adjacent neighbors to political action, or pornographic theaters in residential neighborhoods drive citizens to rewrite zoning codes.

Other activities are hidden from public view and closed to outside observation. Certain activities in private clubs are tolerated, for example, although they would be banned if occurring in public. They are private in the sense that they are reserved to individual places or things, and removed from public scrutiny.[11] There clearly is overlap between this visibility dimension and the exclusion dimension discussed above. Indeed, Pitkin[12] labels the visibility dimension "access," which may be either a matter of visibility or the feasibility of exclusion. The two also may be interconnected, as when the absence of public knowledge about an activity reduces the costs of enforcing exclusion, and vice versa.

Impact is a fifth dimension, ranging from limited effects to widespread or extensive effects, with the former characteristic of the private and the latter of the public. Some activities are simply bounded in their effects. The number of people affected is small, and the kinds and severity of the impacts are limited and inconsequential. For example, the impact of religious rites usually is confined to worshipers, without consequence for nonbelievers.

Table 3.1 Multiple Dimensions of Publicness and Privateness

Dimension	Qualities of: Privateness	Qualities of: Publicness
1. Exclusion	Feasible	Infeasible
2. Consumption	Individual	Joint
3. Property Rights	Individual	Collective
4. Visibility	Concealed	Observable
5. Impact	Limited	Extensive
6. Agency	Individual	Collective

In contrast, other activities have broad effects on all or most members of a society. When religious organizations assert rights of the unborn, these assertions have significance for the larger society and its politics. It is not necessarily the case, however, that activities with broad social consequences are inevitably or automatically recognized as such by those affected. Thus an activity may be public in terms of its impact while remaining unrecognized, private, or hidden in its visibility. The dimension of visibility does not necessarily co-vary with the dimension of impact. The two may be quite separate and unrelated, or made to appear so by the way they are framed for (or disguised from) public consumption. Similarly, the restricted or broad impact of an activity may depend upon the character of property rights assigned to a place, thing, or activity.

There is finally the dimension of *agency*. Some matters are seen as public because they are subject to governmental agency, while other matters are seen as private due to their being reserved to individual choice. Public here refers to the ways social collectivities act through official agencies of government to provide direction or control. An activity is public to the extent that government agents act in official capacities to regulate, subsidize, promote, operate, own or otherwise govern it. An activity is private in the agency sense to the extent that government interjections are absent or prohibited; private individuals or groups act autonomously from the state.[13] The dimension of agency is clearly associated with each of the five prior dimensions defining the publicness or privateness of places, things, or activities.

These dimensions, which are defined by varying qualities of publicness and privateness, are presented in Table 3.1. Seven observations about the public and private may be drawn from the foregoing discussion. First, that which distinguishes public from private is multi-dimensional, ranging across the qualities of publicness and privateness over a half dozen dimensions. These features of the public and the private provide a more complex formulation than the simple dichotomy presented in classic liberalism. This complexity makes the question of what is public and what private more problematic and thereby available to alternative constructions by social elites. Second, the dimensions themselves are interrelated, with the qualities of publicness or privateness of one dimension subject to influence by those same qualities in another. Third, the degrees of publicness or privateness of a thing, place, or activity vary according to the number of dimensions it is subject to and the character of that influence. Thus social and political issues do not necessarily co-vary across the multiple dimensions in the same magnitude or even in the same direction. This also suggests that meaning systems about what is private versus what is public are amenable to manipulation and social construction.

It follows, fourth, that what is thought of as public in one time or place may be thought of as private in another time or place. Fifth, there are contrasts which usefully can be made between the public and the private, but the two are not always opposites nor are they necessarily mutually exclusive "spheres," "realms," "domains," or "sectors." Rather, they penetrate, connect with, and overlap each other in ways defined by the publicness or privateness of the multiple dimensions of a thing, place or activity, or as defined by those able to construct meaning systems for the public and the private.

A sixth observation is that mass publics easily can form and hold multiple and competing cognitions of the public and private; this is due to the many senses in which a place, thing, or activity exhibits qualities of publicness or privateness. Yet mass cognitions are deeply embedded in the received and still dominant tenets of classic liberalism, with its simplified construction and sharp differentiation between the public and private. The need for simplification among mass publics encourages structuring public and private meaning systems as oppositional and autonomous. Social, economic and political elites can and do reinforce such simplifications by symbolizing public and private life as separable and by assigning priority to the latter, particularly when elite interests support such formulations. Finally, the dimension of agency is extremely problematic. Agents of rule or administration may assume formal public office, roles, or powers, but in reality represent or serve the substantive interests of individuals or other private parties. The recent privatization movement is illustrative of these themes.

Privatization

Privatization is the most important domestic reform program initiated by conservative governments in the late twentieth century. In the future, it is likely to outlast the conservative progenitors who spawned it in the 1980s.

Conservative governments in the industrial nations mounted a campaign to denationalize and otherwise privatize a host of publicly owned industries. Thatcher's Britain effectively privatized vast shares of British state-owned enterprises,[14] while simultaneously Reagan's national privatization campaign largely failed.[15] Although a failure nationally, privatization succeeded in significant measure among the states and particularly within municipal administrations. The latter are examined below in order to suggest ways in which different language constructions and symbolizations of public and private are employed in political argumentation over the privatization policy option. Whether privatization has or has not succeeded, is or is not efficient or effective—as well as related questions—are beyond the scope of this discussion. Instead, the focus is on how particular formulations of privatization are constructed and presented in political discourse and argumentation—and with what effects.

Privatization As A Concept

After a decade's experience with privatization, it remains unclear exactly what the term means. Thiemeyer[16] itemizes fully fifteen different ways the term is used. Among the various meanings are: denationalization, deregulation, load shedding, sale of public assets, contracting out, franchising, voucher systems, voluntary service provision, replacing public with private management techniques, quasi-public structures, and reducing the amount and quality of public goods as a stimulus to private goods production. Because of this diversity of usages, privatization has become an uncertain concept with varying meanings in public discourse. Nonetheless, privatization can be reconceptualized according to two primary meaning systems; one economic, the other political.

As a strict *economic* concept, privatization refers to the improved efficiencies realized in the production and delivery of goods and services by private firms in contrast to public agencies. To its proponents, private firm efficiencies are superior to those achievable in public agencies for three main reasons: government monopolies are replaced by competitive firms; economies of scale are realized; and profit incentives are substituted for bureaucratic incentives. Under privatization, the price mechanism and market relationships are said to allocate resources more efficiently than is the case under conventional public agency provision. This is particularly true for all goods and services exhibiting characteristics of individual consumption and feasibility of exclusion. By definition, it is argued, such private goods and services are more efficiently provided by private firms than by governmental agencies.[17]

Privatization in this strict economic sense shifts the locus of service production from public agencies to private firms. But government responsibility for oversight, (sometimes) financing, monitoring expenditures, and program accountability remains in place. Under this technical economic usage, the means of service production are privatized, but government responsibility is otherwise retained. There is simply a shift in methods and procedures, and also a shift in the instrumentalities of service production, with no necessary consequences save for the promise of enhanced efficiency.[18] Privatization in this sense requires public officials to "think like the economist"[19] and strive for greater efficiency. Under this construction, privatization is a means toward the end of achieving market efficiencies in goods and services production and delivery.

This narrow, technical formulation of privatization is not always, or perhaps most often, the way the term is used; instead, an alternative usage has emerged, with broad implications for the meaning of privatization and for the role of government in modern society.

Privatization has both instrumental meanings—as a means toward greater efficiency—and symbolic meanings. Privatization symbolizes a broad movement to roll back the state, shrink the size of government, and withdraw government from the provision of services. As a *political* concept, privatization is no longer a technical means toward the goal of efficiency, but instead an end in itself.

The objective of privatization as a political concept becomes reducing, or withdrawing entirely, the role of government in regulating the economy and providing goods and services. This usage relies upon a simplified model of the public and private sectors, and argues for reducing the size and scope of the former while enhancing the autonomy and status of the latter. Rather than being a strict economic term, privatization becomes infused with the ideology of reduced government, and embraces the political goal of eliminating the state from service production and provision. The means, therefore, have become the end.

Carried to its extreme, the political conception of privatization becomes a misnomer. At times the term refers to the removal of government controls on the private provision of goods and services, an act of deregulation which is separate and distinct from privatization. Also, if a good or service is withdrawn from public provision, and thereafter no substitution occurs by a private agency, technically an act of privatization has not taken place. Instead, there is merely the absence of the good or service.[20] Privatization in this sense is often identified in political argumentation with privatism, the belief system signifying an underlying confidence in the capacity of the private sector to create and sustain the conditions for personal and community prosperity.[21] The political concept of privatization is sometimes acknowledged by its advocates: "In the most general sense, any privatization proposal involves the rolling back of the activity of the state."[22]

The Political Program of Privatization

Alternative usages and meanings of privatization carry equally contrasting implications for the arena of action where public policy is decided. In its technical, economic meaning, privatization urges public officials to identify services better provided by private agencies in order to realize program efficiencies. However, privatization retains for officials decisions about program content, amounts and kinds of services, monitoring, and enforcement. In its broader, ideologically infused, political meaning, privatization recommends elimination of government programs, or reduction in their size and scope. Frequently there is interaction between the two concepts, as when the goal of efficiency in the former is employed rhetorically by proponents of the latter.

Symbolic appeals invoking norms of efficiency, private sector superiority, and market competition that are associated with the instrumental, or economic, concept of privatization resonate with belief systems based on the society's inherited liberalism. Thus Donnison characterizes the political language associated with privatization as follows: "It is designed not to clarify analysis but as a symbol, intended by advocates and opponents of the process it describes to dramatize a conflict and mobilize support for their own side."[23] Privatization in this usage is capable of evoking powerful ideological appeals that have little, if anything, to do with economic efficiency.

As a political concept, privatization is a program of reform that intends a fundamental alteration in the nature of contemporary government beyond the simple efficiency maximand. Savas, a key academic architect of the privatization movement, writes bluntly about the political reform program:

> Long term, incrementalist tactics are needed to implement a privatization strategy, with a research and public relations effort to press for privatization, tax reforms to encourage it, legislation to allow it, and strong coalitions of stakeholders—some newly converted—to support it. It may also be necessary to erode antiprivatization coalitions, for example, by selling or giving shares to workers of an enterprise that is to be denationalized. It must always be borne in mind that privatization is a more *political* rather than an *economic* act.[24]

It is clear, then, that efficiency is only a minor plank in the program of political privatization.

The Effects of Political Privatization

Why, besides efficiency, does privatization matter? This reform program attempts to reduce the size of government, the scope of its activities, its revenue base, and its mode of operations. It represents an attack on the public sector, with foregone public activities either assigned to the private sector or wholly abandoned. Far from solely focusing on efficiency, it is informed by the ideology of attacking government itself with predictable broad-reaching effects. These can be seen in at least four areas: public employment, service delivery characteristics, governmental character and democratic participation.

There are numerous consequences of privatization for municipal public employees. By reducing the number of public employees, privatization weakens the power of public employee unions, reduces the workforce covered by civil service protections, and erodes the wage scales and fringe benefit levels of public employees. To the extent that private firms pay less for unskilled labor and more for professional and managerial occupations, former public employees are similarly affected. The least well paid workers are paid less while the better paid earn more. The lesser adherence to affirmative action and equal opportunity employment norms in the private sector reduces the social mobility structures recently made available to racial minorities and women in public employment. As intended in the political construction of privatization, these reforms serve to reduce the numbers and status of state workers. The political power of state workers, especially at municipal levels where they can control more than a quarter of the electorate, is correspondingly weakened.

Significant alterations in service delivery characteristics also occur under privatization. Besides inefficiency, privatization identifies for attack those special interest groups which are said to be locked into particularistic benefit structures.[25] The special interests targeted for program termination are most often the poorest and neediest recipients, and those most lacking in resources for power, whether in the public or private sectors. Private service providers' profit motive attracts them to the easy and most profitable customers and clients, and causes them to shirk service provision to more difficult or unprofitable recipients. Again, the poorest and neediest recipients are least well served by this market logic. Likewise the practice of "creaming," giving priority to the most lucrative profit centers, is inherent to the profit incentive of private service providers. Private service provision also may result in a decline in service quality and a rise in service inequality. Privatization thus reduces size and scope in the provision of services, and erodes quality in predictable directions.

Government itself is the central target of political privatization reforms. Besides the general effects of reducing the size and scope of government, there are particular consequences emanating from privatization. Privatization changes the incentives of public officials, who claim under declining budgets and employee rolls to be doing more with less.[26] As relations between officials and private firm providers increase, contacts become routine and familiar, with mutual dependencies between the two groups developing over time—the firm on the official for contract renewals, the official on the firm for political support and campaign finance contributions. As new public-private partnerships evolve, inversions of public and private priorities occur, and a private planning system substitutes for a public one. By manipulating political decisions, contracting firms develop capacities for coopting governmental officials, with potentials for fraud, corruption and abuse familiar in the contracting system.[27] The subnational governmental systems, where privatization is most readily adopted, are already an extremely segmented and fragmented political order; they become more so with privatization, further complicating citizen inability to hold officials accountable. Under political privatization, the role of government is said to be largely one of service provision—and the less of this the better—with little regard to alternative roles governments traditionally perform.[28]

More profound implications of privatization as a political construct deal with no less than the reformulation of democracy. Privatization erodes the legitimacy of the public sector and elevates the private to preeminence. Its advocates view political decision-making as fundamentally flawed and inherently inferior to private decision-making. As Savas notes: "Government's decisions are political, thus are inherently less trustworthy than free-market decisions."[29] What debases public decisions is self-interest among voters, precisely that quality celebrated in consumers within private marketplace decisions.[30]

Privatization also tends to diminish the access and visibility of programs. Decisions are removed from open arenas where public disclosure creates opportunities for citizens to become informed, to comment, criticize, react and amend programs. Privatized decision-making shields proprietary information from public scrutiny, narrows opportunities and forums for deliberation, and restricts choice to those elites directly involved in the autonomous marketplace of service providers. Collective decision-making forums are replaced by individual choice, and democratic citizenship is compromised to the watchword of efficiency.

In sum, the Janus-like character of conservative reform reveals two constructions of privatization: one strictly economic, the other composed of a developed political ideology. The former usage asserts the single objective of efficiency maximization in delivery of goods and services; the latter confines government's role to service provision, then argues for its private provision and delivery. Privatization as a political concept is thus an encompassing ideology of less government, fewer governmental activities, and reduced revenue and power allocations to government. Privatization in fact views government as inherently flawed and turns public priorities to private marketplaces whose superiority is founded on beliefs in the individual, competition, market exchanges, and autonomy. Elite appeals to these beliefs resonate with the classic values of American liberalism and so, too, do arguments for the political construction of privatization.

Conclusion

The classic liberal formulation of public and private relationships presents a simple model, where the two realms are sharply separated and autonomous with respect to form and function. This model lacks utility; it confuses more than it clarifies in a world where most issues are neither wholly public nor wholly private. By contrast, a half dozen dimensions of publicness and privateness can be suggested which differentiate between the public and the private. The relationships between the two spheres are multi-dimensional: continuous, not dichotomous; multiple, not singular; and interrelated, not autonomous. Due to these complex relationships, the publicness or privateness of a thing, place or activity does not necessarily co-vary across the multiple dimensions with the same magnitude or even in the same direction. Instead, the public and private overlap, penetrate, and connect in ways that are defined by their publicness and privateness. These complexly-structured relationships create opportunities for elites to manipulate the presentation of the public and private for mass consumption. The symbolism and language associated with the public and private manufacture meaning systems which may or may not bear a close resemblance to reality. Simplification needs among mass publics tend to structure public and private meaning systems as oppositional and autonomous, consistent with the received and still dominant liberal framework. The conception of the public in political argumentation is, more often than not, portrayed as inferior to the private.

Recent privatization movements demonstrate how the symbols and language concerning public-private relations are used to simplify complex matters. There are two formulations of privatization, one economic and the other political. As a strict economic concept, privatization is a means toward an end, an instrument for instilling competition, scale economies, and the profit motive to achieve efficient service delivery. As a political concept, however, the means *become* the end. Privatization symbolizes a broader movement to roll back the state, shrink the size of government, and withdraw government from the provision of services. In this usage, language advocating privatization relies upon the simplified model of separate and autonomous public and private spheres.

Most of the focus of privatization concerns the question of efficiency, quite appropriately so given the first meaning of the term. But efficiency is insufficient, even inappropriate, to assess the second usage. Rather, the question needs to be asked: why else, besides efficiency, does privatization matter? For public employment, it is the poorest and neediest who are most disadvantaged under privatization programs. The quality of service delivery declines as inequalities rise. Privatization threatens the corruption of public-private relations, leads to an inversion of public and private priorities, and erodes the legitimacy of public participation while declaring public decision-making inherently inferior, even debased. Open and accessible democratic decision-making predictably yields to closed and inaccessible private forums beyond the public's view or reach. The sharp private-public distinction elevates the former to primacy, and trivializes the latter.

Notes

1. S. I. Benn and G. F. Gaus, *Public and Private in Social Life* (New York: St. Martin's Press, 1983), p. 33.

2. See Ferdinand Schoeman, *Philosophical Dimensions of Privacy* (London: Cambridge University Press, 1984).

3. A lively and provocative literature has developed within feminist scholarship over this question. For representative treatments, see Jean Elshtain, *Public Man, Private Woman* (Princeton: Princeton University Press, 1981); and Mary G. Dietz, "Citizenship With a Feminist Face," *Political Theory*, 1985, Vol. 13, No. 1, pp. 19–37.

4. Peter Bachrach and Aryeh Botwinick, "The Concept of the Public: A Radical Perspective," paper presented at the 1985 annual meeting of the American Political Science Association, p. 2.

5. Hannah Arendt, *The Human Condition* (Chicago: The University of Chicago Press, 1958).

6. Hanna Fenichel Pitkin, "Justice: On Relating Public and Private," *Political Theory*, 1981, Vol. 9, No. 3, p. 328.

7. See Garrett Hardin, "The Tragedy of the Commons," *Science*, 1968, No. 162, pp. 1243–1248; Elinor Ostrom and Vincent Ostrom, "Public Goods and Public Choice," in E. S. Savas, ed., *Alternatives for Delivering Public Services* (Boulder: Westview Press, 1977); and Robert L. Bish, *The Public Economy of Metropolitan Areas* (Chicago: Markham Publishing Co., 1971).

8. E. S. Savas, *Privatization: The Key to Better Government* (Chatham, NJ: Chatham House Publishers, 1987), pp. 35–37.

9. Ibid, pp. 40–41.

10. Erik Furubotn and Swetozar Pejovich, eds., *The Economics of Property Rights* (Cambridge, MA: Ballinger Publishing Company, 1974); Harold Demsetz, "Toward a Theory of Property Rights," *American Economic Review*, 1967, Vol. 57, pp. 347–359.

11. Richard Sennett, *The Fall of Public Man* (New York: Knopf, 1977).

12. Pitkin, p. 329.

13. Barrington Moore, *Privacy: Studies in Social and Cultural History* (Armonk, NY: M. E. Sharpe, 1984).

14. Heldrun Abromeit, "Privatization in Great Britain," *Annals of Public and Cooperative Economy*, 1986, Vol. 47, No. 2, pp. 153–179.

15. This is partly due, of course, to the greater extent of nationalized industry in Great Britain than in the U.S. Nonetheless, and despite repeated and major efforts to divest the U.S. of national ownership of Amtrak, the BPA and TVA, the Post Office, among others, the Reagan administration succeeded in selling only one major asset (Conrail).

16. Theo Thiemeyer, "Privatization," *Annals of Public and Cooperative Economy*, 1986, Vol. 47, No. 2, pp. 143–146.

17. Savas, *Privatization: The Key to Better Government*, p. 57.

18. Advocates of privatization draw a sharp distinction between the decision to provide a good or service and the means for producing or delivering a good or service, a distinction reminiscent of the discredited separation of politics and policy in administrative management literature. The issue here is that, as a political concept, privatization ignores the conventional wisdom that implementation of policy decisions, whether by public or private agencies, is not a neutral enterprise, but carries its own set of policy influences.

19. Harold Henderson, "Can Business Do It Better?" *Planning*, 1985, p. 19.

20. James L. Sundquist, "Privatization: No Panacea for What Ails Government," in Harvey Brooks, Lance Liebman, and Corrine S. Schelling, eds., *Public-Private Partnership: New Opportunities for Meeting Social Needs* (Cambridge, MA: Ballinger Publishing Company, 1984).

21. Sam Bass Warner, Jr., *The Private City: Philadelphia in Three Periods of Its Growth* (Philadelphia: University of Pennsylvania Press, 1987); Timothy Barnekov, Robin Boyle and Daniel Rich, *Privatism and Urban Policy in Britain and the United States* (New York: Oxford University Press, 1989).

22. J. LeGrand and R. Robinson, *Privatization and the Welfare State* (London: George Allen and Unwin, 1984), p. 3.

23. D. Donnison, "The Progressive Potential of Privatization," in LeGrand and Robinson, p. 45.

24. Savas, *Privatization* . . . , p. 233.

25. Harry P. Hatry and Carl F. Valente, "Alternative Service Delivering Approaches Involving Increased Use of the Private Sector," in *Municipal Year Book* (Washington, D.C.: International Managers Association, 1983).

26. Ira Sharkansky, *Wither the State: Politics and Public Enterprise in Three Countries* (Chatham, NJ: Chatham House Publishers, 1979).

27. While much of the contracting system is relatively new, there are long and well-established contracting relationships which may be instructive on this score. The kinds of relationships developed in the Department of Defense, Housing and Urban Development, or in state highway construction, and the abuses which regularly appear, may signify patterns prospectively for the new contracting arrangements.

28. Besides goods and services provision, among the roles governments may be said to perform are: conflict resolution, providing a bargaining forum, community integration, providing for public health and order, social control, cultural provision, and setting collective goals.

29. Savas, *Privatization* . . . , p. 5.

30. Thus, public employees are viewed as self-interested budget maximizers and spending enthusiasts in their voting behavior, as are descriptive social groups who vote simply to maximize programs benefitting the category of groups to which they belong.

PART TWO

Elections and Symbolism

4

Constructing Explanations for Election Results: When 'The Voters Have Spoken,' Who Decides What They Said?[1]

Marjorie Randon Hershey

Introduction

In *Constructing the Political Spectacle*, Murray Edelman begins with the premise that "reality" is constructed: that "political developments are ambiguous entities that mean what concerned observers construe them to mean."[2] The conduct of politics, then, is the construction of these meanings: the process by which political actors define themselves and their worlds, are defined by others, and attempt to get their own preferred meanings accepted as the basis for allocations of values. As Edelman suggests:

> The critical element in political maneuver for advantage is the creation of meaning: the construction of beliefs about events, policies, leaders, problems, and crises that rationalize or challenge existing inequalities. The strategic need is to immobilize opposition and mobilize support. . . . the key tactic must always be the evocation of interpretations that legitimize favored courses of action and threaten or reassure people so as to encourage them to be supportive or to remain quiescent.[3]

Conflicting interpretations of the qualities of political leaders, the motivations and impact of public policies, are the substance of a nation's political history. Those interpretations are carried by, and powerfully shaped by, language. People do not experience political events directly; rather, we experience language about such events. Edelman sees language, then, as the creator of the social worlds with which people deal:

> . . . it is not 'reality' in any testable or observable sense that matters in shaping political consciousness and behavior, but rather the beliefs that language helps evoke about the causes of discontents and satisfactions, about policies

that will bring about a future closer to the heart's desire, and about other unobservables.[4]

For most people, the news media serve as the major transmitters of language about political events. The media are ubiquitous in American society. They carry a stream of strobe-like images of the political spectacle: slices of social problems, images of national and international threats, views of the character and skill of leaders, a rapidly-changing agenda of crises.

The results of this transmission, Edelman argues, are to distort and to mystify. Political news is a steady parade of threats and reassurances whose impact is to encourage people's acquiescence to the existing power arrangements. The focus of such accounts is frequently on leaders, as symbols of powerful emotions such as hopes and fears, national pride and individual failure, even though leadership is less an autonomous force than a byproduct of fundamental social and economic forces. As Edelman suggests, "Leaders become objectifications of whatever worries or pleases observers of the political scene because it is easy to identify with them, support or oppose them, love or hate them."[5]

Elections are especially prominent in the political spectacle. They are engaging images because they involve such elements of drama as suspense, surprise, victory and defeat. They epitomize the focus on leaders in a particularly compelling setting: as supplicants, whose fate rests on the voters' choice. Further, the meaning and importance of an election result is "always ambiguous and usually controversial,"[6] as will be discussed later. Normally portrayed as unique events, isolated from the structural and historical trends that would help explain them, elections' meaning must be supplied by the media's audience; that further entices audience involvement.

Quantitative analysis is not frequently used to explore this stimulating vision of politics. But there are areas of Edelman's work in which quantitative research can prove useful—for instance, in determining how meaning is attributed to election returns and how that meaning comes to be disseminated and to affect subsequent behavior. This chapter, then, will explore empirically a central element of the vision of elections as political spectacles. It will propose and test some ideas about the process in which explanations are created for election results and will examine the implications for an understanding of politics.

Elections as Political Spectacles

It is part of the mythology of elections in the United States that when "the people have spoken" on election day, what they said will be plainly apparent. Interested observers of the vote totals will know not just who won, but why they won: whether the voters wanted less government, a stronger defense, a cleaner environment, or more conservative leaders.

The mythology can be found not only in popular language but in media accounts as well. Right after the 1984 presidential election, for example, the *Denver Post* divined from the outcome that "Peace and prosperity—not foolish incursions by government into Americans' private and religious lives—are Ronald Reagan's historic mandate,"[7] while the *Washington Post* concluded that the voters "gave the president a mandate and it is very simple. It is a mandate *not* to raise taxes."[8] As Stanley Kelley, Jr. states, politicians and the media frequently subscribe to what he terms "the theory of electoral mandates," whose "first element is the belief that elections carry messages about problems, policies, and programs—messages plain to all and specific enough to be directive."[9]

The mythology has variations. What the voters said will be apparent, in some versions, to those in possession of exit poll data, while in other versions, it will make itself known to leaders with their "ears to the ground," or to anyone who is politically aware.

But the greatest variations are in interpretations of what the voters are supposed to have meant by their votes. Journalists, party leaders, candidates, and political scientists debate the meaning of the vote totals and argue for the interpretation they favor. The mythology, then, leads to agreement that elections convey a message about public policy in the face of obvious disagreement as to what that message is. As Edelman points out, "Beliefs about success and failure are among the most arbitrary of political constructions and perhaps the least likely to be recognized as arbitrary."[10]

In the case of elections, institutional factors add to this tendency. Elections permit voters to make only one kind of choice: a choice among candidates. There is no space on the ballot for citizens to explain why they voted for a particular candidate, much less to detail the policies they would like to see implemented by the winners. Someone may cast a ballot for George Bush, for instance, to protest violent crime, or alternatively, to endorse the vision of a kinder, gentler America. But in either case, it will be a silent statement; all the voting machine registers is "Bush."[11]

Verba and Nie point out other reasons why election results have such limitations in conveying information about the voter's policy preferences, and thus add to the freedom observers have in interpreting them:

> [The voter] does not choose the occasion to vote, nor does he choose the agenda; he doesn't choose the issues that divide the candidates, nor does he usually have much voice in choosing the candidates themselves. And given the fact that his own agenda is quite individual and may contain many and varied issues, it is unreasonable to expect that there will be a voting choice tailored to his own particular policy preferences at the moment.... His vote can only be a rather blunt instrument under these circumstances....[12]

Add to this the findings that many people's votes are determined by factors such as their own party attachment and their perceptions of the candidate's personal qualities, especially in election years when candidates do not distinguish themselves sharply on issues.[13] In consequence, the message that can be drawn from the vote totals about public policy is very likely to be vague, and therefore open to interpretation.

Campaigners can never be entirely sure, then, from reading the returns, what the voters were rewarding or punishing about their expressed beliefs, performance, character, or party.[14] So there will always be some uncertainty about what type of representation voters want *after* election day: what policies they would like to see high on the official's agenda, what stylistic characteristics they trust, what mix of policies and other features they would prefer in the official's "home style."[15]

These limitations on elections as learning situations have major consequences. Given the importance of the election in the life of a democracy—that it is the time when the largest proportion of citizens are attentive to politics, that it is the least costly means for people to have an impact on politics, that it controls the avenue to elective office—and its importance to a wide range of democratic theorists,[16] the fact that elections are so inarticulate is a salient commentary on the nature of democratic rule.

Despite the inevitable ambiguity, however, political leaders have powerful incentives to try to decode messages from the vote totals. After the election, those who won have an interest in finding out what they did right, on the assumption that if they keep doing it, they will continue to reap electoral rewards. Being able to explain the election result, to understand why voters selected or rejected them, offers valuable help in charting their course through the uncertainty of the coming months in public life.

Exit polls help to reduce the uncertainty. But poll data do not speak for themselves; they must be interpreted. Typically, the initial reports based on exit polls offer a range of findings that could support a number of different interpretations of the voters' choices. Sophisticated analysis of the data takes time—time in which politicians must already be making choices relevant to their futures.

Yet analysts and participants often behave as though the election results speak volumes about what voters want. Interpreting the vote totals is a seasonal source of fascination within the political community—a chief means by which activists feel they can detect changes in the national mood.[17]

Learning how these interpretations are developed is important. We need to know how politicians and media people come to perceive the voters' meaning, because those perceptions, whether accurate or not, will affect their actions. Examining the process also directs our focus to elections as institutions. Through survey data, we know a lot about the behavior of individual voters. We know much less than we need to know, as V. O. Key, Jr.

pointed out three decades ago, about elections as aggregate events,[18] which are more than simply the sum of the individual voting decisions that comprise them.[19]

How Explanations for Election Results Are Constructed

Even before the polls close on election night, candidates and other activists are motivated to try to read meaning into the results. Journalists also want to find explanations of the election outcome, and to do so quickly. They will enhance their reputations as political writers by being the first to forward an especially plausible interpretation of the vote totals.

Political activists have a second purpose as well: to construct and quickly spread an explanation of the election result that puts them in the best possible political position; in Edelman's terms, to maneuver for advantage by creating meaning. For example, after the 1988 presidential election, many Democratic activists promoted the view that Michael Dukakis' loss was Dukakis' own fault—his staff was disorganized, he failed to respond to Bush's attacks—because this explanation would imply that the voters had not repudiated the Democratic party or its philosophy, but rather that the party simply needs a more effective candidate in 1992. A number of Republican partisans argued for a different interpretation: it wasn't Dukakis' shortcomings but the fact that he was solidly within the Democratic mainstream that caused voters to reject him. Acceptance of this alternative would suggest that prospective leaders, if they intend to win public support, should abandon the Democratic mainstream in favor of Republican policies.

It will make a big difference in the career prospects of various political actors which of the constructed explanations comes to be widely accepted. So in the hours and days after the vote, I would argue, the electoral contest is followed by another kind of competition: intense efforts by campaigners, consultants, party and group leaders to get their explanation of the election results reported as if it were fact.

In the weeks to come, these explanations will be sifted and winnowed until only a "short list"—explanations congruent with prevailing media values—survives. They will be spread by reporters and columnists, read and repeated by political activists, seeming more credible each time. Through a mechanism like "pack journalism,"[20] in which reporters tend to reach similar conclusions about the importance of a story, what its "lead" should be, and how to interpret it, rough agreement emerges.

These hypotheses imply that voters' choices do not in themselves define the meaning of the vote. Rather, in the election spectacle, activists and the journalists who cover them construct meaning out of the raw vote totals, and create the "conventional wisdom" that soon seems as real as the votes it describes. Their latitude is not infinite; it is guided by the society's ideological underpinnings, and bounded by prevailing assumptions about the meaning of recent elections and other indicators of public opinion. And it must bear some relationship to the vote totals; one could not easily argue, for instance, that Reagan's election in 1984 was a close shave. Nevertheless, the central point is that these explanations for election results are constructed by journalists and activists, not directly by voters.

Nor are they necessarily the same as the explanations constructed by scholars. The process is likely to be well underway before scholars have the time for careful analysis of exit polls and other measures of public opinion. By the time their analyses are completed and published, the conventional wisdom about the meaning of the election will have already been determined and will have affected people's behavior. So the main influences on this process are not, at least initially (and perhaps at all), the sophisticated analyses of voter behavior that scholars can provide, but the quick-and-dirty assessments of political activists and media people.

The 1980 election provides an example. As Ross Baker suggests,[21] public opinion specialists later concluded that the election result was more a rejection of Jimmy Carter than an endorsement of Reagan's conservative program. But Reagan's supporters were able to get their explanation—that the vote was a mandate for conservative policies—widely accepted in the Washington community well before political science journals hit the presses. Exasperated House Speaker Thomas P. (Tip) O'Neill testified to the impact of this process: " 'The record *shows* there was no mandate. But Congress thinks there was and it's reacting in that manner.' "

It is through this process of constructing explanations for the vote totals that elections take on meaning as signs. The blunt impact of an election result comes to be embellished with detail and helps shape the specific decisions of candidates and other leaders as to what they will do next.

Data and Method

This paper tests these ideas in the presidential election of 1984, using a content analysis of media coverage of the election results. Routinely in modern American elections, the mass media report not only the vote totals but the interpretations that a variety of political actors construct for those totals. The media, then, are the means by which these constructed explanations enter broader political discourse. Opinion-leading media in particular become a kind of billboard on which candidates, consultants, party and interest group leaders can read one another's best efforts to account for the vote. In the process, media people play a powerful role as filters, in determining what kinds of explanations deserve coverage, and in creating or synthesizing alternative explanations. In Kelley's words:

Journalists routinely interpret elections, as no other group in society does....
No other interpretations of elections have the political significance that those
of the news media do, at least in the short run. The press gets there first with
the most publicity, and first impressions of elections tend to endure.[22]

Although broadcast media coverage of elections has properly received
a great deal of scholarly attention,[23] there are good reasons to focus here on
newspaper coverage instead. Once its marathon election-night reportage is
over, the evening television news, whose stories typically last two minutes
or less, devotes very little time to explaining the election results. By contrast, coverage in opinion-leading newspapers is more detailed, continues
for a longer time span, and is taken seriously by political activists. Newspapers are at least as widely consumed as television news, and seem to carry
the same emphases as network newscasts, but are not as ephemeral.[24] It is
possible to re-read print media coverage, to clip interesting articles, and to
consider their meaning at leisure, thus increasing their impact among politically-aware people.

Selected for analysis were sixteen influential daily newspapers, four in
each region, that were likely to be widely read by political activists. Northeastern papers included the *New York Times*, the *Washington Post*, the *Boston Globe*, and the *Wall Street Journal*; in the South, the *Atlanta Journal*, the Baltimore *Sun*, the *Memphis Commercial Appeal*, and the *New Orleans Times-Picayune*; in the Midwest, the *Chicago Tribune*, the *Detroit Free Press*, the *St. Louis Post-Dispatch*, and the *Indianapolis Star*; and in the West, the *Los Angeles Times*, the *San Francisco Examiner*, the *Denver Post*, and the Portland *Oregonian*. Two major black-oriented newspapers were also analyzed—the *Chicago Defender* and Baltimore's *The Afro-American*—to include prominent sources that black political activists might monitor, and to expand the possible range of explanations. All major news services were represented in the coverage of these 18 newspapers.

The unit of analysis (termed an "item" or article) in this research is the
individual newspaper story, column (syndicated or local), or editorial.
The content analysis covered two time periods. In the immediate post-election period, I analyzed all items that mentioned the presidential race (other
than in passing) from November 7 (the day after the election) through
November 20, 1984 (the second Sunday following election day).[25] An "explanation" was defined as a reason for, a cause of, or an underlying meaning
of the election result. A statement was classified an explanation only if it
made explicit, or very clearly implied, that a particular factor was a reason
why President Reagan won the election or Walter Mondale lost.[26] A total of
572 items (56% of the total) contained codable explanations in this post-election period.

To learn whether these constructed explanations remained prominent long enough to become "conventional wisdom," at least in the short term, I also coded all items in these newspapers that mentioned the election results, either offering an explanation for the election or a consequence of it, or both, during the period January 20–February 10, 1985. On January 20 President Reagan was inaugurated for the second time. February 10 was the Sunday following the State of the Union address and the delivery to Congress of the President's budget message. During this time, political coverage was dominated by discussion of Reagan's budgetary and policy initiatives and efforts by members of Congress to further or thwart those initiatives. This post-inaugural subsample consisted of 310 stories, columns, and editorials.

To check for inter-coder reliability, a second coder analyzed a sample of these items. Agreement in the post-election sample was 92%; in the post-inaugural sample, 94%.

Explaining the 1984 Vote

The 1984 presidential election, as elections normally do, provided more than enough ambiguity and conflicting evidence for the construction of explanations. As a *Chicago Tribune* editorial put it,

> The question now is: Which Ronald Reagan received the popular mandate? Was it the man who portrayed the Soviet Union as an arch-fiend or the one who encouraged East-West discussion and talked of peace? Was it the President who predicted that tax cuts would eliminate the deficit or the one who recognized that spending more than you take in mortgages the future?"

Out of the wealth of data provided by several exit polls, voting patterns, insiders' and spectators' opinions, what kinds of explanations were constructed for the election results?

How Was the Reagan Victory Interpreted?

Table 4.1 shows the explanations most frequently offered in these newspapers for President Reagan's re-election, in the post-election and post-inaugural weeks combined. The most common explanations referred to issues and policies (of which Mondale's pledge to raise taxes was by far the most frequent) and the candidates' personal and personality characteristics (in particular, references to Reagan's likability). In the latter category, almost three-quarters of the explanations referred to Reagan, and only one-quarter to Walter Mondale.

Almost one-fifth of the explanations cited the political parties, almost exclusively the Democrats, as causes of the election result. Most of these

TABLE 4.1: Explanations Cited Most Frequently*

Nov. 7–20, 1984; Jan. 20–Feb. 10, 1985	N=	%
Issues, Policies	648	29.5
Mondale said he'd raise taxes; Reagan said he would not raise taxes	185	8.4
Voters wanted continuity, wanted Reagan's policies continued (non-specific)	78	3.6
Reagan's commitment to strong defense, anti-communism	60	2.7
Mondale too liberal	49	2.2
Reagan's anti-big-government policies	36	1.6
Voters voted self-interest, fear of losing what they have, or of being identified as "losers"	29	1.3
Candidates' Personal and Personality Characteristics	620	28.3
Reagan		
Attractive personality; people like him	192	8.8
Leadership skills, style; strong leader	51	2.3
Patriotic rhetoric; sense of national unity; makes U.S. stand tall	31	1.4
Mastery of TV; communications skills	29	1.3
Mondale		
Wasn't good on TV	37	1.7
The candidate of special interests/unions	37	1.7
Characteristics of the Political Parties	416	19.0
Democrats		
Party of special interests, minorities; seen as overpromising	89	4.1
New Deal coalition is (in danger of) breaking up, losing demographic base	52	2.4
Lost touch with (turned their backs on) average American/middle class	41	1.9
Too liberal; led by the far left	33	1.5
Republicans		
Philosophy reflects American mainstream, growing majority; realignment	28	1.3
National Conditions	244	11.1
Prosperity; economic improvement	191	8.7
Peace	41	1.9
Characteristics of the Campaigns	121	5.5
Reagan		
"Happy times" campaign, not substantive, optimistic	26	1.2

(continues)

TABLE 4.1: *(continued)*

Nov. 7–20, 1984; Jan. 20–Feb. 10, 1985	N=	%
Group Concerns	61	2.8
Vice-Presidential Candidates	84	3.8
Ferraro		
A drag on the ticket (non-specific)	36	1.6
Husband's finances helped lose the election	27	1.2

* The categories of explanations are underlined; the N's and percentages listed across from them refer to all the various explanations in that category. The specific explanations listed under each category are only those that appear at least 25 times during this period.

explanations referred to the Democrats' image as the party of special interests, the splintering of the New Deal demographic coalition, the liberalism of the party's leadership, and the perception that the Democrats had lost touch with the average American.

Next most frequent were references to national conditions, primarily the economy (prosperity, economic improvement, declining inflation). In spite of the pre-election media emphasis on campaign strategy and organization,[28] the least frequently mentioned types of explanations after the election had to do with characteristics of the candidates' campaigns, concerns of various groups (such as blacks, whites, Hispanics, organized labor, women's groups), and the vice-presidential candidates.

In all, the range of reasons cited for the election result was extremely broad. The 22 specific explanations listed in Table 1 accounted for only 62.8% of the total volume of explanations appearing in the coverage. Fully 115 other reasons were offered at least once to account for the presidential outcome. Events, as Edelman writes, truly have multiple meanings.

But most of these explanations appeared early and then fell away. Figure 4.1 shows that the greatest diversity of reasons for the Reagan victory was found, as expected, in the days immediately following the election. On Wednesday and Thursday after election day (dates 1 and 2), 80 and 87 different explanations, respectively, appeared at least once in the coverage (out of a total volume of 367 and 478 explanations on these dates). Then the period of winnowing began, interrupted only by the Sunday after the election (date 5). In the time-honored tradition of exploring the meaning of the election results on that day, reporters, columnists and editorial writers offered up 91 separate reasons why Reagan won re-election.

The sharp drop in the diversity of explanations can be seen even as early as the following Tuesday (date 7), when fewer than half as many

FIGURE 4.1 Number of Different Explanations

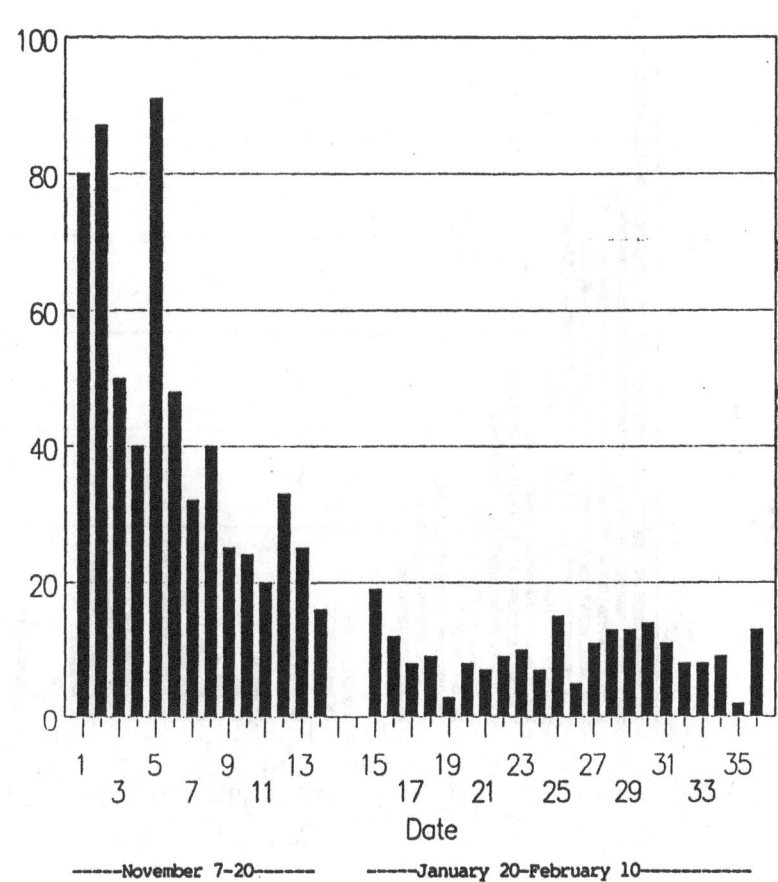

Cited Per Day

explanations appeared at least once in the coverage. A week later, there were fewer than 20. After the inauguration (date 15), only 2 to 15 explanations were cited at least once in each day's stories, columns and editorials.

Along with this decline in the diversity of explanations, the number of explanations cited *per article* decreased as well (see Figure 4.2). On the day after the election (date 1), articles contained an average of 4.5 explanations for the election results, and a maximum of 15. (The coding excludes the simple presentation of demographic correlates of the vote.) This level

FIGURE 4.2 Explanations Per Article

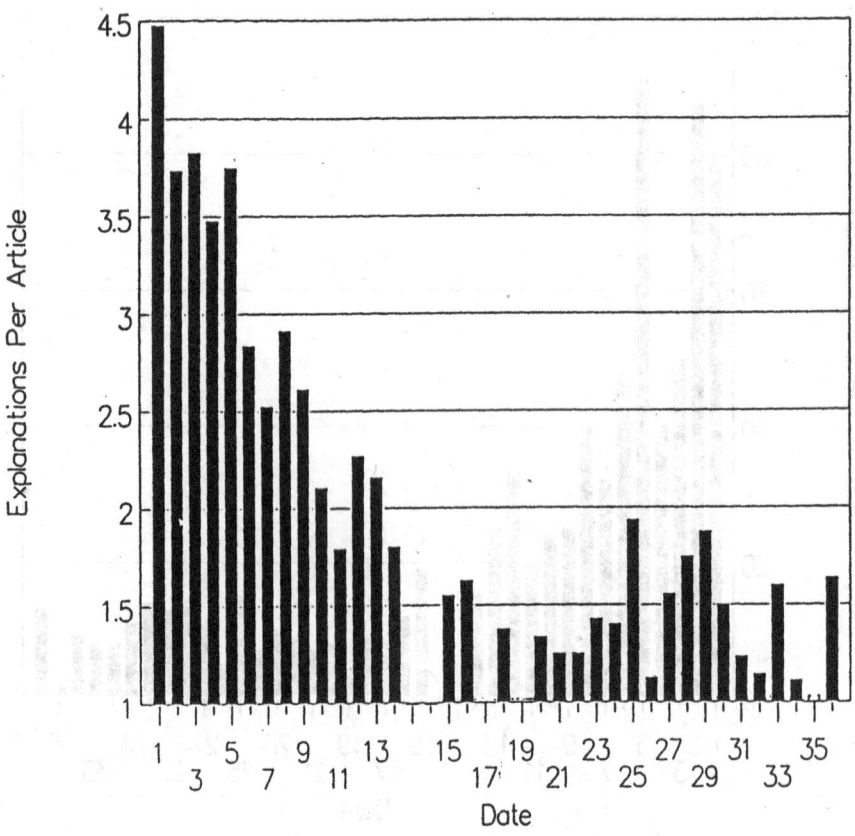

dropped immediately. By late January, there was an average of only 1 to 1.5 explanations of the election results per item, and a maximum ranging from 1 to, in one case, 5.

The effort to explain election results, then, became more parsimonious over time. Both the variety of explanations and the mean number of explanations cited per article declined steadily over the two-week period following the election, reaching a much lower level by the time of the inauguration and remaining at that level through the State of the Union address.

But these data are not sufficient to show that there was increasing consensus on the reasons for the election results. One group of ten explanations might be cited in articles and columns one day, and ten different explanations cited the next. Once the number of explanations was winnowed down to about ten per day, were they the same ten each day?

Which Explanations Became More Prevalent Over Time?

Figures 4.3 through 4.11 plot changes over time in the incidence of various types of explanations, expressed as a percentage of all explanations offered each day. Five-day rolling averages are superimposed on the data, in order to compensate for the small n's on several days in the post-inaugural period.[29]

One of the biggest changes was a marked decline in the prominence of explanations citing the candidates' personalities and personal characteristics as a reason for the Reagan victory. In the first two days after the election, almost a quarter of all the explanations offered had to do with Ronald Reagan: his likability and attractive personality, his image as a strong leader, his skills as a communicator, his identification with traditional values (see Figure 4.3). Here are some examples:

> ... the Reagan campaign knew exactly how to reinforce that impression [of Reagan as a strong leader] by its adroit projection of him through the most powerful political instrument yet developed; and in him they had the best television candidate presidential politics has yet seen.[30]
>
> Liberals and doves [erroneously think Reagan wins because people see him as] Mr. Nice Guy. In reality, he wins because he has demonstrated himself to be Mr. Nice Tough Guy, representing the middle class's long-buried sense of self-worth and newfound freedom from guilt.[31]

A week later (date 8), such explanations accounted for only 15% of the total. And after a brief recovery at the time of the inauguration, when media reports focused extensively on the President's background, character, and other personal qualities, these explanations faded; the rolling average remained at or below 11% for the rest of the post-inaugural period.[32] References to Reagan's attractive personality and leadership skills, the two most frequently mentioned explanations in this group, followed the same pattern as the category measure (not shown).

Explanations citing Walter Mondale's personal characteristics traced a similar pattern, but at a much lower level (Figure 4.4). At their peak, a week after the election, they contributed only 15% of the total. Mondale's personality disappeared even before inauguration day, statistically speaking, and did not re-emerge for the rest of the period coded.

FIGURE 4.3 Reagan's Character and Personality

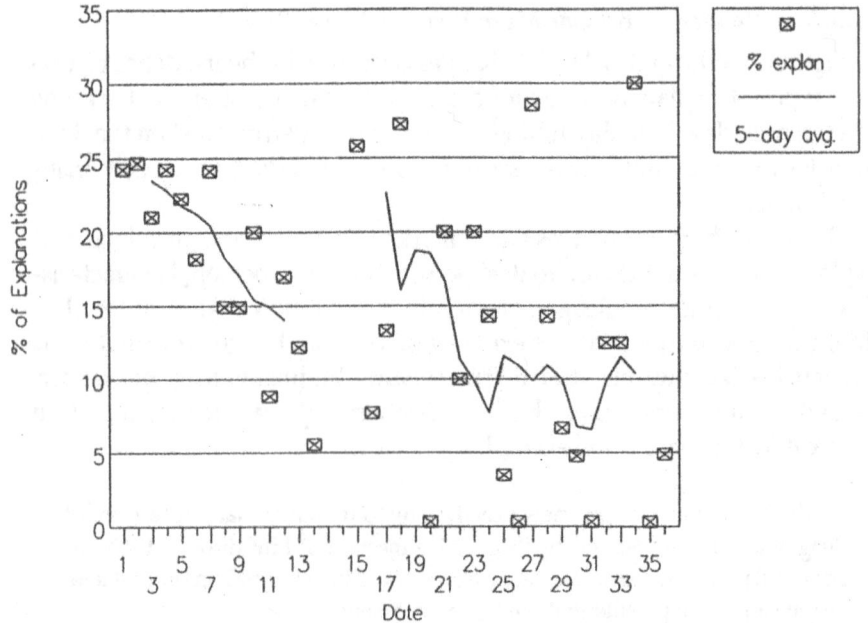

The most prominent components of this category—that Mondale lost because he couldn't match Reagan's skills as a television candidate, and because of his image as the candidate of the special interests—declined dramatically during this period (data not shown), closely matching the trend line of the category measure in Figure 4.4. Columnists Jack Germond and Jules Witcover described Mondale's problems with television:

> From the beginning of the campaign, everyone who knew Fritz Mondale was struck by the difference between the man they knew and what they saw on

FIGURE 4.4 Mondale's Character and Personality

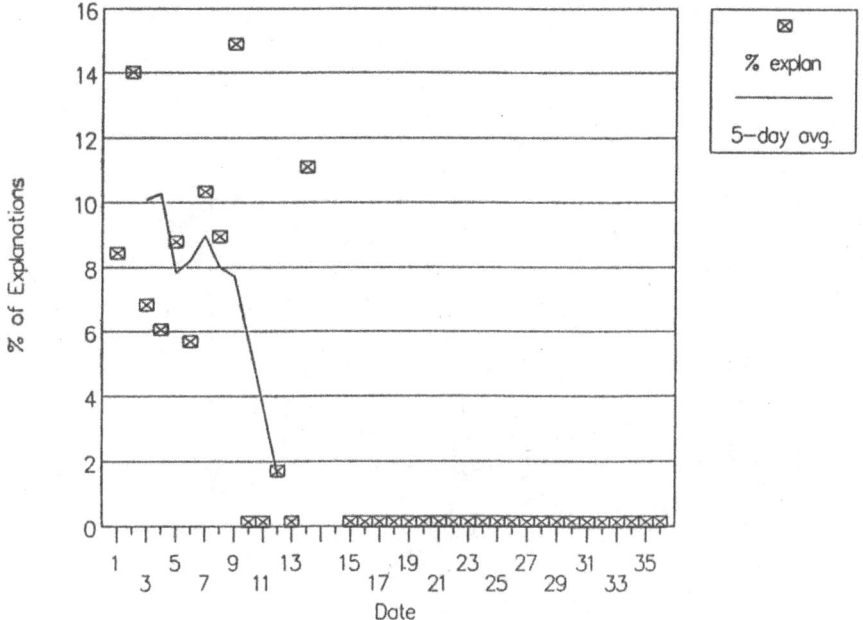

the network news programs. What they knew was a politician of intelligence and wit, but what they saw was a man in a gray suit and red tie who always seemed to be delivering nasal complaints about the state of the nation—and who quickly became tagged by the hecklers with the one unforgivable label of this age, "boring."[33]

As explanations involving the candidates' personal qualities faded from media coverage, those blaming the Democratic party for Mondale's loss were increasing. Immediately after the election, only between 7 and 11% of

FIGURE 4.5 Characteristics of Democratic Party

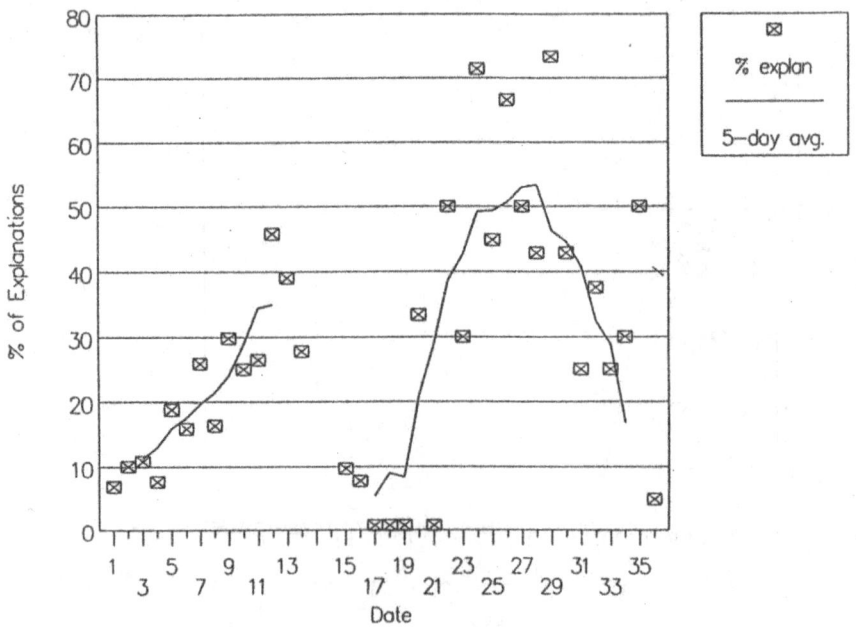

As a Percentage of All Explanations Cited, Per Day

the total volume of explanations referred to Democratic party problems (see Figure 4.5). In the second post-election week, the proportion increased greatly, ranging from 16 to 46%. During the post-inaugural period this pattern was repeated, peaking at around 50% of the total in the five-day rolling averages before dropping off again.

Changes in the two major components of this category are shown in Figures 4.6 and 4.7. The first, the argument that Mondale lost because the Democrats were (or were seen as) the party of special interests, or the captive

FIGURE 4.6 Dems Captive of Special Interests

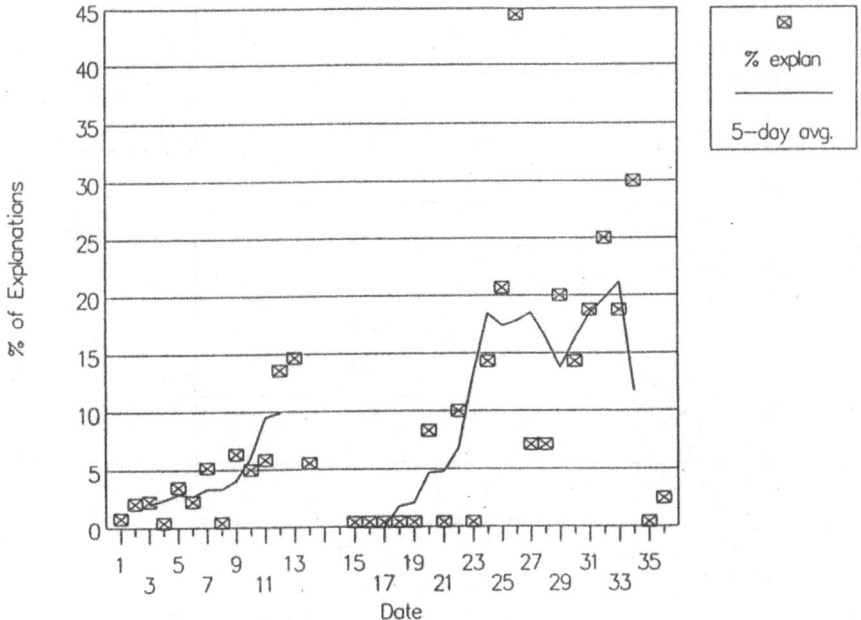

of minority groups, accounts for nearly one-quarter of the explanations involving Democratic party characteristics. The second, only about half as frequent, is that Reagan won because the New Deal demographic coalition was eroding; many of these explanations made specific reference to the loss of southerners, westerners, young people, blue-collar workers, and Catholics from the ranks of Democratic voters.

The trend lines for these two explanations move similarly, except that the "special interests" explanation peaked later than did the demographic

FIGURE 4.7 New Deal Demographic Base Eroding

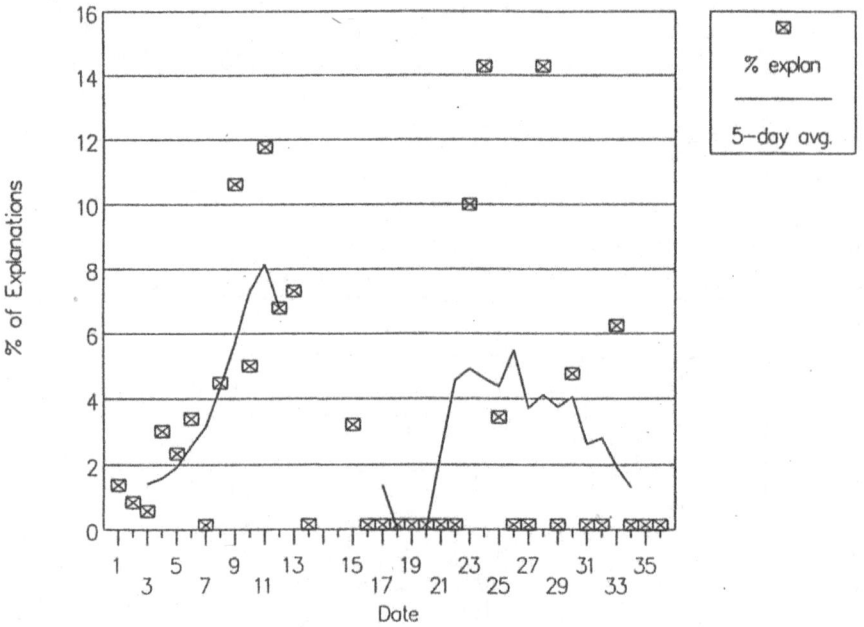

argument; the former reached its high point in the rolling averages (generally 15–20% of all explanations) between January 29 and February 7, and the latter peaked between November 15 and 19, and, to a lesser extent, between January 27 and February 4.

These changes seem to reflect the force of ongoing events. State Democratic party chairs met for an election post-mortem on November 16–18 (dates 10–12)—just when we see an initial peak in Figures 5–7, and particularly in Figure 4.7, the demographic argument. Coverage of the Democratic

National Committee meeting to select a new national chairman concentrated most heavily during the period January 30–February 2 (dates 25–28), which corresponds to the second peak in Figure 5. In this case it is the special interests explanation that attracts the lion's share of coverage.

Claims that the Democratic coalition is faltering and that it is overly dependent on minorities or "special interests" have become staples of the analysis of post-1964 presidential elections.[34] Here are samples of the 1984 coverage:

> ... one of the reasons Mondale was so vulnerable was the lack of restraint on the part of the key groups in the Democratic coalition. In one case after another, the evidence suggests that each of these blocs was so preoccupied with its own narrow concerns they contributed heavily to the image of Fritz Mondale as the candidate of "the special interests" that proved so damaging to him.
>
> The leaders of each of these groups squeezed the candidate for all they could get. And what they got for it on Election Day was a debacle.[35]

> "We have to realize that we're getting out of touch with normal, regular people," [Democratic consultant Mark] Siegel said. "We're forgetting that the white middle-class is rejecting us. We're being wagged by the tail of Jesse Jackson, of feminists or gay activists. The average voter is saying, 'What about me?'"[36]

Explanations referring to issues and policies were the only other category to increase during this period (see Figure 4.8). In the two weeks following the election, the incidence of these explanations hovered around 30%. They received even more attention in the post-inaugural period. The curve in these post-inaugural weeks is the mirror image of the Democratic party curve in Figure 4.5: very high immediately after inauguration day, lower during the following week, and high again during the week of the State of the Union address.[37]

The explanation most responsible for this increase is that Mondale was defeated because of his dramatic pledge to raise taxes. During the week after election day, it accounted for between 4 and 7% of the total number of explanations offered per day. The proportions vary in the post-inaugural weeks, but on about half the days in this latter period, in the raw data, the "Mondale said he'd raise taxes" argument accounted for at least 20% of the total volume of explanations (see Figure 4.9).

Several congressional leaders and administration officials promoted this argument. In the words of Sen. Alan Cranston (D–CA), then Senate Minority Whip: " 'Reagan campaigned against a tax increase and won. Mondale ran for it and lost. Many in the Democratic Party feel it was the major blunder of Mondale's campaign....' "[38] A number of columnists and editorial writers agreed:

FIGURE 4.8 Issues and Policies

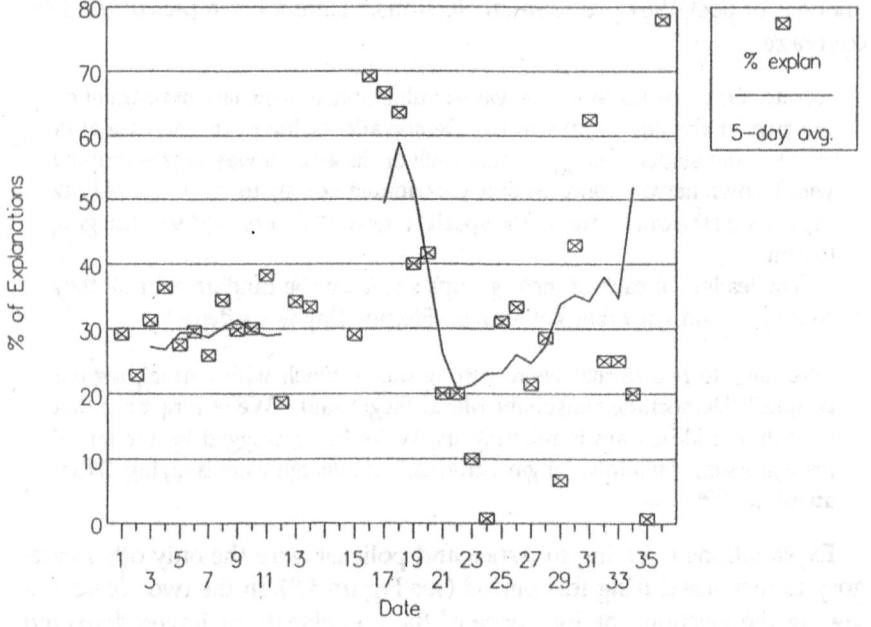

One large reason Mr. Reagan received a purely personal triumph is that until the last week or so of the campaign that is all he asked for; he did not campaign against the Congress with sharp issues. The issues were sharp only where Walter Mondale drew them—in his pledge to raise taxes, and in his TV commercials suggesting that the administration's foreign policy was leading us to nuclear war. These are the propositions the voters rejected by such overwhelming margins; the Democratic campaign succeeded in creating a mandate for Mr. Reagan."

FIGURE 4.9 Mondale Said He'd Raise Taxes

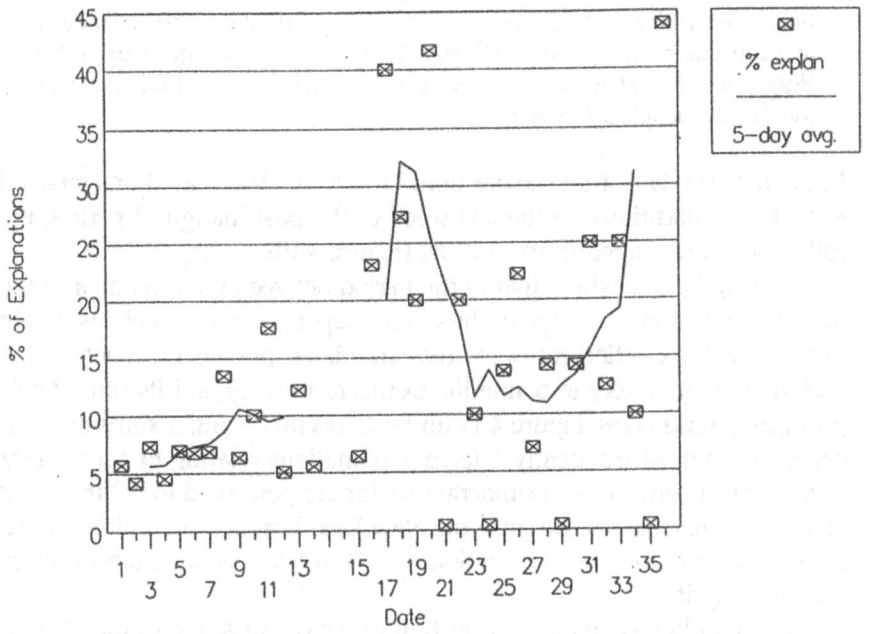

No other issue- or program-based explanation rose to prominence during this period, and most declined.

By the time the next presidential race approached, this explanation had become conventional wisdom. Discussing politicians' reluctance even to talk about tax increases, *Newsweek* recalled the 1984 race this way: "Walter Mondale promised to raise taxes and lost a national election, 49 states to one."[40]

Conventional wisdom also frequently cites the national economy in explaining presidential election results. So do scholars.[41] Yet in the 1984–85 coverage, explanations involving national conditions, most of which had to do with the economy, declined slightly over time. In the early post-election period, commentators frequently suggested that voters had rewarded the President for an expanding economy:

> It is useless to search for deep meaning in the president's landslide re-election. There isn't any deep meaning there. To the extent that issues mattered at all in this campaign, the only significant issue was summed up in Mr. Reagan's rhetorical question: Are you better off than you were four years ago? Most of the people said yes.[42]

In the first six days after the election, 11–15% of all explanations referred to national conditions. In the last week of the post-inaugural period, the rolling average ranged from 5 to 13% (Figure 4.10).

In short, the data show that in the period between the election and the State of the Union, coverage in these newspapers became much less likely to attribute the election results to the candidates' personal characteristics, and much more likely to blame the Democratic party and its candidate's promise to raise taxes. Figure 4.11 underscores this point; it sums the incidence of the most frequently-offered explanations relating to party—that Mondale lost because the Democrats are (or are perceived to be) the party of special interests, and because the New Deal Democratic coalition is no longer viable— and the explanation that Mondale's pledge to raise taxes was the culprit.

This trend line is, in effect, a portrait of the construction of meaning in the presidential election result. In the first week after the election, these three specific explanations combined to account for only about 10% of the total volume of explanations offered for Reagan's victory. In later weeks their prominence increased, to the extent that by early February, the three (in the rolling averages) comprised almost half of all explanations. During this three-month period, then, there was growing consensus that Ronald Reagan's victory was the Democrats' fault: the party, for caving in to special interests and letting portions of the New Deal coalition slip away, and Mondale, for speaking the unspeakable.

Why Did Personality-Based Explanations Give Way to Party- and Issue-Based Explanations?

The patterns in these data suggest some kind of contagion effect: that a few explanations diffuse from some sources to others, gathering adherents as they spread, until they come to dominate the coverage by displacing most of the likely alternatives. Crouse[43] described a similar type of contagion effect among political journalists. In his analysis, "pack journalism" is the tendency for campaign reporters—because they are in close contact with one

FIGURE 4.10 National Conditions

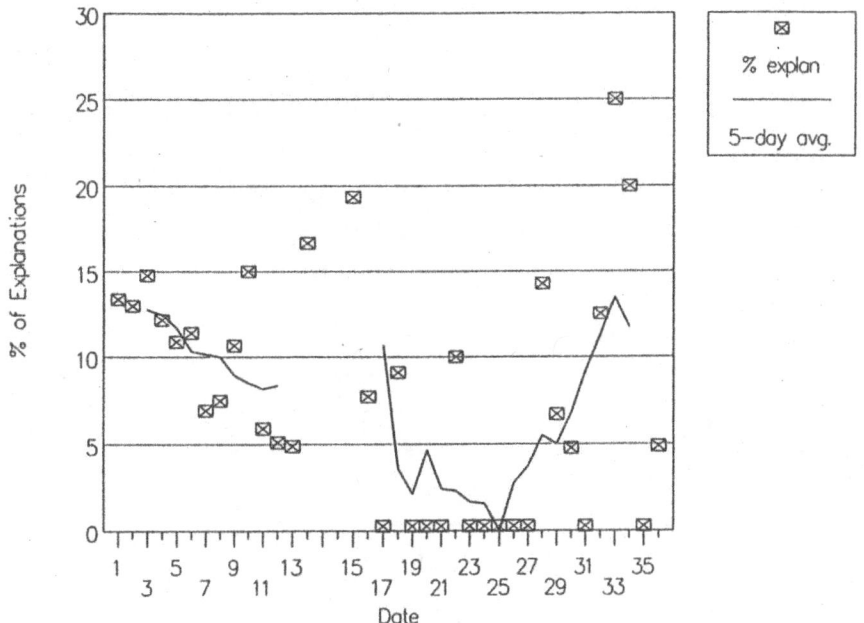

As a Percentage of All Explanations Cited, Per Day

another, and under great pressure to meet deadlines and produce interesting copy—to reach a shared understanding as to what deserves coverage and how it should be covered. The professional socialization that is common to journalists[44] undergirds this tendency toward a shared understanding.

The campaign environment that fosters pack journalism changes a little in the election's aftermath, but not greatly. Journalists covering national politics—especially the White House—remain a kind of "pack," exposed to the

FIGURE 4.11 Taxes and Democrats

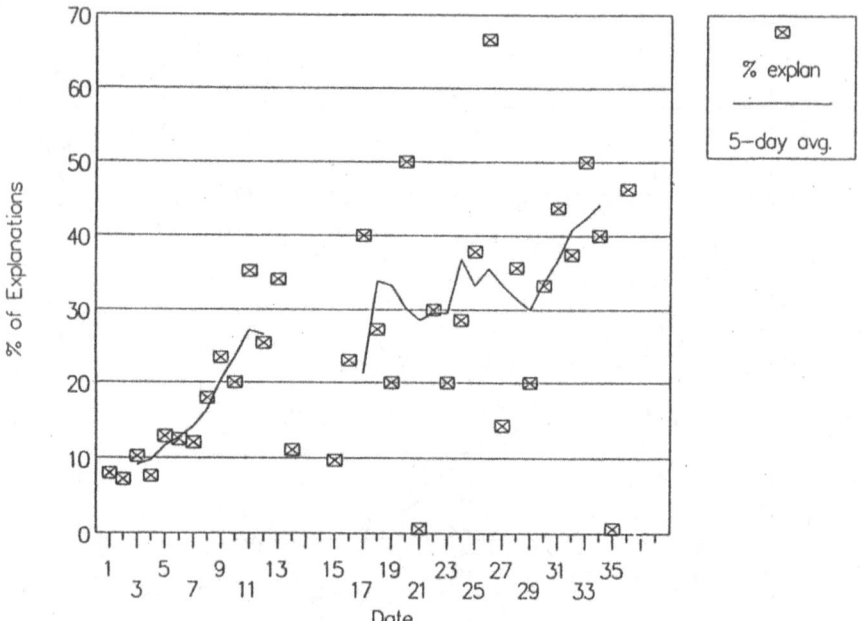

* includes the sum of explanations "Mondale said he'd raise taxes," "Democrats are the party of special interests," and "the Democratic New Deal coalition is eroding."

same news conferences, sources, and ever-present deadlines. There is continuing pressure to take note of the interpretations offered by well-respected White House reporters and columnists, and continuing need to justify to one's editor any interpretation that differs from the evolving wisdom of the pack.

It is significant, then, that in the first five days after the election, several leading journalists cited the arguments that Mondale's descent into truth-telling about taxes and the Democrats' problems with special interests and demographics gave Reagan his re-election. David S. Broder, in his November 8 *Washington Post* news story quoted sources offering all three of these explanations.⁴⁵ Haynes Johnson's news analysis in the *Post* that day cited the Democrats' image as the party of minority interests.⁴⁶ In the *New York Times*, Howell Raines stressed the taxes and demographic explanations on November 7.⁴⁷ Jon Margolis, writing the November 7 headline article for the *Chicago Tribune*, emphasized taxes and special interests.⁴⁸ So did noted columnists Jack Germond and Jules Witcover in several of these newspapers on November 11.⁴⁹

The content analysis alone cannot prove that these explanations rose to such prominence because the judgments of leading journalists such as Broder, Raines, Germond and Witcover gave the explanations credibility with other writers. But the data are consistent with such an interpretation.

It is also plausible that this diffusion stems not so much from the journalists as from the news sources they interview. Political leaders, party and group activists work hard to promote their own interpretations of the election result for the same reason that Kingdon's "policy entrepreneurs"⁵⁰ advocate a particular policy idea: because its widespread acceptance would benefit them or the interests of the group they represent.

Who would benefit from acceptance of the Democrats and taxes explanations? Republican activists might gain by rubbing salt in the Democrats' wounds. But parts of the Democratic coalition might be the promoters too. Those who opposed the policies of their post-reform party might expect to gain more influence within the party if they could move conventional wisdom in the direction of the "special interests" and "New Deal demographic" explanations.

It remains to be explained why these newspapers came to agree that Mondale and the Democrats' problems lost the election, rather than that Reagan and the Republicans won it. Clearly, there were convincing arguments to justify the latter conclusion. Reagan was a personally popular incumbent serving during a period of economic expansion. The kinds of people hurt by Reagan's policies were those least likely to vote. There was never a point, during the year prior to the election, when public opinion polls showed him to be in serious danger of losing.

And in fact, systematic analyses done later by political scientists accepted that latter conclusion. Abramson *et al.*, for example, termed the election a positive retrospective choice: a widespread belief that Reagan had done a good job in his first term.⁵¹

The media emphasis on Democrats and taxes is especially puzzling in light of the long-standing fascination with the possibility of party realignment.⁵² After the Reagan victory in 1980, many observers⁵³ argued that the realization of a Republican realignment would depend in part on Reagan's ability, during his time in office, to transfer his personal popularity into support for his party and policies. Indeed in the 1984 election there were signs that he had been successful, including Republican gains among young voters, increases in Republican party identification more generally, and inroads made by party candidates in the East, Midwest, and South.

Yet characteristics of the Republican party, including the possibility of realignment, accounted for an average of only 2% of the total volume of explanations for Reagan's victory. The 5-day rolling average never exceeded 4.8%. After Reagan's inauguration, explanations mentioning his party were rarely cited.

One possible reason is that the Democrats were a better "story" in light of prevailing media norms.[54] The struggles within the Democratic party had all the qualities the media define as "news": conflict, drama, human interest, timeliness, even oddity. To say that it captured journalists' imaginations is an understatement; Germond and Witcover's book-length treatment of the 1984 election was so preoccupied with the Democratic party's difficulties that fully 13 of the 22 chapters were devoted to the Democrats' nomination race alone, and the concluding chapter stressed the problems the authors found with the party's nominating process and its impact on the general election result.[55]

In addition, the content analysis suggests that Democratic sources were much more available to these journalists than were Republicans. As Table 2 shows, Mondale, Ferraro and their staffs were mentioned as the source of an explanation almost twice as often as was the Reagan/Bush campaign, and Democratic party leaders were quoted almost eight times as frequently as Republican.[56] But the preponderance of Democratic sources certainly did not result in a pro-Democratic slant to the coverage; the majority of Democrats quoted used the opportunity to voice criticisms of their party and its standard-bearer.[57]

A third possibility is that journalists' own predilections led them to pay special attention to the Democratic party's dilemma. It is clear from these data that journalists themselves play a vital role in constructing these interpretations. Throughout the period coded, about 80% of the explanations cited for Reagan's victory were offered with no supporting evidence at all: no poll data, no corroboration from political experts, no argument or examples, thus giving the impression that they were common knowledge. Similarly, 56% of the explanations were presented without attribution to any source (see Table 4.2). The source, then, was the reporter, columnist, or editorial writer him- or herself.

Lichter and Rothman,[58] among others, have found that most prominent journalists are sympathetic with Democratic policies, and also mainstream in their economic orientations. They might, then, be especially sensitive to the concern that the Democratic party had positioned itself too far to the left.

TABLE 4.2 Sources Cited for Explanations of the 1984 Presidential Election*

Source	Number of Citations	% of all Citations
Candidates		
Ronald Reagan	88	
George Bush	1	
Reagan/Bush campaign staff members	11	
Reagan's personal advisers, non-campaign	12	
Total Reagan Campaign		5.1%
Walter Mondale	131	
Geraldine Ferraro	9	
Mondale/Ferraro campaign staff members	17	
Mondale's personal advisers, non-campaign	18	
Mondale's primary opponents	24	
Total Mondale Campaign		9.1
Governmental Sources		
Reagan administration members	36	
House/Senate member from newspaper's district	17	
Other House/Senate members	91	
Elected officials outside of Washington	50	
Total Governmental Sources		8.8
Consultants	31	1.4
Independent analysts		
(social scientists, think tank staff members)	58	2.6
Political party leaders		
Democrats	150	6.8
Republicans	20	0.9
Interest Group Leaders	52	2.4
Broadcast Journalists	7	0.3
Generic Sources		
"Conservatives feel..."	7	
"Liberals feel..."	34	
"Democrats feel..."	11	
"Southern Democrats feel..."	4	
"There is a widespread belief that..."	32	
Total Generic Sources		4.0
Interviews with individual voters	49	2.2
No source: stated without attribution by the reporter/columnist/editorial writer	1234	56.2
Total	2194	99.8**

* For each explanation of the election result appearing in the coverage, I coded the source (if any) to whom the explanation was attributed.
** Due to independent rounding

Interestingly, the charge that the Democrats left the mainstream seems to have had little if any empirical basis. According to Miller and Jennings,[59] survey data show that at least in 1980, the beginning of the Reagan era, Democratic National Convention delegates were closer to the Democratic rank-and-file (party identifiers) on issues than Republican convention delegates were to Republican party identifiers. The empirical data are of interest mainly to academic observers, however. For participants in the process, arguments do not qualify as explanations of election results because they are provable empirically, but because they conform to the presuppositions, or advance the interests, of those who do the explaining.

In that light, it is easy to understand media acceptance of the explanation that Mondale's pledge to raise taxes cost him the election. The belief that government is too large, intrusive, and costly has long been a cornerstone of American public debate—even when much of the remainder of that debate consists of arguments for the provision or expansion of specific government services. Kelley underlines the centrality of this belief when he writes, "Mandates are clearly not impossible; any presidential candidate willing to propose a sufficiently burdensome level of taxation could easily evoke one."[60]

The Role of Events. In short, then, some explanations diffuse and gain adherents because they are promoted by respected journalists and/or persuasive news sources, and because they are consistent with prevailing myths. Another plausible contributor to these patterns of diffusion is that they are event-driven, just as the media are. Media coverage normally centers on discrete and immediate events—leaders' actions, campaign debates and gaffes—rather than on broader concerns of ongoing importance.[61] As journalists whittle down the number of viable explanations to a relative few, they (and their sources) may focus on some subset of those few explanations that is especially relevant to the events being covered at the time, turning to another subset as other events come to dominate.

Right after election day, the event dominating the coverage is the vote itself, its impact and its peculiarities. In the wake of the 1984 election, the biggest puzzle was why Reagan won so big but his party did not; Republicans picked up "the smallest share of House seats won by the party of a victorious presidential candidate in the history of our country."[62] If Reagan was the anomaly, journalists would be very likely to interpret his victory as stemming from his personal characteristics, including elements of his personality and political style.

In subsequent weeks, the story of Reagan as the Teflon candidate faded—inevitably, in the absence of a new "news peg"—and was replaced by coverage of other events. Leaders of state Democratic parties held an election post-mortem and later the Democratic National Committee met to select a new DNC chair; that stimulated journalists to highlight explanations dealing with Democratic party failures from the remaining pool of accepted explanations. The Reagan inauguration led writers to focus again on explanations involving Reagan's personal appeal. After the inauguration, members of the newly-elected Congress got a share of the spotlight, giving speeches and interviews about their legislative priorities. As journalists and their sources paid more attention to policy development, some explanations involving policy became more salient, particularly the ever-interesting matter of taxes.

Thus the unfolding of events that fit the media's definition of "major news stories" may be responsible for pulling some explanations into the media spotlight and letting others rest offstage. But at the same time, as Figure 11 clearly shows, the pool from which these explanations are drawn had been shrinking since the election, so that by the end of January only a relative few were still considered plausible enough to be in the theater at all.

Moving Toward Truth? There is another possible interpretation of the findings in Figure 4.11: that journalists and their sources were steadily uncovering the *real* explanation for the election result. To do so, presumably, they would need to be receiving new data during this time, such as new secondary analyses of exit poll data that confirmed some explanations of the vote and disconfirmed others. If this interpretation is correct, then we should see mentions of new and sophisticated public opinion analyses, especially in the latter part of this time period.

That pattern does not appear. The greatest use of poll data was in the coverage on the day after the election, when exit polls and other survey data were cited as evidence for 23% of the explanations offered. In the second week after the election, poll data were cited as evidence for only 4.9%, and in the last week coded, only 2.3%. These later references did little more than recall earlier coverage of poll findings; no new primary or secondary analyses were cited.

In fact, the coverage of poll data would give an observer little confidence that any careful, empirical explanation of the election result would emerge in the media. Exit polls were treated more as news stories than as data sources. The data were presented most often as marginals, or, at times, as cross-tabulations by party, demographics, or attitude.[63] Many of the early news stories boasted long lists of poll findings, but with little or no indication as to which mattered most in explaining voters' choices. After these early days, references to poll data and other systematic evidence nearly disappeared.

There is no evidence, then, that this is a process in which journalists sift the empirical evidence and finally determine what the "true" explanation of the election result is. As Edelman writes, "If political developments depended upon factual observations, false meanings would be discredited in time and a consensus upon valid ones would emerge, at least among informed and educated observers. That does not happen, even over long time periods."[64]

The Impact of the Explanations

What is the impact of this process by which an election takes on meaning? Do these explanations have consequences, and for whom?

Edelman suggests that news "is not so much a description of events as a catalyst of political support and opposition in the light of the spectator's sensitivities, areas of ignorance, and ideological stance."[65] News takes on meaning as it calls forth people's experiences and prior understanding. In so doing, it influences future actions, future relationships among groups, future power relationships.

Clearly, reporters, columnists, and their interview sources *think* that the choice of constructed explanations has consequences. Consider, for example, these comments on the effects of the explanation that Mondale's promise to raise taxes cost him the election:

> Because Reagan's pledge against a tax increase was a key part of his successful reelection campaign, the political climate makes it virtually impossible to advocate higher taxes. Thus, all of the [tax] reform plans are 'revenue neutral' and would maintain total tax collections at current levels. [referring to the Bradley-Gephardt and DeConcini-Symms tax reform plans then being introduced][66]

> In a secret ballot, that proposition [that a balanced budget isn't possible in the foreseeable future without significant revenue increase] would almost certainly be agreed to by a substantial majority of both houses [of Congress]. But there will be no secret votes and no public ones in support of a tax increase because the president has promised a veto and the Democrats learned last fall what happens to people who speak of such things.[67]

Acceptance of this explanation, then, led to the widely-shared conclusion that voters would not tolerate a tax increase, even in the guise of tax reform. Four years later, the learning was still fresh. Walter Mondale, interviewed on CNN at the 1988 Democratic National Convention, remarked ruefully, "I taught a whole generation of politicians how to handle the tax issue—to not mention it." George Bush and Michael Dukakis did mention it, but only as a preacher might mention sin: Bush with the ever-present phrase, "Read my lips: NO . . . NEW . . . TAXES," and Dukakis with the constant pledge, "only as a last resort."

Newsweek summed it up this way: "Since Walter Mondale's ill-advised promise to raise taxes at the 1984 Democratic convention, tax hikes have joined social-security cuts as lethal 'third rail' issues in American politics.

(Touch them and you're dead.)"⁶⁸ The statement is overdramatized; Mondale's experience was not the first to assume that voters don't like tax increases. But it was a dramatic new indicator that even a mind-numbing national debt might not be enough to soften that aversion.

On the day after the election, only 38.4% of the articles coded cited a link between some explanation of the election results and a consequence of that explanation. During the rest of that post-election week, between half and two-thirds of the articles posited such a relationship. The proportion was 90.9% on the day after the inauguration, and it remained at 88% or over for the remainder of the period. Increasingly, then, journalists were reporting that the choice of an explanation affected, or should affect, the subsequent behavior of some political actor.

As in the case of the constructed explanations, the Democratic party was disproportionately the subject of this coverage. Of the total volume of consequences cited (n=1015), almost half (42.9%) focused on the parties. Of those references to the parties, more than nine in ten had to do with the Democrats. As might be expected from coverage of the political spectacle, fully 33.5% of the consequences referred to the Democrats in strategic terms; an additional 6.1% made recommendations on the party's policy stands. Only 3.3% of the consequences referred to the Republican party in either strategic or policy terms.

Most of the remaining consequences (32.7%) had to do with Reagan's policies: commitments the writer felt Reagan should make or was likely to make as the result of the November vote. Most frequent were judgments that the vote heightened Reagan's determination not to raise taxes, or made him more likely to try to cut the federal budget or freeze spending, or to continue the policies of his first term. Mentioned almost as often was a contrasting, cautionary view: that Congress had received a mandate very different from Reagan's, or that Reagan should not read his mandate to mean that voters wanted an unrestricted extension of his earlier policies.

The highest level of consensus developed with respect to the taxes and special interests explanations. The great majority of conclusions drawn from the taxes explanation (not shown) coincided with the lesson George Bush drew in time for 1988: no new taxes were politically feasible. The most frequent conclusions were that the election result had strengthened Reagan's determination to avoid a tax increase, and that Congress would not cooperate if Reagan *were* to propose new taxes, despite the feeling among many or most members of Congress that a tax hike was necessary. As time passed, these conclusions increased as a proportion of the total.

Similarly, the special interests explanation was linked with a few clearly derived consequences. The general admonition that the party needed to reduce its dependence on these interests predominated in the first two weeks coded. Then, with increasing coverage of the effort to elect a new

DNC chair, the lessons became more fine-tuned: that the Democrats should abolish or freeze the numbers of minority caucuses within the DNC, and choose a non-minority DNC chair. By the last week coded, most mentions of the special interests explanation were linked with one of these concrete proposals.

The conclusions drawn from explanations of the election results are only one of the influences on the agenda of the incoming Congress and administration.[69] But they provide an avenue in which learning prompted by election results helps establish the context for subsequent political action.

Discussion

When "the voters have spoken," who decides what they said? The analysis in this paper suggests that political activists and the journalists who cover them give meaning to the raw vote totals through a process of constructing explanations for the voters' choices. These constructed explanations soon become conventional wisdom about the meaning of the election, and affect the actions and postures then taken by political actors inside and outside of government.

What are the "rules" of the process by which some explanations come to dominate our understanding of an election result? Explanations seem more likely to survive if they are congruent with prevailing ways of looking at the political world. If political discussion, at least in the Washington community, has long centered on the question of the appropriate size and scope of the federal government, or on the problems of the Democratic party, then activists and media people are likely to ask what the election might have to say on that point, and to construct explanations related to it. In particular, explanations may be "winnowed in" because they resonate with the beliefs of opinion-leading journalists or respected sources.

At another level, explanations are more likely to be accepted if they further the prevailing distribution of power. As Edelman argues, "The 'career' of an explanation of a problem manifestly hinges in part on the acceptability of the ideological premise it implies."[70] Figure 11 shows the growing acceptance of three constructed explanations. One is that taxes should not be raised: Those who have money should not be required to put more of it toward public-sector responsibilities. Another is that the Democrats are too concerned with "special interests": They should pay less attention to the needs of blacks, organized labor, and other minorities. The third is that perhaps as a result, more affluent groups—middle-class people, whites, and others—are distancing themselves from the Democratic party. Clearly, these explanations have the effect of protecting privilege.

For an explanation to survive, it would also seem to need a credible promoter. At minimum, the promoter must be accessible to journalists. More likely, the promoter will be actively disseminating his or her ideas to media people (or to *other* media people) to gain widespread acceptance. Further, it doesn't seem to hurt if the explanation has the qualities of a good story: drama, immediacy, conflict. Since the media are central actors in this process, media values help shape it.

What is the impact of this process? During the time period studied, explanations of the election results were increasingly coupled with statements about the consequences of the explanations: for example, if Mondale lost because of his pledge to raise taxes, then it would be unwise for members of Congress to propose a tax increase. By the time of the President's State of the Union address and budget message to Congress, nine in ten explanations of his victory were presented together with a statement of consequences. In other words, the process of constructing explanations had resulted in learning.

There are broader implications as well. This process highlighted Reagan's and Mondale's statements about taxes, their personal qualities, and their parties' alliances. Such a focus encourages the view that leaders are the agent of change, and therefore that dissatisfied people should focus on changing or influencing the leadership rather than on the forces of racial, gender, economic, and other inequalities that shape citizens' lives.[71] The focus on leaders "helps erase history, social structure, economic inequalities, and discourse from the schemas that account for well-being and privations."[72] In short, it encourages a concern with the narrow range of visible choices rather than on basic ideological premises of the society.

These "rules" of news reporting thus make media coverage into a long succession of surface dramas. They draw the audience into the political spectacle, rather than call attention to forces that are both more important and less "newsworthy," such as a small change in the tax code or in a bureaucratic regulation that can affect hundreds of lives. "A free press, competing news media, and alert and competent news staffs are therefore no guarantee that the public can act effectively in pursuit of its interests."[73]

Do these 1984 data provide a basis for drawing conclusions about presidential races more generally, or was this election too unusual to support generalizations? President Reagan ran an image-based campaign in 1984, almost wiped clean of stands on specific issues. Perhaps there is more room for politicians and journalists to impute their own meaning to election results when the winning candidate has failed to, or chosen not to, run on a few clearly-stated, policy-relevant themes. Yet even in the 1980 Reagan victory, often treated as a contrast to the 1984 campaign, there was considerable variation in the explanations offered.[74]

Since 1984 this process has seemed to speed up and to become more self-conscious. As a sure sign of institutionalization, it developed jargon. The effort to construct explanations favorable to one's candidate became "spin," and the people offering those explanations, "spinners" or "spin doctors."

At its heart, however, the meaning of the process remains unchanged. It is that elections have systematic distortions as learning situations. Their limitations as a means of conveying information about voters' preferences inevitably give rise to efforts to interpret what the vote meant. These efforts produce learning that affects future political behavior. Thus "... observers and what they observe construct one another."[75]

The observers, in this case, are political leaders, activists, and media people. It is their constructed explanations that shape the meaning of elections as an influence on public policy. The voters' voice, then, apparently is heard only in translation.

Notes

1. I am grateful to the *Journal of Politics* for permission to reprint a portion of my article, "The Constructed Explanation: Interpreting Election Results in the 1984 Presidential Race" (*Journal of Politics* 54, Nov., 1992). I am also grateful to C. Anthony Broh, Thomas R. Dye, Leon Epstein, Richard F. Fenno, Jr., Jennifer Hochschild, and Gerald Wright for their comments, and to Howard V. Hershey for his invaluable help.

2. Murray Edelman, *Constructing the Political Spectacle* (Chicago: University of Chicago Press, 1988), pp. 1–2.

3. Edelman, pp. 103–104.

4. Edelman, p. 105.

5. Edelman, p. 39.

6. Edelman, p. 95.

7. Editorial "The President's Mandate," *Denver Post*, Nov. 7, 1984, p. 26A.

8. Editorial, "Election Cleanup," *Washington Post*, Nov. 15, 1984, p. A22.

9. Stanley Kelley, Jr., *Interpreting Elections* (Princeton: Princeton University Press, 1983), p. 126.

10. Edelman, p. 43.

11. Different electoral systems may allow more information to come through, as Spitzer (1987) shows with respect to the New York system allowing minor parties to slate candidates who are already running on a major party's ballot line. See Robert J. Spitzer, *The Right To Life Movement and Third Party Politics* (New York: Greenwood Press, 1987).

12. Sidney Verba and Norman H. Nie, *Participation in America: Political Democracy and Social Equality* (New York: Harper and Row, 1972), p. 106.

13. Norman H. Nie, Sidney Verba and John R. Petrocik, *The Changing American Voter*, enlarged ed. (Cambridge: Harvard University Press, 1979); see, further, the argument of Raymond Wolfinger—"Dealignment, Realignment, and Mandates in the 1984 Election," in Austin Ranney, ed., *The American Elections of 1984* (Durham, N.C.: Duke University Press, 1985), p. 293—regarding the inherent implausibility of mandates; also Kelley, pp. 133–137.

14. Marjorie Randon Hershey, *Running for Office: The Political Education of Campaigners* (Chatham, N.J.: Chatham House, 1984).

15. Richard F. Fenno, Jr., *Home Style: House Members in their Districts* (Boston: Little, Brown, 1978).

16. For example, see Joseph A. Schumpeter, *Capitalism, Socialism and Democracy*, 3rd Ed. (New York: Harper and Row, 1950), as compared with John Stuart Mill, *Considerations on Representative Government* (Chicago: Henry Regnery Co., 1962; 1861).

17. John W. Kingdon, *Agendas, Alternatives, and Public Policies* (Boston: Little, Brown, 1984), pp. 153-157.

18. As V. O. Key, Jr. argued in "The Politically Relevant in Surveys," *Public Opinion Quarterly* 24 (Spring, 1960), p. 55:

> If the specialist in electoral behavior is to be a student of politics, his major concern must be the population of elections, not the population of individual voters. One does not gain an understanding of elections by the simple cumulation of the typical findings from the microscopic analysis of the individuals in the system.

19. See Gerald C. Wright, "Level-of-Analysis Effects on Explanations of Voting: The Case of the 1982 U. S. Senate Elections," *British Journal of Political Science* 19 (July, 1989), pp. 381-398.

20. Timothy Crouse, *The Boys on the Bus* (New York: Ballantine, 1973).

21. Ross K. Baker, "The Second Reagan Term," in Gerald Pomper with Colleagues, *The Election of 1984: Reports and Interpretations* (Chatham, N.J.: Chatham House, 1985), p. 134.

22. Kelley, p. 167.

23. E.g., Thomas E. Patterson, *The Mass Media Election* (New York: Praeger, 1980); Shanto Iyengar and Donald R. Kinder, *News that Matters* (Chicago: University of Chicago Press, 1987).

24. Paul Allen Beck and Bradley Richardson, "Personal, Organizational, and Media Intermediaries in the 1988 Presidential Contest," paper presented at the 1989 Annual Meeting of the American Political Science Association, Atlanta, p. 8 and Table 2, for example, found that more of their respondents read a daily newspaper regularly (48%) than watched TV news on a regular basis (34%). And Larry M. Bartels, *Presidential Primaries and the Dynamics of Public Choice* (Princeton: Princeton University Press, 1988), p. 315 discusses studies showing that newspapers and network TV news share the same emphases in campaign coverage.

25. Columns by syndicated columnists such as David Broder and George Will, whose work appears in more than one of the newspapers studied, or wire service stories carried by two or more of these papers, were coded each time they appeared. The more times a column or story is reprinted, the more political activists are exposed to the ideas and explanations it contains.

26. Phrases such as these were considered to indicate the existence of an explanation: "The voters reelected Reagan because . . . ," "The reasons why Reagan was unbeatable are . . . ," "A key element in Reagan's success with the American people is . . . ," "The Democrats lost big because . . . ," "The outcome signified . . . ," ". . . won endorsement from the voters," ". . . helped Reagan win."

27. Editorial, "A Mandate for What?" *Chicago Tribune*, Nov. 7, 1984, sec. 1, p. 2.

28. Marjorie Randon Hershey, "The Campaign and the Media," in Gerald M. Pomper, ed., *The Election of 1988: Reports and Interpretations* (Chatham, N.J.: Chatham House, 1989), pp. 73–102.

29. In the post-inaugural period, the total number of explanations cited per day frequently fell below 20. On these days, the ideas of one columnist, carried in two or more newspapers, might be given disproportionate weight in the percentages. So I calculated a five-day rolling average, which ensured that at least 44 explanations would be represented at any point along that average.

30. Tom Wicker, "GOP ran the textbook TV campaign, *Oregonian*, November 10, 1984, p. C6.

31. William Safire, "The Prairie Fire," *New York Times*, Nov. 8, 1984, p. 27.

32. Other analysts (Paul R. Abramson, John H. Aldrich, and David W. Rohde, *Change and Continuity in the 1984 Elections* (Washington, D.C.: Congressional Quarterly, 1986), p. XV.) also noted that the early efforts to explain the President's re-election focused chiefly on Reagan's personal qualities, or as a "personal triumph" for the President, because his 49-state victory was not accompanied by comparable gains for Republicans running in House and Senate races. But Abramson et al. contend that later explanations emphasized the idea of Republican realignment—a finding not confirmed by my data, as will be seen.

33. Jack Germond and Jules Witcover, "Losers? Mondale's no McGovern, Goldwater or Carter," *The Sun*, Nov. 11, 1984, p. N2.

34. Kelley, p. 174.

35. Jack Germond and Jules Witcover, "Narrow focus of blocs contributed to debacle," *Atlanta Journal*, Nov. 15, 1984, p. 14A.

36. Jon Margolis, "Democrats' middle class slips away," *Chicago Tribune*, Nov. 11, 1984, p. 1.

37. This inverse relationship between the party-based and issue-based explanations is not simply an artifact of the use of percentages. I chose to use percentages in this section because of the widely differing numbers of articles coded per day. Once past the first week, however, where the largest numbers of articles are concentrated, the raw numbers peak on most of the same days as the percentages do.

38. David Hoffman, "The Campaign Begins for the History Books," *Washington Post*, Jan. 20, 1985, p. A1.

39. Editorial, "Four More Years?" *Wall Street Journal*, Nov. 8, 1984, p. 28.

40. "The Politics of Austerity," *Newsweek*, Nov. 23, 1987, p. 18.

41. See Robert S. Erickson, "Economic Conditions and the Presidential Vote," *American Political Science Review* 83 (June, 1989), pp. 567–573; Edward R. Tufte, *Political Control of the Economy* (Princeton: Princeton University Press, 1980); Kelley, pp. 190–210; Barbara G. Farah and Ethel Klein, "Public Opinion Trends," in *The Election of 1988*, pp. 103–128.

42. James J. Kilpatrick, "Because people were better off," *Indianapolis Star*, Nov. 13, 1984, p. 8.

43. Crouse, *op. cit.*

44. See Doris A. Graber, *Mass Media and American Politics*, 3rd Ed. (Washington, D.C.: Congressional Quarterly Press, 1989), chap. 3.

45. David S. Broder with George Lardner Jr., "Democrats Challenge Mandate of President's Landslide," *Washington Post*, Nov. 8, 1984, p. A1.

46. Haynes Johnson, "Voters Sent Up Caution Flags," *Washington Post*, Nov. 8, 1984, p. A48.

47. Howell Raines, "Reagan the Apparent Victor; G.O.P. Heads for Gains in House," *New York Times*, Nov. 7, 1984, p. 1.

48. Jon Margolis, "Reagan Wins 4 More Years," *Chicago Tribune*, Nov. 7, 1984, p. 1.

49. On the influence of such news sources, see Graber, p. 66.

50. Kingdon, p. 129.

51. See Abramson *et. al.*, chap. 7.

52. See Edward G. Carmines and James A. Stimson, *Issue Evolution: Race and the Transformation of American Politics* (Princeton: Princeton University Press, 1989).

53. See Paul Allen Beck, "The Dealignment Era in America," in Russell J. Dalton *et. al.*, eds., *Electoral Change in Advanced Industrial Democracies: Realignment or Dealignment?* (Princeton: Princeton University Press, 1984), pp. 240–266.

54. See Graber, chap. 3.

55. Jack W. Germond and Jules Witcover, *Wake Us When It's Over* (New York: Macmillan, 1985).

56. Note that Democrats outnumbered Republicans in most of the other source categories in Table 2 as well. Of the 91 "other" House and Senate sources (other than the representative from the newspaper's district or state), fully 28 of these citations were to former House speaker Thomas P. O'Neill's office. Only four came from the House and Senate Republican leaders, Robert Michel and Robert Dole. Among pollsters and other consultants identified by party, 14 citations were to Democrats and five to Republicans. In the category of elected officials outside of Washington, 39 were Democrats, compared to 11 Republicans. The great majority of "generic" sources (references to ideological or party groupings) were to liberals or Democrats. And most of the interest group leaders quoted were from groups closely associated with the Democrats: organized labor, black groups, women's groups, and gay activists.

57. There may have been more Democratic sources because Democrats made themselves more available to journalists than Republicans did, or because reporters sought out more Democrats than Republicans to interview. The second alternative might occur because the Democrats' problems made a better story, or because of reporters' own affinities (discussed below).

58. S. Robert Lichter and Stanley Rothman, "Media and Business Elites," *Public Opinion* (October/November, 1981), pp. 42–46.

59. Warren E. Miller and M. Kent Jennings, *Parties in Transition* (New York: Russell Sage, 1986), chaps. 9 and 10.

60. Kelley, p. 140.

61. Graber, p. 216; Edelman, p. 46.

62. Abramson *et. al.*, p. 257.

63. On 1988, see Larry M. Bartels and C. Anthony Broh, "The Polls—A Review: The 1988 Presidential Primaries," *Public Opinion Quarterly* 53 (1989), pp. 568–569.

64. Edelman, pp. 2–3.

65. Edelman, pp. 93–94.
66. Robert A. Rosenblatt, "Key Legislators Vow 'Giant Step' for Tax Reform," *Los Angeles Times*, Jan. 31, 1985, part I, p. 6.
67. Jody Powell, "Frugal Hollings," *San Francisco Examiner*, Jan. 30, 1985, p. B3.
68. "An Economic Scorecard," *Newsweek*, May 16, 1988, p. 42.
69. See Kingdon, op. cit.
70. Edelman, p. 18.
71. See Edelman, chap. 3.
72. Edelman, p. 120.
73. Edelman, p. 92.
74. See Kelley, opt. cit.
75. Edelman, p. 1.

5

The Postmodern Election

W. Lance Bennett

POSTMODERNISM
... *is completely indifferent to the questions of consistency and continuity. It self-consciously splices genres, attitudes, styles. It relishes the blurring or juxtaposition of forms (fiction–nonfiction), stances (straight–ironic), moods (violent–comic), cultural levels (high–low). It disdains originality and fancies copies, repetition, the recombination of hand-me-down scraps. It neither embraces nor criticizes, but beholds the world blandly, with a knowingness that dissolves any commitment into irony. It pulls the rug out under itself, displaying an acute self-consciousness about the work's constructed value. It takes pleasure in the play of surfaces, and derides the search for depth as mere nostalgia.*
—Todd Gitlin

America's national political contests are moments of great opportunity for defining public problems, exploring new directions, evaluating the character of aspiring leaders, and dreaming about the future. Elections are the centerpieces of the civic culture. Yet these grand occasions for stock-taking, consensus-building and renewal are being squandered on a regular basis. Instead of drawing people into the political arena and stimulating wide-open dialogue about the problems that threaten continued national greatness, candidates appear to be walking on eggshells. They not only hide from the press, but with the growing acceptance of image-making techniques, candidates even hide from themselves.

The decline of elections has been a long process, with the contests of recent years merely marking its completion. Pinpoint history, like surgical bombing, is an imprecise art. The argument here is not that before the 1980s and 1990s we were living in one political age and afterwards we entered another. Rather, the last several elections capped a long process in which the very language of public life has been transformed to the point that most citizens can no longer find the sense in it. As writers like Lewis Carroll, George Orwell, Harold Lasswell and Murray Edelman have warned, the quality of political rhetoric holds the key to the satisfactions of public life, and ultimately, to the security of private life as well. *The debasing of language, and more broadly, communications, in American elections is a mystery that needs to be solved. How did it happen? What can be done about it? What are the consequences for the political system as a whole if these trends continue?*

Signs of electoral foolery can be traced to much earlier periods in American history. The historians tell us, for example, that George Washington's campaign practices were anything but models of noble principle. And the likes of Thomas Jefferson, Andrew Jackson and Abraham Lincoln were savaged by opponents in ways that make the negative campaigning of the present seen tame. William McKinley spent most of his election campaign in 1896 pandering to the media from his front porch in Canton, Ohio, mouthing such pithy "sound bites" as "McKinley and A Full Dinner Pail." Franklin Roosevelt's fireside chats were masterpieces of media manipulation. And few latter-day marketing feats can top the selling of the "new and improved" Richard Nixon in 1968.

The difference is that these contests of the past also contained historic choices. Perhaps they were not phrased as eloquently as intellectuals and language lovers would like, but at least there were choices: the Jeffersonian battles over the Alien and Sedition Acts, with their implications for the freedom of speech; the Jacksonian referendum on national monetary policy, and its impact on the growth of the frontier; the social and economic ordeal of the Civil War, and its legacy of industrial growth and the death of agrarian society; the birth of protective government in the New Deal; the promise of civil rights in the New Frontier; and the white conservative backlash contributing to the Republican reformation in 1968.

Meaningful choices in recent years have been harder to find. Even the Reagan presidency could not deliver on its core promise of shrinking the federal government—delivering, instead, a bloated national budget while handing off a long list of underfunded social and regulatory responsibilities to the states. In addition, the Reagan landslides of 1980 and 1984 were delivered by fewer than 30% of the eligible electorate. Perhaps most telling of all is the fact that majorities or near majorities in the opinion polls opposed virtually every major policy that made up the "Reagan Revolution."[1]

The central thesis of this chapter is that we have entered a political era in which electoral choices are of little consequence because an electoral system in disarray can generate neither the party unity nor the levels of public agreement necessary to forge a winning and effective political coalition. The underlying explanation is that the political and economic forces driving our national politics have created a system in which the worst tendencies of the political culture—the hype, hoopla and negativity—have been elevated to the norm in elections, gaining a systematic dominance in campaign content as never before. Meanwhile, the best hopes for creative leadership are screened systematically out of the running by political and economic forces that are only dimly understood, when they are recognized at all.

The result is a new electoral system—one filled with paradox. As voters grow more discontented with elected officials, incumbents grow more likely to win re-election. This result is not accidental—it is systematic. Rather than brand discontented—but seemingly helpless—voters as fools, it makes as much sense to consider the choices they are given. Rather than dismiss declining turnouts as products of apathy, it may be that genuine anger is expressed in opinion polls, but simply has few meaningful outlets.

This system of paradoxes amplifies the meaning of Murray Edelman's concept of *quiescence*.[2] It is easy to assume that the quiescent citizen is one lulled into a state of apathy. While apathy may be one result of the distant and often forbidding dramas of mass politics, much of Edelman's work tells of other political possibilities. Political communication often generates intense human emotions—emotions that simply are not given constructive outlets or tied to satisfying political actions. As the title of one book suggests, it makes sense to think of the politics of the masses as *symbolic* action.[3] Thus, when leaders construct enemies, great human emotion is released by publics as they are led into (quiescent) acceptance of destructive situations that seem beyond their control.[4] Even in more intimate situations, intense emotions often go along with the (quiescent) acceptance of dubious political relationships. For example, the language of the "helping professions" (teaching, social work, therapy, health care) may establish power relations that are anything but helpful for "troubled" individuals.[5]

The point in each case is that quiescence need not involve apathy and withdrawal (although it can). Rather, the hallmark of quiescence is accepting the symbolic definition of a situation, however angering, confusing or crazy-making that definition may be. In this sense, many voters have come to accept, whether angrily, cynically or apathetically, an electoral system that grows more dysfunctional with each election. As society's problems grow in size and number, the political system generates fewer solutions and puts more issues "on hold." Society and politics move awkwardly together, as if in a dream that is all the more troubling because the quiescent citizenry cannot seem to awaken. In short, the voters are mad as hell, but they don't know how to stop taking it anymore.

At some point this political bad dream will end. A social movement may awaken the masses. A crisis of grand proportions could shake the foundations. But will people break their symbolic chains? Will the forces that have corrupted the electoral process be recognized and changed? Not if the citizenry is led into easy analyses and patently unworkable remedies. One of the dangers of an age of cynicism is that easy explanations abound, and frustrated people often settle for them.

The easiest explanation of all for the decline of political ideas is television. Volumes have been written blaming TV for most of our social ills, from the destruction of family conversation, to the senseless violence on our streets, to dismal school test scores and widespread public ignorance of even the barest facts of history, geography and government. Indeed, when the dim electronic glow of the TV screen illuminates the interior of the American home an average of eight hours each day, there is cause for alarm. What can politicians do but fashion their messages to this passive medium, leaving most of the challenging ideas on the cutting room floor? As New York governor Mario Cuomo put it, taking a stand on political principles these days

> requires that you explain your principles, and in this age of electronic advocacy this process can often be tedious and frustrating. This is especially so when you must get your message across in twenty-eight-second celluloid morsels, when images prove often more convincing than ideas. Labels are no longer a tendency in our politics. In this electronic age, they are our politics.[6]

While Governor Cuomo may have perceived correctly the effects of our political transformation, identifying television as the cause of it all is a bit too easy. There is little doubt that television has changed the way we do politics, but it is not the sole or even the major source of our political decline—merely the most visible sign of it. Behind the television images lies a whole set of political and economic changes that limit what politicians say, how they say it, and to whom they can speak. These hidden limits make television the perfect medium for saying nothing, but doing it with eye-catching and nerve-twitching appeal.

The Politics Behind the Images

The declining quality of the national political dialogue is subtle, and, at first glance, hard to define. Neither the amount of verbiage nor the number of position papers has withered away noticeably. But there have been notable deficits in the quality of ideas—the "vision thing" that George Bush confessed having so much trouble with. The quality of political rhetoric has vanished to the point where fewer than 10 percent of those voting in the 1988 presidential election felt the candidates adequately addressed their concerns. At the beginning of the contest, two-thirds of the voters expressed hope that the choices would be meaningful ones. By election day, two-thirds of those still planning to vote wished that two different candidates were running.[7] Despite this lack of runaway enthusiasm, a slim majority felt at least some warmth toward one or the other candidate and made the trek to the polls. For several elections in a row, similar levels of luke warmth have registered on the "feeling thermometer" measure used by the University of Michigan National Election Studies to survey voter feelings about candidates. Perhaps the growing sense of voter distress is due partly to the frustration of going through too many lukewarm elections against the backdrop of so many hot social problems. In any event, it would be too easy to blame voter dissatisfaction on the declining quality of the individuals running for office. The pattern of citizen discomfort and candidate distance has become so familiar and pervasive that one suspects it has roots in the contemporary system of campaigning itself.

Begin with marketing. As the marketplace of ideas has grown unresponsive to the demands of political consumers, many citizens have left public life to invest their human capital elsewhere. Those who continue to participate are regarded by campaign consultants as a marketing challenge. When viewed as marketing rather than a way of life, democracy takes on a different tone. For example, the political consultants who now run election campaigns will tell you in moments of candor that citizen withdrawal is a blessing in disguise. *Political marketing maxim number one: the fewer people voting, the easier it is to sell a candidate.*

Moving candidates off the shelves these days—even to reduced numbers of voters—is still often a "hard sell." The problem is that many political ideas that might attract voter interest have already been bought and taken off the market by political action committees (PACs) and the other political investors who finance candidates. Needless to say, the corporate, labor and special issue PACs have not gone to all this organizational trouble just to give their money away freely. The huge sums of money required to launch a credible bid for office usually come with strings attached. It is not necessary to imagine those strings pulling conspiratorially to the left or the right. A more realistic image is of a mad crosswise pull, leaving the system tied effectively (if unintentionally) in knots. The financial strings can be long ones, reaching far beyond the White House and Congress to smaller state and local offices as well.

An idealistic politician from California recently shared with me the hard facts of running for an assembly seat in his state. He lamented that it takes a staggering sum of money, for which the candidate must go to state party leaders with hat in hand. The leaders first size up the candidate, look at track record and marketability factors, and, finally, ask the big question: Are you willing to "get with the program" on the half dozen or so major issues of interest to the investors who have put their money into the party and its candidates? If the candidate says yes, and the leadership thinks that he or she is electable, the money flows. But, said the young candidate, if you say yes, you have already sold out on the issues that really mattered to you and your constituents in the first place. What are you supposed to go back and talk to the voters about?

In California, candidates for public office spent more than $60 million in 1988, with the legislature costing more than two-thirds of that amount. In 1990, the candidates for governor, alone, spent nearly $40 million. To put this in perspective, a British general election costs a bit more than $10 million. This, for a national contest in a country with more than twice the population of California. By contrast, the total cost of running for public office in the U.S. in presidential years is pushing $2 billion. The average winner in a U.S. Senate campaign spends more than $3 million, and the typical cost of a House seat is over $300 thousand.[8] Unless serious reforms limit campaign spending, restrict television advertising and change financing procedures, these figures will continue to go up with each election.

If the problem of what is left to tell the voters is daunting for a candidate from a small district in California, imagine the dilemma at the presidential level. Candidates who raise the huge sums necessary to launch credible national campaigns (until the federal funding begins to flow) are left with very little to say. This means, of course, that they end up sounding a lot like their opponents, who are competing for much the same financing with the same strings attached. Making this "hard sell" to voters becomes easier when there are fewer voters who need to be convinced. The electorate these days is sized up in much the same way a market is tested and analyzed prior to the release of a new breakfast cereal or underarm deodorant. With any luck, a small segment of that market can be identified as the key group whose votes could swing the outcome of the contest. And so, a whole campaign may be pitched in subliminal images that play in Peoria, or wherever that target audience is found.

In this upside-down world where Madisonian ideals have been traded for Madison Avenue methods, the political challenge is not to inspire and mobilize the great and diverse masses of people, as a romantic notion of democracy might lead us to hope. Rather, the challenge of contemporary politics is to isolate key groups (the smaller and more homogeneous, the better) who can be persuaded to go out and pull their levers in response to test-marketed images like wimpiness, competence, liberalism, prayerless schools, burning flags, tax paid abortions, and weekend rapists on prison release programs. The nervous system of target audiences seems to twitch more violently if the weekend rapist is black, and all of these symbolic effects are enhanced when distracting "noise" is screened out of the communications between candidates and their chosen publics. "Noise" in this age of political unreason consists of things like serious proposals, programs, and spontaneous moments in which candidates act on their own instincts. And so, our electoral process revolves around small but scientifically chosen segments of the public who are bombarded with images of candidates standing squarely behind flags, fetuses, bibles, and other market-tested, and therefore politically unassailable, symbols of the day.

Add to this mix of money and marketing the growing repertoire of techniques for keeping a growling press-pack at bay, and *voila*, a system emerges in which we witness celluloid candidates pronouncing suspect lines to listless voters while a managed media tries to point out the absurdity with mixed success. The elements of this electoral system will be explored in a bit more detail later, but first, let's drop in on a memorable case in point....

Welcome to the Postmodern Election

"Read my lips."
"Senator, you're no Jack Kennedy."
"Make my twenty-four hour time period."
Just a few of the high—or low—points of Campaign '88, depending on one's view of political language and its proper uses.

For most scholars, commentators and the majority of the American public, the Presidential election of 1988 was the worst in memory. And it was no easy last-place finish, considering the stiff competition in recent years. Evidence from polls, editorials, and academic studies suggests that even by minimal standards, the most expensive contest in history failed to accomplish what an election campaign should do: introduce intelligent, well-reasoned and occasionally inspiring debate into the voter choice process.

Yet—and here's the rub—these superficial one-liners and telegenic "sound bites" seem to be what speech writers, consultants and willing candidates aspired to achieve in their communications with the electorate.

Welcome to the postmodern election. All text and no context. All rhyme, no reason. George Bush, Blade Runner. Mike Dukakis, Max Headroom. Dan Quayle, the Happy Camper. And Lloyd Bentsen, the first candidate who couldn't lose.

If the rosy electronic theme fashioned for the election of 1984 was "Morning in America," then 1988 was, in the characterization of a noted political scientist, "Brunchtime."[9]

* * *

Begin with the TV image. Looking at television gives us a rough picture of how political messages have been transformed over the last few decades, (but not much of an idea about what transformed them). Although tantalizing, it is ultimately incomplete to leave our understanding at Marshall McLuhan's household phrase, "The Medium Is the Message." It is useful, however, to begin with this glassy surface of elections—the transparent screen through which most people experience their political "reality."

For several elections, television has been the decisive factor in the reports of voters about how they make up their minds. And, for reasons that will become clear soon, political advertising is often the most influential part of the TV picture. Yet the election of 1988 struck many observers as something of a capstone in the TV age—not so much for voters, who have already adapted to televised information, but for campaigns and candidates. After decades of experimentation and flirting with TV as a strategic weapon in election battles, Election '88 suggested that campaign managers had accepted fully and unashamedly the use of TV technology to reconstruct candidates. The subordination of communication between candidates and public to the dictates of "tele-campaigning" was revealed, among other places, in Democratic candidate Michael Dukakis' transformation *during the campaign* from traditional campaigner to a creature of television (albeit an unsuccessful one).

Many observers agree that something happened in 1988.[10] "Some invisible line has been crossed," said Marvin Kalb, a former network correspondent and, more recently, Director of Harvard's Barone Center on the Press, Politics and Policy.[11] That line, according to John Buckley, a media consultant who has worked for both the Republican Party and CBS News, is between print and video, the image and the word:

> This is the first election of a newly mature style of politics wherein it is accepted as absolute gospel by both sides that what you need to do is create ... a message ... that communicates itself on television ... There is no longer a value judgement on the need to tailor a message to television. It's now a matter of survival, not a matter of ethics or intellectual honesty.[12]

Like most historical changes, this realignment of our political discourse to fit the medium of television did not occur overnight. The first step over the electric line occurred in 1952, the year in which television commercials appeared in campaigns. Another step was taken in 1960, the year that Richard Nixon arguably won the presidential debate in print and on the radio, but lost the same debate, along with the election, on television. Goodbye *logos*, hello *logo*.

> *logos*: reason as constituting the controlling principle of the universe, as manifested by speech.
>
> *logo*: short for logogram: the word replaced by the sign, or the visual image

Crossing the line from intellectual to anti-intellectual discourse has altered the ways in which we (are forced to) understand and participate in politics. The most fundamental change, as noted above, is the decline of traditional political argument itself. A case in point is the now legendary incident in the 1984 campaign involving CBS correspondent Leslie Stahl's attempt to point out the logical inconsistencies between candidate Ronald Reagan's campaign appeals and the contradictory positions and policies Mr. Reagan advocated on the same issues as president. To her amazement, Stahl received a thank-you call from the White House after the lengthy piece was aired. The reason for the thank you: the visual images of Reagan speaking, no matter what the contradictions in his speech, were more powerful than the argument that Stahl fashioned to go along with those images. The moral: political ideas aren't anchored in reason, logic or history anymore. Political ideas as we may have known them once upon a time don't exist.

A number of shock waves flow from this fundamental transformation in our national political communications. Witness, for example, the eclipse of the newspaper as a significant factor for the mass public in the electoral process. It is too easy to blame the decline of the print media on creeping illiteracy or lack of time for reading. To the contrary, we are beginning to learn that printed information is highly valued when it is available in useful form. The key words here are "available" and "useful." Consider the possibility that crossing over to the television side of the communications line has created a political content so disjointed and diminished that it isn't fit to print. Newspapers have become the odd media out in elections because they are literally starved for content.

This judgement on the demise of the newspaper was handed down in the spare postmodern vernacular by ABC correspondent Brit Hume when he referred to the newspaper reporters following the candidates as "printheads." Translation: logocentric throwbacks to the age of reason, the modern era, if you will; people of little consequence for the outcome of the postmodern election. Yet Hume later lamented to colleagues in a post-election seminar, "I'd like to tell you anecdotes about what it's like to cover George Bush up close, but I never got close to George Bush."[13] Nobody ever said that being significant in the postmodern age would be meaningful.

Crossing the rhetorical line to the bullier pulpit of television emboldened ABC News president Roone Arledge (President of ABC Sports at the end of the modern age) to pronounce the Democratic National Convention boring. So boring, in fact, that he threatened to cut back coverage of the Republicans the following month.[14] Something must be going on when a threat like that is issued on the heels of a convention that offered its audience no fewer than four or five excellent speeches by prominent members of the party—speeches recalling a bygone era of rousing, thought-provoking, morally challenging rhetoric.

No matter. Speech of any caliber or length greater than a sound bite seems to be the problem. ABC's executive producer for the conventions dismissed the television coverage of these speech fests as a "dinosaur."[15] And so, we witness the demise of what has been the most important rhetorical form at least since the time of Aristotle: The Speech. Welcome to the postmodern election.

* * *

Basking far too long in the fleeting electronic glow of his convention speech, Michael Dukakis finally woke up to the fact that he was losing the election, and losing it badly. His midsummer dream lead of seventeen points dwindled to a dead heat following the Republican Convention, then plummeted to a fifteen point deficit in October.

Responding to the cries of state and local campaigns and the encouragement of liberal editorialists, the Democrats finally lifted a page from the Republican play book: think short, talk negative, get mediated. In the closing weeks, the Duke's handlers withdrew their candidate from informal contact (especially question-answer sessions) with the press corps, and replaced his basic stump speech (emphasizing competence and economic recovery) with a positive/negative format emphasizing the profound message "I'm on your side. He's on theirs."

Meanwhile, the campaign went after Bush's "negatives" (another key word in the postmodern political vocabulary) with a vengeance. So negative was the closing Democratic campaign that its newly-appointed advertising director estimated an even higher negative-to-positive ad content (60–40) than the Bush campaign's more "balanced" target ratio of fifty-fifty.[16]

Although Dukakis still lost the election, and lost it convincingly, his rhetorical rebirth near the end of the campaign is significant. It suggests that what I propose to call "telerhetoric" really has become the "absolute gospel" that media consultants proclaim it to be. One suspects that Dukakis did not kneel easily before the new rhetorical doctrine. Much of his punishment at the polls and on the editorial pages may well have resulted from his stubborn resistance to the dogma of the electronic age. Yet, convert he did, even if too late.

Once the decision was made, and a new ad man was in place, the candidate went before the cameras with exhausting, if not shameless, determination. A *New York Times* "Campaign Trail" piece on his TV blitz began "H-e-e-e-e-r-e's ... Michael." A splashy front page article the same week aptly summed up the tone now unifying the two campaigns: "TV's Role in '88: The Medium Is the Election." The author, Michael Oreskes, described the last weeks of the Dukakis campaign as an "electronic whistle stop:" "This is the electronic age's equivalent of the final whistle stop tour, seeking Nielsen ratings, not crowds at the tracks."[17]

Once all the candidates were on board, that rhetorical train moved fast down its electronic track. The average length of a TV sound bite plummeted to 9.2 seconds in 1988, down from a robust 14 seconds in 1984.[18]

* * *

As the very concept "sound bite" indicates, the postmodern election comes complete with euphemistic and ambiguous jargon to help bridge the uneasy gap between it and more familiar, and one might add, meaningful, electoral realities past. It is hard to discuss the meaning of any 9.2-second slice of a text, particularly when such slices are constructed to stand alone, rendering the rest of the text something like a serving utensil. But in the new age, it is unnecessary to fret over meaning. Meaning, as it were, is a pre-postmodern phenomenon.

The new language of postmodern politics is preverbal. And it is anything but proverbial. It transcends easy distinctions between issues and candidate images, reason and feeling. May the Greeks forgive us, it throws out the classical categories of *logos*, *pathos* and *ethos*. Indeed, it was when the Bush message, for all its rhetorical hubris, was universally declared effective, and the Dukakis message, for all its traditional tenacity, was pronounced a blur, that Dukakis entered the new age.

What he found on the other side of the line was something the Republicans had known ever since they began winning the presidency on a regular basis. Mike Dukakis, meet Roger Ailes, the electronic guru who brought us Spiro Agnew, the "new" Richard Nixon, Dan Quayle, and the George Bush who parlayed his "wimp factor" into a "kinder, gentler" guy who "goes ballistic" only when he really has to. As Ailes put it, "There are three things that get covered: visuals, attacks and mistakes."[19] As a challenge, try to fit this typology into any of the traditional ways of thinking about argument, debate or public speech.

The new political language is slippery by design. It is as if baseball legalized the spitball as a concession to pitchers, and paid no mind to the inevitable decline in batting averages and fan interest in the game. And so, to pursue the analogy, the new political rhetoric comes as a welcome change only to the political pitch men and the winning candidates. Despite the disapproval of spectators and journalists alike, the place of minimalist, ambiguous language seems secure in the postmodern campaign.

Assuring the marginality and ambiguity of language has become so important that campaigns these days employ people known in the new vernacular as "spin doctors." These specialists come into play when a political pitch is released and heads too straight for the plate. The spin doctors rush out ahead of it, trying to influence or deflect the way reporters pass it along to the mass audience.

In 1988, the Democratic National Convention boasted a Spin Control Coordination Unit. And in October, when Bush campaign chairman Lee Atwater made a rare appearance on the press plane, he was surprised with a chorus of boos and a chant of a "Spin Moratorium." Undaunted, Atwater explained solemnly how Dan Quayle had done a splendid job in the debate. Initially pleased that everyone seemed to be taking him seriously,

Atwater looked up to discover a sign being held above his head. It read: "The Joe Isuzu of Spin—He's Lying."[20] Welcome to the first postmodern election.

Perhaps cartoonist Lynda Barry said more with a picture than those words can convey. Her cartoon version of Election '88 was titled "The Election from Hell." The devil was a journalist.[21]

* * *

Given the decline of traditional concerns about meaning, reason, debate and evidence in postmodern rhetoric, it becomes challenging just to talk about, let alone evaluate, it. For the sake of American democracy, one can only hope, as Mark Twain is rumored to have said about the music of Richard Wagner, that "it is really much better than it sounds."

Unfortunately, the best evidence from consumers suggests that the new "telerhetoric" is really no better than it sounds. As with other products of postmodernism, from slam dancing to gourmet microwave meals, people consume telerhetoric despite (one hopes it is not because of) being actively offended by it.

True, the 1988 voter turnout—the lowest since 1924—indicates that many people chose to preserve their sensibilities at the expense of giving up the franchise. But the more remarkable figure is the fifty percent who made a voting choice despite the self-confessed moral and intellectual pain involved.

What this tells me is that we cannot understand the new rhetoric on traditional grounds; it reflects some sort of positive, responsive communication, however "deep," worked out between candidates and their audiences. There is little that is sympathetic about telerhetoric. Even as they made their decisions, voters told pollsters that they disliked their choices and regarded them as negative, uninteresting and insubstantial.[22] Nevertheless, these same polls, along with other market research studies, showed that the offending political messages "worked."[23]

This perverse dynamic of disaffected voters who tuned in but did not drop out of the election built to a crescendo of sorts on election eve. The *NBC/Wall Street Journal Poll* followed levels of voter dissatisfaction over the contest. At the time of the conventions—the last memorable moments of traditional speechifying—two-thirds of the voting public were satisfied with their choices. By the last week of the campaign, when Dukakis had made his conversion, two-thirds wished that two different candidates were running.[24]

Perhaps the most telling set of statistics on the disjuncture between the popularity and the effectiveness of the new rhetoric came from a *New York Times/CBS News Poll* reported on October 30, 1988. Fully 63% of the voters said that issues were the most important factor in choosing a president. Next, the respondents cited their most important issue. Health, homelessness, education, the economy, the deficit and defense accounted for 64% of the responses. Then, a majority (54%) revealed that neither candidate was talking enough about the issue. Even more telling, only 5% for Bush and 4% for Dukakis felt that either candidate addressed their issue adequately.[25]

Trying to make sense of why people were planning to vote at all in light of the above information, the *Times'* analyst argued to the effect that there really must have been issues out there somewhere, but they just didn't look the way voters expected them to. Credit the *Times* for publishing one of the few pieces anywhere claiming that meaningful issue differences had been located in the campaign. However, the analysis dissolved quickly into the suggestion that many deeper, seemingly personality-related appeals were really issues in disguise. Welcome to the postmodern election. This was precisely how the Bush campaign introduced its personal attacks on Dukakis (e.g., that he was "naive," and "weak" on foreign policy)—namely, as issues.[26]

No wonder voters were fed up. To their credit, many journalists in post-campaign laments recognized this mass disillusionment. At first reading, it seems that few, if any, did much to change their coverage. The press appeared as caught up in the negative thrall of the campaign as the public. Yet, on closer inspection, maybe there was a faint signal from the press. Actually, there may have been two faint signals from the media—a sort of one blink, two blink communication between a paralyzed press and its bed-side public.

The first sign of media dis-ease is revealed in a study by Marjorie Hershey. She found that, on average, print media (largely wire service) coverage from September to election day dealt with issues only one-third of the time, while devoting two-thirds of the content space to campaign strategy. Even though the prestigious *New York Times* tried to hold to issue coverage 50% of the time in September, it was filling less than 20% of its campaign "news hole" with issues by November (when it actually topped the wires in percentage of campaign strategy reports).[27] In short, the campaign became its own news. The media reflected on their own role as never before. Redundancy, self-referential logics, loss of context: the hallmarks of postmodern symbolics. The media couldn't get out of their own loop.

The second signal, or wink, that the media seemed to send to the political audience was an unprecedented number of stories on voter disaffection itself. In the past, reporters generally have been happy to buy the political science dicta that nonvoters would have voted the way voters vote, and that voters find their acts meaningful. This time around, however, the press interviewed thousands of disgruntled citizens who challenged both of the above assumptions.

Typical of these stories is one of a series by *New York Times* senior correspondent R.W. Apple, Jr., titled "From Jersey to Missouri, Voters are Fed Up."[28] In another "fed up" article by another reporter, the wife of a former (read: unemployed or underemployed) steelworker lamented that current voting choices made no sense to people like her who grew up in normal, modern households "with mothers like June Cleaver that stayed home with the children... And now we are in our thirties and forties and, bam! Everything falls apart on you."[29]

When things fall apart (industrial decline, an emerging underclass, homelessness, health care costs, the disappearing dream of home ownership, etc.) people expect election rhetoric to sharpen the issues, define the problems and point to the solutions. Yet just the opposite occurred in 1988. An early warning for voters to disabuse themselves of their normal expectations came in June when two publications no less diverse then *The Nation* and *Time* agreed on what the coming contest held in store. In what may well have been a first, a *Nation* editorial cited *Time* as its source: "... As *Time* aptly put it last week, 'The contest ... will be less about ideas and ideologies than about clashing temperaments and styles.'"[30]

Perhaps it requires greater distance to appreciate the irony here. As Lynda Barry's cartoon cuts to the quick of it, so, too, did French television's response to the first debate (arguably the more "exciting" of the two). After no more than a few words had been exchanged, French viewers were whisked back to the newsroom where a deadpan newscaster pronounced judgement: "This debate is not too exciting. Let's go to the Olympics."[31]

Explaining the New Rhetoric: the View from the Academy

It would be surprising if crossing this thin rhetorical line had been lost on the academy. It is the job of academics, after all, to keep track of the various thin lines within which our realities are contained. To be sure, the importance of television has been a favorite subject of communications scholars since its advent. However, recognition of the transforming effects of television on political rhetoric is a more recent phenomenon.[32] A number of high-quality analyses came along within the year leading up to the 1988 election. Even more notable is that fact that the media latched onto these books and gave them wide play, both in reviews and in interviews with their authors. Such media attention to fine-hewn, often esoteric, scholarly labors is rare. Perhaps it constitutes a third signal from media to audience that something is happening here, and what it is was painfully clear.

Approaching the "rhetorical presidency" from different angles, Jeffrey Tulis,[33] Roderick Hart,[34] and Kathleen Jamieson[35] all concluded that the contemporary presidency has become essentially a rhetorical office increasingly bent to the medium of television. Not only were their books all favorably reviewed by more than one national publication, but similar popular treatment was accorded an even more technical book by Iyengar and Kinder that demonstrated through a series of laboratory experiments that television may not be able to tell us what to think, but is amazingly successful at telling us what to think about.[36]

Of all these analyses, Jamieson's explores most fully the transforming effects of television on political (mainly presidential) communications. Drawing on the traditions of classical rhetoric and modern mass communication research, she concludes that the electronic medium rewards a "feminine" style. (I prefer the concept of an "intimate" political style suggested to me by Swedish professor of rhetoric, Kurt Johannesson.) This style is warm and personal. It emphasizes narrative over reason and logical argument. The intimate style accounts for the "great communicator" in Ronald Reagan, and, I think, helps explain why the unpopular, offending rhetoric of Campaign '88 still had a powerful effect on its audience. Since telerhetoric works at a preverbal, prelogical, affective level, it permits voters to reject its content on logical, rational terms while still being moved at deeper levels that determine attention, commitment and behavior.

The intimate style thus transcends positive and negative. Ronald Reagan was positive. The kinder, gentler George Bush had a negative streak that came out on cue fifty percent of the time. Both moved large audiences who disavowed much of what both men said at the level of truth, logic and reason. For example, polls repeatedly showed that majorities of Americans disagreed with nearly all of Ronald Reagan's specific policy initiatives both as candidate and president.[37] And, as noted above, George Bush's specific issue appeals played to the full satisfaction of a tiny 5% of the voters prior to election day. Yet both men captured the presidency.

Jamieson's view of telerhetoric contains the seeds of an even more important insight into the contemporary electoral and political scenes. During her tour of duty as one of the most cited academic experts on the 1988 election, she told a *New York Times* reporter that there was, in effect, nothing about television itself that really determined the vacuity of the new rhetoric. There was, she said, a glimmer of hope that television might lead the way back to an age of reasonable rhetoric. To put it simply, there is no reason why television couldn't extricate itself from the candidate's loop and create an independent context for viewer evaluation of everything said during a campaign. With the achievable technology of a computerized tape retrieval system, TV could play for its viewers everything a candidate has ever said (and done) about any given subject, and let the audience judge whether the rhetoric of the moment has a historical or other contextual significance. When the networks made brief use of this potential in Campaign '88, Jamieson seized upon it as a ray of hope, saying that ". . . what you're seeing is the very beginning of an attempt to hold candidates accountable for inconsistency without placing the reporter as an intruder."[36]

One can hope that the contextualization of attacks, visuals and sound bites becomes the wave of the future, but I am not so sanguine. To begin with, as the Leslie Stahl incident suggests, it may not be possible to create sensible contexts that unify the disparate images and free-floating messages of video collages, or "clusters" as they are known in the trade. Even if it is possible to contain telerhetoric within some larger logical context, these efforts will surely be condemned loud and long by all candidates as editorializing (for all candidates subscribing to the new gospel will appear heretical by the standards of the old). And, as we know, television does not stand up long in its own defense against a chorus of authoritative condemnation—particularly when it is a chorus that it is compelled to televise. More importantly, however, the media, and especially the electronic media, have no compelling reason and surely no corporate interest in rocking the political boat. No matter how shoddily built, that boat continues to float the phenomenal profitability of the mass media. More on this point later. For now, suffice it to say that the full extent of media response to the perverse politics of postmodernism may well be what we have already seen in 1988: self flagellation and grumbling from reporters, knowing winks and blinks to the suffering voter, and endless media coverage of media coverage of media coverage . . .

There is, however, a less conjectural line of argument in Jamieson's observation: perhaps television isn't inherently to blame for the degradation of contemporary rhetoric. Say what? TV isn't to blame for the decline of elections? Taking off from Jamieson's insight just might get us to a new understanding of the problem. Unfortunately, where I propose to take this line of thought doesn't lead to a very optimistic forecast, but it may offer a better explanation for the current state of affairs than pointing the finger of blame (or in social science, the causal arrow) at television alone.

Toward an Explanation of Elections Without Choices

Consider the possibility that telerhetoric is something known in the academic trades as an epiphenomenon, or, in everyday parlance, a symptom of something deeper. Television, after all, is a passive medium, having the capacity to show us everything from talking heads, the public affairs people, to Talking Heads, the rock band—everything from commentators trying to make sense of it all, to a rock concert video called "Stop Making Sense."

What this means for elections is that television could bring us an entirely different political reality. Debates could become true forensic exchanges. Conventions could be conferred special status rather than threatened with cancellation. Candidates could be grilled one at a time by journalists for extended periods under the television lights as they are in Sweden, for example.³⁹ And, again as in Sweden and many other countries, networks could be required to provide free air time to candidates, and restrictions could be imposed on length and format of political commercials (encouraged, of course, by appropriate legislation).

The list of "coulds" and "what ifs" is too long to continue. The point is that TV isn't an explanation; it is merely a medium. Who uses TV? Why do they use it? How do they employ its mediating potentialities? These are the underlying elements of an explanation of telerhetoric. As for television itself, it may be a worthy object of blame and a useful window on an important problem, but it is not a valid cause in an explanation.

Stepping back, we can view postmodernism in general as the product of deeper social forces. The whole syndrome: multiple realities, strange loopiness, power lunching, slam dancing, microwave meals, nostalgia for *Leave It to Beaver* reruns, the generalized loss of meaning, diminished concern for truth, the spinoff academic disciplines of deconstructionism and Foucault studies, and the pervasive social schizophrenia and collective amnesia that artists and writers have been trying to call to mind. All of these things, including the emergence of the idea-less, choice-impaired election may be traced to identifiable and quite palpable social, political and economic forces.

As a first step toward identifying these forces in the electoral arena, consider the curious role of the political audience. Murray Edelman has argued that this is the age of the political spectator.⁴⁰ Citizenspectators confronted with mass media spectacles may be entertained, dazzled, confused or bored—the normal range of audience emotions. There is even a role for the audience to play: voting. Elsewhere, Edelman has argued that voting and elections are mainly important for legitimizing the governments that are installed in Washington.⁴¹ By giving voters a meaningful part to play in the process, they are more likely to support what governments do to them or don't do for them. However, Edelman argues that meaning for voters tends to be a shallow affair produced by symbol-waving and flimflamming by candidates. These would-be leaders create enemies, announce crises and generally push symbolic buttons in ways that make political audiences see red, or red-white-and-blue. Lacking much policy substance, the most substantial result of voting is that people get meaningfully involved in the battle of symbols, and the seal of public approval is stamped on the government that goes into office. At the very least, then, elections legitimize governments. Or do they?

The decline of voter interest and satisfaction suggests that even the symbolic meaning of electoral choices has become undermined in recent elections, raising questions about the legitimation function of elections and the stability of public support for any elected governments put into office. The main reason for the loss of voter involvement and the declining legitimacy of elected governments is an interesting one. Unlike audiences of other spectator media—even television—the political audience is a captive of a political system with no competition. *Political marketers have finally figured out the beauty of the captive political audience: voters are unable to command new programming when their lack of interest sends the ratings plummeting.* To explore this point a bit further, there are, it seems to me, two important differences between political spectators and the audiences who respond to theatrical performances and other entertainment in various ways from buying tickets to laughing at the funny lines. First, spectator displeasure with the quality of the electoral performance, even to the extent of nonvoting, does not shut down or otherwise "condition" the spectacle itself—as the lack of patronage conditions the content of both the fine arts and popular culture media. Second, the converse also holds true: those who choose to participate in the political audience do not do so because they necessarily enjoy or find meaning in the experience—as one expects audiences for music, theater or film to connect with their chosen medium. Recall here that full satisfaction with electoral choices in 1988 was expressed by a tiny nine percent of those planning to vote for the two candidates.

In most other spectator arenas, decline of patronage and rise of antipathy would be more consequential. Whereas other cultural forums are responsive to the marketplace of popular taste, elections seem relatively immune from the important market forces of consumer dissatisfaction and outright withdrawal from the marketplace. This curious feature of elections helps us recast traditional thinking about candidate-audience communication. *The easy assumption is that the effectiveness of electoral rhetoric turns on some sort of meaningful, positive, responsive exchange between communicator and audience. Throwing out this assumption raises the question of what does shape the content of electoral language these days.*

Begin with Money . . .

Consider this possibility. Instead of competing with each other for audience approval, candidates increasingly compete for the support of a much more select and seldom-recognized group: political campaign contributors. A presidential election these days costs upwards of $100 million, and more than twice that if we consider the uses of party and "independent" campaign funds for support of national campaigns. Although federal funding covers the majority of a candidate's immediate costs, candidates personally must raise five to ten million dollars in order to win the primaries and qualify for the national largesse. Competition for these staggering sums of money is stiff, and the nature of this offstage maneuvering does not reward those who expand the domain of issues and policy proposals. To simplify the point, a restricted range of political ideas makes backing a candidate a safer bet for big money interests. In fact, restricting the range of ideas enables backers to hedge their bets and support both candidates. This is, of course, a bad thing for the health of democracy, but a very good thing for those who invest their money in elections.

The most controversial version of this "investment theory" of elections is developed by Thomas Ferguson and Joel Rogers, who argue that the Republican Party has won over many of the Democrats' big backers.[42] This core of multinational (read: free trade) business and financial interests initially put their money behind the Democrats at the time of the Great Depression to counter the protectionist economic policies of the Republicans. Since the Nixon years, however, the Republicans have recognized the financial and political advantages of adopting the free trade rhetoric. Now, so the theory goes, the two parties compete head-on for much the same core of financial support, with the result that the Democrats have been leveraged to the right on a whole list of major issues like defense and foreign policy, unemployment, domestic industrial decline and the structure of the national budget. This "right turn," as Ferguson and Rogers call it, has put the Democratic Party at odds with sizable numbers of traditional voters who support more liberal policies in areas ranging from defense to social programs.

It is not clear, however, that the Democrats "can go home again" to their old liberalism. Moreover, in a more extensive discussion of this point elsewhere, I suggest that there may be less convergence of interest among financial backers than Ferguson and Rogers claim.[43] *It may be more accurate to say that the pull of interests this way and that simply erodes the abilities of most candidates (at presidential and congressional levels) to express broad policy programs or join in stable political coalitions. After deducting the silent commitments made to the numbers of financial backers required for successful campaigning, candidates are left with little in the way of credible governing ideas to offer voters.*

Next, Add Marketing ...

This brings us to the second major constraint on campaign discourse: the wholesale use of marketing techniques and strategies to generate campaign content. Enter marketing experts into elections in a big way. Their task is to transform a product of diminished or dubious market value into one that wins the largest market share. The result: an emphasis on communication that short-circuits logic, reason and linguistic richness in favor of image-making techniques. This means that candidates are not sold to a broad general public, but to narrow slices or "market segments" of that public. These market segments need not understand the candidates, only vote for them. Thus, people are induced to vote for Candidate A over Candidate B much as soap buyers may favor Brand X over Brand Y, without feeling they have established a meaningful relationship with their laundry detergent in the process. This further diminishes the importance of language, logic and reason in the articulation of campaign issues.

Since at least 1980, the Democrats have encountered a difficult problem that once paralyzed the early Goldwater Republicans until the party solved it with the successful marketing of the "new" Richard Nixon and the even newer Ronald Reagan. The problem is simple: a narrow, unpalatable issue agenda that is hard to sell to the general public. The Republican secret was to turn the liability of voter avoidance into an asset by targeting key segments of the shrinking audience that continued to vote. Since votes aren't dollars, profitability isn't an issue. Only victory counts, no matter how many voters boycott the electoral process altogether.

In a classic commentary on the new political age, a Republican strategist ushered in the election of 1980 with these words: *"I don't want everyone to vote. Our leverage in the election goes up as the voting population goes down."*[44] Borrowing this page from the Republican play book, the Democrats in the 1980s went after the narrow market segment of blue-collar Republicans with a vengeance. Perhaps the most blatant example involved the Dukakis campaign avoiding anything resembling an overt appeal to Jesse Jackson's constituency. This market analysis, even though flawed, was followed to the end: the liberal Jackson wing of the Party was not viewed as essential to victory, while the "Reagan Democrats" were. The constraints on campaign rhetoric and issue definition were equally clear: it was feared that anything said to liberal segments of the fragile voter market would send more conservative segments into the Republican camp. As it turned out, this feared pattern of conservative defection occurred anyway, due in part to Dukakis' withering at the L-word, and in larger part to the inability of strategically hamstrung Democrats to compete rhetorically on remaining issues like prayer, patriotism, civil rights and abortion. Such is political life without a credible rhetorical vision.

Now, Try to Control the News Media ...

In the three factor model proposed here, the above two constraints necessarily engage a third limiting condition operating on electoral communication: the highly controlled use of the news media. The press, like the voters, generally regard issues and ideas as the most important grounds for electoral choice. Idealess elections antagonize reporters searching for meaningful differences between the candidates to write home about. An aroused press can be expected to assume an adversarial role, leaping upon inconsistencies, making much of candidate slips and blunders, seizing upon anything inflammatory in the absence of much to say about policy positions.

As a result, campaigns tend to isolate their candidates from the press corps, and stick to a tightly controlled and carefully scripted daily schedule. This means, in Roger Ailes' words, that reporters are handed a lot of visuals and attacks, while mistakes (and ideas) are held to a minimum.

It is by now well-accepted that good media strategy entails three things: keeping the candidate away from the press; feeding the press a simple, telegenic political line of the day; and making sure the daily news line echoes (magnifies may be the better word) the images from campaign ads, thus blurring the distinction between commercials and "reality."[45] Candidates and their "handlers" vary in the ability to keep the press-pack at bay, but when they succeed, reporters are left with little but an impoverished set of campaign slogans to report. As ABC reporter Sam Donaldson said on an election week news analysis program in a tone that resembled the coroner disclosing an autopsy result: "When we cover the candidates, we cover their campaigns as they outline them."[46] And so, a willing, if unhappy, press becomes a channel for much the same meaningless telerhetoric that emerges from the interplay of advertising strategy and the concessions made to campaign contributors.

In recent years the media have showed signs of becoming more critical of campaigns. Encouraged by a public that is angry at candidates and politicians, the news contains increased coverage of the celluloid world of marketed candidates and media manipulation. This increase in media coverage of media campaigns, however, has not brought candidates out of hiding or appreciably affected the way campaigns are run. The ironic result of media attempts to "deconstruct" candidate images and expose the techniques of news control may be to reinforce public cynicism about the whole process. Taking the public behind the political illusions has not succeeded in bringing the candidates out of hiding behind those illusions. The net result is still an election system dominated by mass-marketed, Madison Avenue messages that deliver quick emotional punches instead of lasting visions and governing ideas to voters. In other words, the way in which news organizations have exercised their critical skills may result less in changing the system than in reinforcing (albeit inadvertently) the public cynicism that helps keep it going. One might think the press would do something bold to elevate election news content above the intellectual level of political commercials. For example, the various news organizations could separate themselves from the pack mentality and develop a thoughtful agenda of important issues (based, if need be, on opinion polls) and score the candidates on how well they address these issues. *Don't hold your breath.* A very modest version of this suggestion was vetoed out of hand by a news executive. When asked why the media did not make more of George Bush's well-documented connections to the Iran-Contra arms scandal and the CIA hiring of Panamanian dictator Manuel Noriega, the producer of one of the three network evening newscasts explained simply, "We don't want to look like we're going after George Bush."[47]

Despite this reluctance to tackle candidates on the issues, it is apparently appropriate to "go after" them on grounds of health (Thomas Eagleton in 1972), character (Edmund Muskie, 1972), gaffes and malapropisms (Gerald Ford, 1976), family finances (Geraldine Ferraro, 1984), extra-marital sex (Gary Hart, 1988) or hypocrisy and gall (Dan Quayle, 1988). However, the press draws the line when it comes to pursuing issues beyond where the candidates are willing to take them.

Never mind the resulting declines in the quality of campaign discourse and citizen interest in politics (not to mention public faith in the press), the media seem determined to steer a passive and safe course of "fairness" (the postmodern version of "objectivity"). Elaborating the doctrine behind Sam Donaldson's earlier words, the ABC vice president in charge of campaign coverage in 1984 and 1988 said: "It's my job to take the news as they choose to give it to us and then, in the amount of time that's available, put it into the context of the day or that particular story ... The evening newscast is not supposed to be the watchdog on the Government."[48]

It is interesting to note that this self-styled impression of what the media are "supposed to be" has changed about 180 degrees from the hallowed role of the press defined by the likes of Peter Zenger and Thomas Jefferson. The new norm of press passivity enables increasingly profitable and decreasingly critical mass media to chase political candidates in dizzying circles like cats after their own tails. To wit, two-thirds of the coverage in 1988 was coverage of coverage: articles on the role of TV, news about campaign strategy, and updates on voter fatigue in response to meaningless media fare. As the irrepressible French social critic Jacques Ellul said about the contemporary mass communications industry: "The media refer only to themselves."[49]

* * *

Each of these related constraints on political communication imposes a substantial limit on what candidates say to voters, creating, in turn, important limits on the quality of our most important democratic experience. Taken together, these limiting conditions go a long way toward explaining the alarming absence of meaningful choices and satisfied voters in recent elections. These restrictions on political speech also explain the mysterious elevation of "telerhetoric" to gospel-standing in contemporary campaigns. With ideas safely out of the way and the press neutralized, television has little use other than as a medium for turning a seemingly endless election process into the world's longest-running political commercial without programmatic interruption.

Other puzzles about the contemporary election scene also become less puzzling. Take the rise of negative campaigning, for example. Due to the severe content restrictions imposed by the three limits outlined above, candidates suffer the marketing problem of appearing unattractive (i.e., negative). In this strange world, victory goes to the candidate who manages to appear the least unattractive or negative. The easiest strategy is to play up the opponent's "negatives," in an effort to look less negative by comparison. (One can hardly hope to look positive in this context.) Hence, the obsession with the opponent's negatives, as emphasized in commercials and played up in news sound bites spoon-fed to the press.

All of the above—the rhetoric without vision, the telegenic sound bites, and commercialized advertising and news production—all happen to play best (or, in keeping with the new spirit, less offensively) on television. In the words of a leading campaign consultant commenting on a race in California, "A political rally in California consists of three people around a television set."[50] Welcome to the postmodern election.

Considering the magnitude of these forces working against the traditional forms and contents of political communication, it is not surprising that candidates say so little these days. One marvels that they are able to say anything at all.

Notes

1. Thomas Ferguson and Joel Rogers, *Right Turn: The Decline of the Democrats and the Future of American Politics* (New York: Hill and Wang, 1986).

2. Murray Edelman, *The Symbolic Uses of Politics* (Urbana: University of Illinois Press, 1964).

3. Murray Edelman, *Politics as Symbolic Action* (New York: Academic Press, 1971).

4. Murray Edelman, *Constructing the Political Spectacle* (Chicago: University of Chicago Press, 1988).

5. Murray Edelman, "The Political Language of the Helping Professions," *Politics & Society*, Vol. 4 (Fall 1974), pp. 295–310.

6. This quote can be found in Kathleen H. Jamieson, *Eloquence in the Electronic Age: The Transformation of Political Speechmaking* (New York: Oxford University Press, 1988), p. 248.

7. The figures cited here will be reintroduced and analyzed in more detail later in this chapter. Full source citations are available there.

8. See Lewis Lipsitz and David M. Speak, *American Democracy*, 2nd ed. (New York: St. Martin's Press, 1989), p. 259.

9. John Aldrich quoted in Ralph Blumenthal, "To Many, the Best Choice on Nov. 8 Is Just Home," *The New York Times*, Nov. 6, 1988, Sect. 1, p. 18.

10. See, for example, R. W. Apple, Jr., "Old Pros Appraise the '88 Campaign," *The New York Times*, Nov. 6, 1988, Sect. 1, p. 18.

11. Quoted in Michael Oreskes, "Talking Heads: Weighing Imagery in a Campaign Made for Television," *The New York Times,* Oct. 2, 1988, Sect. 4, p. 1.

12. Oreskes, p. 1.

13. ABC correspondent Brit Hume quoted in John Dillin, "News Media Critique Themselves: Many Reporters Unhappy with Campaign '88 Coverage," *The Christian Science Monitor,* Dec. 9, 1988, p. 3.

14. Jeremy Gerard, "Convention Coverage: Endangered Species?" *The New York Times,* July 23, 1988, Sect. 1, p. 9.

15. Gerard, p. 9.

16. Michael Oreskes, "TV's Role in '88: The Medium Is the Election," *The New York Times,* Oct. 30, 1988, Sect. 1, p. 10.

17. Ibid., p. 1.

18. Source: NBC Nightly News, March 26, 1989. Also, Marvin Kalb, "TV, Election Spoiler," *The New York Times,* Nov. 28, 1988, Sect. 1, p. 19.

19. Quoted in Ibid.

20. On the Democrats, see: Philip Weiss, "Party Time in Atlanta,: *Columbia Journalism Review,* Sept./Oct. 1988, p. 29. On the Republicans: *New York Times,* "Campaign Trail," Oct. 10, 1988. Sect. 1, p. 10.

21. Lynda Barry, "The Election From Hell," 1988.

22. New York Times/CBS News Poll reported in *The New York Times,* Oct. 25, 1988, Sect. 1, p. 1.

23. Ibid., pp. 1, 10.

24. John Dillin, "Voters on Election '88: Is This It?" *The Christian Science Monitor,* Nov. 2, 1988, p. 1.

25. E.S. Dionne Jr., "The Campaign Has Real Issues in Spite of Itself," *The New York Times,* Oct. 30, 1988, Sect. 4, p. 1.

26. Maureen Dowd, "Bush Lays Out Foreign Policy Tenets," *The New York Times,* Aug. 3, 1988, p. 8.

27. Marjorie Randon Hershey, "The Campaign and the Media," in Gerald M. Pomper, ed. *The Election of 1988* (Chatham, NJ: Chatham House Publishers, 1989), p. 97.

28. *The New York Times,* Oct. 11, 1988, Sect. 1, P. 1. Also: R.W. Apple, Jr., "County That's Always Right Dislikes '88 Choices," *The New York Times,* Nov. 2, 1988, Sect. 1, p. 12.

29. Michael Oreskes, "Steel City Tires of Politics and Promises," *The New York Times,* April 25, 1988, Sect. 1, p. 1.

30. Editorial, *The Nation,* June 25, 1988, p. 1.

31. William Echikson, "Difference Between Bush, Dukakis Lost on French," *The Christian Science Monitor,* Nov. 2, 1988, p. 10.

32. For an excellent discussion of this, see Bruce Gronbeck, "Electric Rhetoric: The Changing Forms of American Political Discourse," Paper presented at the Congress on "Rhetoric and Techniques of Interpretation," Department of Philology, University of Calabria, Italy. September 11–13, 1989.

33. Jeffrey K. Tulis, *The Rhetorical Presidency* (Princeton, NJ: Princeton University Press, 1987).

34. Roderick P. Hart, *The Sound of Leadership: Presidential Communication in the Modern Age* (Chicago: University of Chicago Press, 1987).

35. Kathleen Hall Jamieson, *Eloquence in the Electronic Age: The Transformation of Political Speechmaking* (New York: Oxford University Press, 1988).

36. Shanto Iyengar and Donald R. Kinder, *News That Matters: Television and American Public Opinion* (Chicago: University of Chicago Press, 1987).

37. See, for example, Thomas Ferguson and Joel Rogers, *Right Turn: The Decline of the Democrats and the Future of American Politics* (New York: Hill and Wang, 1986), esp. ch. 1.

38. Quoted in Michael Oreskes, "Talking Heads," Sect. 4, p. 1.

39. Erik Asard, "Election Campaigns in Sweden and the U.S.: Convergence or Divergence?," *America Studies in Scandinavia*, Vol. 21, no. 2, 1989, pp. 70–85.

40. Edelman, *Constructing the Political Spectacle.*

41. Edelman, *The Symbolic Uses of Politics*, (1964).

42. Ferguson and Rogers, *Right Turn.*

43. See W. Lance Bennett, *The Governing Crisis: Media, Money and Marketing in American Elections* (New York: St. Martins, 1992).

44. Paul Weyrich quoted in Thomas Ferguson and Joel Rogers, "The Reagan Victory: Corporate Coalitions in the 1980 Campaign," in Ferguson and Rogers, eds. *The Hidden Election: Politics and Economics in the 1980 Presidential Campaign* (New York: Pantheon, 1981), p. 4.

45. See, for example, Mark Hertsgaard, *On Bended Knee: The Press and the Reagan Presidency* (New York: Farrar, Strauss and Giroux, 1988).

46. "This Week with David Brinkley," ABC, November 6, 1988.

47. Unnamed source, cited in Mark Hertsgaard, "Electoral Journalism: Not Yellow, but Yellow-Bellied," *The New York Times*, Sept. 21, 1988, p. A15.

48. Ibid.

49. Jacques Ellul, "Preconceived Ideas About Mediated Information," in Everett M. Rogers and Francis Bolle, eds. *The Media Revolution in America and Western Europe* (Norwood, N.J.: Ablix Publishing Co., 1985), p. 107.

50. Robert Shrum, quoted in R.W. Apple, Jr., "Candidates Focus on Television Ads," *The New York Times*, October 19, 1986, p. A16.

PART THREE

Policy Implementation, Elite Control, and Political Symbolism

6

Law at the Margins: The Symbolic Power of Professional Discourse

Kristin Bumiller

Professional Violence

The appropriation of violence in the service of social science research often follows from a naive commitment to solving a social problem. In contemporary political discourse about violence against women, a cadre of social scientists assert their authority in the form of strategic knowledge to address a panoply of "distinct" forms of abuse, including wife-battering, child abuse, marital rape, acquaintance rape and sexual harassment. Professional scholars who "appropriate violence" in the production of social science "let [themselves] in for the diabolical forces lurking in all violence."[1] Although the construction of social problems may disengage the social scientist from the actual violence of everyday life, violence as the substance of politics is the *raison d'etre* of their endeavors.

Those who make politics their vocation confront the dilemma of legitimating their exercise of force by means of professional power. This cadre of researchers and practitioners who claim a specialized expertise in these distinct forms of violence establish for themselves a role within the social service delivery systems of the modern welfare state. Their material existence depends upon sustaining the legitimacy of these issues as a "public" problem, while expanding their influence through entrepreneurial skill and the mobilization of sociological knowledge. Yet the social scientists' disengagement from the substance of politics produces a shallow confrontation with the dilemmas inherent in their professional role. Their commitment to the methods of the scientific production of knowledge is tempered by their self-involvement in the social welfare bureaucracy's control over perpetrators and victims. Their internal commitment to act in a "service of a cause" is inhibited by their lack of identification with and professional distance from the "subjects" of violence. This brings to their

151

professional project a mundane commitment to a scholarly constructed community of victims.

In this paper I describe how the production of social scientific discourse that appropriates violence against women is linked to the political structure in which it has recently arisen. I am interested in how these expert discourses translate into regulatory practices that constitute communities with social needs, and how the "diabolical forces" of violence "lurk" within this translation into practice.

The Production of Expert Discourse

The production of a professional language to account for, intervene in, and prevent domestic violence is a means by which violence against women is rationalized as a chronic yet treatable problem.[2] In the professional literature, the choice of treatment strategies may appear to be a controversial issue. Yet the internal divisions in professional literature about the imposition of psychological stereotypes in diagnosis and treatment often fail to raise fundamental questions about the scientific enterprise that monopolizes discourse on violence against women.

The question posed is not only how women are represented in an expert discourse, but how their identities are produced and then utilized by forms of juridical power.[3] I begin to address this question by critically examining the history of domestic violence as a social problem worthy of public recognition and state intervention.

Insurgent Discourse

The term "battered woman" had no political or scientific significance before the feminist movement politicized the issue as one form of violence produced by a system of male domination.[4] The political goal of this era of the feminist movement was to bring into the public realm an everyday event that had previously been hidden by the ideology of privacy surrounding the patriarchal family. An essential part of the movement against wife-battering was the creation of shelters that provided a safe-haven from male violence. The shelters were centers of consciousness-raising and staffed by feminist volunteers, some of whom were previously battered women. A core ideology of this grassroots movement was that the shelter was both a physical and symbolic boundary between women's space and the violence of the male world, and within these homes women would exercise their own strength and autonomy outside of relationships of domination.[5] Beyond a spiritual component that stressed the interconnectedness of women's problems was a practical mission of providing the basic resources needed for the economic sufficiency of the women and their children. The volunteer staff utilized the government service network (although not exclusively) in assisting women's search for housing, jobs, and childcare.

Domestic violence as a social problem entered a new era in the 1970's as it was transformed in response to feminist awareness of the issue. The activists' reading of history characterized the problem of domestic abuse as persistent and age-old, yet accounted for the previous lack of awareness by stressing both the repression of the issue by the old social work bureaucracy and the inability of women to seek assistance backed by even modest claims of rights.[6] Even some of the early shelters had not broken out of the mode of the social work model of family service and consequently sought their start-up funding in conjunction with alcoholic treatment programs.[7]

An integral part of the new movement's agenda was correcting an orientation of the social worker that was seen as unsympathetic to women, favorable to the interests of the father, and devoted to the preservation of the family unit.[8] From the point of view of social work reform, a grave crime was committed by the legal and mental health system's re-victimization of abused women who sought help.

The problem of marital violence gained prominence on the public agenda in the same period that the social work academy strove to solidify its authority through linkages to the expanding social welfare apparatus and its own professionalization. This included two strategies: first, the recruitment of a new professional corps trained in academic schools of social work, mostly young and male, to replace older working class women who often shared some identification with their clientele; and second, the reconstruction of the social work discipline as a composite of the functionalist approaches of psychology, sociology, and other human sciences.[9]

As the centers became more established in the late 1970's they sought state funding, and thus were subjected to review and evaluation by the social work bureaucracies.[10] The issue of battered women drew attention among the traditional enterprises that protected the welfare of the family, including the social work bureaucracy, police, and public assistance agencies, while the whole system of welfare became a "feminized terrain" by constituting women and their children as the needy.[11]

This process is described by Nancy Fraser as the "politics of need interpretation," a process in which social service agencies construct women and their needs in forms that discourage contestation.[12] The social welfare system substitutes the "juridical, administrative, and therapeutic management of need satisfaction for the politics of need interpretation."[13] These expert discourses co-exist with oppositional (politicized or grassroots) discourses, as well as with the rhetoric of conservative political forces attempting to re-privatize the problem.

In this new production of social science knowledge, women's experience of violence is recast in therapeutic and administrative language. This enterprise contributes to the re-privatization of sexual violence and promotes a normative interpretation of the causes of male violence. This normative vision, despite its arcane presentation in the jargon of social science, has an influential presence in the politics of needs interpretation as it gains a monopoly over popular understandings of the social problem and becomes translated for popular consumption as common sense wisdom about the psychology of victims.

The Professional As One and the Other

The dominant mode of understanding in expert discourse on battered women rests upon an internalized debate about the defeat of the "masochist" hypothesis within the social work profession. A strong contrast is drawn between traditional social work agencies that impeded effective service delivery—and may even have harmed women with their "victim blaming" attitudes—and the professional social work approach that has identified the violence as symptomatic of complex social, structural and individual conditions that create stress on normal families.[14]

This powerful theme serves several purposes in positioning the new social work ideology. First, it places the new orientation clearly in the role of "doing good" for the client, as opposed to unprofessional conduct that potentially re-victimized the client. This stance "purifies" the social work apparatus from its stigmatic effects and clearly defines the social worker's role in the field of public service. Second, it locates the problem of inappropriate signification of victims within professional power. The profession is, therefore, engaged in a self-correcting reformulation of the image of the battered woman. And third, it situates the professional in the role of an educator about the true nature of women's victimization.

This professional posture enables the social work academy to speak authoritatively about the identity and needs of abused women by delimiting speculation about the reality of the subject's conditions. And thus, this discursive strategy empowers itself by creating a realm of authority which is "subjectless."[15] Its judgments about the pejorative treatment of abused women is a pre-empirical observation that in fact justifies removing from its empirical analysis inquiries about "what women want"—the gendered subject's deep self of motivation and desire. At the same time, the defeat of the masochism hypothesis disassociates the social worker from the authority of the batterer, as he or she subsumes the interests of the victims.

The Netting of Scholarly Constructed Community

For those battered women shelters guided by feminist ideologies, the act of founding these homes was a political marking of space. These shelters were created as homes in the sense of making an atmosphere of domestic life, yet they were also conceived as spaces in which women would feel free to come and go as they pleased. In essence, these women's lives were to "intersect" with the houses, and their continued connection with this domestic space depended upon their needs and contributions over time.[16]

In the journals of social medicine, "battered women" are measured with regard to their "susceptibility to treatment."[17] The medical profession's effort to provide battered women with the "attention and support they need" requires study of their attitudes toward psychosocial support, as well as their incentives to complete or default on a therapeutic program. This raises the problem of inadequate *surveillance* of battered women after their initial contact with hospital emergency rooms because it is unfeasible to conduct "structured treatment programs" without a high probability of completion.[18]

In the language of administrative goals, the shelter house is an essential part of a *netting* system that brings women in crisis into the domain of therapeutic programs.[19] Clients who enter safe-houses are considered to be at an opportune moment for clinical intervention;[20] these women are ripe for psychological intervention and lifestyle change during "periods of disequilibrium."[21] The social workers' mandate to restructure the service of shelters from self-help and consciousness-raising to the administration of client needs is justified by imposing requirements to document program success. A center is unable to "document client progress" if it fails to outline specific objectives so that the *"client knows what she needs to accomplish."*[22] This "meaningfully stated behavioral objective" is necessary both to measure the overall success of treatment strategies within the center, and as a message to the client of the *"terminal behavior or skills she will need to demonstrate success."*[23] The shelters that have not actively revised their programmatic goals since the 1970's, and therefore offer general statements of purpose (such as providing space for women of need in the community and directing them to the survival resources they need outside of the shelter home), are considered potentially less effective because they offer unspecified expectations of the transformation of the clients' psychological profile. Moreover, the success rate of centers with generalized goals is impossible to document when they release women back into society *without adequate tracking mechanisms.*[24]

The social work model of effective service delivery requires battered women's programs to establish themselves within a network of social service bureaucracies. A shelter is judged successful when it "takes the initiative to ally itself with an established and *respected* [social service agency]."[25] These connections are deemed desirable because they are a part of the process of professionalizing the service personnel and eliminating the high reliance on volunteers, who are labeled "paraprofessionals" (while being "cost effective," they are *"no substitute for professional counseling"*[26]). In fact, the social work profession portrays itself as indispensable to the feminist shelter movement. As a social work "pioneer" in the battered women's field writes, "researchers came forth to *validate* the data gathered by the shelter movement."[27] They offer the expertise and personnel to bring shelters to their full potential: "many times shelters for abused women are staffed by paraprofessionals—people *dedicated to and concerned about the victim's well-being but lacking in the advanced training and skills* to provide individual, group, and family therapy."[28] One member of the social work academy offers an urgent prediction that in times of "shrinking government spending," "unless established social service and traditional mental health agencies incorporate spouse abuse components into their programs, one can predict that the treatment of spouse abuse will disappear."[29]

When shelters are staffed by corps of paraprofessionals, concerns are raised about whether these women possess the expertise required to treat women with "extensive and severe trauma" of such a nature that *only a therapist* can "help them achieve understanding of their past."[30] For example, in the social work literature the worst case scenario of paraprofessional inadequacy is demonstrated by case studies. In one such case study, after a series of emotional outbursts by a shelter resident, a volunteer worker reassures the woman by drawing on personal examples of surviving violent relationships. It is the social worker's contention that such comparisons by a volunteer to her own abilities to cope is inappropriate given differences in individual levels of psychological health and, in fact, demonstrates that the volunteer has "no knowledge of the basics of clinical intervention."[31] The goal of phasing out the untrained volunteer is further mandated by the growing use and success of "couple's counseling," which presents an extremely delicate therapist/client(s) relationship and requires a "skilled therapist to *facilitate the couple's homeostasis.*"[32] In this regard, the forms of self-help at the core of feminist shelter philosophy are rendered useless, if not harmful, to a process of readjustment to a *normal* life.

The Social Construction of Women's Well-Being

The administrative approach, in its effort to institute specific programmatic goals, imposes a definition of needs on battered women; their needs are viewed as derivative of the psychological incapacities that precipitated the crisis, in particular the women's inability to formulate options which would stop physical abuse. The therapeutic model is applied in an effort to move women beyond their self-imposed psychological constraints to participate in a *normal*, nonviolent family.

The most recent articles by social work practitioners stress the desirability of treating battered women as members of violent families.[33] The favored treatment strategies (which emphasize the reintegration of family units) clearly fall in the so-called "family therapy modality;" according to their professional logic, it simply makes *good economic sense* to bring the rest of the family into the social service network.

The couple or conjoint therapy model is based on the therapeutic assumption that marriages exist in equilibrium. Violence is the result of disruptions in that equilibrium, which occur when one individual (presumably the wife) moves to a "higher differentiation of self." In this theory, it is primarily the wife who introduces stresses into the relationship through the imposition of children and childcare responsibilities, or by her demands for employment and recognition outside the family. The husband, in response to the introduction of these new stresses, is sometimes unable to communicate his frustrations or possible counterclaims on family resources. Some men, presumably because they function and communicate intellectually at levels best suited for the economic world outside of the family, are often functionally incapable of emotionally expressing their grievances, and thus violence becomes the outlet for their frustrations.[34]

In the conjoint therapy model, acts of physical violence are translated into communication disorders. The scientific project that verifies and refines this model is referred to as the "comprehensive assessment of the psychological adjustment of wife abusers and their spouses."[35] These studies attempt to establish the causal connections between violent marriages and social skills or impaired communication styles. The results seem to indicate that abusive males have "more speech disturbances ... and [use] less praise/appreciation than satisfactorily married husbands."[36] The data on abused women, by contrast, indicate some similarities between the relationship skills of "abused wives and their nonabused counterparts."[37] Rather than concluding that these results tell us something about the aberrations of violent men, the interpreters of this research emphasize the need to model marital relationships as "interdependent ... on multiple factors" that "influence commission of these violent acts."[38]

In the application of this model as a therapeutic technique, this construction of dysfunctional communication within the family is sometimes coercively imposed to achieve compliance to the conjoint strategy. Social workers advocate conjoint therapy because of its advantages for legitimating professional intervention—couple's therapy promotes trust in the therapist for both partners by ensuring that there are "no secrets" (from the third party husband).[39] Moreover, the frequency with which battered women return to live with their spouses, and the dangers encountered by wives returning to the family, make couple's therapy the more *realistic* option.

In a "model" case study written by one advocate of couple's therapy, the abused wife is advised over the phone during her initial contact with the social worker to convince her husband to come to therapy.[40] When the woman suggested that she would have difficulty persuading her husband to speak with a therapist, she was told to *"find a way to get him in."* After further resistance to the social worker's explicit references to the woman's responsibility to get her husband into therapy, she was told simply to look at her options, one of which was to *"come in alone but the violence wouldn't stop."* The social worker justifies her imposition of responsibility on the wife by linking it to her decision to stay married, yet the exchange reveals how dependent the social worker is on the image of the woman as the instigator of marital disequilibrium—to establish the compatibility of her interests with the abused woman, and to affirm the methodology of conjoint therapy.

In what are termed the "intrapersonal" correlates of domestic violence, the language of therapy reconstructs the feminine personality. As previously stated, the new professional discourse of social work posits itself in opposition to the masochist hypothesis of self-blame. Yet, in actuality, the social scientific project that defines intrapersonal correlates reinscribes these pathologies of the woman in a gender-neutral fashion. As one author maintains: "Although investigations still rely on pathological indexes, women's symptoms are viewed as sequelae of abuse, rather than concomitants or precursors of abuse. These studies indicate, for example, that women who have been battered tend to suffer from depression, anxiety, alcohol abuse, and elevated MMP1 profiles."[41]

In the professional mind, the "sequelae of abuse" approach allows these qualities to be viewed analytically and abstractly. This enables a new approach, given two assumptions. First, these qualities are not gender specific, meaning that these are pathological indicators that would be manifested in response to extreme violence regardless of the sex of the victim. Second, the stigmatic potential of these attributes is mitigated when appropriately employed by the professional for the purposes of prediction, diagnosis, and treatment of domestic violence. The implicit assumption in the professional discourse is that these psychological responses to violence are reasonable reactions of a genderless subject, while their manifestations in a woman's personality is a pathological syndrome reflecting unrealistic fears and the overvaluation of male power. This is only reconcilable if the fear of violence and the bonds of gender exist in a woman's imagination and the psychological construction is the reality.

Moreover, when the psychological theories accounting for battered women are grounded in personal identities, the social workers' impression that every woman's situation is different is likely to mean only that there are differences in relationship skills and levels of emotional stability.[42] The social work language has a universalizing quality in that women are taken out of their gender, class, and racial specifics and the problems are discussed as if all women are equally vulnerable.

The myth of the masochist woman is generated anew in its genderless formation. The language of therapy reconstructs women so that a "degendered" submissiveness is part of a complex of psychological attributes.

For example, the psychological disorder of "parentification" stands in place of the dependence of women structured by the modern conditions of motherhood.[43] Parentification is the condition of battered women that results from their over-involvement with the needs of others, to such an extent that it causes women to disregard their own needs.

In this psychological theory the battered women's dysfunctional obligations to others—in particular, the needs of their children or husbands—preclude action that may not conform to their notion of "doing the right thing." In this potentially sensitive orientation which accounts for the perpetuation of domestic abuse, however, society's undervaluation of motherhood is psychologized as a woman's personal distortion of her situation.[44] The conditions that create women's vulnerability to men's power are reduced to psychosomatic reactions. The concept of parentification is incompatible with the early shelter movement belief that the battered woman's "status as a mother provides the starting point for building a new identity,"[45] and has potentially negative consequences when the social workers' evaluations are used as evidence about the woman's ability to care for or protect her child from her spouse's abuse. The therapeutic model produces a psychological profile that is available as a potential mechanism to remove the children from their home.

Some social workers favor "interpersonal pathologies" as explanatory variables for domestic violence. These researchers pose the question of which family types are potentially "at risk" for wife abuse. The family types "at risk" include couples with rigid sex role attitudes, pairings of traditional husbands with nontraditional wives, relationships in which the male partners have undifferentiated personalities and lower masculinity, and families with a history of acceptance of violence or where there is low self-esteem in either partner.[46] This risk analysis is applied in the development of treatment and prediction models in a manner that reaffirms the rigidity of sexual roles. For example, this theory has been employed to warn against therapeutic applications of patriarchal explanations of family violence because it demonstrates that greater equality within the family, in the short run, may exacerbate tension and promote more family violence.[47]

Yet another facet of the interpersonal pathologies approach is the method by which it constructs women as a threat to men's position within intimate relationships. Women's hyperdevelopment of verbal skills is seen as the precipitating factor in marital disequilibrium. Thus *men's aggression is a response to their wives' "verbal abuse . . . which does much to fuel the fires of domestic strife . . . .[Evidenced by the fact that] most women have a higher verbal IQ score than men."*[48] While the verbal attributes are naturalized as reflective of feminine wiles, these explanations also emphasize their mutability by suggesting the ways in which the female psyche is more differentiated and capable of transformation than the male psychological configuration.⁴⁹ (In discussion of case studies it is often added that the woman is physically attractive and capable of re-entering a non-violent marital relationship.) Social programs designed to *improve battered wives' relationship and problem-solving skills* are suggested as "more cost efficient than secondary interventions."⁵⁰

It is precisely the malleability of gendered relationship attributes that allows the social worker to suggest that women can utilize normal "feminine" coping mechanisms to readjust the dynamics of the violent home. The social workers' strategy to recreate family equilibrium is based upon a construction of the woman in which a gendered-self employs coping mechanisms within the constraints of rigid sex roles, while a therapeutically managed degendered-self facilitates the adaptation to normal life. The construction of the healthy female personality, therefore, does not disrupt "primary gender identifications" as heterosexual or relational.

Lurking Violence

A primary concern of criminologists who study domestic abuse is documenting the pervasiveness of family violence; their project is devoted to the production of more accurate measures of the amount of violence in individual families and the scope of the nationwide problem. This documentation supports the importance of their own research enterprises, and provides the basis of their claim that the family is the "most violent institution in America."⁵¹

The documentation of domestic abuse by academics can be held in stark contrast to the efforts of women in the early shelter movement to represent the violence they experienced as a collectivity. The latter sought to preserve the record of violence against women in an oral history that would gradually grow and be enriched by the reflections of women who sought refuge in the shelter.⁵² Women's participation in the collective story would help them find identities they had lost within isolated and violent homes. The environment of the feminist shelters was a place for women to become whole again after the experience of violence, an experience not simply seen as a series of injurious acts but as a shattering condition of women's lives.

The social scientist studies the family as a "special case of violence,"⁵³ and in so doing inhibits speculation about the social structure of violence. The experience of violence within the home is reduced to a "public interest story" in which private events are brought to public attention.⁵⁴ These images denigrate the everyday concerns of women by ignoring the realities of violent terror and sexual perversity that structure their lives.

The social scientific methodology denies the phenomenology of violence by separating its project from the ideological uses of claims of violence. The research methodology makes distinctions between scales of family violence and the political concept of "wife-beating"—or the use of violence as a "political concept to attract attention to undesirable behavior or situations."[55] The study of the causes of violence in the family is clearly delimited so as not to include emotional abuse or quasi-legitimate forms of physical discipline. Violence is not seen as expressive of irrationality; it is the symptom of a dysfunction in the equilibrium of the family, and a cause of physical injury. In social science research on battered women, the construction of the reality of family life is devoid of symbolic interaction;[56] the dynamics of family life can even be simulated by a computer program, SIMFAM, which manipulates a crisis between real persons. For the social work therapist, the dramatic potential of violence to shape relationships is denied by methods that avoid discussion of the violent incidents (especially in couple's therapy) because the therapist is often fearful of the possibility of provoking further violent confrontation inside the professional's office.

The social work paradigm studies the *correlates* of violence rather than its meanings. The working definition of violence in this field is "an act carried out with the intention, or perceived intention, of physically hurting another person."[57] This definition is designed to include only violence that has "a high potential" for causing an injury. The definition facilitates quantified measurement of harm imposed on others, yet avoids the non-contained qualities of violence that permeate the relationships under study. The researcher may identify the correlates of violence within a discursive strategy that distorts the meanings of violence. For example, a research report that attempted to account for the high prevalence of spouse beating during pregnancy concluded that the "violence grew out of their [the women's] irritability which began when they became pregnant and in some cases it was abuse directed at the unborn child." He concludes that it is "correct that this is prenatal child abuse . . . *this violence may serve as an indicator or predictor of future abuse* of children in these families."[58] This account dismisses the expressive reality of men's complex emotions of hate and jealousy toward pregnant women; the reality of violence is discernible only as a predictor of violence. By ignoring the reality of expressive violence, the social science construction of the problem precludes debate over contested political meanings of violence.

Even when the risk of potential violence is considered, it is often in terms of narrowly framed questions of professional ethics. A mental health official compares her own risk of violence to that of her client: "the danger of violence a professional faces for her/himself parallels that of the battered woman[;] they both have little control over the batterers' violence. The professional has the opportunity to make use of a full range of options to maximize her/his safety, thus providing a positive model for battered women."[59] The statement makes the battered woman's experience of violence appear trivial by comparing it to professional risk, and then affirms the professional's ability to exercise more appropriate forms of control than are available to women. These concerns might even be seen as the professional's vicarious participation in the hazards and "excitement" of the lives of their subjects, a reality of violence that is then buried in the academic construction of their situation.

Juridical Power

The social science theory of domestic violence is connected to practice, in particular, by measures which define concrete state intervention. The modern social paradigm posits a dilemma between strategies of "compassion" and "control." The compassion approach is considered problematic because the professionals' excessive identification with the plight of their clients may lull them into the impression that they actually *"do something" for the person by forming an emotional bond.*[60] Although the model of "compassion" counteracts the indifference of the old social work approach, the more "effective" control model places the professional in the role of "aggressive [user] of intervention to limit, and if necessary, to punish domestic violence." The preference for control strategies legitimates the trend in social work practices to mediate their powers through state agencies (placing the protection of the battered woman within a complex system of government bureaucracies) rather than defend their client against the state's neglect and indifference.[61] The social work bureaucracy assumes a regulatory role over the social welfare apparatus, especially the police. This solidifies the power of the social work profession, and establishes its crucial role in training the police and other contact personnel.[62]

The introduction of the "Battered Women's Syndrome" to criminal defense strategies has created a public forum for the professional construction of abused spouses. These spectacles of the battered women's story have reinforced rather than transformed the dominant sexual stereotypes of victimized women. The linking together of therapeutic and legal discourses, in fact, immunizes the interpretation of the identities of battered women from political critique.

The introduction of expert testimony on the Battered Women's Syndrome is permissible if this evidence is "beyond the ken of the average layman."[63] The relevance of the psychological testimony is, therefore, dependent upon the professional contention that the diagnosis of the syndrome requires specialized expertise and that the techniques are "generally accepted in the psychological community."[64] The claim for psychological expertise is made at the expense of giving credit to the battered woman's self-awareness or her ability to make a defense on her own terms. The woman is considered an ineffective advocate of her own cause and, in most cases, the psychological documentation of her "minimization" of the violence is essential to the psychological verification of the syndrome.

Although these psychological tools are sometimes utilized in legal actions against violent men, the creation of the Battered Women's Syndrome is primarily a defense tactic to introduce testimony about a history of abusive spouses in homicide cases. The labeling of the syndrome has focused public attention on the unusual case of women who kill their violent spouse.[65] As a consequence, the political message of the battered women's movement has been transformed by focusing attention on abused women as fearful, desperate, and driven to murder. The justification of women's violence as self-defense is made at the cost of creating a special category of insanity for battered women for mass public consumption. In fact, the indicators of battered women's syndrome on the prevailing tool, "DSM-III diagnostic criteria for post-traumatic stress disorders,"[66] are exactly the same as the symptoms of schizophrenia and borderline personality disorders.[67] Thus, the professionals' claims to expertise are simply their familiarity with the Battered Women's Syndrome and their ability to make proper distinctions between the tools and how they are used. In this field, psychologists *"read personality tests like judges read the Constitution."*[68] In conjunction, the psychological and legal models bracket the discourse about harm publicized by these trials in terms of the de-gendered psychological self. Moreover, the reification of the passive (yet dangerous) victim of the Battered Women's Syndrome further removes women's everyday experiences of violence from the public imagination.

The fluid boundaries between the expert discourses of law and psychology facilitate the absorption of professional knowledge as well as permit scientific concepts to cross boundaries without contests between competing visions of professional purpose. In the case of battered women, these boundaries preclude contests about the compatibility of women's needs with their rights and interests, and, indeed, presume they are synonymous. This alliance between legal and mental health professionals, formed on their willingness to "educate" each other,[69] serves to enclave their knowledge, vision, and strategies and further isolate any competing versions from public discussion.

The social work profession's assumption of a "helping" role in relation to the legal professional is the fulfillment of its commitment to the control model. This relationship among experts creates a monopoly on the "new social work understanding" of battered women and provides the context to legitimate and disseminate expert accounts of the syndrome. The linguistic attributions constructed by the social work profession concerning the gender relations of women are recreated in these trials; within the legal forum, authoritative messages are projected through language and legal forms about the identity and social relationships of battered women.[70] This professional connection, therefore, is a powerful means by which the expert constructions of women's identity are assimilated in "popular" or "common sense" understandings of women's condition.

The Appropriation of Violence

The production of a professional language for domestic abuse was an integral part of the displacement of the feminist shelter movement's emerging (yet incomplete) articulation of battered women's needs and definition of community. The co-optation of the institutional structures of the movement was accompanied by the expansion of new expert discourses that distorted the political meanings of the insurgent language. While public attention focused on the social problem, the social work profession created new language and practices in the expanding political space for discourse about "doing good" for women.

The politically transforming language of shelter organizers that connected concepts of women's "space" and autonomy was displaced by therapeutic definitions of women's needs. The expression of needs in "women's terms" did not serve the interests of the new social work ideology, which depended upon its application of the scientific model in a gender neutral fashion to justify its authority.

The power of professional language to structure public perceptions contributes to the denial of the multifaceted dimension of women's experiences of violence, and popularizes the constructed identity of the battered woman as a genderless and pathological self. Public acceptance of the professional discourse about domestic violence "closes the door" on linking domestic violence to broader political action, and ripens the political environment for the trivial pursuits of conservative backlash movements such as the protection of "husband battering."

Implicit in this critique of professional power is the view that the study of the phenomenology of violence against women potentially offers a new insurgent discourse. This project would seek to articulate the meanings of violence, recognizing how violence structures social relations and shapes the reality of women's lives. Can the scholar be exorcised from the diabolical forces of violence? Perhaps not; as the post-modern project penetrates the social constructs that hide violence and uncovers the violence of language, it also "appropriates" that violence for the construction of a new privileged discourse of scholars.

Notes

1. Max Weber, "Politics as a Vocation," in *From Max Weber: Essays in Sociology*, eds. H. H. Gerth and C. Wright Mills (New York: Oxford University Press, 1946), pp. 125–126.

2. Murray Edelman, *Political Language* (New York: Academic Press, 1977).

3. See, e.g., Judith Butler, *Gender Trouble: Feminism and the Subversion of Identity* (New York: Routledge, 1990) pp. 2–4.

4. Linda Gordon, *Heroes of Their Own Lives: The Politics and History of Family Violence* (New York: Viking, 1988).

5. Micheline Beaudry, *Battered Women* (Montreal: Black Rose Books, 1985).

6. Gordon, pp. 257–64.

7. Ibid, p. 286.

8. Some of the earliest examples of professional literature on battered women are politically informed; see, e.g., R. Emerson Dobash and Russell Dobash, *Violence Against Wives: A Case Against Patriarchy* (New York: Free Press, 1979).

9. Eve Brook and Ann Davis, eds., *Women, Family, and Social Work* (London: Tavistock Publications, 1985), pp. 3–50.

10. Beaudry, pp. 102–4.

11. Nancy Fraser, *Unruly Practices: Power Discourse and Gender in Contemporary Society* (Minneapolis: University of Minnesota Press, 1989).

12. Ibid, p. 146.

13. Ibid, p. 156.

14. Liane V. Davis, "Battered Women: The Transformation of a Social Problem," *Social Work* 32 (1987): 306–311.

15. For this critique of male language, see Luce Irigaray, *Speculum of the Other Woman*, trans. Gillian C. Gill (Ithaca: Cornell University Press, 1985).

16. Beaudry, pp. 66–70.

17. Bo K. Bergman, et al., "Battered Women—Their Susceptibility to Treatment," *Scandinavian Journal of Social Medicine* 16 (1988): 155–60.

18. Ibid, p. 159.

19. See, e.g., Edward W. Gondolf, "The Effect of Batterer Counseling on Shelter Outcome," *Journal of Interpersonal Violence* 3 (September 1988): 275–289.

20. See, e.g., J. Scott Fraser, "Strategic Rapid Intervention in Wife-Beating" in *Troubled Relationships* eds. Elam W. Nunnally, et al. (New York: Sage, 1988), pp. 163–191.

21. Albert R. Roberts, "Crisis Intervention with Battered Women" in *Battered Women and Their Families*, ed. Albert R. Roberts (New York: Springer, 1984), pp. 65–83.

22. Ibid, p. 69.

23. Ibid.

24. Ibid, p. 70.

25. Ibid, p. 71.

26. Ibid, p. 74.

27. Del Martin, "The Historical Roots of Domestic Violence" in *Domestic Violence on Trial* ed. Daniel Sonkin (New York: Springer, 1987), p. 16.

28. Roberts, "Crisis Intervention," p. 74.

29. Janet A. Geller and Janice Wasserstrom, "Conjoint Therapy for the Treatment of Domestic Violence," in Roberts, *Battered Women and Their Families*, p. 33.

30. Roberts, "Crisis Intervention," p. 75.

31. Ibid, p. 76.

32. Ibid, p. 77.

33. The alternative trend, not discussed here, is the therapeutic approach to the treatment of the male batterer; see, e.g., Daniel Jay Sonkin, et al., *The Male Batterer* (New York: Springer, 1985).

34. The contention among scientists who examine neurological factors is that "normal males are more liable to physical conditions that often spell pathological aggression—the episodic dyscontrol syndrome, the attention deficit disorder, and the antisocial personality disorder." Frank A. Alit, "Neurological Factors," in *Handbook of Family Violence*, eds. Vincent B. Van Hasselt, et al. (New York: Plenum, 1988), p. 262.

35. Randall L. Morrison, et al., "Assessment of Assertion and Problem-Solving Skills in Wife Abusers and Their Spouses," *Journal of Family Violence* 2 (1987): 229.

36. Margaret H. Launius and Bernard L. Jenson, "Interpersonal Problem-Solving Skills in Battered, Counseling, and Control Women," *Journal of Family Violence* 2 (1987): 160.

37. Morrison, "Assertion and Problem-Solving Skills," p. 235.

38. Ibid, p. 236.

39. Geller and Wasserstrom, "Conjoint Therapy," p. 34.

40. Ibid; the dialogue is reported on pp. 35–46.

41. Gayla Margolin, et al., "Wife Battering," in *Handbook of Family Violence*, p. 94.

42. There is controversy within the scientific literature about the degree to which battered women resemble "ordinary" women; see, e.g., Lewis Okun, *Women Abuse: Facts Replacing Myths* (Albany, NY: State University of New York Press, 1986).

43. Margaret Cotroneo, "Women and Abuse in the Context of the Family."

44. See, e.g., Martha Fineman, "Dominant Discourse, Professional Language, and Legal Change in Child Custody Decisionmaking," *Harvard Law Review* 101 (February 1988): 724–74.

45. Beaudry, *Battered Women*, p. 64.

46. Margolin, et al., "Wife Battering," pp. 95–99.

47. Ibid, p. 99.

48. Frank A. Elliot, "Neurological Factors" in *Handbook of Family Violence*, p. 363.

49. Linda Gordon's theory of the hyperdevelopment of the verbal is different, but may be considered problematic for similar reasons: "[W]omen's verbal skills were honed to sharpness precisely to do battle against men's superior power, including violence.... This superiority ... was a collective characteristic developed as a result of the structural position of gender." *Heroes of Their Own Lives*, p. 286.

50. Launius and Jenson, "Interpersonal Problem-Solving," p. 161.

51. David Finkelhor, *Stopping Family Violence* (New York: Sage, 1988); see also U.S Congress, *Women, Violence, and the Law*, Hearing before the Select Committee on Children, Youth, and Families, House of Representatives, 100th Congress, 1987.

52. Beaudray, *Battered Women*, pp. 51–4.

53. Richard J. Gelles, *Family Violence*, 2nd ed. (New York: Sage, 1987), p. 41.

54. See Murray Edelman, *Constructing the Political Spectacle* (Chicago: University of Chicago Press, 1988), pp. 90–102.

55. Gelles, *Family Violence*, p. 32.

56. For an exception within social scientific approaches, see Norman K. Denzin, "Toward a Phenomenology of Domestic Family Violence," *American Journal of Sociology* 90 (November 1984): 483–513.

57. Richard J. Gelles and Claire Pedrick Cornell, *Intimate Violence in Families* (New York: Sage, 1985), p. 22.

58. Gelles, *Family Violence*, p. 129.

59. Mary Ann Douglas, "The Battered Women Syndrome," in *Domestic Violence on Trial*, pp. 52–3.

60. Richard J. Gelles and Murray A. Straus, *Intimate Violence* (New York: Simon and Schuster, 1988), pp. 160–7.

61. See, e.g., Brook and Davis, *Women, the Family and Social Work*, p. 46.

62. Gelles and Straus, *Intimate Violence*, p. 167.

63. Roberta K. Thyfault, et al., "Battered Women in Court: Jury and Trial Consultants and Expert Witnesses," in *Domestic Violence on Trial*, p. 57.

64. Douglas, "The Battered Women Syndrome," p. 45.

65. See Angela Brown, *When Battered Women Kill* (New York: Free Press, 1987).

66. Douglas, "The Battered Women's Syndrome," p. 40.

67. Lynne Bravo Rosewater, "The Clinical and Courtroom Application of Battered Women's Personality Assessments," in *Domestic Violence on Trial*, p. 86.

68. Ibid, p. 88.

69. Thyfault, et al., "Battered Women in Court," p. 60.

70. For the role of the trial as a signifier in legal culture, see Pierre Bordieu, "The Force of Law: Toward a Sociology of the Juridical Field," *Hastings Law Journal* 38 (1987): 805–853.

7

The Neutered Mother

Martha Albertson Fineman

Introduction

Definitions:

Mother; a female who has borne offspring

Female; of or pertaining to the sex that brings forth young

Neutered; neither masculine nor feminine in gender

Gender; the quality of being male or female

Mother as Symbol

I use the term "Neutered Mother" because it represents conflict and contradiction—words in contraposition to each other, incompatible when placed together. The Neutered Mother presents a gendered noun, degendered by the adjective that precedes it—an opposition of meaning that mirrors the conflicts in culture and in law over the significance and potency of the symbol of Mother.

In this essay, I am going to assess the evolution of the symbolic aspects of "Mother" in modern family law reform and offer an argument for revitalization of the powerful and positive aspects of the Mother symbol to effect changes in law for real life mothers.[1] Focusing on Mother in any context is dangerous. Mother is a universally possessed symbol (although its meaning may vary across and within cultures). We all have a mother—some of us are mothers. As a lived experience, Mother is virtually universally shared in our culture and, therefore, more intimately and intensely personalized than many other symbols. Mother, however, is an ambiguous symbol—one about which there is contest. For that reason, the importance of Mother as a symbol is greatly enhanced on both an individual and a societal level. In its various configurations, "Mother" is a significant factor in defining our understanding of our own familial, sexual and social circumstances. In this way, it is also significant in our construction of universal meanings—defining the general qualities of life for us.[2]

In terms of contemporary society, Mother has accumulated negative as well as positive content. Two major twentieth century contributors to the construction and perpetuation of negative images of motherhood have been neo-Freudians (very loosely defined) and contemporary liberal feminists. The reason these two particular discourses have been so significant is due to the coherency and comprehensiveness of their articulations of the negative aspects of Mother. These two groups, for different purposes and in different contexts, have typically constructed Mother as a problem-laden social and cultural institution. In both discourses, the symbol of Mother is negatively implicated by the specter of her dependence on husband and child. In both, she is marred by burdens of obligation and intimacy in an era where personal liberation and individual autonomy are viewed as both mature and essential. However, the focus of the discourses is different. Neo-Freudians seem more concerned with the ability of the child to extricate himself (and I do mean *himself*) from the clutches of Mother,[3] while liberal feminists are concerned with the ability of women to avoid the psychological and material burdens Mother has placed on them through the generations.[4]

My particular focus in this essay will be on those law reform activities consistent with the stated position of liberal legal feminists. In their increasingly important role of effecting changes in law and legal institutions, liberal legal feminists have represented women's issues and concerns as though they are due in part to pathology in the traditional institution of motherhood. The result is that their rhetoric surrounding issues of potential law reform constantly reaffirms the notion that Mother must be overcome—refashioned so that the individual woman is left unencumbered. To a great extent the law and legal language have begun to incorporate the liberal legal feminist notion that Mother is an institution which must be reformed—that is, contained and neutralized. In law, this has been accomplished through the transfiguration of the symbolically positive cultural and social components of parenting typically associated with the institution of motherhood into the degendered components of the neutered institution of "parenthood."

The Law of the Mother

It is important to position the discussion of the neutering or degendering of Mother within the confines of traditional family law discourse. Family law is that area of law whereby the state regulates certain intimate relationships by defining a legal family relationship and assigning formal legal consequences and obligations within the context of that definition. Family law both reflects and contributes to our cultural understandings of the traditional family roles of mother, father, husband, wife and child.

Early Law

Early and well-defined references to Mother are found in the Anglo-American rules regulating custody decisions at divorce. Mother was clearly designated the "inferior" parent and it was a battle getting her established in law as a contender with respect to the custody of her children. Under English common law, fathers had an absolute right to "ownership" and control over their children, as if they held title, and a corresponding duty to support them. Mothers, according to Blackstone, were entitled to "no power, but only reverence and respect."[5] Early American custody law operated in a relatively simple and straightforward manner. Judicial decision-making was limited to determining if a particular set of circumstances was one of the exceptional cases which required deviation from the stated standard of father custody and control.

It was not until the latter part of the nineteenth century that the notion of paternal possession was successfully challenged. Invoking the powerful cultural Mother imagery of the day, domestically oriented feminists stressed the importance of the mother's special nurturing and caregiving roles to the welfare of her children.[6] This feminist agitation, coupled with the efforts of turn-of-the-century welfare state do-gooders, was instrumental in shifting the focus of custody law towards concern for the child's right to the best custodial situation, and away from the property interest of the father.[7]

The move away from automatic paternal right came with the adoption of the "best interest of the child" standard as the governing substantive principle in custody adjudications. Instead of merely implementing a father's right to custody, the courts were directed to select the best custodial placement for the child.[8] The indeterminacy of this test created problems for the legal system, however, as it required judges to assess a multitude of factors in making substantive comparisons and judgments on a case-by-case basis. Many jurisdictions developed subsidiary rules to give coherence (from their perspective) and content to the best interest standard. One such rule was the presumption in favor of maternal custody based on the belief that in most instances it would be in a child's best interest to continue to be nurtured by its mother. This rule became known as the "tender years doctrine." It incorporated the positive symbolic aspects of Mother, favoring and fostering mother custody, by implementing the best interest rule.[9]

The movement away from the father's absolute right incorporated the notion of custody as a legal companion to domestic ideology that recognized a mother's socially productive labor in raising future citizens. Although the custody rules were predicated on positive perceptions about Mother, they were not problem-free when viewed from a contemporary feminist perspective.[10] The revised custody rules were premised on the middle-class gendered assumptions and assertions of the late nineteenth and early twentieth centuries. The contemporary norms sanctioned women's exclusion from the public or market aspects of life under the guise of protecting or sheltering women so they could fulfill their true roles as bearers and nurturers of the species.

In addition, even women's gains in the family arena were ambiguous. Both social and legal systems conditioned women's enjoyment of their newfound custodial rights on their submission to patriarchal norms such as fidelity, temperance, and so on. For that reason, these apparent gains may be better understood as consistent with the dominant paternalistic rhetoric of the time.[11] While the wave of domestic feminist ideology that raised Mother as a powerful symbol initially challenged patriarchy, its more radical implications were inevitably absorbed and deflected—illustrating the elastic nature of patriarchal ideology.[12] Individual men had to relinquish some control over the private or domestic sphere, in that they did not retain an absolute right to their child's custody, but the basic structures as well as the ideological underpinnings of the system remained patriarchal. Women's role within the private sphere did not alter and codes of wifely conduct could be enforced through a custody doctrine that denied deviant mothers custody of their children. Mothers received custody of young children unless they were "unfit" to provide care for them. Sexual indiscretions, in particular, provided grounds upon which to base a finding of unfitness and to deny mothers custody under the tender years doctrine. Common bases upon which to establish unfitness included adultery, cohabitation, and sexual orientation.

In spite of its limitations, this early law of the Mother had unrealized radical potential to empower Mother within the family. Once this potential was complemented by the economic gains women made during the last half of this century, it became apparent that women could practice motherhood independent of men. This potential necessitated that Mother be explicitly controlled and reconfined—hence, the direction of modern reforms in family law.

Modern Trends

The maternal preference embodied in the tender years doctrine stood relatively unchallenged for decades. However, as the incidence of divorce increased in the early 1970s, so did conflicts over the law governing child custody determinations. The conflicts were generated in part by the formation of gendered interest groups with family law as their focus. For example, stringent state and federal provisions for the collection of past due child support fostered the formation of fathers' rights groups which expressed resentment that men were not equal parents in regard to child custody. To a great extent these groups represented a backlash to some of the successes of the feminist movement, such as the impetus to take child support awards seriously.

The fathers' groups advocated reforms in the family law area that had as their subtext the perceived inequality in the family law process.[13] In efforts to exonerate "deadbeat dads," for example, the widespread nonpayment of child support was justified by images of beleaguered fathers victimized by a court system which consistently awarded mothers custody and treated fathers as nothing more than "walking wallets."[14]

Predating the fathers' groups assertion of their interest in achieving equality within the family, mainstream liberal feminists were attacking gender-specific legal tests in the public sphere as inherently discriminatory. They also articulated the ideal of an egalitarian, genderless family where child care and household responsibilities were equally shared by husband and wife. The fathers' rights movement picked up on the idea of gender neutrality and turned it to their rhetorical advantage in the custody area. They effectively criticized child custody rules and decision-making for manifesting what they perceived to be a "pro-mother" bias.[15] Their attacks seemed all the more forceful because of the equality reforms that were being implemented in response to the economic consequences of divorce.

Male backlash to family law economic reforms and the liberal feminist equality and gender neutral rhetoric it appropriated helped to set the stage for challenges to custody rules and processes of decision-making that relied on the positive aspects of Mother.[16] Both the liberal feminists and the fathers' rights groups undermined the earlier acceptance of Mother as being something distinct, separate, and, perhaps, superior to the generic term "parent." Some commentators even went so far as to assert that gender neutrality requires that considerations of "typically Motherly" characteristics be eliminated from judicial consideration.[17] In place of the maternal presumption, custody arrangements that formally equated parents, such as joint custody, were proposed and defended on the grounds of furthering equality between the sexes.[18]

Liberal legal feminists, the most obvious potential source for the articulation of an alternative, non-patriarchal legal discourse about Mother, seem disinterested in the undertaking, perhaps even in the subject. Legal feminists have for the most part centered their attention on non-family circumstances and have expressed ambivalence about challenging concepts of family relationships except insofar as they are viewed as hindering or assisting market and economic equality for women. The existence of women in law, as practitioners, judges and teachers, and the fledgling movement among some female legal academics to develop feminist legal theory have yet to substantially alter the nature of legal discourse or the dominant legal concepts and constructs.

Liberal legal feminists constantly reaffirm their commitment to gender neutrality in the family context. Gender neutrality is the paradigmatic expression of the values and norms of the dominant legal concept of equality which, even if—perhaps, especially if—rephrased in feminist terms, precludes the consideration of Mother as something different or distinct from father. In legal texts, statutes, and cases, Mother is collapsed into the legal generic category of "Parent" and is suppressed. However, Mother has only disappeared rhetorically. In social and extra-legal institutions that embody cultural expectations—idealized and practical—Mother continues to exist and to function. It is the legal discourse, not society, that is now formally Mother-purged.

A Return to the Law of the Father

Neutering Mother

As a result of the push to gender neutrality, Mother as an explicitly positive symbol with unique connotations and significance in regard to her relationship with her child has been moved out of the text and into the margins of family law discourse. Mother is neutered into Parent and is, at the same time, transformed into "Wife"—a role considered to be more appropriate as it connotes an equal or full partner in the family and extra-family contexts. This emphasis on adult roles and relationships facilitates the tendency to perceive the family as peripheral to the public arena. The focus in that arena is on women as economic actors, a role that requires a degree of independence that is difficult to reconcile, if not incompatible, with the demands of traditional motherhood; changes in family law will be justified by the need to refashion Mother, manipulating her to permit the construction of an appropriate egalitarian legal position for women in the market and public sphere.

Furthermore, one consequence of this emphasis has been the alteration of women's relationship to the market. Women and wives as equal partners are expected to work—to be self-sufficient and to assume equal financial responsibility for their children. This is now true at divorce. However, the implications of neutering Mother are not confined to custody questions or to the re-ordering of families that takes place when "private" middle class families encounter the divorce system. Liberal legal feminist arguments for gender neutrality and family structuring to facilitate market participation have had an impact on "public" family law as well.[19] The way we have refashioned Mother has created significant consequences in areas of law and policy making outside of the traditional family form. It is the neutering of Mother that has paved the way for acceptance of workfare solutions to the persistent poverty of many mother-child families in this country. Requiring single mothers (or any mothers) to engage in market work and/or to train for work is viewed as compatible and complementary to their status as mothers, not in conflict with it.

The liberal feminist valuing of market work for women has been broadened from its initial conception as an ideal *option* for middle class and professional women. The current rhetoric on the appropriate relationship between women and market work establishes work as a universal and *mandatory requirement* for all women, mothers or not. The image of women as independent, economic equals is the mainstay of public and private family policy. The question that arises, of course, is what is the harm in that?

Needless to say, the shift in policy has operated to harm the most disadvantaged and defenseless mothers. The unanticipated by-product of earlier liberal feminist attempts to achieve economic equality has been that the new images of Mother operate to disadvantage many women encountering the law in the context of nonmarket circumstances. Such women are caretakers, nurturers who live lives of dependency—their child's and their own—which is generated by their roles as Mother. The institutions with which they have to deal, the worlds of work and market, are places in which there are no mothers. Workers are motherless, neither having nor being a mother. The very gendered and Mothered lives most women live are not accommodated in the liberal legal concept of gender equality.

The boundary between gender neutral legal discourse and the gendered operation of society cannot be maintained. The significance of Mother as an institution and cultural symbol continues to have a shadowed impact on law. Equality rhetoric successfully employed to neuter Mother as a unique legal construct has failed to erase Mother on the societal level, and it has not removed the material manifestations of the institution of Motherhood. The disparity between the experience of Mother and its neutered legal presentation is potentially threatening to the maintenance of the legal system's commitment to gender neutrality. If Mother is and continues to be experienced as different, legal accommodations for Mother will be demanded even within a formally neutral family law system.

Women who are Mothers are not well represented in the political process. It is essential, however, that their perspectives be articulated in the context of law and policy proposals. Yet, liberal feminists have been reluctant to make Mother a legislative agenda. An over-riding commitment to the equality objective seems to preclude these feminists from conceptualizing and becoming proponents of a gendered analysis of the policy and politics of families in the United States. This is an essentially assimilationist stance which does not challenge existing structures of dominance and control. The liberal legal feminist position on family reforms, which is exemplified in the paradigm of gender neutrality, makes it likely that equality will remain the ideological medium for the construction of legal images—a medium that threatens further destruction of Mother.

Even if a demand for a reexamination of the legal implications of the institution of motherhood from a feminist perspective were generated, it is not clear how successful it would be. The nature of law is conservative. It tends to reformulate, not render obsolete, the core tenets of our society, and challenges that are too radical or extreme are typically deflected. In the family context, the basic ideological construct is patriarchy—a decidedly anti-Mother perspective reflecting power relationships in which pater consistently trumps mater and the law assists in this endeavor.

The Sexual Family

The reflection of the family presented in family law doctrine may be distorted or fragmented, but it constitutes a "reality" and forms the basis for the regulation of actual lives. Because the legally constructed image of the family expresses what is appropriately considered "family," it also constitutes the "normal" and defines the "deviant." The designation of some intimate relationships as deviant legitimates state intervention and regulation.

Our continued adherence to patriarchy is inevitable given the tenacity and singularity of our prevalent conception of the family as an institution of horizontal intimacy, based on the romantic sexual affiliation between a man and a woman. The idealized "nuclear family" is a sexual family and its dominance in social and legal thought has restricted real reform and doomed us to recreate patriarchy.

The basic familial connection in our society is the sexual bond. For example, one of the central assumptions underpinning our conceptualization of family is that the entity is dependent upon a heterosexual relationship between a man and a woman.[20] This form of affiliation, romanticized in the glorification of the nuclear family, is central to traditional family law ideology. Politicians as well as religious leaders extol this relationship (if it is sanctified) as the core of the family.[21] While it is true that there is a great deal of emotionally charged rhetoric directed at children, it seems clear that its primary focus is on the traditional family model. Under this rhetoric, children's problems are created, to a large extent, by the fact that they are trapped in a deviant family situation.

Historically, in order to qualify as the foundational family relationship, a heterosexual union had to be legally privileged through marriage. There is a great deal of current agitation to eliminate this formality. Liberals seek to expand the traditional nuclear family model, urging the recognition of "informal" heterosexual unions within the definition of "family." There are also calls for acceptance and legal legitimation of same-sex relationships in the form of proposed domestic partnership laws.

Note, however, that even in the context of the proposed liberalized definitions of family, it is still the adult sexual affiliation that is central. The very existence of a sexual relationship is what provides the basis for arguing that these non-traditional unions should be included within the formal legal category of family. The form of argument is by analogy. Non-traditional unions are equated with the paradigmatic relationship of heterosexual marriage.

Formal, legal heterosexual marriage continues to dominate our imagination when we confront the possibilities of intimacy and family. This domination is evident in the language we use to describe the effect of the end of the relationship through divorce when we speak of the "broken" family. It is also evident in the way we characterize the growth of unwed mother-child units as constituting a threat to the family.

In contrast to the construction of family around a sexual affiliation, a non-sexual construction would not categorize families based on the relationship of men and women (or its adult members). Instead, it might begin with the premise that the basic family unit consists of mother and child. Although this is the family form experienced for significant time periods by many women and children in our society, it has never been accepted as a positive ideological or rhetorical alternative to the sexual family. A woman and her children "alone" are considered *incomplete*, and thus a deviant unit. They are identified as a source of pathology, generators of problems such as poverty or crime.[22]

That the relationship between men and women has been at the core of our perception of family is also evident when we see how it has defined other family members. For example, the historic characterization of children as "legitimate" or "illegitimate" depended on whether or not their parents were married. The significant reference in defining the status of the child was the nature of its parents' relationship. While such children today are more apt to be labeled "non-marital," the focus is still the same—the child is defined by the relationship between its parents.

The problem with a notion of family that is culturally and legally dependent upon the formal (or informal) relationship between adults is the inevitable focus on "doing justice" between the adults in public policy and political discussions. Of course, the conclusion that something is just heavily depends upon the articulation of the problem and the context in which any solution is considered. As with all systems of rules, family law cannot help but reflect the society's values and choices. When codified as legal standards, the privileging of the sexual tie stands as an eloquent, and potentially coercive, statement about our understanding of the nature of family. The potential negative effects of this codification are apparent when it is considered in the context of the contemporary hostility between the sexes and the status of equality as the dominant legal framework for discussions about fairness and justice. With high divorce rates and the organization of women and men into gendered interest groups when confronted with family issues, we should not be surprised that assets of the family, including children, are considered prizes, providing an arena for competition between women and men when their relationships fail.

In fact, the coalescence of interests along gendered lines is inevitable. The family represents the most gendered of our social institutions and this remains true even after decades of an organized women's movement. While other, nonfamily, transformations have fostered male-female competitiveness, the family is the one area where tensions generated by perceived changes in the position of women seem most clearly visible.

Historically, the family was the "private sphere" to which women were assigned in their roles as wife and mother. In recent decades more and more women have escaped the exclusivity of this assignment and they theoretically have more options available now. To the extent that today's society has developed a system of easy access to divorce and provided some economic security for women, women now combine private and public roles or reject the imposition of a historically defined role altogether. A woman may choose both work and family or decide to become a mother *without* being a wife. They can choose to end a marital relationship or never formally establish one and need not fear that their own or their children's futures in such circumstances will involve total impoverishment and social ostracization. Such changes have not come without costs, however.

Some women feel the changes have been expensive for all women while benefiting only a few. Others question whether such changes have been "advances" or whether they operate to further disadvantage many women. In earlier work, I asserted that it seems that our response to changing behavior on the part of women in the evolution of family law only reasserts, in different forms, the power men implicitly enjoyed within the context of indissoluble marriage and traditional patriarchy.[23]

While Mother has become potentially empowered by these changes, patriarchy has not been displaced. And, its beneficiaries (female as well as male) are displaced. Its norm of the male-defined and male-headed family, with heterosexual union at its core, is threatened by the changes that have occurred. Consequently, the desire is to contain and undo the reform. Part of the contemporary attack (or backlash) against the changes in women's options is found in the neutering of Mother evident in contemporary family law rhetoric.

The Legacy of the Neutered Mother

Consistent with the feminist commitment to gender neutrality, parenthood (like personhood) has become the preferred designation because it encompasses both father and Mother without the idealized distinctions associated with the terms. The desire to have only gender-neutral rules represented an important symbolic component of the legal feminists' battle to demonstrate that there were no relevant differences between the sexes and thus no basis for treating them unequally in law. Certain feminists even anticipated that the rise of these egalitarian expectations in language would have concrete effects on behavior patterns in marriage and divorce situations.

Consistent with the goal of gender neutrality, the legal system had to eliminate any preferences based on gendered concepts of Motherhood.[24] This had to be accomplished for important symbolic reasons, regardless of whether a gendered rule accurately conformed to either intuitive or empirical evidence as to which parent actually was most likely to systematically and continuously invest time and effort into child care.[25]

The law's reluctance to recognize and accommodate the uniqueness of Mothers' role in child rearing conforms to the popular gender-neutral fetish at the expense of considerations for mothers' material and psychological circumstances. Even if the *ultimate* goal is gender neutrality, the immediate imposition of rules embodying such neutrality within the family law context is disingenuous. The effect is detrimental to those who have constructed their lives around gendered roles. In this regard, reformed divorce laws impose the risk of significant emotional as well as economic costs for such Mothers. For example, shifting custody policy means the threat of potential loss of children for many mothers at divorce. To Mother, this risk is too great to contemplate. As a result, many mothers exchange a bargained-down property settlement to avoid a custody contest because they tend, in contrast to fathers, to consider custody a nonnegotiable issue.

Conclusion

As with all symbols about which there is contest, some positive components can be extracted from the negative and neutered construction of Mother. Certainly, the power of Mother is conceded in the very recognition that it must be contained. The strands for weaving a feminist legal theory of Mother may even hide in the discourse of patriarchy itself. The question is how to shift contemporary legal discourse, feminist and otherwise, in such a way as to empower Mother. Legal discourse, even in its feminist forms and even in the family law area, continues to be guided by the male normative and confined by concepts such as equality. For those who believe any recognition of differences between men and women will inevitably lead to the designation of an inferior status for women, this is good news. However, for those who believe that acceptance and accommodation of differences is necessary (whether they are viewed as essential and inherent or as socially constructed), the marginalization of Mother in law and in legal theory is cause for concern.[26]

One lesson feminists must learn from the neutered Mother is to be wary of equality. The dominant ideology of equality carries with it a powerful interpretive history which defines and limits the context for change. Liberal legal ideology is rarely compatible with "different" or "special" treatment. It assumes that the ideal must be equality of circumstances (or at least of opportunity). This legal context has made it difficult for reform to take into account the persistent, far-reaching, unequal and different circumstances that many women experience as a result of Motherhood and the dependency of children.

Equality ideology may resolve some of the problems revealed by focusing on the political and public interaction between men and women. However, this does not mean that it is the inevitable legal context for the entire endeavor of restructuring the legal position of women in the family or in their roles as Mother. Within the family, women are not only Wives or partners, but also Mothers—and it is this latter role, in particular, that continues to bear gendered consequences and expectations.

In an earlier work I argued for the concept of "gendered lives" in order to legitimate differences based on women's perspective. In a world in which gender is more than semantics, feminist legal theory *cannot* be gender-neutral, nor can it have as its goal equality, in the traditional, formal legal sense of that word.[27] Addressing the material consequences of women's gendered life experiences cannot be accomplished by a system that refuses to recognize gender as a relevant perspective, thereby imposing "neutral" conclusions on women's circumstances. Women's existences are constituted by a variety of experiences—many of them gendered. The potential for reproductive events such as pregnancy, breast feeding and abortion certainly have an impact on women's constructions of their gendered lives.[28]

This concept of gendered life is my attempt to create a vehicle for arguing that a concept of differences is necessary to remedy harms to women. There are totalizing social and legal constructions that do not conform to our experiences or our needs as mothers. The concept of a gendered experience is an attempt to simultaneously open a space for women's perspective in law, as distinct from men's, while providing the occasion for unity among women over some specifics of their lives. Attention to the force that an imposed (and in that sense, therefore, "common"), socially constructed concept of neutered motherhood exercises upon aspects of all mothers' lives presents an opportunity for participation by diverse women in resisting that imposition.

Women can coalesce across differences to work together on the project of defining for ourselves the implications and ramifications of this gendered aspect of our lives. Women have an interest in the institution of Mother—how it is understood and given social and legal significance. Therefore, women have a basis for cooperation and empathy across their differences. The experience of struggling with the unreality of the idea of a neutered Mother provides the potential for this cooperation and empathy.

The recognition that women now face an inappropriately neutered concept of Mother reaffirms that the struggle over content and meaning in law is inherently political and that perspectives count. Any focus on perspectives that asserts as a basic premise that there are significant differences between women and men which must be addressed in law is fraught with potential pitfalls. On the other hand, given that male-defined and controlled notions of law systematically disadvantage women in a variety of contexts, it seems essential that legal feminists affirm the need for law to respond to what women experience in their gendered lives. Adopting Mother's perspective will, of necessity, call into question the very core of patriarchy and force us to consider how the institution of Motherhood should be defined.

Notes

1. My arguments in this essay are fairly abstract. In earlier work I provided the details that inform the theoretical stance taken here. I see no need to repeat them, though when appropriate they are summarized in the text. For further information on the specifics of family law reform, see Martha Albertson Fineman, *The Illusion of Equality: The Rhetoric and Reality of Divorce Reform* (Chicago: University of Chicago Press, 1991).

2. This particular idea is based on statements in Murray Edelman, *Constructing the Political Spectacle* (Chicago: University of Chicago Press, 1988), p. 8., but I am deeply indebted to Murray's work in general for educating me about the significance and power of analyzing rhetoric and symbolism in political thought.

3. See e.g., Nancy Chodorow, *The Reproduction of Mothering* (Berkeley: University of California Press, 1978); Dorothy Dinnerstein, *The Mermaid and the Minotaur: Sexual Arrangements and Human Malaise* (New York: Harper and Row, 1977; 1976); Carole Klein, *Mothers and Sons* (Boston: Houghton Mifflin Co., 1984), pp. 121–140; David Levy, *Maternal Overprotection* (New York: Norton, 1966).

4. The concern with the burdens of motherhood was seen most vividly in the feminist literature of the 1970's. See e.g., Simone de Beauvoir, *The Second Sex* (New York: Vintage Books, 1974; 1952), p. 586, where the author extols the popular view among feminists of the day that too much Mother, that is too much self sacrifice, makes for inferior mothering. ("The woman who works . . . is the one who undergoes pregnancy most easily . . .; the woman who enjoys the richest individual life

will have the most to give her children and will demand the least from them; she who acquires in effort and struggle a sense of true human values will be best able to bring them up properly.") To de Beauvoir a "rich individual life" does not consist entirely or even primarily of mothering, and demanding the least from one's child is an ideal.

More recently there has been a trend in feminist writing not to totally disavow the role of mother but to simultaneously praise and reject it. Mother is seen as a desirable status at the same time that it is viewed as a threat to one's personal autonomy. For an illustration of this ambivalence see e.g., Nancy Rubin, *The Mother Mirror* (New York: Putnam, 1984), p. 263: ("Mother isn't forever. It's a limited altruistic and narcisstic endeavor, albeit one of the most important experiences a woman can have, ... Somehow we have to maintain a balance between our feelings of empathy, devotion, love, and identification with our children without losing the whole of ourselves to it.")

The idea of mother as a gendered concept seems particularly threatening, and feminists continue to contribute to the neutering of Mother. See Barbara K. Rothman, *Recreating Motherhood* (New York: Norton, 1989), p. 260: ("I would like us to get rid of our 'mommy' and 'daddy' language. We are individuals, in individual relationships with our children, and not the embodiment of gender-based parental roles.")

5. See William Blackstone, *Commentaries on the Laws of England* (Washington, D.C.: Washington Law Book Co., 1941).... James Schouler, *A Treatise on the Law of Domestic Relations* (Albany, N.Y.: M. Bender & Company, Inc., 1921; 1870), pp. 61, 233.

6. See Michael Grossberg, *Governing the Hearth* (Chapel Hill: University of North Carolina Press, 1985), pp. 244–247.

7. See, e.g., Michael Grossberg, "Who Gets the Child? Custody, Guardianship, and the Rise of a Judicial Patriarchy in Nineteenth-Century America," 9 *Feminist Studies* 235, 239, 246, 254–55 (1983).

8. For a general description of the development of state supervision of parental duties, see Grossberg, *supra* note 6, pp. 289–91.

9. For a discussion of the origins of the "tender years doctrine," see Jamil S. Zainaldin, "The Emergence of a Modern American Family Law: Child Custody, Adoption and the Courts," 1796–1851, 73 NW. U.L. REV. 1038, 1072–74 (1979).

10. Ibid. at 237–53. See also Robert J. Levy, "Custody Investigation in Divorce Cases," 1985 AM. B. FOUND. RES. J. 713.

11. This focus on conduct within the context of custody determinations endures in some jurisdictions today, even though there has been a retreat from fault-based divorce. Some of the states with express statutory grounds require that denial of custody on the grounds of conduct be based on a finding that the child is adversely affected by the behavior in question. For data supporting the proposition that women are treated more harshly than men in such instances, see Linda K. Girdner, "Child Custody Determination: Ideological Dimensions of a Social Problem," in *Redefining Social Problems*, eds. Edward Seidman and Julian Rappaport (New York: Plenum Press, 1986), pp. 165, 175–176.

12. Norma Basch, *In the Eyes of the Law* (Ithaca: Cornell University Press, 1982), pp. 179–180. See also Frances E. Olsen, "The Family and the Market: A Study of

Ideology and Legal Reform," 96 HARV. L. REV. 1974, 1530–35 (1983). It is also relevant to note that, at this time, there were few divorces, particularly among middle and upper-class couples, those most likely to be concerned with the content of family laws.

13. See Nancy Polikoff, "Custody and Visitation: Their Relationship to Establishing and Enforcing Support" (1989—on file with author).

14. See, e.g., the primary field research of Michael Raschick Wisconsin Non-Custodial Parents' Groups (May 16, 1985) (unpublished manuscript, on file with author). For a discussion of the various ideological strains within the men's movement, see Michael Shiffman, "The Men's Movement: An Exploratory Empirical Investigation" (paper prepared for presentation at the 80th Annual Meetings of the American Sociological Association, Washington, D.C.) August 26–30, pp. 3–4, (draft 2.1 on file with author).

15. See Jay Folberg, "Custody Overview," in *Joint Custody and Shared Parenting* (Washington, D.C.: Bureau of National Affairs, 1984), pp. 3–10; see also Letter from Neal Skrenes, Secretary, Custodial Parents' Rights Coalition, Inc., to Wisconsin Representative Jeannette Bell, Chair, Special Legislative Committee, Custody Arrangements (on file with the author).

16. For an analysis of the tender years doctrine under the equal protection clause, see *Ex Parte Divine*, 398 So. 2d 686 (Ala. 1981), which held that the doctrine constituted unconstitutional gender discrimination. Most state statutes now specifically provide that both parents are "equal," thus forbidding consideration of gender in custody cases. *See State Divorce Statutes Chart and Summary Sheet Introduction*, FAMILY LAW REPORTER (BNA) 5–6 (Mar. 25, 1986). For example, the relevant Wisconsin statute reads: "In making a custody determination, the court . . . shall not prefer one potential custodian over the other on the basis of the sex of the custodian." WIS. STAT. ANN. § 767.24(2) (West 1981).

17. See, e.g., William Everett, "Shared Parenthood in Divorce: The Parental Covenant and Custody Law," 2. J.L. & REL. 85, 85–89 (1984).

18. Several commentators extended this equality goal to its most extreme limits in their suggestions that custody disputes be resolved by a toss of the dice. See Robert Mnookin, "Child-Custody Adjudication: Judicial Functions in the Face of Indeterminacy," 39 LAW AND CONTEMPORARY PROBLEMS, 226 at 289–291 (1975) and, more recently, John Elster, "Solomonic Judgments: Against the Best Interest of the Child," 54 UNIVERSITY OF CHICAGO LAW REVIEW 1 (1987).

19. I develop these concepts of "private" and "public" families in Martha A. Fineman, "Intimacy Outside the Natural Family: The Limits of Privacy," 23 *University of Connecticut Law Review*, 955 (1991). See also, Martha A. Fineman, "Images of Mothers in Poverty Discourse," 1991 *Duke Law Journal* 955 (1991).

20. This view was explicitly and forcefully expressed recently in a speech by California Governor Pete Wilson. Speaking over a chorus of chants protesting his veto of a bill outlawing employment discrimination against homosexuals, the Governor made a plea for a return to the values more common in the 1950's—a time he characterized as when the family was cherished as a "sacred union born from romantic love" and "hard work was rewarded." Daniel M. Weintraub and Scott Harris,

"Gay Rights Protest Disrupts Wilson Speech," *Los Angeles Times*, Oct. 2, 1991; at 1A col.2.

21. A stark example of this was found in the speech that the governor of California made justifying his veto of an anti-discrimination employment bill designed to protect homosexuals. Governor Pete Wilson warned young people against a "headlong rush into mindless hedonism," and praised "the sacred union born from romantic love." Richard L. Berke, "Aids Battle Reverting to Us Against Them," *New York Times*, Oct. 6, 1991, at 4–1.

22. For a particularly potent example of the persistence of this idea it is illuminating to trace these assertions of pathology in single parent families over the twenty year period from the issuance of the Moynihan Report. See, Daniel P. Moynihan, "The Negro Family: The Case for National Action," in *The Moynihan Report and the Politics of Controversy* eds. Lee Rainwater and William L. Yancey (Cambridge, Mass.: M.I.T. Press, 1967), p. 41; *The Vanishing Family: Crisis in Black America*, (CBS Television broadcast, Jan. 25, 1986); see also, Daniel P. Moynihan, *Family and Nation* (San Diego: Harcourt Brace Joranovich, 1986) . . . For a critique of this rhetoric, see, Fineman, *supra*, note 19.

23. See. Fineman, *supra*, note 1.

24. For an extensive discussion of this point regarding the reform of divorce and property division laws, see Martha L. Fineman, "Implementing Equality: Ideology, Contradiction and Social Change; A Study of Rhetoric and Results in the Regulation of the Consequences of Divorce," 1983 WIS. L. REV. 789, 851, 852 (1983).

25. For an illustration of the gap between these reform efforts and reality in contemporary custody practice, see Girdner, *supra*, note 11, at 174–175.

26. This opportunity to define the significance of differences should be welcomed. The traditional legal discourse about motherhood exemplified and reinforced patriarchal values—it was the patriarch who initially defined Mother. Removal of the patriarchal definition is necessary, but the institution must then be redefined and the discredited discourse must be replaced with a non-patriarchal one.

27. Catherine A. MacKinnon, "Feminism, Marxism, Method and the State: An Agenda for Theory," 7 SIGNS 515 at 535–541 (1982) (discussing human sexuality as a gendered experience) and at 535 (discussing feminism as "the theory of women's point of view").

28. Martha A. Fineman, "Challenging Law, Establishing Differences: The Future of Feminism Legal Scholarship," 42 FLA, L,REV. 25, 1991.

8

Museums, Zoos, and Ecology: Animal Displays on Display

Michael Lipsky

Introduction

When we go to a zoo or a museum of natural history we expose ourselves to a political institution that intends to instruct and entertain us. It does not matter that *our* intentions may be to do something with the family or pass the time between conference sessions. The zoo and museum are produced and sustained by political processes. Moreover, they currently present themselves as playing political roles appropriate to contemporary circumstances. Zoos and museums propose to prepare citizens to understand the full meaning of ecological interdependence and to appreciate the need for conservation in the coming decades. They lay claim to influencing the public on such issues as species extirpation, deforestation, and global warming.

In this essay I will suggest a framework for analyzing zoos and museums as subsets of a larger group of public activities whose political place and character tend to be neglected. These are public activities that provide facilities intended to be used by masses of people on a voluntary basis. Museums, zoos, but also war memorials, parks, beaches, wildlife preserves and other "outdoor resources" may be valued by citizens but still tend to be taken for granted when it comes to the processes which produce them and the roles in society that they play. Perhaps these institutions are taken for granted because they provide "services" on a collective rather than individualized basis. Perhaps it is because they are associated with diversion and leisure. Perhaps it is because they are often not directly connected in the public mind with government.

Whatever the reason, I will explore in this essay the unexamined political roles of two of these institutions—zoos and museums of natural history.[1] I will proceed, first, by treating these as service providers. Second, addressing aspects of zoos and museums that are unique to these institutions, I will examine their implicit communications about the relationship of humans and nature.

Museums and Zoos: Definition and Purposes

Museums and zoos may be defined as institutions that collect, conserve and display objects for public edification and enjoyment. A great deal of discussion has taken place within the museum industry (which arguably encompasses zoos) concerning a proper definition of the institution. A definition produced in 1974 by the International Council of Museums defined museums' purposes as conserving, researching, communicating and exhibiting, and added, notably, that museums were "open to the public" and, superfluously, that they were "permanent institutions in the service of society and its development."[2]

The balance between museum purposes is currently in flux. Education and the presentation of exhibits, and entertainment—indeed, one might say the selling of zoos and museums—are now ascendant objectives over the older purposes of research and conservation.[3] Museums today are very conscious of marketing strategies. This is perhaps a predictable development among non-profit and governmental institutions which need to justify themselves to financial supporters but lack a "bottom line" to demonstrate their worth.[4] It also reflects a period in which fees for services are an increasingly important component of the institutions' budgets, and the fact, to be discussed shortly, that they are activities for which charging fees is entirely feasible.

Museum and Zoos as Public Institutions

Museums and zoos not only cater to the public; they are often supported by public funds, indirectly subsidized by favorable tax treatment of contributions to nonprofit organizations, and governed in ways intended to secure the public interest. Most European museums had their origins in private collections, while most American zoos and museums were public institutions from the start. But in both cases, in their earlier histories museums were governed by elites, sponsored by rich people performing their civic duties, and catered to a bourgeois clientele.[5] Today these institutions have changed a great deal. They may still be governed by elites, but museums and zoos today promote outreach to a broader clientele; they are concerned as never before with school children and racial and ethnic minorities. Many zoos and museums receive subventions from city or county budgets, or are run outright by local public agencies. In addition to commitments to the Smithsonian Institution, there is today also the beginning of federal support for museum activities.[6]

The governance of museums and zoos can take several forms: they can be direct activities of government, activities of government corporations or authorities established for special purposes, or activities of non-profit corporations established privately or under the aegis of public authorities. Each form implies different forms of accountability: bureaucratic accountability in the case of government agencies; more remote public accountability in the case of special government corporations; accountability to privately appointed boards of directors with fiduciary and programmatic responsibilities in the case of non-profit corporations. The differences in accountability stemming from governmental or non-profit status are less important than the fact that, in general, governance of zoos and museums is guided by responsibility to a set of public objectives.

We should not be distracted from thinking about zoos and museums as public institutions because some of them are formally non-profit corporations. For one thing, non-profit corporations enjoy a variety of advantages that arguably render them government-sponsored activities, including treatment of contributions as tax deductible and land and buildings as tax exempt. Furthermore, to the extent public funds play an important part in the budgets of these institutions, this is likely to bring them more into line with public priorities.[7] Moreover, the formal governing structure of an institution hardly tells the most important part of the story. Organizations with different governing structures but similar tasks, clients and technologies often come to resemble one another. Thus, service delivery patterns may not be importantly affected by organizations' status as non-profit or government entities.[8]

Collections of animals and artifacts offered to the public as businesses perhaps belong in a different category. Disneyland, Seaworld and other such businesses share much in common with zoos and museums and will undoubtedly share even more in the future as public and nonprofit institutions adopt lessons in marketing from their for-profit counterparts. Nonetheless, these businesses belong in a separate category than zoos and museums because they ultimately are judged by their profitability. By contrast, zoos and museums are not judged primarily by how much money they make. And because profitability is not their primary objective, zoos and museums are recipients of funds from a variety of sources, including charitable contributions and public subsidies as well as fees and, controversially, income from quasi-commercial activities such as bookshop sales and space rental.

To summarize, museums and zoos may be considered public institutions because they are supported by public funds and implicit subsidies, and governed in ways designed to realize public purposes. Before moving to analyze the policies that are pursued by these institutions, however, I must mention two other characteristics of museums and zoos that distinguish them from other public institutions and provide something of a guide for assessing them. First, they are institutions whose benefits can be shared without using up the benefits, and to which access can plausibly be restricted. In the language of economists, they are toll goods. Second, they are transformative.

Museums and Zoos as Toll Goods. Museums and zoos share with transit systems and libraries qualities of certain public goods that critically affect their delivery of public policies. First, (up to a point) these public services can be consumed by one user without diminishing the ability of other users to enjoy them. In contrast, job training programs, public universities with limited places for students, and breadlines differ from museums and zoos because admission of one individual to the institution or program denies admission to someone else. Consequently, museums and zoos as public institutions are free from problems associated with *having* to ration scarce resources.[9]

Instructively, as crowds become a problem the policies of zoos and museums begin to resemble those of public services in which rationing has to take place. Thus, free hours may be restricted, lotteries and additional fees may be adopted for special attractions, and so forth. Also, patrons may be divided according to their willingness to pay. Contributors may be rewarded with invitations to attend members' nights and their visits may be enhanced by special tours.

Second, potential users may be excluded from the service. Unlike a public beach, clean air, and the economists' fabled lighthouse, museums and zoos do not in theory require public funding or have to attend to other free rider problems. They *can* restrict access to users who choose not to pay. They may still enjoy public subsidies in order to provide and sustain the activity, or to help keep fees down. But the public subsidies are not related to the institution's inability to implement a fee structure.

What goods are and are not toll goods is a political matter of considerable importance. It may appear that beaches and parks are public goods from which free riders cannot reasonably be excluded. But access to beaches and parks, via roads and parking facilities, can be restricted, thereby turning otherwise public goods into toll goods. Kruger National Park in South Africa, the third largest game park on the continent, has effectively been turned into a toll good by fencing the entire domain, an area larger than Israel.

The ability to implement a fee structure makes zoos and museums more vulnerable to claims that they should be supported by user fees than services such as public radio, from which it is not technically feasible to exclude the free rider. In an era of declining public resources, this weakens the claims of toll good institutions to public support. Relatedly, dependence on fees helps to explain the ascendance of entertainment as an institutional objective.[10]

Museums and Zoos are Transformative. Zoos and museums, among other things, aspire to be transformative. They intend to influence or change their patrons in some way. Like schools and many social services, but unlike transportation systems and public beaches, museums and zoos expect that they will interact with patrons so that patrons will be affected in some way by their visits.[11] In other public institutions—public transportation, for example—patrons' experiences matter primarily because their utilization of the service will be affected by their experiences. In zoos and museums, as well as schools and welfare agencies, for that matter, the rationing effect of patrons' experiences also are germane. But in addition, how they are affected by the institutions is important in its own right.

Museums and Zoos in Service Delivery

With respect to their effects on individuals, public institutions may be analyzed on three dimensions. One is the accessibility of the institution, which ultimately determines people's exposure to the policy of the institution. A second is the material impact of the institution. This refers to what people receive from the institution that directly affects their well-being. A third is the symbolic impact. Here I refer to the contributions of institutions in shaping the way people come to fix and attribute meaning to objects and events, to themselves, and to their relationship to the world.[12]

The first dimension, accessibility, is a category common to all public institutions and invariably provides a means to assess them. The other two dimensions, however, vary in importance. Traffic citations and motor vehicle registration renewal policies may have real but ultimately trivial symbolic implications with respect to people's conceptions of themselves as citizens. Analyses of these policies would likely be most useful if they focused on whether services were fair, efficient, and accountable. Institutions such as schools and courts, which dispense rewards and sanctions and make judgments about childrens' behavior and potential, clearly must be assessed on both material and symbolic grounds.

Some public activities, however, are most fruitfully understood by focusing primarily on the symbolic. These are activities with only modest claims to provide services to individuals, but which have high potential to excite the imagination and treat people as part of collectivities. This is surely the case with public buildings,[13] and, less clearly, with public institutions such as zoos, museums and parks, which do not provide services person to person.

In this essay I will concentrate on the symbolic effects of museums and zoos in the contemporary climate of ecological concern. I will also treat issues of accessibility, which bear relationship to the institutions' symbolic role. Although zoo and museum personnel are vitally interested in their cognitive impact, spending considerable effort to discover who their patrons are and what they actually learn from visits, this aspect of these organizations' operations will not concern me here.

Rationing and Institutional Openness

Zoos and museums are open to the public, but they can and do vary in their openness over time, among each other, and with respect to different constituencies. Museums historically were often criticized for being inaccessible to lower class patronage. At one time working people were able to visit the museums in London only if they were vouched for by a member of the gentry.[14] In 1891, 80,000 workers in New York City petitioned to obtain admission to the Metropolitan Museum of Art on Sunday, so they could attend when they were not obliged to work.[15] Today one can still rate the accessibility of these public institutions by their degree of openness.

The extent to which museums and zoos are fully inclusive of all citizens is a matter of deep concern to the public sector. During the 1960s and 1970s museums were heavily criticized for their indifference to the patronage of blacks and other minority groups. They were criticized as well for mounting exhibits that were insensitive to indigenous cultures. The visitor can see this conflict played out in the American Museum of Natural History's magnificent Man in Africa hall, where treasures of traditional cultures are presented according to their anthropological uses—religion, agriculture, war, ceremony, and so forth. At one entrance to the exhibit, presented apparently as an afterthought, is a montage, now shabby, of photographs of contemporary, urban Africa. In an alcove apart from the main exhibit, another sequence presents artifacts of slavery and the middle passage. These components, apparently appended to the main exhibit, give the appearance of having been responses to social pressures rather than having been organic parts of the primary exhibit.

Concern about issues of outreach is illustrated in the self-reflective document developed by the museum profession to provide a guide and vision for the future. "Museums for a New Century" includes, as one of its sixteen recommendations, the need to "address the underrepresentation of minorities," to "reflect cultural diversity and equal opportunity."[16] Many museums today reflect sensitivity to the issue of inclusion by soliciting the participation of indigenous South Sea Islanders, Maori, Australian Aboriginals and Native Americans in the planning of exhibits on their cultures.

Inclusiveness and openness are not the only factors in rationing service. Another is cost. Many museums originated as commercial exhibitions whose proprietors hoped to profit. In recent years, of course, admission to public museums and zoos has been free or at only nominal charges, with the bulk of expenses paid primarily out of public and private subventions. Increasingly, it would seem, admission fees are the norm, and they are sometimes quite substantial, particularly among new institutions that have no history of free admission to rile long-time users who would object to the change. High admission charges are particularly noteworthy among aquariums, which have no history of free or only nominal admission fees, are sometimes built with funds from bond issues and thus must have a high fee structure to support the debt, and are particularly popular among tourists who may be less sensitive to price than local residents.[17]

These two aspects of rationing interact. The more an institution is dependent on fees, the more it will be driven to offer generous admission hours to reach the optimal balance between income and costs. Those more dependent on other sources of revenue will be freer to set their hours independent of the effects on attendance. The latter are also more free to choose among objectives, such as conservation and research, that compete with consumer satisfaction.

Museums and zoos have tried to cushion public resentment against high fees. They offer free days, or evenings, to accommodate those who may object, for whatever reason, to fees. They discount admission charges to consumer groups deemed worthy or lacking in funds. Perhaps the classiest fee policy has been that of the American Museum of Natural History, which posted a recommended fee schedule along with a notice informing patrons: you may pay any amount, but you must pay something.

Still another dimension of rationing is accessibility. The location of a facility is critical to its availability to all segments of the population. The Central Park Zoo, in the middle of Manhattan, has an ideal location in terms of general accessibility, although it is so small by contemporary standards that in its recent reconstruction zoo officials had to reduce radically the number of animals on display in order to conform to minimum display standards. The Bronx Zoo in New York has the advantage of being accessible by public transport as well as private auto.

These public institutions tend to stay fixed while cities ebb and flow around them. The American Museum of Natural History in New York was built on swampy land in the outer reaches of the city when construction was started in 1874.[18] Today it sits in the middle of a fully developed Manhattan. If today the Museum is perceived as located in the heart of the upper middle class West Side, it should be remembered that a generation ago its environs were the setting for the gang wars of "West Side Story." Yesterday the National Zoo in Washington was located in the countryside of upper Connecticut Avenue; today the Metro brings it close to all residents of the city.

In terms of access museums and zoos are not separable from the transportation systems to which they are tied. The availability of inexpensive public transportation, parking, and road networks mediate the availability of the institution to broad groups of clients. As decisions to establish and then locate new facilities, or to relocate existing institutions get made on the basis of their potential contribution to development, they may be judged on how well they meet public needs for accessibility. But ongoing decisions about public transportation will determine their accessibility in the future.

In dealing with the access question museums and zoos have not been confined to their primary location. Through outreach programs they have loaned collections to exhibitors outside the museum world—such as the lobbies of private office buildings. They go into schools, establish museum "satellites," and take their collections on the road.

Symbolic Roles

Public institutions affect the way people locate their place in the society and understand their relations to others, and to societal institutions. To analyze the symbolic roles of public institutions we must try to clarify the postures of the institutions and reflect on the ways in which people extract meaning from them. I mean to suggest that an institution may be presumed to present itself in a particular way, and that that posture may be perceived and comes to have meaning for those who attend the institution. But the institution is not necessarily explicit about its meaning, nor does it interact with people to explain itself or clarify ambiguities. Even if institutions do articulate their purposes and objectives for clients, a symbolic analysis would regard as problematic what the institutions may take for granted.

I am deliberately ignoring the extent to which the potential audiences of symbolic messages are disposed to be subject to their content. After all, the crowds at the zoo or museum on any given day will include a fair proportion of children and their harried parents, teenagers, couples looking for a dry refuge on neutral territory, and others who are indifferent to the exhibits and the institutional experience. Thus like other analysts of symbolic political messages, I am willing to hazard the meaning and character of the symbolic messages without being able to specify precisely who is affected and with what degree of intensity.

Postures

The importance of understanding the postures of public institutions will be familiar to observers of public institutions to which such analyses have previously been applied. Institutions of social control, such as schools and courts, organize their settings to reinforce authority. The high bench of the courtroom, the flag, judicial robes (and in some courts ceremonial wigs), the witness box, the separation of observers from those with courtroom roles all reinforce the authority of the court and convey its noble and solemn purposes. Modern courthouses are particularly interesting in the way they reproduce traditional courtroom settings even while using modern materials and new design conventions. Schools reinforce authority through the arrangement of desks and chairs, institutional colors, bells, and the interchangeability of learning materials. These are the visible signs of schools as teaching factories where the workers are standardized and replaceable. It is instructive that even today, vivid colors and informal seating arrangements signify non-traditional education.

The architecture of museums of course varies greatly from one institution to another, but some generalizations still may be made. The great older museums were magnificent Victorian shrines to the collections. With their high ceilings and soaring columns they suggest for that imperial time the power of their custodians and sponsors, the dominance of humans over nature. (Indeed, the European museum seems based on the imperial desire to display artifacts of conquest and colonization.)

As in most public buildings, public areas may be magnificent while secondary space and work areas are more banal. But on the whole, buildings of natural history were temples to the natural order. This idea seems less farfetched when one realizes that the national parks, founded in the second half of the 19th century, were consecrated to similar purposes by their champions.

If the history of the neon CITGO gasoline sign that blinks as a historic landmark in Boston's Kenmore Square is at all instructive, the ugliest and most brutal constructions can be regarded as charming if given enough time to become familiar over generations. As the novelist John Updike recently put it: "Time deposits upon even the satanic mills of Lowell a nostalgic patina."[19] So it is with old museums and zoos. Their architecture, imposing and speaking of authority in the early days, becomes overlaid with meanings associated more with the charms of days gone by. Particularly if restored or redecorated according to modern sensibilities, the old buildings begin to convey continuity, stability, and links with previous generations of visitors more than the imposing grandeur of the original presentation.

Some old zoo buildings can come to have a similar antiquarian appeal. Early zoo architecture attempted to heighten the exotic aspects of presenting animals from afar by exploiting architectural elements of human cultures related to the animals' habitats (Islamic architecture for North African animals, for example).[20] Most of these buildings are now obsolete. Although entirely inadequate for keeping animals according to modern standards, more modern but still strictly functional zoo architecture sometimes features whimsical murals, ironwork and stonework that add charm to the structures when zoo buildings are recycled as gift shops and restaurants. Amidst the spartan old zoo architecture, these motifs perhaps suggest today that in zoos at least the people were supposed to have fun.

Time is often unkind to large public buildings, no less to zoos and museums. The fading, chipping and peeling that affects all structures over the years lends to public buildings a tendency to look seedy. In the perpetual fiscal crises of these public institutions, maintenance often is neglected and patchwork repair becomes the normal practice rather than the exception. A good measure of this can usually be found in the public toilets, where over the years multiple holes have been punched in walls and poorly replastered to repair plumbing, and once magnificent tiles have been torn out and replaced with concrete. The effect left by the neglect of maintenance is to devalue the institution, to convey better than words that the institution and its patrons once were highly esteemed, but now are of little account.

Cost saving activities and piecemeal redesigns also contradict the messages of respect for the visitor that were perhaps conveyed by the original buildings. Through renovations ceilings have been lowered, room partitions and other developments to improve lighting, save heat, provide storage space and change circulation have been erected which destroy the buildings' integrity. These alterations literally break up messages of respect for the enterprise and its patrons which once prevailed.

We may also consider the symbolic meaning of the literal messages that accompany exhibits, reflecting the primacy of communication to the institutions' administrators. Is the signage at the eye level of an average adult? Of a child? Is it well-lighted? Is it readable from a distance or only close-up? These physical qualities of signs demonstrate degrees of concern for the audience.

Another critical aspect of signage is the language level of explanatory materials. With visitors of all ages, signage exclusively for adults or children will neglect the other constituency. More thoughtful exhibits combine two or more degrees of language levels into their signs so that children and casually interested adults may gain information at an elementary level, while more complex information is conveyed elsewhere for those with greater interest in the material.

The neglect of the visitor is surely signalled by the failure of most zoos and museums to post explanatory materials in foreign languages. Although zoos in particular are havens for families of non-native speakers, with rare exceptions they neither offer materials in native minority languages (such as Spanish in the United States) or in the language of foreign visitors (such as, in the United States, Japanese). Monolingual policies not only deny full access to non-native speakers; they also convey to *native* speakers that the institutions do not seek to be fully accessible to all visitors.

Perplexing signals are given off by exhibit spaces without exhibits. Zoo and museum visitors often encounter exhibit spaces which are empty or darkened, without explanation. The visitor is led to feel as if he or she has come early to a party and the hosts have not yet picked up around the house.

Almost as dispiriting are such spaces accompanied by cryptic messages such as "exhibit discontinued," or "closed for repair," particularly if there are more than one or two such signs. Like patchwork physical repairs, these messages also convey that the institution is being neglected.

There are alternatives. Explanations of where the animals have gone, why they have been removed and how the zoo plans to reconstruct the site has the effect of including the visitor in the plans of the zoo. The animals may be on loan for breeding purposes or removed because they have been fighting. The zoo may be building a new aviary and the birds formerly exhibited do not fit into their plans. Such signs have the effect of anticipating the visitors' disappointment and reflecting the respect shown to people who are considered to be interested in and capable of understanding the zoo as an institution.

Informative signs convey respect for the visitor but also draw attention to the zoo as an institution, and thus break the illusion of contained wildness that zoo administrators often seek to cultivate. It is not that zoo administrators believe they can persuade visitors that they are truly in the jungle. But they do often seem to take actions as if the zoo can be presented as a seamless *presentation* of nature, self-contained and regenerating, like nature itself. As I will argue, such a message is intrinsically paradoxical, cannot be fully realized, and ultimately conflicts with zoos' teaching potential.

Zoos and museums have two sorts of messages for their patrons. One, which we have just discussed, reflects the institutions' regard for their consumers. The extent to which they are welcomed, respected, controlled and directed is conveyed as much by the setting as by specific injunctions in these matters. A second concerns the specific objectives of zoos and museums in communicating information in the broadest sense about their collections.

Information

Museums and zoos not only collect, clarify and conserve—they present and exhibit as well. Moreover, they do so with particular educational objectives in mind. The early museums may have been hodge-podges of curios, specimens and fakes, but museums displaying natural artifacts soon strove to make their collections scientifically sound—as much for study as for public education and display. Similarly, menageries went from displaying animals in random fashion to grouping them according to classification or geographic logic.

Just as curators of a previous era wanted to classify and catalog to convey information according to prevailing scientific canons, curators today want to do the same according to contemporary agendas for zoos and museums. This means, among other things, presenting ecological perspectives on natural phenomena and preparing patrons to be ecologically minded in their public and private actions. Zoos and museums aspire not only to provide information, but also to influence consciousness. Indeed, they see themselves at the forefront of ecological consciousness-raising.

To explore the ways in which museums and zoos as institutions mobilize social values, let us consider for each institution three kinds of exhibits that typify the presentational style of each. They are described below, roughly in the order in which they were historically developed.

A first exhibition style for museums is the display of specimens in vertical and horizontal cases. The typical exhibit consists of bird skins, mounted insects or sea shells arranged according to their scientific classification. In a modern variant the animals are at least stuffed so that the exhibit is not entirely morbid.

A second exhibit style is that acme of taxidermy, dioramas of mounted animals displayed in simulated natural settings, complete with accurate painted backgrounds to complement the representative foregrounds. At the turn of the century, in a world before color photography, the best of these exhibits must have been sensational.[21]

A third type of museum exhibit is the "explainer." Combining specimens with charts and diagrams, these exhibits show how things work. They lead the viewer through a particular lesson—soil hydrology, asexual reproduction, functional adaptation in fish—with specific learning objectives. These are the kinds of exhibits from which "you could take good notes." The flowering of the explainer exhibits may be understood in historical terms, developing in concert with mass education but before the full development of television as we now know it. Today the role of the museum as teacher is under threat. Documentary nature films are widely available on television and for school use. The museums' collections no longer give the institutions the special role they played when attractive and informative materials were less available.

The zoo presentation styles I want to analyze are as follows. First is the bare, barred cages representative of old zoo architecture. These typically house individual creatures who sometimes have access to mates or other animals through gates that open into adjacent pens. These cages are of the simplest construction: iron bars and cement floors. A perch or sleeping shelf (to get the animals off the ground) are the amenities. In cold climates the cages are organized around the periphery of aromatic animal "houses" (the cat house, the elephant house, etc.), with access to outdoor extension cages for warm weather use. These are the earliest of zoo animal accommodations.

A second style of animal presentation is the simulation of natural settings. Bears and seals are displayed in simulated pools and rocky outcroppings, for example. Big cats will have simulated "dens." The exhibit may be sunken, with the sheer walls substituting for bars to keep the animals confined. Monkeys will be isolated on an artificial island where they can scamper and scratch over rocks and dead tree limbs. Water birds will be shown in a water course rather than bird by isolated bird, which is more typical of the earlier mode of presentation.

Third, modern zoos have begun to show animals in capacious enclosures in which there appears to be enough space for them to move about spontaneously, rather than keep to the routines required by greater confinement. For gregarious animals, such as zebras, truly large areas allow them to sort themselves out according to their social as well as physical needs. For the human visitor these settings offer an illusion not available in any other zoo presentation: the animals can appear to hide. They are like trout ponds. The angler knows the fish are there in great number, but the impenetrable surface of the water hides the manipulation of nature.

Human visitors may have to pass through such enclosures rather than stand outside looking in. This is the case with modern aviaries, and with large facilities such as Northwest Trek in Washington State, where the visitor has to ride a monorail to see the animals. At Tidbinbilla, in the Australian Capital Territory, visitors enter the enclosures to search out the kangaroos (easy to find) and the koalas (harder to find).

Of the many zoos and museums I have visited recently virtually all of these six forms of presentation may be found at the same time, although many modern museums have fully retired their systematic collections, and in most urban zoos space constraints restrict their ability to build natural enclosures.[22]

Messages of Museums

Increasingly, museums have been giving over the space occupied by their systematic collections and their less elegant dioramas in favor of exhibits that explain natural processes. In doing so they may be maximizing their potential for teaching subject matter, and surely have fitted themselves more effectively into school curricula. But when they have done so it has been at the expense of another, less didactic role.

Explainer exhibits can be very successful in their own terms, but they have liabilities as well. They are not open to the visitor who might be inclined to attach a wide range of meanings. They are, instead, preemptive.[23] They dictate to visitors the subject and the content of what should be learned. As such they appeal not to those aspects of the "marvelously sensitive" human mind that "readily reflect[s] a wide range of perceptions and beliefs, even when they are logically incompatible," as Murray Edelman has put it in a somewhat similar context. Instead they appeal to the duller aspect of human cognition that seems to require answers and gravitates toward condensation symbols that reduce complexity to manageable proportions.[24] In the case of museums, this means a reduction into lessons to be learned. "When is an exhibit not an exhibit?" queries a museum professional who seems to share this viewpoint. He answers: "when it is a booklet pasted on the walls of a museum."[25]

Explainer exhibits often seem to bear little relationship to the museum's other functions of collecting and preserving; when they do they can redeem themselves from the appearance that the explainer exhibits are simply three dimensional "wallboards." A case in point is the memorable display of the massive leg bones of the largest bird that ever lived (now extinct) in the American Museum of Natural History's exhibit on bird morphology. Pinned to one of the enormous bones is the analogous bone from the leg of a tiny hummingbird. The presentation of this dramatic contrast draws attention to the museum as a human activity which collects and preserves specimens for uses such as this.

In contrast to the didactic exhibits, the older exhibition forms are more open. They are better at encouraging the imagination. Moreover they can present themselves without words or text and therefore can appeal to all ages (although there are always labels or text for people who want more information). Mounted specimens and wildlife dioramas are never age-specific by virtue of the vocabulary or the complexity of the concept.

Museum professionals are not unconcerned with effective communication and educational theory. Display designers, for example, are instructed to promote learning and retention by asking questions based on materials presented in the texts of exhibits, rather than simply providing the information. This sort of advice takes for granted that there are learning objectives toward which the exhibits aspire. Although they are designed to be scientifically accurate the older exhibition forms, by contrast, have only the most diffuse goals for viewers. The natural history diorama and even the specimen displays are open, perhaps even indifferent to visitors' objectives.

At the same time, they stimulate certain questions. The systematic specimen collections invite contemplation of similarity and order in nature, and of the origins of variation among similar species. If a visitor has a rudimentary understanding of natural history, he or she will here be able to contemplate the functions played by variations in structural forms (the beaks of birds, the coloration of insects). The dioramas, staged as they may be, draw the viewer into contemplation of the relationship of animals to their surroundings, and to the variety of environments that make up the natural world.

Here, I would maintain, is where museums of natural history play their most important role: engendering curiosity, generating awe in the contemplation of the natural world. The visitor can learn from books and television how natural processes "work." But museums are unusually suitable for staging confrontations between visitors and artifacts of nature, creating a context in which visitors can be led to wonder.

Kenneth Hudson, who has written extensively about museums, reflects this perspective when he quotes approvingly the remarks of Marshall McLuhan at a seminar sponsored by the Museum of the City of New York. McLuhan drew attention to the design of Montreal's Expo 67. It had no story line, he explained, but was instead "just a mosaic of discontinuous items in which people took an immense satisfaction precisely because they weren't being told anything about the overall pattern or shape of it, but they were free to discover and involve themselves in the total overall thing."[26]

What some educators say about childrens' experiences in museums might well be applied to all visitors. "Young children," according to some specialists, "should be allowed to have direct encounters with natural objects. . . . No adult interpretations should interfere with the important emotional responses of a child of seeing the exhibits placed in the room for his [sic] enjoyment."[27]

The evocation of such regard identifies the special role of museums in the ecology movement. Museums have always symbolized the world beyond the city limits. As those limits are extended farther and farther out from the center, museums can inspire visitors to reflection, can validate their instincts that it is important to understand and preserve natural settings and their inhabitants. Urban populations have several sources to learn how the world works, but only a few places which can inspire uninstructed people to care.

There is another and mostly unintended role that museums' older styles of exhibition play in forging ecological consciousness: they draw attention to humans' involvement with and efforts to understand and command the natural world. The ranks of bird skins, the butterfly collection, the mammals of the region to the thoughtful visitor raise questions about how and why these specimens were sought out, collected and killed, mounted and preserved, displayed. "Someone killed these birds and bugs and put them here" is one of the messages the visitor takes away. What is the purpose of such an activity? Is such killing ethical? If it seems unethical now, was there a time when it was considered ethical? What does this say about ethics and nature?

The dioramas raise similar questions. Someone went to this location and shot these magnificent creatures. Why did he do it? Are such things still being done? How do the animals come to look so life-like?

The dioramas are not representations of nature so much as uncanny stagings of natural settings. Who has visited one of these exhibits and not sought to discover where the line was between the representative foreground and the painted background? Like the theater, the museum asks the visitor to accept the story behind the proscenium, but part of the enchantment is the knowledge that it is real people who are putting on the play.

Sometimes museums draw attention to themselves as collectors and conservers in ways that enhance their role in nature study. The American Museum of Natural History has done this in recent years with exhibits organized around the adventures of particular explorers and naturalists, and the paintings of the Museum's most famous muralist. The recent exhibition on the LaBrea tarpits also exploited popular interest in the collection of artifacts rather than focusing on bones alone.

The twin roles of the museums as trigger to the imagination, and as human activity, can be illustrated by a visit to the Discovery Room of the new museum in Brisbane, Australia. The Discovery Room, incidentally, is designated for children, as if only children can make discoveries. The room is lined with cases representing all the Queensland vertibrates, grouped scientifically and stuffed in natural poses. In the center of the room are artifacts chosen apparently in order to provoke the imagination. The most memorable is the mummified remains of a goanna, a large lizard, and an echidna. The goanna and echidna had died together when the goanna could neither swallow the echidna nor expel it because the spines stuck in its throat. The death throes of these two animals could be easily imagined.

One of the artifacts on display during a recent visit was a grooved rock. A label explained that people often bring artifacts to the museum for identification; the rock had been brought in by someone who thought it might be a sharpening stone and wanted an expert opinion. However, museum personnel had tested the rock and had discovered it was too soft for such use. The label concluded: "what do you think the rock was used for? We don't have any idea!"

Messages of Zoos

The typical zoo is inherently more open and less didactic than the modern museum. It presents its specimens straightforwardly. What information is provided is usually restricted to common and Latin names, the animal's range, and perhaps whether it is endangered in the wild. The zoo is also typically less physically controlling than the museum. Museum exhibits are often accessed room by room and floor by floor, whereas the zoo invites visitors even more than the museum to make their own itinerary. A visit to the zoo is inherently an outing; the climate of the visit is beyond the control of zoo officials.

The experience of contemplating the natural order is encouraged for visitors, of course, primarily by the animals themselves. Their individual movements and interactions with one another appear to provide a chance to contemplate what the animals are like in the wild. But captive animals are intrinsically paradoxical. They have qualities that can be observed by the visitor, but whether the qualities are natural to them or conditioned by being captive and on display cannot be known. To start with, most wild animals would flee or hide from humans, while zoo animals cannot escape and often become inured to being objects of human attention. This is clearly a profoundly unnatural state of affairs, although zoos almost always ignore this aspect of animal display. The animals that are least paradoxical are those that are nocturnal or sleep a lot, since they appear in zoos to behave much as they would in the wild. Nocturnal houses, instructively, give the illusion of minimal behavioral distortions resulting from captivity.

Perceptions of zoos, like other institutions, change as our understanding of the world changes. Some zoos of the past may have enjoyed popular support as imperial institutions bringing the wonders of the empire home. Societies supporting such zoos unquestioningly approved of collecting specimens from around the world for popular edification. Zoos today have become more humane through advancements in nutrition and animal medicine, and by abandoning when practical their cell-like architecture in favor of more naturalistic settings. They also recognize the importance of respecting and somehow integrating into their displays the social needs of gregarious animals. Moreover, they have carved out for themselves a separate role in species preservation, cooperating with each other to breed genetically diverse populations of endangered species while wild populations are threatened and in decline.

Nonetheless, the modern zoo has come to occupy an ambiguous moral position in today's world. While the zoo has become more "humane" in its handling of animals, scientific and moral perspectives have changed radically. Space, climate and other resource limitations prevent modern zoos from ever keeping animals in fully natural settings. Most zoos are at best in transition to a greater naturalism which still falls far short of the natural environment. And in many zoos, progressive philosophies for keeping wild animals aside, the old bleak cages are still much in evidence. There are also inherent limitations to the pursuit of naturalism. Excessive movement toward natural settings at some point interferes with the accessibility of the animals to visitors. There is a point beyond which zoos will not want to go if research and naturalistic settings require radical restriction of visitors' access to the animals.

But the challenge to zoos is not just that their settings are often barren. Zoos are also criticized as cruel simply because they incarcerate animals for display purposes. They are also charged with "bestializing" the zoo visitor, who comes to accept as proper the capture and display of animals. This criticism arises not because zoos are doing anything differently. If anything, they are getting better at keeping animals in decent environments. Rather, it arises because philosophic perspectives on interactions of humans and animals are changing radically, and are increasingly becoming matters of public concern.

The morally ambiguous position of zoos undoubtedly is a matter of concern and discomfort to zoo officials, but it actually represents a great opportunity. Like some aspects of the museum, the zoo inevitably presents itself in ways that draw attention to the perspective and role of humans in the order of the zoo, and, by extension, in the natural order.

Zoos have keepers. They clean cages. They sweep up after their charges. They groom the animals' environments. Order and cleanliness depend upon visible keepers. The animals depend upon keepers to get food, and zoos exploit the feeding of the animals to entertain visitors, as animals are most lively when they are hungry or consuming food. Of course the humans who feed the animals are only the keepers who are visible to the public.

The exhibits also convey messages about the history of the relationship between people and the natural order. The sterile cages of the older zoos reflect what according to today's standards might seem cruelty to animals. If anything, the remnants of the old zoos clearly indicate that the human visitor, not the animal, is the client of the zoo keepers. Consider the gorilla, alone in a cage with his thoughts, slumped on a huge scale which announces his weight for the edification of his watchers. Or the murals of jungle scenes on the walls of zoo houses, at one time intended to provide atmosphere for the crowds, but which, now in disrepair, mock the inhabitants of the cages. Certainly the old zoo remnants convey indifference to all but the animals' minimal food and shelter requirements. In these cages animals, particularly the large carnivores, are from a contemporary perspective most evidently "specimens."

One step up from the barren cages stage of zoo architecture are attempts to make the same cages interesting to animals and viewers alike. The monkey bars and ropes that are provided to engage the primates (and to keep the monkeys entertaining for the visitor) represent progress, but they also call attention to the absence of the very thing they are supposedly replacing—the highly complex arboreal environment to which the monkeys are naturally adapted. The inevitable inadequacy of the intellectual stimulation provided for caged chimpanzees was reflected memorably in the favorite pastime of chimps in the San Francisco zoo: throwing their feces at the crowds.

The result of efforts to make the cages more complex and closer to nature, if they indeed are stimulating to the animals, still draws attention to what cages currently lack. An eagle in a small cage is a pathetic specimen. An eagle that has enough room to fly twenty feet from one dead tree limb to another is a caged bird unable truly to soar.

The same is true for the simulated natural environments that zoos often present. The giraffe house where the animals are caged without any pretense of freedom or stimulation is simply cruel and unnatural. But enclosures that provide a bit of room, including a few trees with the trunks wrapped in chicken wire, draw attention dramatically to the predicament of the animals which can now walk around a bit, but cannot range freely or feed naturally. These enclosures represent progress in the humane keeping of wild animals. But they convey mixed messages to zoogoers.

Modern zoos are experimenting with ways to allow animals much more space and freedom, permitting some species perhaps to have a semblance of communal existence. This means enough space for wild dogs or wolves to form packs, zebras to form herds, and so forth. These initiatives are expensive, require enormous space, and make sometimes difficult demands on visitors. They also clearly place zoos in the business of worrying about ecology. Zoos justify the new approach in terms of accurate and effective display, and research into the needs of endangered and soon-to-be endangered species. (Zoos have always had to make themselves knowledgeable about animal requirements. Animals cannot be held captive unless they can be fed properly.)[28]

Whatever sense this makes for research and entertainment, it ultimately heightens the contradiction as a message about captive animals. The more that freedom for zoo animals is faked, the clearer it becomes that keeping animals locked up contradicts at least some important ethical and aesthetic values. It would appear that the only thing left to do would be to take down the fences, or not create zoos in the first place. In this age of television and documentary nature programs, is there any justification for keeping animals confined—aside, that is, from providing entertainment and important opportunities for research?

There are two inter-related responses to this apparent dilemma, although it may remain ultimately unresolvable. First, the direct exposure of people to species in distress builds support for wilderness habitats. As zoos self-consciously explain the reasons for the threat to species and their own roles in species preservation, they educate zoo visitors while reinforcing the information by providing direct, emotionally powerful encounters with representatives of the species. The pandas that China has sent around the world create constituencies for saving panda habitat that cannot otherwise be created. By extension, people who are led to concerns over emotional lead species like pandas are that much more prepared to understand the challenges confronting other species.

The same argument may be made about whale watching. Some people argue that whale watching is highly intrusive, so much so that they speculate harassment by humans may interfere with whale reproduction. Regulations to reduce excessive human intrusiveness make sense, but it would be mistaken to end whale watching entirely, because whale watching recruits human supporters to take an interest in the conservation of marine mammals.

Should the rare mountain gorilla be tracked down by tourists in their remote West African habitat? Perhaps tourism will endanger their communities in some way. But the gorilla communities are more threatened by disappearing habitat than they are by groups of tourists under the restraints of local guides. Opening up the jungle to gorilla watchers creates local economic stake-holders in the continued viability of the gorillas, and provides an opportunity to create an international constituency of people who support gorilla preservation. Properly displayed, zoos can build constituencies for endangered species in a similar way.

The message zoos convey must respect the autonomy of the captives and beware of suggesting that human imperialism is right and proper. Displays of small endangered whales may be acceptable if they build support for whale protection. Trained animal acts such as porpoise shows, by contrast, present a moral order in which the purpose of the animal performers is strictly to entertain humans. The more passive displays of animals in simulated natural settings at least hold out the hope of displaying animals with greater respect and autonomy.

A second response is contained in confronting the inherently problematic nature of the modern zoo. Zoos cannot remain simply as exhibitors, yet they cannot realize the goal of providing truly natural habitats either. Only the most well-endowed zoo extending over remarkably large acreage can even aspire to such visions. Otherwise, institutions must divide among urban zoos, which are inevitably even more compromised, and game parks, which may accommodate visitors but offer qualitatively different experiences from those we normally associate with zoos.

If they are to make sense to themselves and play a significant role in ecological consciousness-raising, zoos must actively embrace this contradiction. They must incorporate recognition that the entire world has become a zoo. Animal populations in the wild, particularly large animal populations such as those typically kept by zoos, are all more or less subject to human intervention. Zoos influence their animal populations deliberately and under controlled conditions. Outside the zoo, animal populations are manipulated inadvertently. Although there is a sense in which zoos cannot truly be showcases of nature, they are nonetheless emblematic of a critical aspect of human society. Perhaps it is not too far-fetched to say that zoos confront in microcosm problems that must be confronted worldwide.

The key to negotiating this new role is to confront as directly as possible the fact that it is the zoo, not the animals, which is on display. Zoos could explicitly draw attention to the artificial environments of animal captivity even as they try to provide increasingly natural settings. Zoos could involve visitors in the scientific basis for removing and returning animals to and from the wild, as well as displaying the animals for visitors' amusement. Zoos could devote more space to animal displays involving efforts to restore wilderness, and less space to displaying animals for their own sake. Some zoos have already moved in this direction. Above all, they could create and develop policy as extensions of the message that zoos regularly communicate but in the past have not acknowledged—that the zoo is the place to go to see how humans treat and regard animals.

Notes

1. For the most part I restrict discussion to museums of natural history in order to pursue the relationship between museums, zoos and ecology. But some of the analysis also draws on and applies to other kinds of museums as well.

2. Kenneth Hudson, *Museums for the 1980s: A Survey of World Trends* (Paris: UNESCO, 1977), p. 1.

3. For a discussion of the tensions between museum curators and museum display presenters, see William Honan, "Say Goodbye to the Stuffed Elephants," *New York Times Magazine*, January 14, 1990, pp. 34–38.

4. A good discussion of the efforts of non-profit organizations to operate according to the exigencies of profitability is Estelle James, "How Non-Profits Grow: A Model," *Journal of Policy Analysis and Management*, 2, 3 (1983), pp. 350–366.

5. Kenneth Hudson, *A Social History of Museums* (London: Macmillan Press, 1975).

6. Five federal agencies provided $7 million to the nation's museums in the early 1980s through the National Science Foundation, Smithsonian Institution, National Endowment for the Arts, National Endowment for the Humanities and the Institute for Museum Services. *Museums for a New Century: A Report of the Commission on Museums for a New Century* (Washington, D.C.: American Association of Museums, 1984), pp. 43–44.

7. For a discussion of the circumstances under which nonprofit or government status is likely to affect the operations of nonprofit organizations, see Michael Lipsky and Steven Rathgeb Smith, "Nonprofit Organizations, Government, and the Welfare State," *Political Science Quarterly*, 104, 4 (Winter 1989–90), pp. 625–648.

8. See Paul J. Dimaggio and Walter W. Powell, "The Iron Cage Revisited: Institutional Isomorphism and Collective Rationality in Organizational Fields," *American Sociological Review*, 48 (April, 1983), pp. 147–160.

9. On the character of toll goods see Vincent Ostrom and Elinor Ostrom, "Public Goods and Public Choices," in E.S. Savas, ed., *Alternatives for Delivering Public Services* (Boulder, Colorado: Westview Press, 1977), pp. 7–49.

10. See Denise L. Stone, "The Use of Advertising to Attract the Museum Public," *Curator* 31, 2 (1988), pp. 123–30.

11. Zoos and museums deliberately construct themselves to influence their patrons. They seek to know who their patrons are and how they are influenced by their encounters with the institution. See, e.g., the American Museum of Natural History's "A Profile of Consumer Use and Evaluation," unpublished, in the Museum's library, April, 1983.

12. I take this to be the essence of what Murray Edelman has called the "symbolic process." See Edelman, *Politics as Symbolic Action* (Chicago: Markham Publishing Co., 1971), p. 2.

13. See Murray Edelman, "Space and the Social Order," *Journal of Architectural Education*, 32, 2 (1978), pp. 2–7.

14. Hudson, *A Social History of Museums*.

15. Lilian Wald, *The House on Henry St.* (1915, reprinted 1971), pp. 80–81. Thanks to Ros Baxandall for the reference.

16. *Museums for a New Century*, p. 32.

17. Andrew J. Nelson, "Going Wild," *American Demographics* (February, 1990), pp. 34–37, 50.

18. A delightful informal history of the Museum is Douglas J. Preston, *Dinosaurs in the Attic* (New York: St. Martin's Press, 1986).

19. *The Boston Globe*, March 4, 1990, p. B35.

20. See, generally, Kenneth J. Polakowski, *Zoo Design: The Reality of Wild Illusions* (Ann Arbor: University of Michigan, School of Natural Resources, 1987).

21. See Preston, ch. 7.

22. Listing only cities in which I have visited zoos and museums since taking a conscious interest in the political role of public spaces, institutions and environments, I have drawn on experiences, in the United States, in: Boston, Cambridge, MA., Washington, D.C., Seattle, Tucson, San Francisco and New York; in Australia, in Sydney, Melbourne, Adelaide, Darwin, Canberra and Brisbane, and in Denmark, Copenhagen. Earlier visits to Milwaukee, London and Berlin have also shaped my thinking.

23. Thanks to John Iremonger for the phrase.

24. Murray J. Edelman, "Space and the Social Order," p. 2.

25. Joseph V. Noble, "When is an Exhibit not an Exhibit," *Curator*, 31, 3 (1988), pp. 178–180.

26. Hudson, *Museums for the 1980s*, p. 7.

27. Judy Diamond, *et al*, "The California Academy of Sciences Discovery Room," *Curator*, 31 8 (1988), p. 157.

28. Kenneth Hudson, *Museums of Influence* (Cambridge: Cambridge University Press, 1987), p. 76.

PART FOUR

Culture and Political Domination

9

False-Consciousness, or Laying It on Thick

James Scott

Most of Murray Edelman's work, as I read it, has centered on questions of ideological domination. In the Gramscian sense he has asked, again and again, under what circumstances and through what mechanisms has ideological hegemony and mystification prevailed. By virtue of its thematic unity and its steady elaboration, Edelman's corpus has a kind of intellectual cohesion and power that is comparatively rare. Even a close exegesis would not reveal many contradictions. Thus it is possible to talk about an Edelmanesque position on ideological processes in a fairly unambiguous way.

Edelman has consistently taken a very pessimistic, even despairing (he would say realistic) view of the degree to which powerful groups and institutions can shape the perceptions and values of ordinary people. The Lockean man of classical liberalism or of "public choice theory" fares badly in the political world as Edelman reconstructs it. Beset by normal hopes and fears, having relatively little first-hand information about the threats they face, Edelman shows how ordinary people are prey to the strategies of the powerful. Much of his work could be described as a particularly influential view of how institutions of hegemony in the Gramscian sense (school, political leaders, churches, the media) influence the values and attitudes that prevail in civil society.

The essay that follows is, like much of the rest of my work, an extended dialogue with this view. I have found Edelman's view far too pessimistic for the social facts which have preoccupied me; namely, peasant rebellions, resistance, dissident utopian thought, satire and carnivalesque parody, and so forth. How much of the difference in our views can be accounted for by the difference in social settings we examine is hard to say. Edelman examines modern, capitalist, liberal societies while I examine more traditional, rural, illiberal societies. No doubt this difference is influential. It is not, I think, decisive. Traditional societies, after all, have hegemonic institutions of their own in religious structures, sacred texts, myths of kingship, and metaphors of kinship that serve the same function as Gramsci's instruments of hegemony in modern society. Even after differences in social context and conceptual tastes are allowed for, there is, I think, a substantial difference of opinion that remains and is important. That we have a difference of opinion at all, of course, is only possible because I have the benefit of setting out from Edelman's provocative and original position.

The powerful have a vital interest in keeping up the appearances appropriate to their form of domination. Subordinates, for their part, ordinarily have good reasons to help sustain those appearances or, at least, not openly contradict them. Taken together, these two social facts have, I believe, important consequences for the analysis of power relations. In what follows, I examine how the concepts of the public and hidden transcript can help us to a more critical view of the various debates swirling around the troubled terms, "false-consciousness" and "hegemony." A combination of adaptive strategic behavior and the dialogue implicit in most power relations ensures that public action will provide a constant stream of evidence which appears to support an interpretation of ideological hegemony. This interpretation may not be mistaken, but I will argue that it cannot be sustained on the basis of the evidence usually presented and that, in the cases I am examining, there are other good reasons for doubting this interpretation. I conclude with a brief analysis of how forms of domination generate certain rituals of affirmation, certain forms of public conflict, and, finally, certain patterns of profanation and defiance. Throughout, my aim is to clarify the analysis of domination in a way that avoids "naturalizing" existing power relations and that is attentive to what may lie beneath the surface.

The Interpretation of Quiescence

Much of the debate about power and ideology for three decades or more has centered around how to interpret conforming behavior by the less powerful (e.g. ordinary citizens, the working class, peasants) when there is no apparent use of coercion (e.g. violence, threats) to explain that conformity. Why, in other words, do people seem to knuckle under when they appear to have other options? In North America, the arguments about the reasons for quiescence are to be found in what is known as the "community power" literature based on local studies demonstrating relatively low levels of political participation despite marked inequalities and a relatively open political system.[1] In continental Europe and England the arguments have been conducted on a larger social terrain and in largely neo-Marxist terms employing Gramsci's concept of hegemony.[2] Here, the attempt is to explain the relative political quiescence of the Western working class despite the continuing provocation of inequities under capitalism and access to the political remedies which might be provided by parliamentary democracy. Why, in other words, does a subordinate class seem to accept or at least consent to an economic system which is manifestly against its interests when it is not obliged to by the direct application of coercion or the fear of its application? It is worth noting that each of these debates begins with several assumptions, any one of which might plausibly be contested. Each assumes that the subordinate group is, in fact, relatively quiescent, that it is relatively disadvantaged, and that it is not directly coerced. We will, for the sake of argument, accept all three assumptions.

With the exception of the "pluralist" position in the community power debate, virtually all other positions explain the anomaly by reference to a dominant or hegemonic ideology. Precisely what this ideology is, how it is created, how it is propagated, and what consequences it has, is hotly contested. Most of the disputants, however, agree that while the dominant ideology does not entirely exclude the interests of subordinate groups, it operates to conceal or misrepresent aspects of social relations which, if apprehended directly, would be damaging to the interests of dominant elites.[3] Since *any* theory which purports to demonstrate a misrepresentation of social reality must, by definition, claim some superior knowledge of what that social reality is, it must be in this sense a theory of false consciousness.

Simplifying things greatly, I believe that we can discern a *thick* and a *thin* version of false-consciousness. The thick version claims that a dominant ideology works its magic by persuading subordinate groups to believe actively in the values which explain and justify their own subordination. Evidence against this thick theory of mystification is pervasive enough to convince me that it is generally untenable[4]—particularly so for systems of domination such as serfdom, slavery, untouchability in which consent and civil rights hardly figure even at the rhetorical level. The *thin* theory of false-consciousness, on the other hand, maintains only that the dominant ideology achieves compliance by convincing subordinate groups that the social order in which they live is natural and inevitable. The thick theory claims consent; the thin theory settles for resignation. In its most subtle form, the thick theory is eminently plausible and, some would claim, true by definition. I believe, nevertheless, that it is fundamentally wrong and hope to show why in some detail after putting it in as persuasive a form as possible, so that it is no straw-man I am criticizing.

Within the community power literature, the debate is essentially between "pluralists" and "anti-pluralists." For the pluralists, the absence of significant protest or radical opposition in relatively open political systems must be taken as a sign of satisfaction or, at least, insufficient dissatisfaction to warrant the time and trouble of political mobilization. Anti-pluralists reply that the political arena is less completely open than pluralists believe and that the vulnerability of subordinate groups allows elites to control the political agenda and create effective obstacles to participation. The difficulty with the anti-pluralist position, as their opponents lost no time pointing out, is that it creates a kind of political Heisenberg principle. That is, if the anti-pluralists cannot uncover hidden grievances—grievances which the elite is presumed to have effectively banished—then how are we to know whether apparent acquiescence is genuine or repressive? An elite which did its "anti-pluralist work" effectively would thereby have eliminated any trace of the issues they had suppressed.

In an attempt to sustain the anti-pluralist position and to clarify how issues are, in fact, banished, John Gaventa proposes a third level of power relations.[5] The first level is the familiar and open exercise of coercion and influence. The second is intimidation and what Gaventa calls "the rule of anticipated reactions." This second effect typically arises from experience of subordination and defeat in that the relatively powerless elect not to challenge elites because they anticipate the sanctions that will be brought against them to ensure their failure. Here there is no change in values or grievances presumably, but rather an estimate of hopeless odds that discourage a challenge.[6] The third level of power relations is more subtle and amounts to a theory of false-consciousness that is both thick and thin. Gaventa claims that the power afforded to a dominant elite in the first two dimensions of power "may allow (them) further power to invest in the development of dominant images, legitimations, or beliefs about (their) power through control, for instance, of the media or other socialization institutions."[7]

The result, he claims, may well be a culture of defeat and non-participation such as he found in the Appalachian coal valley he studied. What is not clear is how much of the "mystification" Gaventa points to is presumed to actually change values and preferences (as his term "legitimations" implies) and how much is a reinforcement of the belief in the power of dominant elites to prevail in any encounter. Nor is it apparent why such ideological investments should be convincing to subordinate groups beyond the inferences they draw from their direct experience. Gaventa, at any rate, supports both a thick theory of false-consciousness *and* a thin theory of naturalization.

When it comes to understanding why the Western working class has apparently made an accommodation with capitalism and unequal property relations despite its political rights to mobilize, one finds, again, both thick and thin accounts of ideological hegemony. The "thick" version emphasizes the operation of what have been called "ideological state apparatuses" such as schools, the church, the media, and even the institutions of parliamentary democracy which, it is claimed, exercise a near monopoly over the symbolic means of production just as factory owners might monopolize the material means of production. Their ideological work secures the active consent of subordinate groups to the social arrangements which reproduce their subordination.[8] Put very briefly, this thick version faces two daunting criticisms. First, there is some rather compelling evidence that subordinate classes under feudalism, early capitalism, and late capitalism have not been ideologically incorporated to anything like the extent claimed by the theory.[9] Second, and far more damaging, there is no warrant for supposing that the acceptance of a broad and idealized version of the reigning ideology prevents conflict—even violent conflict—and some evidence that such acceptance may, in fact, provoke conflict.[10]

The thin theory of hegemony makes far less grandiose claims for the ideological grip of ruling elites. What ideological domination does accomplish, however, according to this version, is to define for subordinate groups what is realistic and what is not realistic and to drive certain aspirations and grievances into the realm of the impossible, of idle dreams. By persuading underclasses that their position, their life-chances, their tribulations are unalterable and inevitable, such a limited hegemony can produce the behavioral results of consent without necessarily changing people's values. Convinced that nothing can possibly be done to improve their situation and that it will always remain so, it is even conceivable that idle criticisms and hopeless aspirations would be eventually extinguished. One sympathetic and penetrating account of English working class culture by Richard Hoggart captures the essence of this thin theory mystification.

> When people feel that they cannot do much about the main elements of their situation, feel it not necessarily with despair or disappointment or resentment but simply as a fact of life, they adopt attitudes toward that situation which allow them to have a liveable life without a constant and pressing sense of the larger situation. The attitudes move the main elements in the situation to the realm of natural laws, the given and now, the almost implacable material from which a living has to be carved. Such attitudes, at their least adorned a fatalism or plain accepting, are generally below the tragic level; they have too much of the conscript's lack of choice about them.[11]

At one level it is simply undeniable that this account is entirely convincing. No one will doubt that the actual situation of subordinate groups throughout their history has seemed an unmovable "given," and realistically so.[12] If such a claim is plausible for the contemporary working class with its political rights and its acquaintance with would-be revolutionary movements, not to mention actual revolutions, historically it should be true in a far more overwhelming way for slaves, serfs, peasants, and untouchables. As an illustration, imagine the situation of an untouchable in 18th century rural India. In the collective historical experience of his or her group, there have always been castes; his caste has always been most looked down upon and exploited, and no one has ever escaped his caste—in his lifetime. Small wonder that in such circumstances the caste system and one's status within it should take on the force of natural law. There is also no standard of comparison which can be used to find the caste system wanting, no alternative experience or knowledge to make one's fate less than inevitable.[13]

This apparently compelling, thin version of the false-consciousness argument is not incompatible with a degree of distaste for, or even hatred of, the domination experienced. The claim is not that one's fated condition is loved, only that it is here to stay whether one likes it or not. On my reading, this minimal notion of ideological domination has become almost an orthodoxy, one encountered again and again in the literature on such issues. As Pierre Bourdieu puts it, "Every established order tends to produce (to very different degrees and with very different means) *the naturalization of its own arbitrariness*."[14] Other formulations vary only in particulars. Thus, Anthony Giddens writes of "the naturalization of the present" in which capitalist economic structures come to be taken for granted.[15] Paul Willis echoes both in claiming that "One of the most important general functions of ideology is the way in which it turns uncertain and fragile cultural resolutions and outcomes into a pervasive naturalism."[16] Quite often, however, there is an attempt to take this more defensible notion of hegemony and, as it were, to fatten it back up to the thick theory of false consciousness. This transmutation is accomplished by arguing—and occasionally simply asserting—that what is conceived as inevitable becomes, by that fact, just. Necessity becomes virtue. As Bourdieu puts it epigrammatically, subordinate groups manage ". . . to refuse what is anyway refused and to love the inevitable."[17]

Barrington Moore raises this same equation into something like a psychological universal, claiming that "What is or appears to human beings unavoidable must also somehow be just."[18] The logic behind this position is not unlike the logic underlying some of the earlier studies of the personality structure of American blacks.[19] It is of the "face-grows-to-fit-the-mask" variety, beginning with the need for the black in a racist society to act a role and to continuously monitor his or her behavior by the standards imposed by the dominant, white, world. It is difficult if not impossible, the logic goes, for an individual constantly to act a role and to hold a view of the self apart from that role. Since, presumably, the individual has no control over the roles imposed by powerful others, whatever personality integration takes place must bring the self into line with the imposed role.[20]

A Critique of Hegemony and False Consciousness

A great many objections can be made to the case for hegemony and false-consciousness. Taken singly, many of them are crippling; taken together, I believe they are fatal. Our interest, however, lies for the most part in understanding how the process of domination generates the social evidence that apparently confirms notions of hegemony. For this reason, and because lengthy critiques are available elsewhere, this critique will be brief and even schematic.[21]

Perhaps the greatest problem with the concept of hegemony is the implicit assumption that the ideological incorporation of subordinate groups will necessarily diminish social conflict. And yet, we know that any ideology which makes a claim to hegemony must, in effect, make promises to subordinate groups by way of explaining *why* a particular social order is also in their best interests. Once such promises are extended, the way is open to social conflict. How are these promises to be understood? Have they been carried out? Were they made in good faith? Who is to enforce them? Without elaborating, it is reasonably clear that some of the most striking episodes of violent conflict have occurred between a dominant elite and a rank-and-file mass of subordinates seeking objectives which could, in principle, be accommodated within the prevailing social order.[22] The myriad complaints voiced from all over France in the *cahiers de doléances* prior to the Revolution give little if any evidence of a desire to abolish serfdom or the monarchy. Virtually all the demands envisioned a reformed feudalism with many "abuses" rectified. But the relative modesty of the demands did not prevent—one might even say they helped stimulate—the violent actions of peasants and *sans culottes* which provided the social basis for the actual revolution. Similarly, what we know of the demands from the factory committees formed spontaneously throughout European Russia in 1917 leaves no doubt that what these workers sought "was to improve working conditions, not to change them" and certainly not to socialize the means of production.[23] And yet, their revolutionary actions on behalf of reformist goals, such as an eight-hour day, an end to piecework, a minimum wage, politeness from management, cooking and toilet facilities, was the driving force behind the Bolshevik revolution. Further examples abound.[24] The point is simply that the subordinate classes to be found at the base of what we historically call revolutionary movements are typically seeking goals well within their understanding of the ruling ideology. "Falsely-conscious" subjects are quite capable, it seems, of taking revolutionary action.

Even if we were, for the sake of argument, to grant that ideological hegemony, once achieved, should contribute to the quiescence of subordinate classes, it *then* becomes highly questionable whether such hegemony has often prevailed. The problem with the hegemonic thesis, at least in its strong form proposed by some of Gramsci's successors, is that it is difficult to explain how social change could ever originate from below. If elites control the material basis of production, allowing them to extract practical conformity (what Marx called the "the dull compulsion of economic relations"), and also control the means of symbolic production thereby ensuring that their power and control is legitimized, the system has achieved a self-perpetuating equilibrium which can only be disturbed by an external shock. As Willis observes:

> Structuralist theories of reproduction present the dominant ideology (under which culture is subsumed) as impenetrable. Everything fits too neatly. Ideology always pre-exists and preempts any authentic criticism. There are no cracks in the billiard ball smoothness of process.[25]

Even in the relatively stable industrial democracies to which theories of hegemony were meant to apply, their strongest formulation simply does not allow for the degree of social conflict and protest which actually occurs.

If social conflict is an inconvenience for theories of hegemony as applied to contemporary societies, it is a massive, intractable contradiction when applied to the histories of peasant societies, of slavery, and of serfdom. Considering only agrarian Europe in the three centuries before the French Revolution, the proponents of hegemony or naturalization are confronted with a host of anomalous facts. What is remarkable about that period, surely, is the frequency with which peasants were seized with a sense of historical possibilities—possibilities on which they have acted and which, it turned out tragically, were not objectively justified. The thousands of rebellions and violent protests from Wat Tyler's Rebellion in the late 14th century, through the great Peasant War in Germany, to the French Revolution are something of a monument to the tenacity of peasant aspirations in the face of what seem, in retrospect, to have been hopeless odds. As Marc Bloch put it,

> A social system is characterized not only by its internal structure but also by the reactions it produces... To the historian, whose task is merely to observe and explain the connections between phenomena, agrarian revolt is as natural to the seigneurial regime as strikes, let us say, are to large scale capitalism.[26]

For slavery in North America where the odds were even longer against rebels, surely the remarkable thing is that revolt occurred at all and that for every actual rebellion, there were scores of plots which never came to fruition. Given the dispersion of slaves among farms with relatively few hands, the fact that they were less than one quarter of the population, and an active surveillance, the observer does not have to assume that slaves came to believe the "unavoidable" was just in order to account for the paucity of rebellion.[27]

If there is a social phenomenon to be explained here, it is the reverse of what theories of hegemony and "false-consciousness" purport to account for. How is it that subordinate groups such as these have so often believed and acted as if their situations were not inevitable when a more judicious historical reading would have concluded that it was? It is not the miasma of power and thralldom that require explanation. We require instead an understanding of a *misreading* by subordinate groups which seems to exaggerate their own power, the possibilities for emancipation, and to underestimate the power arrayed against them. If the elite-dominated public transcript tends to naturalize domination, it would seem that some countervailing influence manages often to denaturalize domination.

With this historical prespective in mind, we may begin to question the logic of the case made for hegemony and naturalization. The attempt to turn a thin theory of naturalization into a fat theory of hegemony seems, in my view, clearly unwarranted. Even granting the historical fact that subordinate groups of serfs, slaves, or untouchables have often had no knowledge of a social order founded on different principles, the inevitability of domination does not necessarily make it just or legitimate in their eyes. Let us instead assume that the inevitability of domination for a slave will have approximately the same status as the inevitability of the weather for the peasant. Concepts of justice and legitimacy are simply irrelevant to something that is inescapably *there* like the weather. Here it is perhaps relevant to note that traditional cultivators effectively *denaturalize* even the weather by personifying it and developing a ritual repertoire designed to influence or control its course.[28] Once again, what we might assume to be inevitable is brought into the realm of potential human control. When such efforts appear to fail, traditional cultivators, like their scientific, modern counterparts, are prone to curse the weather. They, at least, do not confound inevitability with justice.

The thin theory of naturalization is far more persuasive because it claims nothing beyond the acceptance of inevitability. It is, nevertheless, mistaken in assuming that the absence of actual knowledge of alternative social arrangements produces automatically the naturalization of the present, however hated that present may be. Consider two small feats of imagination which countless numbers of subordinate groups have historically performed. First, while the serf, the slave, and the untouchable may have difficulty imagining other arrangements than serfdom, slavery, and the caste system, they will certainly have no trouble imagining a total reversal of the existing distribution of status and rewards. The millenial theme of a world turned upside down, a world in which the last shall be first and the first last, can be found in nearly every major cultural tradition in which inequities of power, wealth, and status have been pronounced.[29] In one form or another, most folk utopias have included the central idea behind this Vietnamese folk song:

The son of the king becomes king.
The son of the pagoda caretaker knows only
   how to sweep with the leaves of the banyan tree.
When the people rise up,
The son of the king, defeated, will go sweep the pagoda.[30]

These collective hidden transcripts from the fantasy life of subordinate groups are not merely abstract exercises. They are embedded, as we shall see later, in innumerable ritual practices (e.g. carnival in Catholic countries, the Feast of Krishna in India, the Saturnalia in classical Rome, the water festival in Buddhist Southeast Asia) and they have provided the ideological basis of many revolts.

The second historical achievement of popular imagination is to negate the existing social order. Without ever having set foot outside a stratified society, subordinate groups can, and have, imagined the absence of the distinctions they find so onerous. The famous ditty which comes to us from the English Peasants Revolt of 1381: "When Adam delved and Eve span, who was then the gentleman" was imagining a world without aristocrats or gentry. In the fifteenth century the Taborites anticipated both a radical equality and the labor theory of value. "Princes, ecclesiastical and secular alike, and counts and knights should only possess as much as common folk, then everyone would have enough. The time will come when princes and lords will work for their daily bread."[31] Lest one confine such levelling beliefs to the Judeo-Christian tradition with its myth of a perfect society before the Fall, note that similar levelling beliefs of religious and secular lineage may be found in most, if not all, highly stratified societies. Most traditional utopian beliefs can, in fact, be understood as a more or less systematic negation of an existing pattern of exploitation and status degradation as it is experienced by subordinate groups. If the peasantry is beset by officials collecting taxes, by lords collecting crops and labor dues, by priests collecting tithes, and by poor crops, their utopia is likely to envision a life without taxes and dues or tithes, perhaps without officials, lords and priests, and with an abundant, self-yielding nature. Utopian thought of this kind has typically been cast in disguised or allegorical forms, in part because their open declaration would be considered revolutionary. What is beyond doubt is that millenial beliefs and expectations have often provided, before the modern era, a most important set of mobilizing ideas behind large-scale rebellions when they did occur.

On the historical evidence, then, there is little or no basis for crediting either a fat theory or a thin theory of hegemony. The obstacles to resistance, which are many, are simply not attributable to the inability of subordinate groups to *imagine* a counter-factual social order. They do imagine both the reversal and negation of their domination and, most important, they have acted on these values in desperation and on those rare occasions when the circumstances allowed. Being at the bottom of the heap, it is little wonder that they should have a class interest in utopian prophesies, in imagining a radically different social order from the painful one they experience. In concrete terms, the seventeenth century broadsheet depicting a lord serving an elegant meal to a seated peasant was bound to evoke more pleasure from the peasantry than from their social-betters.[32] Nor, having imagined a counter-factual social order, do subordinate groups appear to have been paralyzed by an elite-fostered discourse intended to convince them that efforts to change their situation are hopeless. I do not by any means wish to imply that the history of peasants and slaves is a history of one quixotic adventure after another, nor to ignore the chilling effects a crushed insurrection must certainly have had. Nevertheless, since slave and peasant uprisings occurred frequently enough and failed almost invariably, one can make a persuasive case that whatever mis-perception of reality prevailed was apparently one more hopeful than the facts warranted. The penchant of subordinate groups to interpret rumors and ambiguous news as heralding their imminent liberation is striking.

A Paper-thin Theory of Hegemony

What, then, is left of the theory of hegemony in this context? Very little, I believe. I do, however, want to suggest the very limited and stringent conditions under which subordinate groups may come to accept, even to legitimate, the arrangements which justify their subordination.[33]

Ideological hegemony in cases of *involuntary* subordination is, I believe, only likely to occur if either of two rather stringent conditions are met. The first of these conditions is that there exists a strong probability that a good many subordinates will eventually come to occupy positions of power. The expectation that one will eventually be able to exercise the domination that one endures today is a strong incentive serving to legitimate patterns of domination. It encourages patience and emulation and, not least, it promises revenge of a kind, even if it must be exercised on someone other than the original target of resentment. If this supposition is correct, it would help to explain why so many age-graded systems of domination seem to have such durability. The junior who is exploited by elders will eventually get his chance to be an elder; those who do degrading work for others in an institution—providing they can reasonably expect to move up—will eventually have that work done for them; the traditional Chinese daughter-in-law can look forward, if she has a son (!), to becoming a domineering mother-in-law.[34]

Onerous and involuntary subordination can also, perhaps, be made legitimate providing that subordinates are more or less completely *atomized* and kept under close observation. What is involved is the total abolition of any social realm of relative discursive freedom. In other words, the social conditions under which a hidden transcript might be generated among subordinates are eliminated. The society envisioned is rather like the official story propagated in the public transcript or in Bentham's Panopticon, inasmuch as all social relations are hierarchical and surveillance is perfect. It goes without saying that this ultimate totalitarian fantasy, in which there is no life outside relations of domination, does not even remotely approximate the reality of any real society as a whole. As Foucault has noted, "... solitude is the primary condition of total submission."[35] It is perhaps only in a few penal institutions, thought-reform camps, and psychiatric wards that one is afforded a glimpse of what is involved.

The techniques of atomization and surveillance were employed with some success in the prisoner-of-war camps in North Korea and China during the Korean War. For our purposes, what is remarkable about these camps was the lengths to which captors had to go in order to produce the confessions and propaganda broadcasts they required.[36] The prisoners were driven to extreme physical exhaustion, denied any contact with the outside world, *separated* and *isolated* for weeks at a time during constant interrogation. The interrogator alternated between favors and threats, telling the prisoner that he received no mail because his relatives at home didn't care what became of him. Above all, the captors endeavored to minutely control every action and communication of the captives and to eliminate, with isolation or informers, any possible solidarity or affiliation between them. Draconian conditions did, in fact, produce a small harvest of confessions, and a good many prisoners reported suddenly feeling great affection toward an interrogator who had treated them ruthlessly. What apparently had happened was that the impossibility of validating one's feelings and expressing anger with others in the same situation—of creating an off-stage hidden transcript, a different social reality—had allowed the captors to exercise a temporary hegemony.

I want to emphasize exactly how draconian were the conditions which produced this compliance. Captors were not successful when they permitted prisoners to associate with one another; they had to concentrate on destroying any autonomous subordinate group contact. Even then it was often possible for prisoners to communicate secretly under the noses of the authorities. Taking advantage of small linguistic nuances that their captors would not notice, they often managed to insert in a publicly read apology or confession before other prisoners an indication that their performance was forced and insincere. The degree of policing and atomization required were in keeping with what we know from social psychology about acts of obedience to authority which offend one's moral judgement. In Stanley Milgram's famous experiments in which volunteers gave what they thought were shocks to subjects who failed to answer questions correctly, several small variations dramatically reduced the rate of compliance.[37] First, if the experimenter (the authority figure) stepped out of the room, the subject would disobey and lie to the experimenter about the shocks he or she had administered. In another variation of the experimental situation, the subject was provided with one or two peers who refused to administer increasingly severe shocks. With even this modicum of social support, the vast majority of subjects rebelled against the authority of the experimenter. Willing compliance in this context thus evaporates the moment the subject is not under close observation *and* whenever the subject is afforded even a small degree of social support for resistance from peers in the some boat.[38]

It is plausible then, under certain conditions, to imagine that even an onerous and non-voluntary subordination can be made to seem just and legitimate. Those conditions, however, are so stringent that they are simply not applicable to any of the large-scale forms of domination that concern us here. Slaves, serfs, peasants, and untouchables have had little realistic prospect of upward mobility or escape from their status. At the same time they have always had something of a life apart in the slave quarters, the village, the household, and in religious and ritual life. It has neither been possible nor desirable to entirely destroy the autonomous social life of subordinate groups that is the indispensable basis for a hidden transcript. The large historical forms of domination not only generate the resentments, appropriations, and humiliations which give, as it were, subordinates something to talk about; they are also unable to prevent the creation of an independent social space in which subordinates can talk about it in comparative safety.

The Social Production of Hegemonic Appearances

If much of the criticism of theories of hegemony offered above is valid, we would be obliged to find other reasons for compliance and quiescence than the internalization of the dominant ideology by subordinate groups. There are, certainly, a host of factors which might explain why a form of domination persists despite an elite's failure to incorporate ideologically the least advantaged. To mention only a few: subordinate groups might be divided by geography and cultural background; they may judge that the severity of possible reprisal makes open resistance foolhardy; the daily struggle for subsistence and the surveillance it entails may all but preclude open opposition; or they may have become cynical from past failures.

What remains to be explained, however, is why theories of hegemony and ideological incorporation have nevertheless retained an enormous intellectual appeal for social scientists and historians. We must remember, in this context, that theories of ideological incorporation have been equally seductive both to mainstream social science and to neo-Marxist followers of Gramsci. In the structural-functional world of Parsonian sociology, subordinate groups came naturally to an acceptance of the normative principles behind the social order without which no society could endure. In the neo-Marxist critique it is also assumed that subordinate groups have internalized the dominant norms but, now, these norms are seen to be a false view of their objective interests. In each instance, ideological incorporation produces social stability; in the former case, the stability is laudable; in the latter case, it is a stability that permits the continuation of class-based exploitation.[39]

The most obvious reason why notions of ideological incorporation should find such resonance in the historical record is simply that domination, as we have seen, produces an official transcript which provides convincing evidence of willing, even enthusiastic, complicity. In ordinary circumstances subordinates have a vested interest in avoiding any *explicit* display of insubordination. They also, of course, always have a practical interest in resistance—in minimizing the exactions, labor, and humiliations to which they are subject. The reconciliation of these two objectives, which seem at cross purposes, is typically achieved by pursuing precisely those forms of resistance which avoid any open confrontation with the structures of authority being resisted. Thus the peasantry has historically preferred to disguise, in the interest of safety and success, its resistance. If it were a question of control over land, they would prefer squatting to a defiant land invasion; if it were a matter of taxes, they would prefer evasion rather than a tax riot; if it were a question of rights to the product of the land, they would prefer poaching or pilfering to direct appropriation. Only where less dramatic measures failed, where subsistence was threatened, or where there were signs that they could strike with relative safety, would the peasantry venture on the path of open, collective defiance. It is for this reason that the official transcript of relations between the dominant and subordinate is filled with formulas of subservience, euphemisms, and uncontested claims to status and legitimacy. On the open stage, the serfs or slaves will appear complicitous in creating an appearance of consent and unamity; the show of discursive affirmations from below will make it seem as if ideological hegemony were secure. The official transcript of power relations *is* a sphere in which power appears naturalized because that is what elites exert their influence to produce and because it ordinarily serves the immediate interests of subordinates to avoid discrediting these appearances.

The "official transcript" as a social fact presents enormous difficulties for the conduct of historical and contemporary research on subordinate groups. Short of actual rebellion, the great bulk of public events, and hence the great bulk of the archives, is consecrated to the official transcript. And, on those occasions when subordinate groups do put in an appearance, their presence, motives, and behavior are mediated by the interpretation of dominant elites. Where the subordinate group is almost entirely illiterate, the problem is compounded. The difficulty is, however, not merely the standard one of records of elite activities kept by elites in ways that reflect their class and status. It is the more profound difficulty presented by earnest efforts of subordinate groups to conceal their activities and opinions which might expose them to harm. We know relatively little about the rate at which slaves in the United States pilfered their masters' livestock, grain, and larder. If the slaves were successful, the master knew as little about this as possible although he could certainly know that there were losses. We know even less, of course, concerning what slaves said among themselves about this re-appropriation of value from the masters. What we do know typically comes to us, significantly, from ex-slaves who had been able to escape this form of subordination—e.g., from narratives given by runaways who had made it to the North or to Canada and from accounts collected after emancipation. The goal of slaves and other subordinate groups, as they conduct their ideological and material resistance, is precisely to escape detection; to the extent that they achieve their goal, such activities do not appear in the archives. In this respect, subordinate groups are complicitous in contributing to a sanitized official transcript, for that is one way they cover their tracks. Acts of desperation, revolt, and defiance can offer us something of a window on the hidden transcript but, short of crises, we are apt to see subordinate groups on their "best behavior." Detecting resistance among slaves under "normal" conditions, then, would seem rather like detecting the passage of sub-atomic particles by cloud chamber. Only the trail of resistance—e.g., so much corn missing—would be apparent.

Consider, for example, the difficulties reported by Christopher Hill in his attempts to establish the social and religious antecedents of the radical ideas associated with the Levellers in the English Civil War.[40] It is, of course, perfectly clear that the social gospel of the Levellers was not invented on the spot in 1640, but it is another thing to track down its origins. The religious views associated with the Lollards are the obvious place to look. Examining Lollardy, however, is vastly complicated by the fact that the adherents of such heterodox religious views were considered, and correctly so, dangerous to the established order. As Hill observes, "By definition, those who held them [these views] were anxious to leave no traces."[41] Lollardy was, given the circumstances, a fugitive and underground sect with no means to enforce an orthodoxy on those who believed. It can be glimpsed in reports of illegal preaching, in occasional anti-clerical incidents, and in some radically democratic readings of the scriptures later echoed by the Baptists and Quakers. We do know they preached the refusal of both "hat honor" and the use of honorifics in address, that they believed as early as the fifteenth century in direct confession to God, in the abolition of tithes for all those poorer than the priest, and that, like the Familists, Ranters, and Levellers, they would preach in taverns or in the open air. They thrived best in those areas where surveillance was least—the pastoral, moorland, and forest areas with few squires or clergy. And when they were challenged, they, like the Familists after them, were likely to disavow holding any heterodox views.

> This unheroic attitude was related to their dislike of all established churches, whether Protestant or Catholic. Their refusal of martyrdom no doubt helped their beliefs to survive but it increases the historian's difficulty in identifying heretical groups with confidence.[42]

The last thing the Lollards or Familists wanted, in this period, was to stand up and be counted. In fact, it is significant that the interest in Lollardy derives, in this case, from the public, open explosion of radical heterodoxy that so typified the English Civil War beginning in 1640. Their subterranean history became a matter of some historical importance because the ideas it embodied could, in the political mobilization and power vacuum of the Civil War, finally find open expression. Without such favorable moments, which cast a retrospective light on a previously hidden transcript, one imagines that much of the off-stage history of subordinate groups is permanently lost or obscured.

A parallel historical argument could be made about the dissimulation deployed by subordinate groups to conceal *practices* of resistance. Malay paddy farmers, in the region in which I have conducted field work, have resented paying the official Islamic tithe.[43] It is collected inequitably and corruptly; the proceeds are sent to the provincial capital and not a single poor person in the village has ever received any charity back from the religious authorities. Quietly and massively, the Malay peasantry has managed to nearly dismantle the tithe system so that only 15% of what is formally due is actually paid. There have been no tithe riots, demonstrations, protests—only a patient and effective nibbling in a multitude of ways: fraudulent declarations of the amount of land farmed; simple failures to declare land; underpayment; and delivery of paddy spoiled by moisture or contaminated with rocks and mud to increase its weight. For complex political reasons, the details of which need not concern us, neither the religious authorities nor the ruling party wish to call public attention to this silent and effective defiance. To do so would, among other things, expose the tenuousness of government authority in the countryside and perhaps encourage other acts of insubordination.[44] The low profile adopted by both antagonists amounts to something of a joint conspiracy to keep the conflict out of the public record. Someone examining the newspapers, speeches, and public documents of the period a few decades hence would find little or no trace of this conflict.

The seductiveness of theories of hegemony and false consciousness thus depends in large part on the strategic appearances which elites and subordinates alike ordinarily insert into the public transcript. For subordinates, the need for protective ingratiation[45] ensures that, once they come under scrutiny from above, the Lollard becomes an orthodox believer, the poacher becomes a peaceful respecter of gentry property, and the tithe evader a peasant ready to meet his obligations. The greater the power exercised over them and the closer the surveillance, the more incentive subordinates have to foster the impression of compliance, agreement, deference. By the same token, we know that compliance extracted under such draconian circumstances is less likely to be a valid guide to offstage opinion. Elites also, as we have seen, may have their own compelling reasons to preserve a public facade of unity, willing compliance and respect. Unless one can penetrate beyond the official transcript of both subordinates and elites, a reading of the social evidence will almost always represent a confirmation of the status quo in hegemonic terms. Just as subordinates are not much deceived by their own performance, there is, of course, no more reason for social scientists and historians to take that performance as, necessarily, one given in good faith.

The Interrogation of Power, or the Use Value of Hegemony

The only irony allowed to poverty is to drive Justice and Benevolence to unjust denials.
Balzac, *The Country Doctor*

We must, on my reading of the evidence, stand Gramsci's analysis of hegemony upside-down in at least one respect. In Gramsci's original formulation, which has guided most subsequent neo-Marxist work on ideology, hegemony works primarily at the level of thought as distinct from the level of action. The anomaly, which the revolutionary party and its intelligentsia will hopefully resolve, is that the working class under capitalism is involved in concrete struggles with revolutionary implications but, because it is in the thrall of hegemonic social thought, is unable to draw revolutionary conclusions from its actions. It is this dominated consciousness which, Gramsci claims, has prevented the working class from drawing the radical consequences inherent in much of its action.

> The active man-in-the-mass has a practical activity, but has no clear theoretical consciousness of his practical activity ... His theoretical consciousness can indeed be historically in opposition to his activity. One might almost say that he has two theoretical consciousnesses (or one contradictory consciousness): one which is implicit in his activity and which in reality unites him with all his fellow-workers in the practical transformation of the real world; and

one, superficially explicit or verbal, which he has inherited from the past and uncritically absorbed. But this verbal conception is not without consequences ... the contradictory state of consciousness does [often] not permit of any action, any decision, or any choice, and produces a condition of moral and political passivity.⁴⁶

We have explored, however, something of the imaginative capacity of subordinate groups to reverse or negate dominant ideologies. So common is this pattern that it is plausible to consider it part and parcel of the religio-political equipment of historically disadvantaged groups. Other things equal, it is therefore more accurate to consider subordinate classes *less* constrained at the level of thought and ideology, since they can in secluded settings speak with comparative safety, and *more* constrained at the level of political action and struggle where the daily exercise of power sharply limits the options available to them. To put it crudely, it would ordinarily be suicide for serfs to set out to murder their lords and abolish the seigneurial regime; it is, however, plausible for them to imagine and talk about such aspirations, providing they are discreet about it.

My criticism of Gramsci, a skeptic might object, is only applicable at those times when power relations virtually preclude open forms of resistance and protest. Only under such conditions are the constraints on action so severe as to produce near hegemonic appearances. Surely, the skeptic might continue, at times of open political struggle the mask of compliance and deference may be shed or at least lowered appreciably. Here would certainly be the place to look for evidence of false-consciousness. If, however, in the course of active protest, subordinate groups still embrace the bulk of the dominant ideology, then we can reliably infer the effect of a hegemonic ideology.

It is true that protest and open struggle by subordinate groups has very rarely taken truly radical *ideological* turns. This undeniable fact has been used to reclaim a thin version of the theory of hegemony. One persuasive formulation comes from Barrington Moore.

> ... one main cultural task facing any oppressed group is to undermine or explode the justification of the dominant stratum. Such criticisms may take the form of attempts to demonstrate that the dominant stratum does not perform the tasks that it claims to perform and therefore violates the social contract. Much more frequently they take the form that specified individuals in the dominant stratum fail to live up to the social contract. Such criticism leaves the basic functions of the dominant stratum inviolate. Only the most radical forms of criticism have raised the question whether kings, capitalists, priests, generals, bureaucrats, etc., serve any useful social purpose at all.⁴⁷

Moore implicitly asks us to imagine a gradient of radicalism in the interrogation of domination. The least radical step is to criticize *some* of the dominant stratum for having violated the norms by which they claim to rule; the next most radical step is to accuse the entire stratum of failing to observe the principles of its rule; and the most radical step is to repudiate the very principles by which the dominant stratum justifies its dominance. Criticism of virtually any form of domination might be analyzed in this fashion. It is one thing to claim that *this* king is not as beneficent as his predecessors, another to claim that kings in general don't live up to the beneficence they promise, and still another to repudiate all forms of kingship as inadmissible.

As one, among many, plausible ways of distinguishing how deeply a particular criticism cuts into a form of domination, I have no quarrel with this scheme. My quarrel is rather with the use of this criterion to infer the degree of ideological domination which prevails in a particular setting. By itself, I am convinced the fact that social criticism remains ideologically limited can never justify the conclusion that the group which makes that criticism is prevented by a hegemonic ideology from consciously formulating a more far-reaching critique. To conclude that slaves, serfs, peasants, untouchables, and other subordinate groups are "ethically submissive" merely because their protest and claims "conform to the proprieties" of the dominant class they are challenging would be a serious analytical error.

The fact is that the public representations of interest and claims by subordinate groups, *even in situations of conflict*, nearly always have a strategic or dialogic dimension which influences the form they take. Short of the total "declaration of war" that one does occasionally find in the midst of a revolutionary crisis, most protests and challenges—even quite violent ones—are made in the realistic expectation that the central features of the form of domination will remain intact. So long as that expectation prevails, it is impossible to know from the public transcript alone how much of the appeal to hegemonic values is prudence and formula and how much is "ethical submission."

The potentially strategic element in appeals to the hegemonic values is apparent from almost any setting of inequality; it follows from the domination of language. To take a banal example, imagine someone appealing to his superiors in a capitalist firm for a raise or protesting his failure to receive a raise which others have been given. So long as he anticipates remaining within the structure of authority, his case will necessarily be addressed to the institutional interests of his superiors. He may, in fact, want a raise to, say, buy a new car, support a gambling habit, or help fund a fringe political group and feel he is entitled to it for having faithfully covered for his boss' mistakes—and he may say as much to his family and closest friends. None of this, however, will have a legitimate place in the official transcript. He will, therefore, probably emphasize his loyal and effective contribution to the institutional success of the firm in the past and what he can contribute in the future. Strategic action always looks upward, for that is frequently the only way in which it will gain a hearing. The appeal may, of course, be entirely candid, but we cannot judge its candor on the basis of the official transcript alone.

Most acts of protest from below, even when they are protests—implicitly or explicity—will largely observe the "rules" even if their objective is to undermine those rules. Apart from the homage to the official transcript implied by invoking such rules, they may often be seen as habitual and formulaic, implying little in the way of inwardness. The *lettres de cachet* addressed directly to French kings, and typically complaining about a personal injustice they wish to see righted by the monarch, make liberal use of grandiloquent language in addressing the crown. The formulas were known and a notary could be hired to surround the substantive complaint with the appropriate euphemisms stressing the grandeur and beneficence of the crown and the humility and loyalty of this particular petitioning subject. As Foucault notes, such formulas

> cause beggars, poor folks, or simply the mediocre to appear in a strange theatre where they assume poses, declamations, grandiloquences, where they dress up in bits of drapery which are necessary if they want to be paid attention to on the stage of power.[48]

The "strange theatre" to which Foucault refers is deployed not merely to gain a hearing but often as a valuable political resource in conflict and even in rebellion. Examples drawn from a civilian prison and from patterns of peasant petitioning and revolt should help convey how euphemized power provides that basis for appeals from below.

In his careful description of public strategies used by inmates in a relatively progressive Norwegian prison, Thomas Mathiesen explores how they manage to advance their interests against those of the treatment staff and administration.[49] It matters little for our purposes whether the prisoners view the institution with cynicism or with legitimacy; their conduct is perfectly compatible with either assumption, so long as their strategic understanding is that they will have to continue to deal with the prison authorities, in one form or another. Deprived of realistic revolutionary options and having few political resources by definition, inmates nevertheless manage to conduct an effective struggle against the institution's authorities by using hegemonic ideology to good advantage. What the prisoners resent most about daily prison life is their powerlessness before the seemingly capricious and unpredictable distribution of privileges and punishments by administrative personnel. In their dogged attempts to domesticate the power arrayed against them and to render it predictable and manipulatable they pursue a strategy that Mathiesen characterizes as "censoriousness." This consists in stressing the established norms of the rulers of their small kingdom and claiming that these rulers have violated the norms by which they justify their own authority. Prisoners press constantly for the specification of procedures, criteria, and guidelines which will govern the granting of privileges (e.g., residence in a minimum security block, good jobs, furloughs). They are partisans of seniority as the major criterion, inasmuch as it would operate automatically and mechanically. The wider society from which they come has established values of law-regarding procedures and mechanical equality for citizens which they deftly employ to make their case. Their behavior in this respect is moralistic; it is the staff who are deviating from legitimate norms, not they. The principle of radical indeterminacy once again prevails. It is virtually impossible to know from the official transcript to what degree the argument of the prisoners is strategic in the sense of being a conscious manipulation of the prevailing norms. The officials of the prison would, in any event, be the last to know.

The treatment and administrative staff have, with limited success, attempted to resist the logic of the inmate's case. Their power quite clearly rests on maximizing their personal discretion in apportioning benefits and discipline; it is virtually their only means of gaining conformity from a population which has already been denied its basic freedoms. Without discretion their social control evaporates, and in arguing for some latitude of action they have recourse to the "treatment ideology" of tailoring their conduct to the individual needs of the particular prisoner. For the prisoner, this may simply represent their capacity to punish him for sullenness or sloppy clothes. We have here, then, a useful illustration of how a set of given normative or ideological rules come to help constitute the exercises of power and conflicts which are easily available within its ambit. The plasticity of any would-be hegemonic ideology which must, by definition, make a claim to serve the real interests of subordinate groups provides antagonists with political resources in the form of political claims which are legitimized by the ideology.[50] Whether he believes in the rules or not, only a fool would fail to appreciate the possible benefits of deploying such readily available ideological resources.

Using the ideology of the dominant stratum does not by any means prevent violent clashes of interest; it may in fact be fairly viewed as a common justification for violence. Peasant petitions to the lord of the daimyo in Tokugawa Japan were frequently a prelude to riots and insurrections. Despite capital penalties for petitioning, village leaders did occasionally take this dramatic step and, when they did, their petitions were invariably cast in deferential terms, appealing for the "mercy of the lord" in reducing taxes and invoking a tradition of "benevolent social aid from their superiors."[51] Such wording—even as a prelude to an insurrection—is often taken as a privileged glimpse into the true peasant world view of "benevolent lords and honorable peasants," when, in fact, we are observing a dialogue with power which may have a greater or lesser strategic dimension. One thing, however, is clear. By making appeals which remain within the official discourse of deference, the peasantry may somewhat lessen the mortal risks incurred by the desperate act of petitioning. In the midst of a collective provocation heavy with implicit threat, peasants attempt to cede the symbolic high ground to official values and imply that their quiescence and loyalty will be assured if only the lord abides by their understanding of the hierarchical social contract. Everyone involved knows, certainly, that the petition carries a threat, as virtually all such petitions do, but the document begins by invoking the hierarchical verities that the peasantry professes to accept as given.

The collective insistence, through petitioning, on the "rights" to which subordinate groups feel entitled carries an understood "or else," with the precise consequences of a refusal left to the imagination of the lord. If one can speak of the self-disciplined adherence of an aristocracy to its own code of values when that adherence is painful, as *noblesse oblige*, then one can speak of peasant insistence on elite adherence to its own understanding of the social contract as *paysans obligent*. Such petitions usually refer to the sufferings, the desperation, the tried patience of loyal peasants under taxes, conscription or whatever and, as a seventeenth-century French historian correctly observed: "he who speaks of desperation to his sovereign, threatens him."[52] A petition of desperation is therefore likely to amalgamate two contradictory elements: an implicit threat of violence and a deferential tone of address. It is never simple to discern how much of this deference is simply the formula in which elites are addressed—with little significance beyond that—and how much is a more or less self-conscious attempt to gain practical ends by disavowing, publicly, any intention of challenging the basic principles of stratification and authority. We know, for example, from Le Roy Ladurie's reconstruction of the uprising in Romans in 1580, that an insurrectionary atmosphere among the artisans and peasants had taken shape by early 1579. And yet when the Queen Mother Catherine, on a visit to the town, asked Paumier why he was against the king, he is reported to have replied, "*I am the king's servant*, but the people have elected me to save the poor folk afflicted by the tyranny of war, and to pursue *humbly*, the *just remonstrances* contained in their Cahier."[53] Since the moment was not ripe for an open rebellion, it is plausible that Paumier chose to speak prudently. It is also plausible that he used the formulas of respect unreflectively in much the way that standard salutations and closings are employed in contemporary business letters. There is, however, a third alternative, which I wish to explore in more detail. It is that subordinate groups have typically learned, in situations short of those rare "all-or-nothing" struggles, to clothe their resistance and defiance in ritualisms of subordination which serve both to disguise their purposes and to provide them with a ready route of retreat which may soften the consequences of a possible failure. I cannot prove an assertion of this kind, but I believe I can show why it should be seriously entertained.

Naive Monarchism: "Long Live X"

In sketching the case for a not-so-naive interpretation of naive monarchism among the peasantry, I rely very heavily on Daniel Field's thoughtful study of the phenomenon in Russia.[54] The "myth" of the Tsar-Deliverer, who would come to save his people from oppression, was generally believed to have been the great conservative ideological force in Russian history. Until Bloody Sunday in 1905, when the Tsar was known to have given orders for troops to fire on peaceful demonstrators, Lenin believed that it was naive monarchism that had been the major obstacle to peasant rebellion.

> ... until now [peasants] have been able naively and blindly to believe in the Tsar-*batiushka* [Deliverer], to seek relief from their unbearably hard circumstances from the Tsar-*batiushka* "Himself," and to blame coercion, arbitrariness, plunder and all other outrages *only* on the officials who deceive the Tsar. Long generations of the oppressed, savage life of the *muzhik*, lived out in neglected backwaters have reinforced this faith ... *Peasants could not rise in rebellion, they were only able to petition and to pray.*[55]

Lenin notwithstanding, there is simply no evidence that the myth of the Tsar promoted political passivity among the peasantry and a fair amount of evidence that, if anything, the myth facilitated peasant resistance.

The myth itself appears to have been developed in the 17th century during the "Time of Troubles" and dynastic crises. In one more-or-less standard variant, the Tsar-Deliverer desires to free his loyal subjects from serfdom—but wicked courtiers and officials, hoping to prevent this, try to assassinate him. Miraculously, he survives (often saved by a loyal serf) and hides among the people as a pilgrim, sharing their sufferings and revealing himself to a faithful few. At length he returns to the capital, is recognized by the people and enthroned, whereupon he rewards the faithful and punishes the wicked. As a just Tsar, he inaugurates a reign of peace and tranquility.[56]

Perhaps the most remarkable feature of the myth was its plasticity in the hands of its peasant adherents. First and foremost, it was an invitation to resist any or all of the Tsar's supposed agents who could not have been carrying out the good Tsar's wishes if they imposed heavy taxes, conscription, rents, military corvée, and so forth. If the Tsar only knew the crimes his faithless agents were committing in his name, he would punish them and rectify matters. When petitions failed and oppression continued, it may simply have indicated that an imposter—a false Tsar—was on the throne. In such cases, the peasants who joined the banners of a rebel claiming to be the true Tsar would be demonstrating their loyalty to the monarchy. Under the reign of Catherine II there were at least twenty-six "pretenders." Pugachev, the leader of one of the greatest peasant rebellions in modern European history, owed his success in part to his claim to be Tsar Peter III—a claim apparently accepted by many. As a practical matter, the wishes of the benevolent Tsar were whatever the pressing interests and tribulations of the peasantry projected onto him; and this, of course, was what made the myth so politically incendiary. The myth of the Tsar could transmute the peasantry's violent resistance to oppression into an act of loyalty to the crown. Defending themselves before the magistrate, Ukranian rebels in 1902 claimed that the Tsar had given them permission to take grain from the gentry and that they had heard there was a *ukase* (decree) from the Tsar to this effect which had been suppressed. Peasants might resist local authorities, claiming they (the officials) were acting against the will of the Tsar, and then reject messages and messengers to the contrary as fraudulent. They might rebel on behalf of reforms in serfdom, or its abolition, which had been decreed by the Tsar but concealed from them by cruel officials.

In a form of symbolic jujitsu, an apparently conservative myth counseling passivity becomes a basis for defiance and rebellion which is, in turn, publicly justified by faithful allegiance to the monarch! Once the serfs were convinced that their resistance was serving the Tsar, the submissive patience and prayer advised by the myth was of no avail to officialdom. As Field concludes,

> ... naive or not, the peasants professed their faith in the Tsar in forms, *and only in those forms*, that corresponded to their interests. Peasant leaders, finding the myth ready to hand in its folkloric expressions, used it to arouse, galvanize, and unify other peasants. It was a pretext to resistance against heavy odds, and there was not other likely means to that end.[57]

In each of the two cases examined in depth by Field, it was not entirely implausible to believe that local officials were defying the Tsar's wishes. After the Emancipation in 1861 the peasants in Biezdne (Kazan Province) were demoralized to discover that with redemption payments, labor dues, and taxes their burdens were, if anything, heavier than before. When one of their number claimed that the Emancipation Decree granted them complete freedom from such dues—the term *volia* for "freedom" appeared in many contexts in the decree—but that the squires and officials had kept it from being implemented, they leapt at the opportunity, now sanctioned from on high, to refuse payment. Given the fact that they had been formally freed from serfdom, the notion that its full import was being kept from them was not so far-fetched. It would not have been the first time nobles and officials had ignored or distorted a decree from the Tsar. At the same time, they drew up a petition to the Tsar and sent three of their number to Petrograd to deliver it by hand. Whatever they might be charged with, their actions *seemed* to disavow any temptation to sedition or treason. They avoided question and, when pressed, "dissimulated."[58]

The second case occurred in Chigirin District, Kiev Province in the Ukraine. It involved a dispute about land allocations—whether they were to be individual or communal—which had continued for more then seven years. A majority was opposed to the allocations imposed earlier and finally, in 1875, refused to make redemption payments and petitioned the Tsar in the most deferential terms, referring to a more generous *ukase* which had been kept from them. One unique feature of the Chigirin episode is that a populist agitator, hoping to spark an insurrection in these troubled waters, arrived in the area with cash and a bogus imperial charter supposedly from the hand of the Tsar granting them all their demands. He was attempting to use peasant gullibility and naive monarchism to launch a rebellion. The peasantry treated him as they might any outsider: they relieved him of his money, "they were obsequious and compliant in his presence and otherwise went their own way."[59]

When the imposter was arrested, local villagers, fearful of the consequences for themselves, drafted their own petition to the Tsar to explain why they might have believed that the Tsar had decided in their favor. It began, "How could we, simple, backward people, not believe in the kindness of our beloved monarch when the whole world attests to it, when we know of His love and trust for His people, His concern for them . . . ?"[60] Here it is not a question of peasants hilariously slapping their sides or cynically calculating the effect of their phrases. It *is*, however, a question of understanding at some level the usefulness of naiveté, simplicity, and backwardness in appeals to the Tsar. If the official view of the peasants as childlike, unenlightened, God-fearing, and basically loyal led to a philosophy of rule that emphasized both strictness and paternal indulgence, this official view was not without its advantages to peasants in a tight spot. By invoking their simplicity and loyalty, they might hope to invoke his generosity and forgiveness as well as that of the judges and police officials they might encounter. And if peasants were notoriously gullible, they could hardly be entirely responsible if they fell prey to clever, seditious propaganda. One can, under the circumstances, scarcely imagine a more effective symbolic rationale for acts of rebellion and insubordination—a rationale which was likely to minimize the consequences of failure in the struggle with gentry and officials over taxes, land dues, conscription, and grain. A history of the need to dissimulate, as well as long practice in the strategic use of hegemonic values, are all we need to grasp the use value of naive monarchism.

The usefulness of naive monarchism to the peasantry sprang in part from its value to the Tsarist bureaucracy. Above all, naive monarchism represented the most comforting interpretation of peasant disorder for those with most to gain from the existing distribution of property, status, and wealth. If there was discontent, it could be explained by a momentary disturbance of a fundamentally sound and just social order. The serfs/peasants were devoted to the Tsar and generally met their obligations to the state except when a few agitators or a few rapacious officials or aristocrats provoked them from their allegiance. It sufficed, then, to round up a few agitators or dismiss a few officials and order would be restored. No fundamental changes need be contemplated and no mass deportations of peasants to Siberia were required. Dealing leniently with the peasants who had expressed their repentance would further confirm the Tsar's reputation for paternal indulgence, thereby justifying the naive monarchism of the peasantry. And because the peasantry were still naive, backward and so easily misled—didn't they admit as much in the petitions?—they needed a strong, authoritarian monarch and his agents to guide and instruct them.

The tacit ideological complicity apparently at work here is a product of the very logic of Tsarist paternalism. While the peasants could make of naive monarchism an incitement to revolt, they also may well have appreciated the value of "the myth of the peasant"—the stereotype of the ignorant, "dark" *narod* could be as handy on occasion as a simple faith in the Tsar's concern for his people. In this respect, we must not see the myths of the Tsar and peasant as an ideological creation of the monarchy, then appropriated and reinterpreted by the peasantry. These myths were instead the joint product of an historic struggle, rather like a ferocious argument in which the basic terms ("simple peasant," "benevolent Tsar") are shared—but in which the interpretations follow wildly divergent paths in accordance with vital interests.

The not-so-naive use of naive monarchism by Russian peasants should give us pause about the analysis of those numerous occasions on which a rebellious subordinate group invokes the ritual symbols of a conservative hegemony. Throughout Europe and in Southeast Asia, for example, there are long traditions of the return of a just king or religious savior, despite great differences in cultural and religious lineages.[61] Such traditions have figured prominently in peasant rebellions and may have served much the same ideological function as the myth of the Tsar-Deliverer in Russia. The many variations in what have been, in England, called "Church and King" riots may well, on closer examination, have an important strategic element to them. In France and Italy in the sixteenth and seventeenth centuries, it was common for insurgent rioters to cry "Long Live the Virgin" ("Viva Maria") followed by particular demands. As Peter Burke has observed, "But it is unlikely that all the rebels were unaware of the strategic value of shouting, 'Viva Maria!' a cry which like 'Vive le Roi!' made their cause respectable. In that limited sense religious ideas were instruments in the struggle . . . "[62] We might, in this context, think of shouts of "Vive le Roi," when they come first in a series, just before, say, "Down with feudal dues and the salt tax" as having the same performative force as the deferential opening of a petition demanding redress for bitter grievances.[63] It is the "accepted" form of address, costs little, reassures one's antagonist that one is not out utterly to destroy him, claims loyal intentions, allows the king to grant the petition while appearing to enhance his prestige, and offers a welcome defensive posture which may help limit damage if the initiative fails. Such gestures may, in some cultural contexts, become as habitual as the ordinary conversational prefaces to complaints by subordinates who are not yet so alienated as to declare war. I have in mind sentences that might begin with: "I don't mean to complain but . . .;" "With all due respect . . ." Any dominant ideology with hegemonic pretensions must, by definition, provide subordinate groups with political weapons which can be of use in the public transcript.

Let us return briefly to the issue of "ethical submission" and hegemony by way of placing the public transcript in its political context. I believe the historical evidence clearly shows that subordinate groups have been capable of revolutionary *thought* which repudiates existing forms of domination. Schwabian artisans and cultivators in the German Peasant War could imagine that Christ's crucifixion had redeemed all believers from serfdom, bondage, and taxes; untouchables can and have imagined that orthodox Hinduism has hidden the sacred texts proving their equality; slaves can and have imagined a day when they would be free and slaveowners punished for their tyranny.

What is rare, then, is not the negation of domination in thought, but rather the occasions on which subordinate groups have been able to act openly and fully on that thought. Only under the most extraordinary historical circumstances, when the nearly total collapse of existing structures of domination open unprecedented new vistas of new realistic possibilities, can we expect to witness anything like an unguarded discourse by subordinate groups. In Western history, the German Peasant War, the English Civil War, the French Revolution, the Russian Revolution, and the Spanish Republic of 1936 offered such brief and privileged moments.[64] Here one glimpses something of the utopias of justice and revenge which are ordinarily marginalized in the hidden transcript.

Under any other circumstances, which is to say for the great bulk of political life, including most violent conflict, the stakes are less than the conquest of a new world. The conflict will accordingly take a dialogic form in which the language of the dialogue will invariably borrow heavily from the terms of the dominant ideology prevailing in the public transcript. If the official discourse is one of a Christian ruler and pious peasants, the ideological struggle will swirl around the interpretation of these terms.[65] We have seen similarly how, in a dominant discourse of benevolent Tsar and loyal serf, the ideological struggle will swirl around the interpretation of these terms and need not exclude violent conflict. A dominant ideology of paternalistic lords and faithful retainers does not prevent social conflict, but is simply an invitation to a structured argument. We may consider the dominant discourse as a plastic idiom or dialect which is capable of carrying an enormous variety of meanings, including those which are subversive of their use as intended by the dominant. Appealing to would-be hegemonic values sacrifices very little in the way of flexibility, given how malleable the terms are, and has the added advantage of appearing to disavow the most threatening goals. For anything less than completely revolutionary ends, the terrain of dominant discourse is the only plausible arena of struggle.

Exactly how deep this apparent acceptance of the dominant discourse goes is, again, impossible to judge from the public evidence. If we were to be exceptionally meticulous about the conclusions we could legitimately draw from such appearances, we might say that (addressing the dominant elite under less than revolutionary circumstances and given certain constraining assumptions about the distribution of power) the use of the terms of the dominant ideology in the course of political struggle is both realistic and prudent.

Minding the Public Discourse:

You have got to be a model thief if I am to be a model judge. If you are a fake thief, I become a fake judge. Is that clear?

—Genet, The Balcony

Any ruling group, in the course of justifying the principles of social inequality on which it bases its claim to power, makes itself vulnerable to a particular line of criticism.[66] Inasmuch as these principles of inequality unavoidably claim that the ruling stratum performs some valuable social function, its members open themselves to attack for the failure to perform these functions honorably or adequately. The basis of the claim to privilege and power creates, as it were, the groundwork for a blistering critique of domination on the terms invoked by the elite. Such a critique from within the ruling discourse is the ideological equivalent of being hoisted on one's own petard. For any particular form of domination, one may specify the claims to legitimacy it makes, the discursive affirmations it stages for the public transcript, the aspects of power relations which it will seek to hide (its "dirty linen"), the acts and gestures which will undermine its claim to legitimacy, the critiques that are possible within its frame of reference, and, finally, the ideas and actions which will represent a repudiation or profanation of the form of domination in its entirety.⁶⁷

The analysis of forms of domination might well begin by specifying the ways in which the structure of claims to power influences the sort of public transcript domination requires. It might then examine how such a public transcript may be undermined or repudiated. If, for example, we were studying the relation between warrior aristocrats of feudal Europe and their serfs, it would be important to understand how their claim to hereditary authority was based on providing physical protection in return for labor, grain, and military service. This "exchange" might be discursively affirmed in an emphasis on honor, *noblesse oblige*, bravery, expansive generosity, tournaments and contests of military prowess, the construction of fortifications, the regalia and ceremony of knighthood, sumptuary laws, the assembling of serfs for work or military campaigns, acts of deference and humility of serfs before their lords, exemplary punishment for insubordination, oaths of fealty, and so forth. The feudal "contract" could be *discursively negated* by any conduct that violated these affirmations: e.g., cowardice, petty bargaining, stinginess, runaway serfs, failures to physically protect serfs, refusals to be respectful or deferential by serfs, and so forth. A parallel kind of analysis might be applied to relations between the Brahmin (or high-caste superior) and the lower caste. Here the claim to power is based on sacred hereditary status, superior karma, and on the provision of certain presumably vital ritual services which can only be performed by Brahmins due to their status and knowledge. Discursive affirmations might include all the ritual separations of purity and pollution; diet; dress; refinement of manner; presiding at key rites of birth, marriage, death; observance of taboos on commensuality; other forms of segregation by occupation, residence, drinking wells, temples, etc. The discursive negation of these expressions of hierarchy might take the form of refusing to abide by rules about pollution and purity, failure by Brahmins to provide ritual services, insubordination in terms of address or posture by untouchables, and so on. This pattern of analysis might be extended, of course, to any particular historical form of domination in comparable terms; e.g., certain forms of priestly rule, specific forms of slavery, various monarchical systems, religious prophets within a specified tradition, modern managerial authority in the firm in Italy or in Japan. Having elaborated the public transcript required by a specific form of domination, one has gone far to specify precisely what a subversive act in this context would look like.

Regardless of the particular form of domination, it is a safe bet that a vital sector of the elite-choreographed public transcript will consist of visual and audible displays of rank, precedence, and honor. Here I have in mind such expressions of domination as terms of address, demeanor, speech levels, codes of eating, dressing, bathing, cultural taste, who speaks first, who gives way to whom. By the same token, whenever the public transcript is breached—whether inadvertently or by design—it is also a safe bet that such breaches will disrupt or desacralize the ceremonial reverence.⁶⁸ For acts of insubordination of this kind represent a small insurgency within the public transcript.

Just as the official transcript helps define what counts as an insult to the dominant—as *lèse majesté*—it also helps to define which of the practices that comprise the inevitable dirty-work of power must be screened from public view. The very operation of a rationale for inequality creates a potential zone of "dirty linen" that, if exposed, would contradict the pretensions of legitimate domination. A ruling stratum whose claim to authority rests on the provision of institutionalized justice under law with honest judges will have to go to exceptional lengths to hide its thugs, its hired assassins, its secret police, and its use of intimidation. An elite which bases its power on its self-sacrificing, public spirited probity will be damaged more by an exposé of corruption in high places than a patronage machine. Every publicly given justification for inequality thus marks out a kind of symbolic Achilles heel where the elite is especially vulnerable.

Attacks which focus on this symbolic Achilles heel may be termed "critiques within-the-hegemony." One reason why they are particularly hard to deflect is simply because they begin by adopting the ideological terms of reference of the elite. Although such critiques *may* be insincere and cynical, they cannot be accused of sedition inasmuch as they clothe themselves in the public professions of the elite, which now stands accused of hypocrisy, if not the violation of a sacred trust. Having formulated the very terms of the argument and propagated them, the ruling stratum can hardly decline to defend itself on this terrain of its own choosing. The cowardly lion is a staple of pathos, if not humor, in the folklore of those who have regarded the lion as a metaphor for courage. An ascetic priestly caste is profoundly damaged if shown to be promiscuous and gluttonous; the benevolent Tsar is profoundly damaged if shown to have ordered the troops to fire on his peacefully assembled, respectful subjects; the slaveowner's claim to paternalism is hollow if he can be shown to whip his slaves *arbitrarily*; and the general is compromised if he abandons his troops in fear for his own life. Any dominant group is, in this respect, least able to take liberties with those symbols in which they are most heavily invested.⁶⁹

It is perhaps for this reason why, as we have indicated earlier, so many radical attacks originate in critiques within-the-hegemony—in taking the values of ruling elites seriously, while claiming that they (the elites) do not. To launch an attack in these terms is to, in effect, call upon the elite to take its own rhetoric seriously. Not only is such an attack a legitimate critique by definition, but it always threatens to appeal to sincere members of the elite in a way that an attack from outside their values could not. The Soviet dissident Voinovich captures the critical force of disillusioned believers:

> I was a completely harmless member of society. It is the young people, those who display a serious interest in the theoretical foundations of communism and begin immersing themselves in Marx, Lenin and Stalin who pose a much greater danger to the regime. The Soviet authorities realize this. A person who takes theory seriously will, sooner or later, begin comparing it with practice, and will end up rejecting one or the other, and, later on, the two of them together. But a person who has not been seduced by theory will view the practice as a common and immutable evil—one that can be lived with.[70]

The remarkable fact may be that it is when a would-be hegemonic ideology does manage to convince members of subordinate groups to take it to heart that a potentially radical chain of events is set into motion. That is, contrary to the usual wisdom and to Gramsci's analysis, radicalism may be less likely to arise among disadvantaged groups (the vast majority, it appears) who fail to take the dominant ideology seriously than among those who, in Marxist terms, might be considered falsely-conscious. In a perceptive study of working class secondary school students in England, Paul Willis discovered a strong counter-culture that produced a cynical distance from dominant platitudes but *not* radicalism.[71] Paradoxically, it was the "conformists" who appeared, in form at least, to accept the values of the school (the hegemonic instrument par excellence in modern society) who posed the threat. Because they operated as if they accepted the implicit promise of the dominant ideology (if you work hard, obey authority, do well in school, and keep your nose clean you will advance by merit and have satisfying work), they made sacrifices of self-discipline and control and developed expectations which were, usually, betrayed. Employers preferred *not* to hire them because they were "pushy" and "hard to deal with" as compared with the more typical working-class youth who were realistic, expected little, and put in a day of work without too much grumbling. The "system" may have to fear most from those subordinates among whom the institutions of hegemony have been most successful.[72] The disillusioned mission boy (Caliban) is always a graver threat to an established religion than the 'pagans' who were never 'taken in' by its promises. The anger born of a sense of betrayal implies an earlier faith.

Notes

1. Some of the representative voices in this debate may be found in Robert A. Dahl, *Who Governs? Democracy and Power in an American City* (New Haven: Yale University Press, 1961); Nelson W. Polsby, *Community Power and Political Theory*

(New Haven: Yale University Press, 1963); Jack E. Walker, "A Critique of the Elitist Theory of Democracy," *American Political Science Review*, vol. 60 (1966), pp.285–95; Peter Bachrach and Morton S. Baratz, *Power and Poverty: Theory and Practice* (New York: Oxford University Press, 1970); Steven Lukes, *Power: A Radical View* (London: Macmillan, 1974); and John Gaventa, *Power and Powerlessness: Quiescence and Rebellion in an Appalachian Valley* (Urbana: Univ. of Illinois Press, 1980).

2. Some of the representative voices in this debate are Antonio Gramsci, *Selections from the Prison Notebooks*, ed. and trans. Quinten Hoare and Geoffrey Nowell Smith (London: Wishart, 1971); Frank Parkin, *Class Inequality and Political Order* (New York: Praeger, 1971); Ralph Miliband, *The State in Capitalist Society* (London: Weidenfeld and Nicholson, 1969); Nicos Poulantzas, *State, Power, Socialism* (London: New Left Books, 1978); Anthony Giddens, *The Class Structure of Advanced Societies* (New York: Harper, 1975); Jürgen Habermas, *Legitimation Crisis* (Boston: Beacon Press, 1975); and Louis Althusser, *Reading Capital* (London: New Left Books, 1970). For penetrating critiques of these approaches see especially, Nicholas Abercrombie, Stephen Hill, and Bryan S. Turner, *The Dominant Ideology Thesis* (London: G. Allen and Unwin, 1980), and Paul Willis, *Learning to Labour* (Westmead: Saxon House, 1977).

3. The sort of misrepresentation referred to might, for a liberal democracy, include the effects of official beliefs in equality of economic opportunity, an open, accessible political system, and what Marx called "commodity fetishism." The effect of each belief in turn might be to stigmatize the poor as entirely responsible for their poverty, to mask the inequalities in political influence underwritten by economic power, and to misrepresent low wages or unemployment to workers as an entirely impersonal, natural (i.e., not social) occurrence.

4. See Abercrombie, *The Dominant Ideology Thesis* and Willis, *Learning to Labour*.

5. Gaventa, *Power and Powerlessness*, ch. 1.

6. The appropriate analogy here is that of an electric fence, which repels intruders.

7. Gaventa, *Power and Powerlessness*, p. 22, emphasis added. For a "thicker" version of this argument see Parkin, *Class Inequality and Political Order*, pp. 79–91.

8. Not, however, without real concessions as the price of hegemony on the Gramscian view.

9. This criticism is best summarized in Abercrombie, *et al.*, *The Dominant Ideology Thesis*, passim.

10. Some of this evidence is summarized in my *Weapons of the Weak: Everyday Forms of Peasant Resistance* (New Haven: Yale University Press, 1985), ch. 8, where I rely heavily on Barrington Moore, Jr., *Injustice: The Social Bases of Obedience and Revolt* (White Plains, N.Y.: M.E. Sharpe, 1978) and Willis, *Learning to Labour*.

11. Richard Hoggart, *The Uses of Literacy: Changing Patterns in English Mass Culture* (Fair Lawn, N.J.: Essential Books, 1957), p. 77–78.

12. Hoggart also implicitly asks us to agree that people do not dream much about what they are convinced they cannot have, nor do they waste time railing against what they believe they cannot change. These claims are far more contestable, as we shall see later.

13. The doctrine of karma and reincarnation, the ultimate in ideologies of hegemony, promise that a conforming and humble untouchable will be rewarded by

rebirth in a higher status. Justice is promised, and in an entirely mechanical fashion; it is just that justice only operates between lifetimes, not within them.

14. Pierre Bourdieu, *Outline of a Theory of Practice* translated by Richard Nice (Cambridge: Cambridge Univ. Press, 1977), p. 164.

15. Anthony Giddens, *Central Problems in Social Theory: Action, Structure, and Contradiction in Social Analysis* (Berkely: University of California Press, 1979), p. 195.

16. Willis, *Learning to Labour*, p. 162. Zygmunt Bauman sees hegemony as a process by which alternatives to the current structure of power and status are excluded: ". . . the dominant culture consists of transforming everything which is not inevitable into the improbable . . . and overrepressive society is one which effectively eliminates alternatives to itself and thereby relinquishes spectacular, dramatized displays of its power." *Socialism, The Active Utopia* (New York: Holmes and Meier Publishers, 1975), p. 123.

17. Bourdieu, *Outline of a Theory of Practice*, p. 77. In a later work the same point is put somewhat more obscurely, and it is difficult to discern whether "consent" means resignation to the inevitable or the embracing of the inevitable. He writes,

> Dominated agents . . . tend to attribute to themselves what the distribution attributes to them, refusing what they are refused ('That's not for the likes of us'), adjusting their expectations to their chances, defining themselves as the established order defines them, reproducing in their verdict on themselves the verdict the economy pronounces on them, condemning themselves to what is in any case their lot . . . consenting to be what they have to be, 'modest,' 'humble,' and 'obscure.'

Distinction: A Social Critique of the Judgement of Taste, translated by Richard Nice, (Cambridge: Harvard Univ. Press, 1984), p. 471.

18. Moore, *Injustice*, p. 64.

19. For a discussion of such theories see John D. McCarthy and William L. Yancey, "Uncle Tom and Mr. Charlie: Metaphysical Pathos in the Study of Racism and Personality Disorganization," *American Journal of Sociology*, Vol. 76 (1970-71), pp. 648-72.

20. If we substitute "servility" for "friendliness" in the following quote from Nietzsche, the process being imagined is apparent: "He who *always* wears the mask of a friendly (servile) man must *at last* gain power over friendliness [servility] of disposition, without which the expression itself of friendliness [servility] is not to be gained—and finally friendliness [servility] of disposition gains the ascendancy over him—he is benevolent [servile]." We will have ample reason, later, to reject this logic, but is important to recognize the nature of the argument being made. Nietzsche implies that the mask must never be removed and that the transmutation occurs after a long, but unspecified, period. Notice also that the substitution of "servility" for "friendliness" may fundamentally change the logic. We assume that the man who "wears the mask of a friendly man" actually wishes to become genuinely friendly, whereas there is every reason to assume that the man who "wears the mask of servility" wears it because he has no choice and wishes he could discard it. In the case of servility, the principal motive which might remake a face to fit a mask may well be lacking. Quoted in Arlie R. Hochschild, *The Managed Heart* (Berkeley: University of California Press, 1983), p. 35, emphasis added.

21. See, for example, ch. 8, Scott, *Weapons of the Weak: Everyday Forms of Peasant Resistance* (New Haven: Yale University Press, 1985) and Abercrombie, et al., *The Dominant Ideology Thesis, passim.*

22. We shall later have reason to ask whether or not these objectives are not, themselves, partly an artifact of power relations which preclude voicing more ambitious objectives.

23. Moore, *Injustice*, pp. 369–70.

24. Examples that come to mind are those of the German working-class in the "near-revolution" after World War I or the peasantry of Morelos under Zapata in the Mexican Revolution. To put it another way, what Lenin saw as "trade-union consciousness"—modest objectives pursued in this case with ferocious intensity—is very common in revolutionary situations.

25. Willis, *Learning to Labour*, p 175.

26. Marc Bloch, *French Rural History: An Essay on its Basic Character*. Trans. by Janet Sondheimer, (Berkeley: Univ. of California Press, 1970), p. 169.

27. In the West Indies where agricultural units were much larger on average, where slaves comprised the vast majority of the population, and where conditions were materially worse as well (judging from the mortality rates), rebellion was far more common.

28. Traditional peasants not only denaturalize the weather. In rebellions it is common to find traditional peoples wearing charms, amulets, or reciting magic formulas which they believe will make them invulnerable to the weapons of their enemies. For several examples of colonial rebellions in which such "denaturalization" occurs, see Michael Adas, *Prophets of Rebellion: Millenarian Protest against European Colonial Order* (Chapel Hill: University of North Carolina Press, 1979).

29. For a more elaborate argument along these lines, see my "Protest and Profanation: Agrarian Revolt and the Little Tradition," *Theory and Society*, Part I, Vol. 4 (1977), pp. 1–38; Part II, Vol. 4 (1977), pp. 211–46. The subject of inversions and reversals in art and social thought is examined in Barbara A. Babcock, ed., *The Reversible World: Symbolic Inversion in Art and Society* (Ithaca: Cornell Univ. Press, 1978). In this collection see, particularly, David Kunzle, "World Upside Down: The Iconography of a European Broadsheet Type," pp. 39–94.

30. Nguyen Hong Giap, *La Condition des paysans au Viet-Nam à travers les chansons populaires* (Paris, thèse 3ème cycle, Sorbonne, 1971), p. 183.

31. Norman Cohn, *The Pursuit of the Millenium* (London: Secker and Warburg, 1957), p. 245.

32. David Kunzle, "World Upside Down," pp. 80–82.

33. We should, of course, set aside from this discussion two kinds of subordination. First, we exclude the voluntary and revocable subordination typified by entering a religious order. The fact that someone who enters such a life makes a voluntary commitment to the principles which underlie the subordination, principles which are usually marked by a solemn oath, but which may be renounced at any time, fundamentally changes the nature of domination. Hegemony, if one could call it that, is established by definition since only true believers enter and when they cease being believers, they may leave. Voluntary servitude for a specified time of voluntary enlistment in the military or merchant marine, which it resembles, is less

clear cut. Entry may not be experienced as voluntary if, say, few other economic opportunities exist and one may not escape subordination until the term of enlistment or servitude expires. In principle, however, the greater the freedom of choice in entry and the greater the ease of withdrawal, the more legitimate the subordination. The second form of subordination we exclude is that of infants and children to parents. The asymmetry of power in this situation is extreme—hence the possibility for abuses—but it is typically benign and nurturant rather than exploitative, and it is a biological given.

34. The promise of being set free in return for a record of service and compliance can also produce a pattern of conformity that looks very much like hegemony. This is an excellent example of how the prospects for the future exert a palpable influence on the evaluation of one's present conditions. This effect is vastly magnified if the possibility of emancipation is mediated solely by the will of the dominant. As Orlando Patterson, *Slavery and Social Death: A Comparative Study* (Cambridge, MA: Harvard University Press, 1982), p. 101 has observed in the case of slavery, holding out the promise of eventual manumission upon the death of the master was more effective than any whip in gaining steady compliance. The logic is precisely the same as that of those prison systems which hold out the promise of time off for good behavior. And like the incentive of "good time," the possibility of manumission can never produce hegemony because it is, after all, the slave's desire for emancipation, the prisoner's desire for liberty, which is being manipulated. The very premise of the manipulation is that the subordinate will do almost anything—including faithful compliance for an extended period—if that is the price of liberation. Such a pact or contract is possible only on the assumption that the ideology of domination is *not* hegemonic.

35. *Discipline and Punish: the Birth of the Prison* (New York: Pantheon Books, 1977), p. 237. Solitude, atomization, and domination are also the themes of some influential interpretations of schizophrenia. Since the experience of victimization and control is an individual one (and not a social one shared by others similarly placed) for the schizophrenic, the boundary between fantasy and action disappears. See, for example, James M. Glass, *Delusion: Internal Dimensions of Political Life* (Chicago: University of Chicago Press, 1985), chapter 3, and Harold F. Searles, *Collected Papers on Schizophrenia and Related Subjects* (New York: International Universities Press, 1965), chapter 19.

36. Denise Winn, *The Manipulated Mind* (London: Octagon Press, 1983), *passim*.

37. Stanley Milgram, *Obedience to Authority: An Experimental View* (New York: Harper and Row, 1974), pp. 116–21. Milgram's experiment showed how easily subjects could be induced to do something against their better judgement and might, from one angle, be seen as proving the ease of indoctrination. The key fact, however, is that Milgram's subjects were all volunteers rather than unwilling conscripts. As we have seen in Chapter 2, this makes all the difference in readiness to be persuaded.

38. Subordinates are never, of course, in precisely the same boat. This raises another question: that of divide and rule. If we imagine, say, that each slave of a given master is treated differently on some uniform scale of harshness or benevolence, then it follows that one half of the slaves in question are treated better than

average. This being so, should they not be grateful to be among the privileged and should they therefore not internalize the ideology of slavery? While it is surely true that slaves and other subordinates might strive to please their masters to win such privileges, this does not imply internalization of hegemonic standards. To assume that it does is to assume that slaves and others are incapable of simultaneously understanding that a form of domination is unjust *and* that they are relatively better off than other slaves. Consider the following statement made by a recently emancipated slave about her ex-mistress:

> Well, she was as good as most any old white woman. She was the best white woman that ever broke bread, but you know, honey, that wasn't much, 'cause they all hated the po' nigger.

Quoted in Eugene G. Genovese, *Roll, Jordan Roll* (New York: Pantheon Books, 1974), p. 125.

39. There are also interests involved here. For conservative social theorists, the notion of ideological consent from below is obviously comforting. For the Leninist left, on the other hand, it offers a role for the vanguard party and its intelligentsia who must lift the scales from the eyes of the oppressed. If the working class was capable of generating not only the force of numbers and economic leverage but also the ideas of their own liberation, the role of the Leninist party becomes problematic.

40. Christopher Hill, "From Lollardy to Levellers," pp. 86–103 in Janos M. Bak and Gerhard Benecke, eds., *Religion and Rural Revolt: Papers Presented to the Fourth Interdisciplinary Workshop on Peasant Studies*, University of British Columbia, 1982 (Manchester: Manchester University Press, 1984).

41. Hill, p. 87.

42. Hill, p. 93.

43. For an extended account comparing this resistance to the resistance of French peasants to the Catholic tithe in the seventeenth and eighteenth centuries, see my "Resistance Without Protest and Without Organization: Peasant Opposition to the Islamic Zakat and the Christian Tithe," in *Comparative Studies in Society and History* 29:3 (July, 1987).

44. This raises a political variant of the philosophical question: Does a tree falling in the forest, and unheard by any living creature, make a sound? Does "resistance" by subordinates, which is purposely overlooked by elites or called by another name, qualify as "resistance?" Does resistance, in other words, require recognition as resistance by the party being resisted? The issue points to the enormous importance of the power and authority to determine (never entirely unilaterally) what is considered the public transcript and what is not. The ability to choose to overlook or ignore an act of insubordination as if it never happened is a key exercise of power.

45. The term comes from Edward E. Jones, *Ingratiation* (New York: Appleton-Century-Crofts, 1964), p. 47. He defines the term as follows:

> In protective ingratiation, the goal is not to improve one's outcomes beyond some otherwise expected level, but rather to blunt a potential attack . . . farsightful defensive planning. For the protective ingratiator, the world is

peopled with potential antagonists, people who can be unkind, hostile, brutally frank. Ingratiation can serve to transform this world into a safer place by depriving the potential antagonist of any pretext for aggression.

46. Gramsci, *Selections from the Prison Notebooks*, p. 333.

47. Moore, *Injustice*, p. 84.

48. Michel Foucault, *Michel Foucault: Power, Truth, Strategy*, edited by Meaghan Morris and Paul Patton (Signey: Feral Publications, 1979). "Working Papers Collection #2," p. 88.

49. Thomas Mathiesen, *The Defenses of the Weak: A Sociological Study of a Norwegian Correctional Institution* (London: Tavistock, 1965).

50. Over time, of course, the use and manipulation of the ideological rules for novel purposes will transform them in important ways.

51. Tetsuo Najita and Irwin Scheiner, *Japanese Thought in the Tokugawa Period* (Chicago: University of Chicago Press, 1978), pp. 41, 43.

52. Le Roy Ladurie, *Carnival in Romans* (New York: G. Braziller, 1979), p. 257. The Dauphinois historian quoted here is N. Chorier, *Histoire Generale de Dauphine*, II 1672, p. 697.

53. Ladurie, p. 152, emphasis added. At the same time Paumier did not kneel before Catherine while saying this, an omission which the enemies of the popular movement found insolent.

54. Daniel Field, *Rebels in the Name of the Tsar* (Boston: Houghton Mifflin, 1976).

55. Quoted in Field, p. 2, emphasis added.

56. The parallels with the life of Christ can hardly be inadvertent but, as in other cultures, there were in Russia long traditions of the return of a just king. As in Western Europe, the anti-Christ and the tyrant were often assimilated to one another.

57. Field, p. 209.

58. Field, p. 79.

59. Field, p. 201.

60. Field, p. 198. Speculatively, the form of the classic petition is a threat embedded in a rhetoric of deference. One imagines it being read by officials who routinely skip the rhetoric of deference in order to get to the operative clause which may state (though in more decorous terms): "If you don't lower taxes we may make big trouble." But in the dramaturgy of naive monarchism the petition says, in effect, "Alright, we'll pretend to be loyal peasants so long as you pretend to be the beneficent Tsar, which, in this case, means lowering taxes."

61. For a brief discussion of these traditions in Europe, see Peter Burke, *Popular Culture in Early Modern Europe* (New York: Harper and Row, 1978), ch. 6. For similar traditions in Southeast Asia, see Michael Adas, *Prophets of Rebellion*.

62. Peter Burke, "Mediterranean Europe, 1500–1800," in Janos M. Bak and Gerhard Benecke, eds., *Religion and Rural Revolt*, p. 79.

63. This particular shout is reported for sixteenth-century Normandy by David Nicholls, "Religion and Peasant Movements during the French Religious Wars," in Bak and Benecke, pp. 104–22.

64. For a pathbreaking analysis of utopian moments in French history—all recapturing in some sense the initial promise of the Revolution of 1789, see Aristide R. Zolberg, "Moments of Madness," *Politics and Society* 2:2 (Winter, 1972), pp. 183–207.

65. The Filipino revolutionary leader Andreas Bonifacio, for example, issued a manifesto charging the Spanish with having betrayed a pact of brotherhood in which they promised their Filipino younger brothers knowlege, prosperity, and justice. "Do we see them fulfilling their side of the contract which we ourselves fulfilled with sacrifices? We see nothing but treachery as a reward for our favors." (Quoted in Reynaldo Clemeña Ileto, *Pasyon and the Interpretation of Change in Tagalog Society*, Ph.D. thesis Cornell University, 1975, p. 107.) As the Spanish have betrayed the self-proclaimed terms of their domination, the Filipino people are absolved from any obligation to obey. Bonifacio, of course, necessarily implies that if the Spanish had lived up to their Christian professions, the Tagalogs would have remained loyal. Did Bonifacio believe this? We cannot know. What we do know, however, is that he chose to address the Spanish in terms they could understand—in the terms of their own rhetorical discourse and which, on this interpretation, justified armed defense.

66. Moore, *Injustice*, p. 84.

67. A very suggestive analysis along these lines, dealing with conflicts in the jute mills of Bengal earlier in this century, will serve to indicate how valuable such an inquiry might be. Dipesh Chakraberty shows how the patron-client style of authority exercised by supervisors in the mills required personal discretion, direct relations of both benevolence and brutality, and the display of power in the form of dress, retenue, housing, and demeanor. By adopting the parental model as the pattern for the relationship, the supervisor was experienced along a continuum from personal despot to kindly father-figure. Unlike relations of industrial discipline derived from contract, the labor market, the division of labor, and the organization of work, control was phrased in entirely personal, direct, and often violent terms. One result, as Chakraberty shows, is that the resistance to the supervisors, in turn, tended to take the form of personal vengeance and violence. Insults to the dignity of the worker, used as a form of social control, were repaid in insults to the supervisor when that was possible. The form of resistance mirrored the form of domination. Dipesh Chakraberty, "On Deifying and Defying Authority: Managers and Workers in the Jute Mills of Bengal circa 1900–1940," *Past and Present* no. 100 (August, 1983), pp. 124–46.

68. See Ranajit Guha, *Elementary Aspects of Peasant Insurgency in Colonial India* (Delhi: Oxford, 1983), ch. 2 especially.

69. Bourdieu, *Toward a Theory of Practice*, pp. 193–94. The constraint, I believe, is also self-imposed in part since these claims are rarely just a cynical facade for the dominant.

70. Vladimir Voinovich, *The Anti-Soviet Soviet Union*, translated by Richard Lourie, (New York: Harcourt Brace Jovanovich, 1985), p. 147.

71. Willis, *Learning to Labour*, pp.110–11.

72. One might argue similarly that the institutional centers of the civil rights movement in the U.S. in the early 1960's were churches and universities precisely because the contradiction between principles of equality and the reality of segregation was particularly striking in institutions making strong moral claims. See Sara Evans, *Personal Politics* (New York: Vintage Books, 1980), p. 32.

10

Challenge and Resistance: Two Cases of Cultural Conflict in the United States

Richard M. Merelman

Introduction

Analysis of the relationship between dominant and subordinate groups has preoccupied political sociology from its classical period onward. Conflict theories in political sociology—whether Marxist or Weberian—assume that dominants and subordinates normally contest each other for power. By contrast, consensus theories in political sociology assume that functional interdependencies normally hold dominants and subordinates peacefully together. Struggles for power therefore become the exception, rather than the rule.

Conflict theorists have generally attempted to explain the struggle between dominants and subordinates by reference to economic and political factors. To Marx, of course, increasing capitalist exploitation of workers created a process of confrontation between the two groups.[1] Weber argued that the market and the state were principal foci of conflict between subordinates and dominants over unequal "life chances."[2] Even Durkheim —usually viewed as the father of modern consensus theory—argued that conflict in industrialized societies reflected economic factors: a "forced" division of labor within the productive process.[3] Thus, to all three theorists conflict was economically and politically motivated.

Of course, these theorists did not ignore value differences as possible sources of conflict between dominant and subordinate groups. The most famous example is Weber's analysis of the way Protestantism helped destroy feudalism.[4] However, Weber argued that in modern societies value-driven struggles between dominants and subordinates would diminish in the face of bureaucratic power. Conflict generated by culture would give way to the instrumental rationality of the bureaucratic stratum.[5]

Recently, however, conflict theorists have begun to reassess the contribution of cultural factors to social and political conflict. Sometimes overlooked in discussions of Gramsci, for example, is his insistence that cultural hegemony has two faces: one which favors capitalist domination, the other which supports worker resistance. Gramsci described at some length the indispensable contribution of "organic intellectuals" to the formation of subordinate classes. As Bocock puts it:

> Gramsci was concerned with arguing that Marxism needed an elite who were to be well educated in philosophy and political economy, but who would also be in touch with the masses and not only with other intellectuals.[6]

This process of the social construction of a class involves organic intellectuals actively helping to produce the class as a change agent. Classes do not arise already formed as agents of change within the relations of production.[7]

Moreover, Gramsci also argued that workers needed to develop an ideology of populism if they were to reach a *national* constituency of all the oppressed, including peasants and farmers.[8] In short, to Gramsci new cultural formations helped to *create* and *disseminate* class interests. Culture and ideology did not simply reflect objectively determined group struggle.

Recently, Paul DiMaggio has argued that cultural symbols have increasingly become sources of group conflict, and determinants of group power. As DiMaggio puts it:

> Symbols . . . become increasingly important to the organization of social life as the division of labor and the number of human contacts increase . . . Subjects of conversation supplant objects of display as bases of social evaluation. This process is accompanied by the rise of meritocratic ideology and the substitution of 'cultural capital' for direct inheritance in the mobility strategies of the upper middle class.[9]

In an important empirical study, DiMaggio demonstrates that participation in a symbol-based "status culture" influences the academic success of American high school students, regardless of the students' inherited class position. DiMaggio also found that participation in a "high status culture" disproportionately assisted students from lower economic classes.[10] This finding implies that cultural distinctiveness may be a useful weapon in the struggle to overcome economic and political subordination.

The fullest modern theory of cultural conflict between dominant and subordinate groups may be found in the work of the British Cultural Studies school.[11] These theorists concentrate on popular culture as a terrain of cultural conflict. A typical statement is that of Janet Woollacott: "Works of fiction and specific genres are popular precisely because they articulate, work upon and attempt in different ways to resolve contemporary ideological tensions."[12] This statement specifically denies any mechanistic cultural domination exerted by the powerful over the powerless; instead, popular culture constitutes a site within which conflicts over ideology are made explicit, debated, and possibly even resolved in a transformative direction.

The present essay takes up ideas put forth by Gramsci, DiMaggio, and Woollacott, among others. By examining two cases it attempts to describe some features of cultural conflict between dominant and subordinate groups in the United States. The first case—the Martin Luther King, Jr. federal holiday—involves the symbolic recognition of a subordinate racial group. The second— the films of Spike Lee—involves a cinematic challenge to the interpretation of race relations traditionally favored by white dominants.

My hope is to lay some groundwork for a theory of cultural struggle in liberal democracies, drawing upon recent American racial experience. The essay is divided into three parts: (1) a discussion of the King holiday, (2) a discussion of Spike Lee's films, and (3) a conclusion containing some tentative generalizations from these two cases about the nature of contemporary cultural conflict between blacks and whites in the United States.

The Martin Luther King Jr. Federal Holiday

One form which cultural challenge assumes is symbolic commemoration of subordinate group achievements and leaders. Memorials, in the form of holidays, monuments, or public ceremonies, represent a limited step in the struggle for cultural power. Symbolic recognition permits members of dominant and subordinate groups to interpret these events largely as they choose. This indeterminate quality is a considerable advantage for the subordinate group. Subordinates need not squabble among themselves about tactics to attack the economic or political power of the dominant group, for no such power is directly at stake. Therefore, symbolism allows subordinate groups to unite, rather than to fragment over riskier proposals which threaten the material well-being of dominants.

Moreover, chances of symbolic success are good, for commemorations pose little immediate psychological threat to dominants. Indeed, few members of the dominant group need even be inconvenienced by memorials to subordinates. After all, memorials are quite delimited in time and space. By definition, a holiday occupies a designated period of time; and a memorial plaque occupies a single location, which dominant group members can choose to avoid. Therefore, from the dominant point of view, ceremonial, ritual, or commemorative symbols honoring subordinate groups represent little immediate threat.

However, symbolic commemorations may also spread, penetrating sites of power normally controlled by dominants, and exposing dominants to subordinate group achievements, personages, grievances, and values. For example, observances of the Martin Luther King, Jr. federal holiday have diffused widely throughout sites controlled by dominants. In the Washington, D.C. area, the overwhelming majority of private schools—attended and controlled largely by affluent whites—extensively celebrate the King holiday. These celebrations include classroom lessons, dramatic presentations, voluntary pledges to carry on King's work ("Living the Dream" pledges), and school-community programs.

Still, despite diffusion, it is easy to dismiss symbolic challenges to dominants as trivial or even counter-productive. Edelman, for example, treats symbolic victories by subordinates more as placebos than as assertions of subordinate group power. Edelman argues that symbolic events often divert subordinate groups from threats to the structural foundations of dominant group power.[13]

This perspective, however, is limited. As Kertzer points out, symbolic events sometimes stimulate revolutionary outbreaks against dominant groups.[14] There is nothing about symbolism *per se* which inherently deflects or accelerates subordinate demands for political change. Both outcomes seem equally possible.

In fact, commemorating subordinates can significantly weaken dominants. After all, symbolic recognition requires the dominant group to accept the history and experience of subordinates at least as a worthwhile object for its own attention. Perusing this history may precipitate a novel construction of the past for dominants. Not only is this reconstruction of the past a crucial step for subordinates wishing to advance their struggle,[15] but it may also require dominants to concede that they have caused much pain and deprivation to subordinates. This concession represents a useful victory for subordinates.

Brief examination of the Martin Luther King, Jr. federal holiday is therefore instructive. The campaign to secure the holiday demonstrates how legislative and electoral politics in the United States sometimes favor subordinate group cultural demands. The King episode shows that a few determined members of Congress who play by standard Congressional rules can by themselves effect a considerable symbolic advance for subordinates. Moreover, examination of classroom curricula devoted to the King holiday reveals an interesting ideological framework within which King appears, in Lucaites and Condit's words, as a "culture-type," i.e., a leader who "... revivifies ... ideographs central to the process of social change."[16]

Demands by Coretta Scott King and other civil rights leaders that King's birthday be declared a federal holiday emerged soon after King's assassination. Not until 1983, however, did Congress declare it thus. The main reason for this delay, of course, was King's controversial status. For some time, political entrepreneurs were afraid to promote the enabling legislation. However, Congress Member Katie Hall of Gary, Indiana—otherwise little known—eventually began to lobby her colleagues tirelessly for the proposal. Her efforts brought the idea from the shadow of civil rights controversy to the light that only serious Congressional consideration could provide.[17]

Soon other, more powerful members of Congress took up the King holiday proposal. Particularly significant was Congress Member John Conyers, the Democrat from Detroit. While Hall lacked seniority and clout in Congress, Conyers possessed both. As early as 1976 Conyers introduced legislation favoring the holiday, advocating it in every session thereafter. He also made certain the Judiciary Committee in the Senate gained jurisdiction over the bill. Conyers knew that Edward Kennedy, chair of the appropriate Judiciary sub-committee, had both political and personal reasons for supporting the legislation. Thus, Conyers ultimately proved to be the chief legislative catalyst on the issue.

Although Congress finally proved receptive, the King holiday also reveals some of the limits of symbolism in promoting cultural conflict. For one thing, proponents of the King holiday found it necessary to endorse symbols of the dominant group in order to advance their cause. The House bill, for example, described King as "a person who shook the moral conscience of this nation,"[18] a formulation which assured the "nation" (i.e., the dominant group) that King possessed the same moral conscience as did they. As the Congressional debate reached its climax, John Conyers argued in *The New York Times* that King "renewed our alliance with democracy and the Constitution."[19] References to "our" democracy and Constitution, of course, invoke the most sacred symbols of the dominant group, further assuring dominants that subordinates are loyal to these symbols.

It was easy for Conyers to make this argument, for King was in fact a social reformer attempting to advance and make complete—not overturn—the values of the dominant group. ". . . King's life experiences reinforced the virtues of the dominant American commitment to [equality] and the hope that it held out to black Americans who kept a Christian faith in the 'American dream.' "[20] For this reason, King argued that racial integration was a value white Americans already held in embryo, not a deviation from American values.[21] As a Christian minister, an egalitarian, and a believer in "Americanism," King in fact personified the "American Dream."

Despite these facts, opponents argued that supporters of the King holiday were surreptitiously pursuing a separatist, perhaps even subversive, agenda. Senator Jesse Helms of North Carolina launched a brief filibuster against the bill, charging that King was a Marxist. Helms petitioned the Federal Bureau of Investigation for sealed files which, he argued, would support his charge. By invoking Marxism and the FBI, Helms constructed a Cold War scenario consisting of virtuous Federal investigators protecting gullible Americans from Communists.[22]

The outcome of Helms's ploy was paradoxical. Initially, by rejecting the Helms charge, Congress implicitly endorsed the position that King was indeed an extension of constitutionalism and democracy. In so doing, Congress insured the adoption of the King holiday. But this argument ignored King's radical challenge to capitalist domination at the time of his death. Thus, the condition for the King proposal's success was the reproduction of some dominant group symbols and practices (e.g., capitalism) which King himself rejected, with a constituency newly enlarged to include subordinates. In sum, adoption of the King holiday represented a partial symbolic triumph by subordinates, and a partial incorporation of subordinates within a dominant economic ideology.

The victory was also cheapened by the argument that some Republican Congress Members supported the holiday proposal for purely political reasons. For example, *The New York Times* reported that many Republicans endorsed the measure in order to placate black voters at a time when the Reagan administration's policies of "benign neglect" and reduced social services were costing Congressional Republicans black support.[23] Indeed, *The New York Times* attributed Reagan's own decision to support the bill to this same motive.[24] Such interpretations, by questioning the motives for symbolic commemoration, devalued the King holiday victory. More important, they implied that symbolic victories are much less significant than grubby political deals. Journalistic interpretations thus diminished the value of the King symbolism.

Supporters of the King holiday also had to confront opposing symbols favorable to dominants. For example, President Reagan suggested that a King holiday would be too expensive for the government during a period of economic difficulty. As a compromise, Reagan advocated a public observance, but no holiday for government workers.[25] Reagan thus turned dominant group symbols of government service, economic efficiency, and hard work against the King proposal; by so doing, he strengthened these traditional dominant group symbols.

Opponents also argued that a federal holiday for King was inappropriate because only one other comparable holiday existed—Presidents' Day, which honors Presidents George Washington and Abraham Lincoln. This argument takes Washington and Lincoln as the standard of comparison, thus subtly demoting King.[26] Inadvertently, therefore, the King holiday promoted the symbols of Washington and Lincoln, heroes of the dominant group.

Significantly, President Reagan explained his eventual decision to sign the bill by referring to its "symbolic importance."[27] It is rare for political leaders to cite symbolism alone as the reason for making a decision. Usually, they deny symbolism, and exaggerate the "real" (i.e., material) benefits of their actions. Given this rhetorical context, by labelling the holiday "symbolic" Reagan subtly questioned its importance, while appearing to commend it. Of all our modern Presidents, Reagan most conscientiously practiced the politics of symbolism; therefore, what he perhaps intuited is that symbols exert their greatest power when no one calls attention to them *as* symbols. Perhaps he realized that *naming* something a symbol immediately diminishes its power in a predominantly materialistic political context.

My observations so far speak to limitations in the *production* of symbolic challenges to dominant groups. An additional limitation of symbolic challenges lies in the nature of public response. Ultimately, symbolic challenges can alter the distribution of power only if they gain sympathy for subordinates. The King holiday indicates the difficulty of securing a sympathetic public response. As the bill was in its last stages of debate, Senate Minority Leader Robert Dole reported that mail and phone calls were running overwhelmingly against a King holiday. This announcement emboldened the persistent Jesse Helms to charge that the legislation represented a "tyranny of the minority."[28] In so doing, Helms found another way to invoke a traditional (in this case, Madisonian) symbol of the dominant group to discredit the legislation.

More important than public reaction to the legislative process is the public response to the King holiday once in place. How do people react to the King holiday? Although almost all states have legislated their own observances of the holiday, some (most conspicuously, Arizona) balked. In many places the King holiday has stimulated school teachers to design lessons about King, an obvious step forward for subordinates. Yet public observances of the King holiday—though not yet systematically studied—may well be confined mainly to blacks. A virtually all-black congregation attended a major memorial service to celebrate the King holiday in Washington, D.C. in 1986. Barely ten percent of the congregation at the massive Shrine of the Immaculate Conception was white. Even in 1991, public assemblies to commemorate the holiday remain primarily black.

Studies of the mass media support somewhat guarded conclusions about the persuasive effects of symbolic events. Particularly suggestive is evidence which demonstrates that opposed social groups often draw quite divergent conclusions from media coverage of the identical event. For example, "after viewing identical samples of major network television coverage of the Beirut massacre, both pro-Israeli and pro-Arab partisans rated these programs, and those responsible for them, as being biased against their side."[29] This "hostile media phenomenon" may also apply to symbolic events, such as the King holiday. White dominants may perceive the holiday as an illegitimate assertion of black power, while blacks may view the holiday as a long overdue recognition of a black hero.

Finally, favorable symbolism may be open to revision. Recent revelations about King's private life and academic career have prompted divisions among blacks, and somewhat tarnished the symbol of King. *The New York Times* recently advocated a less "sanitized" picture of a great man, citing a widespread perception that "many of Dr. King's followers have become more attuned to preserving his name than perpetuating his work..."[30] This last observation implies that favorable symbolism may eventually come to restrict subordinates even as it weakens dominants. Subordinates may become the victims of their own social construction, which in any case supports many values of the dominant group.

A useful description of the particular values the King holiday promotes may be derived from the "Learn-A-Bration," a kindergarten-eighth grade curriculum guide distributed by the Martin Luther King, Jr. Federal Holiday Commission to school teachers interested in designing lessons about King. Inspection of the guide reveals an interesting affirmation of traditional dominant values for younger students, and a modification of those values for older students.

For younger children the curriculum guide emphasizes King's affirmation of such traditional dominant values as national unity, individualism, and personal initiative. For example, in her "A Call to Celebrate" Coretta Scott King emphasizes "the important challenge... of making the holiday an all-American one. Martin Luther King, Jr. gave his life that all might be free, regardless of race, color, religion, politics or economic status."[31] This formulation, repeated in various ways throughout the guide, casts King not as a leader of *blacks* alone, but as a great *American* devoted to the elimination of invidious racial distinctions.

Interestingly, the pedagogical techniques the guide recommends emphasize individual activities by students, rather than group enterprises. Prominent among the activities suggested are assemblies which feature dramatic skits and readings about King the individual, and competitions between individual students in the production of original poems, compositions, etc. These activities make King the occasion for individual dramaturgical expressions, rather than the object of group projects which would somewhat submerge individual student expressions.

The guide also treats the King holiday as an occasion for younger students to affirm such traditional values as initiative, self-discipline, and hard work. For example, on page thirty-two the guide suggests that teachers: "Ask students to think about the hard work and determination Martin Luther King must have displayed in order to be successful in school. Point out that his early pattern of hard work prepared him to make great contributions to his nation."

Of course, the issue here is not the truth or falsity of these characterizations of King, nor about the worthiness of individualism, competition, or self-discipline. The point, instead, is that these particular values represent *selections* which accommodate King within beliefs traditionally shared by dominant groups in the United States.

However, for older students the guide construes King in a more challenging fashion. For example, teachers of grades four through six are encouraged to offer a three-day lesson on "Civil Rights: Individual Contributions to a Major Movement." The lesson introduces students to "the contributions of other individuals" to King's activities. In this way, "students will gain a clearer view of the civil rights movement."[32] This lesson—which requires students to investigate the connections between King and many others, such as A. Philip Randolph and Andrew Young—helps students to appreciate the organizational structure of a mass movement. No longer can students concentrate on the false picture of King as a charismatic hero who, through the sheer force of his own rhetoric, personality, and example, moved an entire nation virtually by himself.

In summary, judging from this examination of the King holiday, symbolic commemorations of subordinate group achievements usually accept the value parameters established by the dominant group. However, such commemorations undercut the dominant group in two ways: first, by forcing dominant groups to include some subordinate group members, and, second, by suggesting that without subordinate group struggle, including mass movements, inclusion would never occur. In these two ways, symbolic commemorations contribute to subordinate cultural challenges to dominant groups.

The Early Films of Spike Lee

While symbolic commemorations of subordinate groups often accept the dominant group's terms of discourse, more direct cultural challenges emerge when subordinate groups induce dominant groups to consider the *subordinate* version of events. In recent years a number of film makers have specialized in stories which provide dominants a subordinate vision of the world.[33]

The commercial film medium has considerable potential to diffuse subordinate visions. Films appeal through their emotional impact and their capacity to divert, not through their educative value. This fact does not diminish the film's potential political influence, however. Indeed, the contrary is the case, for, like all dramatic presentations, films can be "truer" emotionally than can real life. Films can portray the practices, values, and beliefs of subordinates in a uniquely powerful, visually dramatic way. For this reason, members of dominant groups who are entertained by films about subordinates may get more than they expected.

However, making films which dispute domination is not easy. In particular, film makers from subordinate groups often have difficulty financing and making profitable their projects. Perhaps this is why even the most prominent of such film makers often adopt aesthetic forms which implicitly ally the subordinate group with dominant group aesthetic traditions. While the *content* of films by subordinates often challenges dominants, *form* may not.

Film makers from subordinate groups also find themselves in a socially ambiguous position. Though wishing to tell a "true" story about "their" group, they have in fact become intellectually and socially distant from most subordinates. As commercial film makers, they are comparatively advantaged, precisely because they enjoy acceptance among many dominants.[34] It is hardly surprising, therefore, that counter-dominant films by subordinates often contain mixed messages. Firm assertions of subordinate group pride often coexist uneasily alongside graphic portrayals of weakness and degradation among subordinates. In sum, counter-dominant films are often complex and internally fissured, qualities which weaken their message.[35]

A particularly revealing example of counter-dominant film making is the career of Spike Lee. As a black making films about blacks, Lee is doubly significant, not least because he is the first black film maker to enjoy a level of success comparable to that of leading white directors. Most important, Lee views himself—and intends other to see him—as making counter-dominant films. Indeed, it is perhaps not too much to call Lee a kind of postmodernist Gramscian "organic intellectual."[36]

Lee is quite explicit about his counter-dominant project. He states, ". . . I really write for black people. I'm not going to lie. That is not to say that other audiences can't or won't understand my films."[37] Lee also rejects a position of financial dependence in a film structure dominated by whites. Blacks, he claims, must make their own films in order to help blacks; they should not depend on white movie makers to assist them.[38] Lee also argues that white film makers such as Steven Spielberg, who directed *The Color Purple*, cannot accurately portray the lives of blacks. Lee therefore uses blacks in all phases of his films—as actors, writers, crew, etc.—in order to create a "black cinema."[39] Lee's success in reaching a wide audience signifies a newfound receptivity among both dominant and subordinate groups to counter-dominant cultural representations.

The four major feature films Lee has written and directed portray blacks defending themselves against oppression, trying to overcome white domination, and disputing dominant stereotypes which divide blacks as a group. For example, *She's Gotta Have It*, Lee's first feature success, challenges dominant stereotypes about powerless black women; the heroine is a young black woman who lives her life freely without becoming subordinated to any man. Instead, her sexual freedom, coupled with her considerable intelligence, becomes an instrument by which she controls potentially overpowering circumstances. She deliberately disputes the white stereotype of promiscuous black women who are helpless victims of men.

In *School Daze*, his second major film, Lee decried divisions within a black university between light-skinned "Wannabees," who imitate whites, and "Jigaboos," whose dark skin relegates them to the bottom of the college status hierarchy. In the movie's climax the film's hero calls upon all factions of the black community to unite in order to resist white oppression.[40] The final scene of the movie depicts the hero ringing the school bell to bring all factions of the university together at dawn. Then, speaking directly to the camera, he implores the audience to please "wake up." The metaphor of waking from sleep, of course, has been used to describe revolutionary transformations from Plato to H.G. Wells. Lee's counter-dominant message thus draws on a rich history of literary imagery.

In his most famous film, *Do the Right Thing*, Lee portrays conflict between the black residents of Brooklyn's Bedford-Stuyvesant and the Italian-American owners of a local pizzeria. In the film's climactic scene, the character played by Lee initiates a riot which ends in the burning and looting of the pizzeria. Though he himself works at the pizzeria and is fond of its owner, Lee's character nevertheless begins the violence. The epilogue to the film consists of quotations from Martin Luther King, Jr. and Malcolm X which, in effect, debate appropriate responses to oppression. The epilogue takes for granted—as does the entire film—that blacks must engage in collective resistance, rather than submit peacefully or play by the constricting rules of liberal individualism. The only question is one of strategy.

Finally, in his more recent film *Mo' Better Blues*, Lee portrays two white owners of a nightclub as crude, callous exploiters of black jazz musicians. This portrayal elicited charges that Lee was anti-Semitic. Although *Mo' Better Blues* is the least directly political of Lee's major films, it still managed to stimulate controversy, a sign perhaps that Lee has attained the political salience he has always coveted.

Features other than film content also mark Lee's career as a counter-dominant film maker. For example, Lee has himself entered into and drawn from the political arena. When *School Daze* entered production in Atlanta, Jesse Jackson endorsed the project in a speech to cast and crew. Jackson said, "It's just a tremendous statement if you just make sure that Dr. King and Medgar Evers did not die in vain."[41] After whites recently killed a black teenager in Brooklyn, Lee was a prominent figure at the funeral. Lee's career demonstrates how rapidly film makers and entertainers can become parts of both subordinate and dominant political coalitions. In turn, these political coalitions may help promote both subordinate and dominant group cinematic representations.

Finally, Lee enjoys the support of many associates who promote both his films and himself. Veteran actors such as Ossie Davis not only appear in Lee's films but also publicize Lee the man. When Davis compares Lee in print to Malcolm X, the galvanizing political potential of the film maker becomes evident.[42] Most important, Lee has established a viable organization that no longer relies upon white-dominated studios for financial backing. Lee thus enjoys an unparalleled opportunity to make counter-dominant films.

Significantly, Lee's cinematic project has attracted considerable media attention. Lee, like other film makers, has capitalized on the fact that in media-pervasive societies, the making of images itself stimulates new image making.[43] Lee appeared on the usual round of television talk shows and morning news programs to promote *Do the Right Thing* and *Mo' Better Blues*. He has also published books about each of the four major films he has made; as an ensemble, print, television, and film magnifies the reach of his message.

Lee's career also demonstrates that media reflexivity may significantly advance subordinate group cultural representations. Perhaps the most interesting example of this reflexivity in Lee's case is a magazine article describing the making of a film documentary about *Do the Right Thing*. The author, St. Clair Bourne, recounts how Lee asked him to "make a documentary about the filming of Lee's new feature in the Bed-Stuy community."[44] The article then goes on to describe the documentary itself. Media reflexivity may thus assist subordinate groups to transmit their messages throughout the culture.

Elle—the magazine in which Bourne's article appeared—is a decidedly chic fashion periodical which reaches few blacks. By turning *Do the Right Thing* into a reflexive media reality, the story in *Elle* serves to distance the film's message. A magazine article about the making of a documentary film about a feature film may be considered appealing to dominants; by contrast, an article describing *real* subordinates in real circumstances might not find its way into *Elle*.

While Lee's project marks a distinct "moment" in subordinate film-making, aspects of his work undercut his counter-dominant message. To begin with, his counter-dominant theme competes against commercial and aesthetic considerations. Lee experienced considerable difficulty raising money for his two early films. Initially he turned to white distributors and investors, but then backed off when he was asked to soften the messages he wanted the films to send. Ultimately, the original production-distribution company for *School Daze*—Island Pictures—rejected the project when it learned the content of the film. In response to these experiences, Lee has become an excellent independent businessman; he now finances his own productions, and has become successful enough to attract money on his own terms. Yet this success should not obscure the point that the criterion of profit, to which Lee pointedly adheres, descends directly from the dominant group which he otherwise criticizes. In this sense, he continues to inhabit a somewhat contradictory ideological universe.

Lee also respects traditional, dominant-based standards of dramatic excellence. As he puts it, "[b]eing a Black film maker isn't a novelty anymore. It's about the work, 'cuz all that other shit won't matter. People aren't gonna shell out six bananas to see any Black film. The question is: *Is the work good or not?*"[45] This observation raises the question of whether Lee's social message is consistent with his aesthetic vision. Of course, there is no inherent conflict between the two things; yet other film makers, most conspicuously Eisenstein, found it necessary to invent a new cinematic aesthetic to advance progressive social visions. Lee never defines the particular aesthetic criteria to which he adheres; but it is plausible that the dominant group aesthetic values he absorbed (albeit reluctantly) at New York University might well influence his judgement of dramatic worth. Thus, while Lee's message is decidedly counter-dominant, his aesthetic standards may remain within a dominant group framework. Indeed, his formal traditionalism— shortly to be examined—reinforces this suspicion.

Lee himself epitomizes the social ambiguity of a commercially successful counter-dominant film maker drawn from the subordinate group. For example, he is anxious to celebrate the street life of blacks; yet, having "escaped" the street himself, he is acutely sensitive to the many ways street life harms subordinates. Not surprisingly, some blacks have complained that Lee stigmatizes the very group he purports to advance, as well as other subordinate groups, such as women.

Lee is painfully conscious of these complaints. For example, he feared that feminists would dislike *She's Gotta Have It* and prevent his getting funds even to make the film on the grounds that a male could not do a "sensitive piece about a woman."[46] His anxiety demonstrates how conflicts between two subordinate groups—women and blacks—diminish the impact of subordinate group representations.

Criticism became more directly racial with *School Daze*. Lee stated that the film "would allow Black folks to see themselves up on the screen and really feel proud."[47] But the presidents of the black universities in Atlanta— where Lee shot the film—did not agree. They objected to the portrayal of color prejudice within black universities. Nor were they thrilled to see portrayals of presidents of black universities condoning apartheid in South Africa in order to raise money from white contributors. So they banned Lee from their campuses.

Lee's response to this action reveals some of the tension inherent in his role as a subordinate group film maker:

> The AUC (Atlanta University Colleges) presidents were after squeaky clean images of Black colleges. I refuse to be caught in the 'negative image' trap that's set for Black artists. Yes, Black people have been dogged in the media from day one. We're extrasensitive and we have every right to be. But we overreact when we think that every image of us has to be 100 percent angelic....[48]

Finally, some unkind critics of *Do the Right Thing* argued that Lee's description of a black underclass actually reinforced white stereotypes of poor blacks. As Brent Staples noted, while Lee originally claimed he was going to portray a stable black working class in Bedford-Stuyvesant, only one of the Black characters—Mookie (Lee)—holds a steady job.[49] Moreover, the film depicts illegitimate children neglected by their parents, alcoholism, and other forms of behavior which provide the raw material for white prejudice against blacks. Therefore, argued Staples, many viewers will identify with the Italian-American pizzeria owners, who at least manage to keep a useful business going against considerable odds in their old neighborhood which demoralized blacks have newly "taken over." The message of *Do the Right Thing*, implies Staples, is that enterprising Italian-Americans and Korean immigrants are much to be preferred to blacks.

Equally restrictive is Lee's formal traditionalism. Traditional aesthetic conventions reflect both the role of dominant groups in shaping Lee's approach to film making, and Lee's need to attract a white audience to his work. While traditional aesthetics promote this latter goal, it also accords deference to white cinematic masters. For example, the major dance sequence in *School Daze* is a gloss on the gymnasium scene in *West Side Story*. Lee in fact intended this to be the case, rejecting the objections of his father, who composed the film's music:

> My father's worry was that Otis (the choreographer) was trying to make it too much like a Hollywood film ... too much like *West Side Story*. He thought that Otis would leave none of the negritude in the dance.... Even though my father objected to the *West Side Story* comparison I still saw this production as a gang fight....[50]

Do the Right Thing is even more traditional. The story, shot almost entirely in exteriors, takes place on a single street in Bedford-Stuyvesant. Its rendition of ethnic group tensions is a throwback to earlier "street scene" dramas on the same theme. The progenitor of this quite conventional form in modern American theater is Kurt Weill and Langston Hughes's *Street Scene*. Other, more recent versions include Arthur Miller's *A View from the Bridge* and, of course, *West Side Story* itself.

Interestingly, both Miller and Bernstein relied upon classical sources for their plots and formal structures. Miller intended *A View from the Bridge* to reinstate Greek tragedy in a New York tenement setting; therefore, people in the neighborhood function in his play as a Greek chorus. Bernstein, of course, used *Romeo and Juliet* as the basis of *West Side Story*. The wellsprings of *Do the Right Thing* are thus infused with theatrical antecedents which prepare dominants to feel comfortable, even though the film's message attempts to challenge their view of the world.

Nor is the argument of *Do the Right Thing* wholly counter-dominant. As the title indicates, the film focuses on a single character ("Mookie") who must decide how to react to events. Should he fight white oppression violently or non-violently? The focus upon one individual's moral decision is thoroughly traditional in the American context, well within the dominant group's film ideology. Lee's film uses group conflict to promote individual choice just as much as it uses individual choice to promote group conflict.[51]

Lee's next film, *Mo' Better Blues*, reinforces these indications of formal traditionalism and substantive compromise. The film's focus is jazz, a music invented by and expressive of the black experience. Lee intends the film to reflect and capture a specifically *black* view of jazz, as opposed to previous white efforts to portray the subject. He writes:

> I saw *Bird*, Clint Eastwood's portrait of Charlie Parker ... Bertrand Tavernier's *Round Midnight* ... was a slightly better film. ... Both were narrow depictions of the lives of Black musicians, as seen through the eyes of White screenwriters and White directors. Two of the three main characters in *Bird* are White. And of all the accounts of Parker's life that Eastwood could have based the film on, he chose a book written by Bird's white wife, Chan Parker.[52]

Yet, even if *Mo' Better Blues* does depict jazz from a distinctly subordinate perspective, jazz itself is hardly an effective vehicle for articulating subordinate group *political* perspectives. *Do the Right Thing* and *School Daze* directly confront social conflict; by contrast, *Mo' Better Blues* does not. Thus, *Mo' Better Blues* cannot be as threatening to dominants as Lee's earlier work.

Indeed, the central conflict in *Mo' Better Blues* is a rather traditional struggle between artistic genius and moral obligation. As Lee puts it, "Bleek's (the central character) obsession with his music makes him a great musician, but it also makes him selfish ... Tragedy forces Bleek to turn his life around."[53] By the end of the film, Bleek has given up his music in favor of his newly-formed family, a decision which reflects the hard-won maturity of a responsible adult. This theme—the "child genius" learning to accept his dependence upon others—is not only a familiar one to dominants, but is also far from Lee's earlier focus on social and political conflict.

Other themes in the film are similarly conventional from a dominant perspective. For example, Lee lauds the value of family bonds, as reflected in Bleek's closeness to his father-confidant, with whom he often begins the day by playing catch. There is also a prototypical "good girl" in the film (Indigo, a school teacher whom Bleek eventually marries), and a "bad girl," (Clarke, a fledgling jazz singer who eventually leaves Bleek). The "good girl/bad girl" dichotomy is a familiar motif in American films.[54] Another conventional theme is the struggle between career and family. Equally conventional is the theme of personal development through adversity; in this case, Bleek's career as a jazz trumpeter is ended by an injury to his lip. Finally, Bleek incurs his injury when he attempts to defend his friend Giant, who is attacked by gamblers to whom Giant owes money. Throughout the film Bleek protects Giant, though Giant is a chronic gambler and an incompetent band manager. *Mo' Better Blues* thus includes a "buddy" theme found in many films about white dominants such as *Rainman* or Neil Simon's *The Sunshine Boys*.

Certainly film makers need hew to no particular ideological line in their work. Lee is rightly free to pursue his own artistic muse. Nevertheless, it is clear that *Mo' Better Blues* moves Lee away from the political themes which animated his earlier work.

Finally, there is the question of Lee's impact on white audiences. Simply put, do white viewers "get" the political messages Lee intends them to get? I have encountered no studies which assess the interpretations white audiences place upon Lee's films. Certainly commercially the message is positive for Lee; each of his films has reached large and growing white audiences. For example, after only seventeen days of release *Do the Right Thing* reported box office receipts of $13,447,107; by contrast, it took 59 days for *School Daze* to accumulate $11,064,115 in receipts. There is no doubt that commercially Lee is a success.

Yet commercial success does not necessarily translate into counter-dominant impact. It is perhaps significant that white audiences responded less favorably to test showings of *School Daze* than did blacks, although the reasons for this response seem more related to the length of the film than its content.[55] Nevertheless, it is distinctly possible that whites use portions of Lee's films to reinforce their prejudices against blacks. Even as Lee's films entertain (indeed, possibly *because* they entertain) they may make prejudice easier. Thus, the question of Lee's counter-dominant impact remains open. While Lee's career demonstrates that opportunities have improved for subordinates to use films in order to advance a counter-dominant argument, the verdict is out on the effectiveness of this strategy.

Conclusion

Several tentative generalizations about subordinate group cultural challenges to domination emerge from these two case studies. These generalizations involve the *sites* of cultural challenge; the *forms* of cultural challenge; the *content* of cultural challenge; and the *effects* of cultural challenge.

The two cases we have examined take place in very different social locations. The King holiday is an official governmental function, which developed through a formal process of legislation and implementation. It now enjoys the imprimatur of state and federal law.[56] By contrast, Lee's films are the works of a private entrepreneur whose cultural challenges enjoy only the "imprimatur" the box office can bring them.

Yet despite their different locations, both Lee's films and the King holiday are real cultural challenges. The first tentative generalization we can advance, therefore, is that in the United States opportunities for subordinate groups to advance cultural challenges exist at several key locations of social control and coordination—in these cases, the polity and the market-controlled mass media.

The two cultural challenges we have examined take contrasting forms. The King holiday is a commemorative ritual which is publicly supported, sanctioned, and controlled. For this reason, as a *narrative* the King holiday must accommodate itself rather closely to the demands of dominant groups. Moreover, it cannot carry the same story-telling power as can a film created by a single film maker who wishes to convey his own vision of subordinate group ideology. After all, the King holiday is an effort to instruct and celebrate; by contrast, a Lee film aims mainly to excite, entertain, and create viewer identification with characters and setting.

These observations allow us to advance a second generalization: diversity in the sites of subordinate group cultural challenge stimulates diverse forms of challenge. As a result, there may be variety among the audiences for different cultural challenges. For example, people who are attracted to a Lee film may find the King holiday boring, overly sentimental, or sententious; by contrast, people who are drawn to the King holiday may find Lee's films undignified, disturbing, or even tasteless.

This diversity of forms and audiences is an advantage for subordinate group cultural challenges. In fact, diverse forms of cultural challenges work as a single *ensemble* to promote social change.[57] Governmental rituals such as the King holiday present a consensual, inclusionary model of change that is connected dialectically to the conflictive model of group protest presented by Lee. The two models benefit from each other in sharpening their respective messages. Most important, the choice the two pose as a *single* ensemble is not between change and stasis, but between different processes of change. We may thus generalize that a chief effect of subordinate group cultural challenges is to deflect dominant group attention away from the legitimacy of change itself to the appropriate method of change.

Yet we have seen that cultural challenges by subordinate groups are often double-edged and halting. Those launching challenges often find themselves conflicted and estranged from the groups whom they promote. Moreover, the values embodied in subordinate group challenges often turn out to be less distinctive than they initially appear. In a sense, dominant groups are protected by several *layers* of values; penetration of any single layer therefore cannot be decisive. For example, Lee's depiction of group cohesion in the Black community (in both *Do the Right Thing* and *Mo' Better Blues*) does not supplant the value of individual moral choice or liberal politics, core beliefs among whites. Because dominant groups possess multiple ideological fortifications, breaches of one line of defense are never decisive.

Yet, though almost never apocalyptic or rapid, cultural struggle does yield real change. The rise of Christianity and the growth of Abolitionism are two signal cases in point. In the former case, a novel religious vision took hundreds of years to produce a major redistribution of power from pagan to Christian Romans.[58] In the second case, a new philosophy of group relations took over one hundred years to help end slavery.[59] Though it is too soon to decide whether contemporary cultural challenges by subordinate groups will have similarly major effects, the length, complexity, and difficulty of cultural struggle hardly counts against so fateful an eventuality.

Notes

1. Karl Marx and Frederick Engels, *Manifesto of the Communist Party* (New York: International Publishers, 1948).

2. Max Weber, *The Theory of Social and Economic Organization*, trans., A. M. Henderson and Talcott Parsons (New York: Oxford University Press, 1947), 181–4; 329–41.

3. Emile Durkheim, *The Division of Labor in Society*, trans., George Simpson, (New York: The Free Press of Glencoe, 1964), chap. 2.

4. Max Weber, *The Protestant Ethic and the Spirit of Capitalism*, trans., Talcott Parsons (New York: Scribner, 1958); for a careful critique, see Gordon Marshall, *In Search of the Spirit of Capitalism: An Essay on Max Weber's Protestant Ethic Thesis* (New York: Columbia University Press, 1982). See also Randall Collins, "The Durkheimian Tradition in Conflict Sociology," in Jeffrey C. Alexander, ed., *Durkheimian Sociology: Cultural Studies* (Cambridge: Cambridge University Press, 1988), 107–29.

5. Weber, *The Protestant Ethic* . . .

6. Robert Bocock, *The Concept of Hegemony* (London and New York: Tavistock, 1986), 97.

7. *Ibid*, 106. A quite different interpretation is Chantal Mouffe, "Hegemony and Ideology in Gramsci," in Mouffe, ed., *Gramsci and Marxist Theory* (London: Routledge and Kegan Paul, 1979), 168–205.

8. Roger Simon, *Gramsci's Political Thought: An Introduction* (London: Lawrence and Wishart, 1982), 42–5.

9. Paul DiMaggio, "Classification in Art," *American Sociological Review*, 1987, 440–55, 443.

10. Paul DiMaggio, "Cultural Capital and School Success: The Impact of Status Culture Participation on the Grades of U.S. High School Students," *American Sociological Review*, 1982, 189–201.

11. For example, see John Fiske, "British Cultural Studies and Television," in Robert C. Allen, ed., *Channels of Discourse: Television and Contemporary Culture* (Chapel Hill: University of North Carolina Press, 1987), 254–91.

12. Janet Woollacott, "Fictions and Ideologies: The Case of Situation Comedy," in Tony Bennett and Janet Woollacott, eds., *Popular Culture and Social Relations* (Milton Keynes: Open University Press, 1986), 196–219, 215.

13. Murray Edelman, *The Symbolic Uses of Politics* (Urbana: The University of Illinois Press, 1964).

14. David I. Kertzer, *Ritual, Politics, and Power* (New Haven: Yale University Press, 1988), chap. 8.

15. Here I build on R. W. Connell, *Ruling Class, Ruling Culture: Studies of Conflict, Power and Hegemony in Australian Life* (Cambridge: Cambridge University Press, 1977), 201.

16. John Louis Lucaites and Celeste Michelle Condit, "Reconstructing 'Equality': Culturetype and Counter-Cultural Rhetorics in the Martyred Black Vision," *Communication Monographs*, 57, March, 1990, 5–25, 6.

17. See reports in *Jet*, December 3, 1984.

18. *The New York Times*, August 3, 1983.

19. *The New York Times*, October 17, 1983.

20. Lucaites and Condit, 15.

21. *Ibid.*

22. For a full investigation of this scenario in films, see Michael Rogin, *Ronald Reagan, The Movie* (Berkeley and Los Angeles: University of California Press, 1987).

23. *The New York Times*, October 21, 1983.

24. *The New York Times*, August 7, 1983.

25. *The New York Times*, August 3, 1983.

26. For an engaging study of how Washington came to be the standard of comparison, see Barry Schwartz, *George Washington: The Making of an American Symbol* (New York: The Free Press, 1987).

27. *The New York Times*, October 20, 1983.

28. *Ibid.*

29. R. P. Vallone, L. Ross, and M. R. Lepper, "The Hostile Media Phenomenon: Biased Perception and Perceptions of Media Bias in Coverage of the Beirut Massacre," *Journal of Personality and Social Psychology*, 1985, 577–585, 577. I am grateful to Diana Mutz for bringing this study to my attention.

30. *The New York Times*, January 14, 1990.

31. "The Martin Luther King, Jr. Holiday Learn-A-Bration," Compiled by the Education Committee, Martin Luther King, Jr. Federal Holiday Commission, 1986, 6.

32. *Ibid*, 39.

33. For example, see John Sayles, *Thinking in Pictures: The Making of the Movie "Matewan"* (Boston: Houghton Mifflin, 1987), 10.

34. But see Thomas Cripps: "Film," in Jannette L. Dates and William Barlow, eds., *Split Image: African Americans in the Mass Media*, (Washington, D.C.: Howard University Press, 1990), 125–175.

35. For comparison, see Goran Therborn, *The Ideology of Power and the Power of Ideology* (London: Verso, 1982), vii.
36. Cripps, 166–7.
37. Spike Lee, *Spike Lee's Gotta Have It: Inside Guerilla Filmmaking* (New York: Simon and Schuster, 1987), 58.
38. *Ibid*, 17.
39. *Ibid*, 15.
40. Spike Lee, *Uplift the Race: The Construction of School Daze* (New York: Simon and Schuster, 1988), 112–3.
41. *Ibid*, 22.
42. Davis's commendation appears in *Ibid*, 15.
43. Stuart Ewen, *All Consuming Images: The Politics of Style in Contemporary Culture* (New York: Basic Books, 1988).
44. St. Clair Bourne, "Brothers Under the Skin," *Elle*, August, 1989, 100–106, 100.
45. Lee, *Uplift the Race*, 17.
46. As Lee put it, "There are feminists running that place so my chances are slim to none." *Spike Lee's . . .* , 140–1.
47. Lee, *Uplift the Race*, 23.
48. *Ibid*, 62.
49. Brent Staples, "Spike Lee's Blacks: Are They Real People?" *The New York Times*, July 2, 1989.
50. Lee, *Uplift the Race*, 150, 146
51. See, for comparison, Michael Moffatt, *Coming of Age in New Jersey: College and American Culture* (New Brunswick and London: Rutgers University Press, 1989), 166 ff.
52. Spike Lee with Lisa Jones, *Mo' Better Blues* (New York: Simon and Schuster, 1990), 40.
53. *Ibid*, 41.
54. Nathan Leites and Martha Wolfenstein, *Movies: A Psychological Study* (Glencoe: The Free Press, 1950)
55. *Uplift the Race*, 172–3.
56. For a further consideration, see Lawrence H. Fuchs, *The American Kaleidoscope: Race, Ethnicity, and the Civic Culture* (Hanover and London: University Press of New England, 1990), 363–71.
57. Lucaites and Condit, *loc. cit.*
58. See, for example, Michael Walsh, *The Triumph of the Weak: Why Early Christianity Succeeded* (San Francisco: Harper and Row, 1986).
59. See, for a history, Robert W. Fogel, *Without Consent or Contract: The Rise and Fall of American Slavery* (New York: Norton, 1989).

PART FIVE

Symbolic Representation and Power

11

Language and Power: The Spaces of Critical Interpretation[1]

Michael J. Shapiro

Introduction

Critical interpretation appears in many forms, but virtually all of them—from the mildly critical, as in some versions of the liberal democratic and hermeneutic, to the more critical as in Marxist, Frankfurt/critical, and post-structural—derive their political significance from an attempt to disclose the operation of power in places in which the familiar social, administrative and political discourses tend to disguise or naturalize it. Thus we learn from Marx and his successors that social processes which appear simply to involve the creation and exchange of value also embody relations of domination and subjugation. And we learn from Gramsci, Adorno and modern culture theorists that although it would appear that simple matters of taste drive the production and consumption of both high and popular culture, it is the case, rather, that (with the exception of some resistant forms) music, theater, TV weather forecasts, and even cereal box scripts tend to endorse prevailing power structures by helping to reproduce the beliefs and allegiances necessary for their uncontested functioning.

The analysis here draws its inspiration from many different critical approaches, but the primary purpose is to isolate some aspects of the genealogical mode of critical interpretation. Genealogical interpretation (or anti-interpretation)[2] is most familiar as an approach to power in the later historical investigations of Michel Foucault. His investigations can be distinguished from other forms of critical interpretation on the basis of both his textual and spatial practices, significantly interrelated elements whose connections are elaborated below.

As a form of textual practice, the Foucauldian genealogy is driven by a commitment to a process of disruptive inscription, where the *process* aspect is especially important. This commitment is obliquely expressed in the concept of patience with which Foucault began his essay on Nietzsche. Noting that genealogy is "gray, meticulous, and patiently documentary," he outlined a mode of inquiry aimed at the continuous disruption of the structures of intelligibility which provide both individual and collective identities for persons and peoples, and construct the spaces as well as the more general assumptions of the order within which they are confined.[3]

Foucault's writing has a defamiliarizing effect. By producing unfamiliar representations of persons, collectivities, places and things, and by isolating the moments in which the more familiar representations have emerged, his texts disclose the instabilities and chance elements in meaning-producing practices. For example, in order to show how arbitrary and fragile are the interpretations constituting the person, Foucault substitutes violent imagery for the more benign representations of social learning process found in sociological discourse. In a phrase such as "The body is the inscribed surface of events...,"[4] intrinsic to the approach is the grammar, which renders the person as the passive receptor of meanings rather than its initiator, and the figuration, which represents persons as bodies rather than in terms of the cognitive orientations familiar in approaches that locate the impetus of the social bond in purposive mentalities.

The critical posture achieved with such linguistic impertinence is not justified with a parallel attempt, characteristic of some forms of critical theory, to seek the authentic essence of the self hidden by mystifying representations. Unlike, for example, most Marxian inspired critical analyses, genealogy does not presume the validity of a particular construction of the self and the order—such as one in which the self masters "nature" rather than succumbing to self-defeating ideologies of subjectivity (a version associated with critical theory). Whereas the general tendency of critical theory is toward critique of ideology, based on the presumption of an authentic model of intelligibility, the genealogical imagination construes all systems of intelligibility as (in Nietzschean terms) false arrests, as the arbitrary fixings of the momentary results of struggles among contending forces, struggles that could have produced other possible systems of intelligibility and the orders they support.

What makes genealogy "patient" is therefore the ontology within which it functions. Rather than presuming an underlying system of order, a form of life in which the self can achieve authenticity or non-alienation, it assumes that Being is fundamentally disordered and that every interpretation of the order is an arbitrary imposition or a violent practice. There is no natural limit summoning the process of inquiry.

> We must not imagine that the world turns toward us a legible face which we would have only to decipher; the world is not the accomplice of our knowledge; there is no prediscursive providence which disposes the world in our

favor. We must conceive discourse as a violence which we do to things, or in any case as a practice which we impose on them.⁵

Within this ontology, the question that has been familiar within traditional interpretive practices (from Kant onwards), "who is man," is displaced by the question, "which one?", which possible self is being imposed on the basis of what attempt to naturalize and thereby maintain the order? For genealogy, *every* form of life creates its modes of subjectivity or kinds of human identity and its systems of meaning and value in a struggle with other possible forms of life.

This ontology is intimately associated with genealogical historiography. The typical modern version of history, influenced by Hegel, tends to regard the present as a moment whose meaning is based on a trajectory reaching into the past. Everything that has emerged as substantial in earlier periods maintains vestiges of its existence in the present according to this view. The genealogical (or postmodern) approach, by contrast, views the present as peculiar.

Against the Hegelian view of the contemporary self as a product of a continuously more edified form of self-consciousness, the genealogist inquires into the different periods in which different forms of the self emerge—for example, the dangerous individual or "criminal" who does not show up until the middle of the nineteenth century. Within such a view, knowledge of the self is not a process of accretion but rather a form of power, a way of imposing an interpretation or, within Foucault's figuration, of imposing a topography on the body. It is a form of subjugation rather than part of a process of enlightenment.

Put in spatial terms, what is understood about the self at a given time is a matter of local practice, where "local" partakes of temporality as well as spatiality. A given historical period has forces at work producing interpretations and overcoming rival ones. The present is not a product of accumulated wisdom or other dynamics reaching into the distant past. It comes about as one possible emergence from an interpretive agonistics. It is the arbitrary result of modernity's configuration of self-producing forces. "We are," Foucault has noted, "much more recent than we think."⁶

Genealogical patience thus resists the moralizing exhortation to recover authenticity from the past or to transcend an inadequate present by either imagining a natural attunement between the self and order produced by a process of mutual adjustment over the centuries, or imagining a future situation with a more shared communicative competence (à la Habermas). Instead it is aimed at offering a history of the body, which reflects a history of the exercise of power. This is not the form of power described in traditional histories of political theory, which have emphasized power as a possession of an individual sovereign or class, a form of power analyzed by focusing on geopolitical space rather than the topology of the body, but a power that functions through discursive strategies and tactics, through the identities produced in the forms of knowledge and interpretation that normalize human subjectivity in various historical periods.

Genealogy and the Practice of Political Theory

To situate genealogical strategies with respect to more traditional forms of political theory, it is important to note that inasmuch as all discourse is spatially situated, all forms of political theory that are comprehensive and totalizing presume elaborate spatial strategies. To say this is to invoke a recognition that "space" designates not only the boundary practices dividing a given society into recognized public and private, industrial and leisure, political and administrative and other domains, but also the temporal practices which give both shape and definition to various historical epochs and thereby contribute to the meanings of written and oral statements.

The historical dimension of this relationship between spatial and discursive practices requires the kind of specification it achieves in a recent investigation of the differences in the relationship between people and animals in both peasant and bourgeois classes. Focusing especially on "transformation of La Pensée Bourgeois"[7] over the past few centuries, the analyst concentrates on the way the bourgeois class came to distinguish itself by ascribing callousness, brutality and indifference to the peasant and proletarian classes in their treatment of animals.[8] What appears immediately peculiar about this bourgeois claim is that one can discern no consistent pattern of generalized kindness in *their* treatment of animals. They have been alternately kind and cruel, depending on the species of animal and the sphere of activity. While the bourgeois class has tried to legitimate its moral and cultural supremacy by seeing itself "as treating animals in a much more civilized and sensitive way . . . than the callous proletarians who flogged their horses or the ignorant peasants who maltreated their dogs,"[9] there have remained such paradoxes as "that of an industrialist who was a member of *The Society for the Friends of Small Birds*," and "could be moved to tears about the problems of the little thrush but may have shown a marked indifference to the sufferings of his own workers."[10] And certainly such people did not have sentimental regard for all animals, only those domesticated as pets or held up as special examples for aesthetic appreciation.

However, the paradox dissolves when one heeds spatial practices. Bourgeois life has come to embody a "sharp division of labor between spheres of production and non-production."[11] Kindness and sensitivity have operated not at the work place but in the domain of leisure and domesticity, and the animals participating in this latter sphere have enjoyed the kind of "humane" treatment of which the bourgeois class has been so proud.

More generally, then, to be able to regard a discursive commitment—in this case claims about the comparative degrees of humane treatment of animals by different classes—as unambiguous and uncontestable, one has to treat the spatial practices necessary to predicate such a claim as natural or uncontestable. To express the relationship more positively and comprehensively: a politics of discourse is inextricably tied to a politics of space. Moreover, this intimate relationship between space and discourse is not one between disparate modes. Because "space" is constituted by the way locations are imagined or given meaning, it is always already a largely discursive phenomenon. For this reason the domains or spaces within which conversations take place can be thought of as "proto-conversations," for they amount to the already established, if now silent, conversations which shape the voluble ones taking place. And because they are a silent force in conversations, they are difficult to draw into discursive processes.

Accordingly, one interested in politicizing elements of a social formation will find spatial practices more resistant than discursive practices to contestation. This proposition is central to the thinking of Henri Lefebvre who has done for space what Marx did for the commodity by recognizing that it is a "social product."[12] Because space, like all fetishized or reified things, does not yield its productive dynamic up to the immediate exercise of perception, the politics of space is not readily discernible.

> If space has an air of neutrality and indifference with regard to its contents and thus seems to be "purely" formal, the epitome of rational abstraction, it is precisely because it has already been occupied and used, and has already been the focus of past processes whose traces are not always evident in the landscape.[13]

While much of "social space"—the practices through which locations are formed and provide the implicit context for human relations (discursive and otherwise)—remains uncontested, there are arenas within which contention is invited. Of interest here are those domains constructed especially for purposes of affording critical reflection on the other non-reflective domains of human interaction, and perhaps the most venerable of these is the theater.

Although the theater is a venerable institution, its relationship with other aspects of social space has been historically inconsistent and problematic. This is brought out in an insight of playwright Arthur Miller during an excursion in Sicily. One afternoon, while being squired around by a minion of the famous "mobster," Lucky Luciano, the driver, who had said nothing for miles, stopped in the town of Siracusa, "and with a gesture behind him said, 'teatro.'"[14] When Miller got out of the car he saw a very large ancient Greek theater, which provoked a long meditation:

I felt something close to shame at how suffocatingly private our theatre had become, how impoverished by a psychology that was no longer involved with the universalities of fate. Was it possible that fourteen thousand people had sat facing the spot on which I stood? Hard to grasp how the tragedies could have been written for such massive crowds when in our time the mass audience all but demanded vulgarization. If the plays were not actually part of religious observances, it is hard to imagine what it was that fenced them off from the ordinary vulgarity of most human diversions . . . .Surely one sound was never heard in this place—applause; they must have left in amazement, renewed as brothers and sisters of the moon and sun.[15]

To cast these observations within the relevant theoretical problematic—linking space and discourse, what Miller is recognizing is that in the Greek polis there was, at various moments, a virtual correspondence between theatrical space and social space. By dint of both the size of the audience and the dimensions of social thought being addressed, the Greek playwright was not one standing apart inventing a performance to be applauded, criticized or remunerated, but was one who stood among the citizens, encouraging a reflection on questions of identity and social practice, and on the conditions of possibility for coherent community, given the emotions and passions which impede such possibilities and the chance events intervening and mitigating them.

Juxtaposed with this recognition of the space of drama, and thus the social location of the playwright in ancient Greece, is Miller's insights into *his* location in private, commercial space. In addition to his seeing the modern theater as relatively distant from most critical personal and political aspects of social space, he recognizes that the theater has become both a commodity and an item in a highly restricted system of prestige. The former aspect of its location, the existence of the playwright in commercial space, is reflected in Miller's remarks on his royalties—as he appreciates the fact that his plays are "work" and products being sold. They are therefore occupying commercial space as much as social and intellectual space: "It occurred to me three or four times a day that if I did no work I would still be earning a lot of money, and by the end of the week would be richer than at the beginning."[16] And he goes on to ask himself what is left of his contact with life now that he is no longer on the outside of commercial success looking in. His problem, he notes, is to keep "trying to maintain contact with the ordinary life from which [my] work had grown."[17]

The latter aspect of theatrical space—its significant drift toward a space enclosed by elite criticism—also hounded Miller. In this connection, he speaks of the significance of the reaction to his work by other playwrights, such as Clifford Odets and Lillian Hellman.[18]

The contrast between the spatial exclusiveness of theatrical discourse in modernity as opposed to ancient Greece that Miller's reflections suggest is not paralleled in the case of social and political theory. Certainly the Platonic version of the relationship between intellectual discourse and the discourse of everyday life suggests a radical separation of the two spaces. In the Platonic version, this separation is based on the superior vision of the philosopher who is thought able to see beyond the veil enclosing the immediate life of the polis into the transcendental domain of the "real," of which everyday life is but a pale, symbolic reflection.

One of the best exemplars of the modern version of Platonism was Leo Strauss, who, along with his many students, also held to a radical separation between intellectual and mundane (non-philosophical) social space. But the Straussian position is not based upon the Platonic imaginative geography, for Strauss saw the "real" not as a special transcendent place of perfection but as lexical, as that which yields itself up to those able to successfully gloss the wisdom of ancient texts.

Ironically, this wisdom points in the direction of a secular enlightenment, but—fearful of the dangerous instability that might flow from a mass acceptance of an impious, secular view of reason—Strauss wrote in a code meant to be penetrated only by intellectuals. His textual practice was, in effect, designed to maintain a separation between intellectual and social space. Despite giving up on the ancient and medieval commitments to a vertically shaped world in which there is a marked separation between the sacred and secular or transcendent and mundane worlds, the Straussian position nevertheless incorporates what "the 'ancients' (meaning Plato and Aristotle) knew and which we have forgotten . . . that philosophy and society are irreconcilable."[19]

However modified the Platonic separation is within the modern, Straussian format (which is secular and even relativist in its more esoteric level of expression), it is useful for purposes of illustration to analyze the Platonic use of the transcendent as a form of spatial strategy, and the relationship of this strategy to Plato's textual practice. To oversimplify, Plato's strategy consisted in the invention of an imaginary space, a domain of perfect things or referents, on the basis of which he could then judge (or demonstrate in dialogues) the adequacies of conversations purporting to treat both questions of individual propriety and the value and meaning of collective arrangements.

As is well known, Plato's invention of the transcendent is represented as a discursive discovery, so that the transcendent becomes the "real," and the mundane venues of everyday life, the situation of his contemporary conversations, are consigned to the realm of the imaginary. It is this spatial strategy that enables Plato to privilege certain interlocutors in his dialogues (e.g. Socrates) and diminish others (e.g. Thrasymachus), for their argumentative success is a function of their varying abilities to create trajectories for their utterances that can aim at Plato's invented/real space. Of course, if Plato is being ironic, and intends to accord privilege in the reverse way (as some commentators have argued), the same spatial strategy enables the ironic trope. Moreover, the dialogic structure of Plato's style articulates well with his spatial strategy as his interlocutors become positioned vis-a-vis each other on the basis of the two-domained spatial structure, which renders some referents as illusory (existing in the world of appearances) and others real (existing in the transcendent world).

A variety of modern social theorists pursue variants of Plato's spatial strategy in that they are also involved in inventing imaginary spaces. For example, Jürgen Habermas's original version of critical theory is based on his invention of a conversational space that is removed from the political conversations of everyday life in order to transcend the ideologies immanent in different forms of interest-driven or partisan positions. Embracing (unlike Plato) non-absolutist notions of the real, the good, and the true, Habermas envisions the possibility of a form of utopian politics that can only be approached within a conversational space that exists outside of the impositions of partisan forms of power on language.[20] There is a shift in Habermas's more recent perspective toward a different imaginative geography to situate critical discourse. It involves a temporal broadening of the terrain within which discourse is deployed.

In his recent writings, Habermas has lent critical discourse two trajectories, one extending into the past to illuminate the background conditions which enable rational communication, the other extending into the future, anticipating a condition of unforced intersubjectivity, which encourages a form of community in which partisanship is not totally overcome but muted and aimed at reconciliation because the participants are able to transcend their particular solidarity groups.[21] This more recent spatial strategy still involves the invention of a separate space of intersubjectivity freed from the attractions that people's group commitments exert on them. It amounts, in short, to an attempt to free thought from its social determinants, not through reflecting on them but through aiming them (in a motivational sense) toward a transcendent ideal of intersubjectivity. Ironically, this attempt to build a freer condition in the present is both illusory and politically insensitive. As Pierre Bourdieu has succinctly put it, "It is through the illusion of freedom from social determinants ... that social determinants win the freedom to exercise their full power."[22]

There is thus still a significant degree of detachment for the conversational space that Habermas invents. He seeks a discursivity that is wholly separated from the field of practices that is productive of and orienting for statements. His spatial strategy amounts to an attempt to replace a false present, one with no utopian or emancipatory aim, with a true or authentic present, one able to dissociate itself from a false past and envision an authentic future capable of sustaining an ideal form of discursivity. Habermas's version of the role of the intellectual is very much like Plato's, but the textual practice is different. Replacing the philosopher's superior vision of a transcendent real, which is conveyed through a process of dialogic argumentation, is a more democratic notion of "competence." This competence is articulated not in terms of a dialogic process, which sweeps aside positions with the wrong trajectory, but in more abstract terms linking it with the ability to communicate while resisting some contentious aspects of past situations and anticipating a less contentious and fractionated life-world.[23]

This is not the place for an elaborate evaluation of Habermas's position. Here it is worth noting briefly the critical losses associated with his communication and intersubjectivity imagery. His position assumes that speakers have a large measure of intentional control over the meaning of their locutions, that the meanings of their statements are wholly present to them and under their control. This logocentric view of language has been effectively criticized by Derrida.[24] What is most relevant here is that, ironically for one influenced by the classic writer on rhetorical force, Habermas's view of communication as a relatively non-situated process deprives discourse of the deep rhetorical force it has by virtue of two of its fundamental aspects: (1) its connection with the historical traditions that have given rise to the meanings of its utterances, and (2) the more immediate force it acquires from the spatial and temporal moments from which it issues.

A recognition of the dependence of intelligibility on such dimensions of positioning requires an attunement to textuality. For example, in Stanley Elkin's novel, *The Magic Kingdom*, a story about a group of terminally ill children taken to Disney World, this relationship between positioning or space and meaning is made evident. At one point, the children are taken on a river ride on a "tiny steamer that vaguely resembled the *African Queen*." Their conversational exchange is rife with irony both because of the long tradition of meaning ordinarily associated with the kind of remarks being made and the special circumstances of the location of the conversation. It takes place in a section of "nature" that has been invented. "Nature is amazing," remarks one of the children, and in response the boat pilot says, "I learned all my lore here on the river."[25] What makes both remarks in this fragment of the conversation ironic becomes evident as Elkin describes the setting. As the boatman makes his response it is noted that, "with a broad sweep of his arm he indicated the rubber duckies floating on the surface of the water, the mechanically driven wind-up sharks, the needlework palm fronds along the banks."[26]

The irony made possible by the invented nature of Disney World is more obvious than in other aspects of Elkin's novel, but his ironic stance is nevertheless a pervasive part of his textual strategy. And once one diminishes the significance of the traditional boundary between the literary or fictional text and the non-fictional one, Elkin's recognition, built into his writing, can be extended to the general relationship between statements and the spaces of their articulation. The fiction-fact boundary tends to dissolve with the recognition that all places have a meaning which is mediated by an imaginative geography. Insofar as space is a set of imaginative practices, all statements can have an ironic dimension. What an ironic gesture requires is a textually registered recognition that the spatial context of an articulation is contestable or in some way peculiar.

Elkin's textual practice is pervasively ironic because it registers his attitude toward both location in space and time as peculiar human practices, as peculiar acts of imagination rather than as outer structures of the world. This ironic, distancing view of the world is constitutive of the genealogical imagination, for it is organized by the recognition that such spatial imaginings are often well-entrenched historical scripts, not immediate acts of meaning-giving perception. Therefore, genealogy involves a significant departure from both the emphasis on dialogue or conversation evidenced in the history of political thought and from the view that there can be a space within which the partisan/ideational, interest-laden political impetus of language can be escaped. Conversations always take place in a preconstituted meaning system; they are always in a world. It is in this sense that the spacio-temporal location of a conversation is proto-conversational; it shapes the economies of the said and unsaid as well as providing a structure of intelligibility for the said.

The genealogist seeks to describe such proto-conversations, to provide an insight into the power relations existing in the present. This spatial strategy contrasts dramatically with those based on the invention of imaginary spaces which are either transcendent or ideal. Indeed, rather than employ such extensions of vision, Foucault has argued that forms of power are disclosed when one's vision is shortened: to focus, for example, on how the body is constructed by the prevailing interpretations in the present—its "nervous system, nutrition, digestion, and energies," i.e., on all the imposed interpretations which reveal the preoccupations of power.[27]

Consider this seeming paradox: a historian, who writes on such domains as medicine, punishment and sexuality as they have been practiced over several centuries, calling for a shortening of vision, disappears when the aim of these histories is understood. The genealogist does not use history to lament the wandering away from a past ideal or the failure to move toward an ideal future but to point to current dangers—in Foucault's case to warn about the dangers of modern biopower represented in seemingly benign individual and collective identities. A genealogical history loosens the hold of present arrangements by finding their points of emergence as practices and thus, by opposing the forces, tending to naturalize them.

Genealogy and Policy

This impetus of genealogy can be demonstrated with an example from a public policy episode that occurred several years ago in Australia. The government commissioned an investigation to discover why the aboriginal part of the "population" manifested what, in world statistical terms, was interpreted as a high infant mortality rate. In another place I subjected their conclusion, in which they blame the "semi-nomadic life of some of the aborigines," to political critique,[28] arguing that it represented a particular politics of explanation. It is a politics which treats as unproblematic the position that it is the aborigines who should adjust their mobility patterns to western, sedentary medicine rather than the medical system adjusting their delivery facilities to keep up with aboriginal migration.

A genealogical approach would add a more basic dimension to such a political analysis. Rather than simply pointing to the forms of implicit partisanship *in* population control politics, it would seek to disclose the politics immanent in the production of the collective identity known as the "population." This has been a key term in Foucault's analysis of modern biopower; he has traced the modern concern producing the idea of a population and found it to be associated with a change in political treatises on the art of government. He found that these treatises emerged in conjunction with the dual movement of state centralization and the divisive tendencies associated with religious dissidence. By the mid eighteenth century, this art of government, a problematic evidenced in canonical political theory, had been extended to the economy, and the "population" had displaced the family as both the target of—and legitimation for—control.

> Population comes to appear above all else as the ultimate end of government, that is the welfare of the population since this end consists not in the act of governing as such but in the improvement of the condition of the population, the increase of its wealth, longevity, health, etc.[29]

This brief genealogy of state problematics places the pressure to investigate the aboriginal mortality rate in a broad political context of governmental management of the collective entity, the "population," which the aboriginal people are necessarily a part of, given the dominance of the interpretive practices (among others) of the European segment of Australian society.

Foucault's advocacy of a shortness of vision is therefore supplemented by a glance at the past, a glance aimed not at the production of a developmental narrative but at showing what we are now. This "what we are now" is not meant as a simple description of the current state of things. Rather, it is an attempt to show that the "now" is an unstable victory had at the expense of other possible nows. The theoretical regard, the short vision, is therefore aimed at the present, but it is important to note where the gaze is directed *from*.

The gaze is not coming from an imagined transcendent or otherwise dematerialized place. To locate the genealogical spatial strategy in such a way as to include the locus of the theoretical regard as well as the world within which it is deployed, one needs to avoid the more familiar geographic metaphors—the now and the then, the now and the yet-to-be, the real and the ideal, the symbolic and the real. What must be emphasized instead is the idea of force. The systems of meaning or intelligibility associated with forms of power are seen as forceful interpretations, impositions that succeed within an interpretive agonistics.

In order to show the lines of force that are no longer visible in the present, genealogy goes back to the point of emergence, the historical moment at which an interpretation emerges as dominant. Such a point is, in Foucault's explication of its spatial significance, a "non-place," in which the adversaries representing different positions—e.g., different models of space such as the medieval, vertical spatial practice and the modern, more horizontal one—are in contention.

In order, then, to show the textual practice associated with genealogy, it is necessary to heed the identification of the historically shifting interpretations of space which give the contending discourses their predicates.

Exploring the Space of Writing

In the Middle Ages, the spaces of European societies were imaginative constructions produced within the dominant religious discourses of the period.

> In the Middle Ages there was a hierarchic ensemble of places, sacred places and profane places; protected places and open, exposed places (all these concern the real life of men). In cosmological theory, there were supercelestial places, as opposed to the celestial, and the celestial place in its turn opposed to the terrestrial place.[30]

Accordingly, much of medieval writing, whether religious, political, or biographical, had the effect of retracing and reinforcing the medieval practices of space. For example, medieval biographies placed their subjects within spiritual odysseys whose textual structures reinforced the morality implicit in the design of medieval space.[31]

By the late seventeenth and early eighteenth centuries, space had become more contentious as commercial impulses produced imaginative cartographies at odds with those that had been generated by spiritually oriented forms of authority. Such a loosening of the dominance of one spatial view invites new forms of thought, so not surprisingly various thinkers began to clear an ideational space for commerce by mounting critiques of the political space of the estate-based society. Whereas the estate system was static in that it was conceived as a stipulation of divine will,[32] liberal political economy, as formulated by Adam Smith, recast divine will as a set of dynamic mechanisms regulating the process of production.[33]

The Creator was banished from the world and was replaced by a view of nature as a series of mechanisms *in* the world regulating the play of interests and exchange of value. A genealogical gloss on this important period in the eighteenth century provides a more politically enabling view of the present. For example, a traditional rendering of the contribution of Adam Smith would emphasize his critical contribution, including not only his above-mentioned move toward desacralization but also his critical departure from the mercantilist view of economy.

The Smithian system was quintessentially critical inasmuch as it took what was regarded as a thing—wealth—and replaced it with the dynamic process through which it was produced. In effect, Smith created first a space for conversations about the practices through which wealth is made, and, second, a space for a political conversation silenced within the old mercantilist system. By constructing a political economy that shifted the emphasis from a concern with national rivalries to the conditions of production or work, he drew attention to a neglected constituency, the working poor, who could now be the object of conversations about problems of equity.[34]

This opened the way for an analysis of political economy (especially the Marxist), which increasingly was able to theorize about the overlap between economic and social/political space. Certainly there is an important degree of desacralization of space associated with Smith's system, for much of his position involves replacing piety with calculation as wealth shifted from a form of bounty to a product of labor power.

However, from a genealogical point of view, the Smithian system can be read more in terms of its continuities within rather than its departures from its age. Smith's *Wealth of Nations* is contiguous with texts, appearing in the seventeenth and eighteenth centuries, which reorganized political space. The emphasis in a series of political treatises after Machiavelli, who had focused on the problem of a ruler governing a territory and its inhabitants, was, rather, on "the complex unit constituted by men and things."[35]

This marks the beginning of theorizing the state as a complex governing entity which has to conceive of itself as managing an economy, where "economy" had begun to emerge from its ancient connotation associated with families or households into its modern sense of a field of calculation applied to the new collective identity known as the "population."[36]

These political treatises, Smith's included, operated within the unstated problematic, which Foucault has called a concern with the "art of government." One might protest that Adam Smith's argument was at odds with positions urging a state control over the economy, but what is important in asserting the continuity of his position is that while Smith may have taken a heterodox position in arguing for less state intervention in controlling commerce, he nevertheless belongs to the reigning doxa;[37] he conceived the problem of governance in terms of the state's relation to the economy in the new, seventeenth and eighteenth century sense, and he had adopted, as well, the then-reigning sovereignty problematic, one associated not with ruling territories and their inhabitants but with "men in their relations, their links, their imbrication with those other things which are wealth, resources, means of subsistence . . ."[38]

Text and Space

What remains in elaborating this genealogical strategy is, once again, to specify its textuality and spatiality. In identifying the cluster of texts (to which Smith's practice belonged), Foucault employs the phrase "the governmentalizing of the state."[39] Textually, this move, which substitutes for the static noun "government" the idea that the state has been governmentalized (a temporal process), helps to loosen the grip of the present facticity and allow for recognition of an institutionalized mentality (a "governmentality") realized as a reigning discursive practice, and the recognition that such practices have won out in the process of struggle. The task, as Foucault has put it, is to "seek to awaken beneath the form of institutions and legislations the forgotten past of real struggles, of masked victories or defeats, the blood that has dried on the codes of the law."[40] Thus insofar as one succeeds in loosening the bland facticity of the present, contention is discerned where quiescence was supposed, and claims to authority become contentious rather than unproblematic. The way is then opened to inquire into the forms of power and authority that the practices of the present help to sustain.

Now how does this gesture work as a spatial strategy? Genealogy is a locational strategy for theorizing, based on a particular view of language. It is a locational strategy for theorizing, but it does not invent utopian spaces as has been the tradition in the history of political theory. Traditional political theory treats language as referential, and the utopian impulse is an impulse toward an ideal as opposed to an interest-laden referent. But the utopian impulse fails to open the political space that is made available by genealogy. Seeing language not as simply referential but as a stock of discursive assets that constitute sets of enabling and disenabling human identities and enabling versus disenabling social locations, genealogical writing is oppositional. It intervenes in existing discursive economies and disrupts the entrenched systems of value by rendering political what has been passed off as natural or uncontentious. For example, while Habermas is trying to improve conversations, genealogists remain suspicious of all conversation, because they recognize that systems of intelligibility exist at the expense of alternatives. Therefore to strive to deepen intelligibility and provide more access *within* available conversations is to consolidate the power arrangements that the persistence of such conversations helps to maintain.

From Political Theory to Literary/Political Space

With a focus more directly on the literary dimension of genealogical strategy, the imbrication of textual and spatial practice becomes more evident. This literary dimension emerges dramatically in connection with an intellectual triangle connecting the writings of Franz Kafka, Michel Foucault, and Maurice Blanchot. The comparison takes as its starting point some remarks by Blanchot which bring Kafka's project into a critical intersection with that of Foucault. According to Blanchot, Kafka designated impatience as the gravest fault.[41] We must read this with the recollection of Foucault's concept of patience (expressed in his above quoted remark) that genealogy is "gray, meticulous, and patiently documentary."

While there are several important dimensions of the Kafka-Foucault-Blanchot connection, patience is the most significant because it is a code for the concept of *process*, which is central to genealogical analysis. Genealogy aims at incessantly dissolving interpretations. Decrying the leap from the laboratory to the cathedral, it militates against any attempt to arrest inquiry by enshrining a particular interpretation. Genealogy, thus understood, is a process designed to interrupt another process. This is summed up in the translator's gloss on Blanchot's idea of the purpose of literature, which is "to interrupt the purposeful steps we are always taking toward a deeper understanding and a surer grasp on things."[42] Impatience is therefore the impetuous attempt to grasp, instead of maintaining the process of inquiry.

Focusing, then, on Kafka with "process" in mind, we are inevitably reminded of *The Trial* (*Der Prozess*), the significance of which Blanchot helps us to heed. Kafka's trial is a process of error that is mistaken for truth. Joseph K.'s mistake is his reliance on functionaries (including his lawyer), for he thinks that they stand on the path toward certitude—an end to the trial/process. But truth for the genealogist is uncertainty, the dissolving of all finalities, and Kafka, through his writing sought to escape the maze, the sets of endless passages that depend for their power on a thought of a final authority or sponsorship. Like the Ulysses in his very short version of the Ulysses and Sirens episode, Kafka resorted to writing fiction because he recognized that a consciousness motivated by a search for finality is an enemy rather than an ally. It is a structure of apprehension that tends merely to reproduce the puzzles that power articulates. The resort to fiction provides the escape from the traps set by the search for certitude.

The Foucauldian version of "patience" is based on the same suspicion of finalities, on a recognition that one cannot envision discovering an interpretation that will end interpretation. And like Kafka, Foucault's resistance to finalities is represented in his writing. For example, characteristic of his genealogically inspired textual practice is his above-noted treatment of the body as "the inscribed surface of events."[43]

The construction of the "body" as an object-effect of discursive practices rather than as an independent referent of statements effects a powerful reversal. The text does not accord responsibility for statements in some natural aspect of the body, but locates it instead in body-making discursive practices. The "real," in this case the body, results from the set of interpretive practices through which the body becomes significant as one thing rather than another. This reversal is not meant to encourage a passive acceptance of authoritative scripts with which selves are fashioned. In particular, what is to be resisted is western metaphysic's model of subjectivity, which Nietzsche disparaged, the assumption that there is a "stiff, steadfast, *single* individual."[44]

To resist this depoliticizing assumption, the Foucauldian textual practice is a writing against a mode of interpretation that naturalizes prevailing human identities and operates within the pretense that all possibilities are exhausted. It is not the typical critical theory style of writing that is aimed at overcoming an estrangement between an adequate self and a mystified one, constructed within dominant discourses. Foucault, like Nietzsche, assumes that there is an indeterminant range of possible selves and that every institutionalized version of the self represents a political victory.

In keeping with genealogy's commitment to patience, Foucault's style is documentary rather than polemic, for it is not aimed at establishing a particular model of the self. It is aimed instead at opening a broader terrain within which the self (and the order) can be thought. In addition, departing as it does from the elucidation of power characteristic in traditional political theory, Foucault's genealogy identifies a form of power other than that associated with traditional relations between heads of state and their subjects.

This elaboration of the epistemic function of genealogy's textuality provides preparation for raising the question of the spatial predicates of such a textual practice. Where does one reside while engaging in such an analysis? Foucault's case seems to be that genealogical writing, as an imaginative enactment, will reveal and thereby oppose the institutionalized acts of imagination that have sustained existing spaces and thereby reinforced existing forms of power. Those engaged in critical interpretation do not invent places apart from the social order; they write within it. The imaginative function of the critical interpreter is, in Foucault's words, "to create a space of illusion that exposes every real space, all the sites inside of which human life is partitioned as still more illusory."[45]

It must be recognized that the production of all texts (as well as their reading or consumption) involves acts of imagination. There are thus no firm boundaries between the fictional and non-fictional genres. If my analysis appears to favor the critical capabilities of what are recognized as fictional texts, it is because in the case of those I have selected, there is an inward gaze; the writing is informed by a recognition of the critical relationship between textuality and interpretation. And those non-fictional texts toward which I am particularly critical are disparaged because they attempt to look only outward, holding the world responsible for the forms of imagination they enact or reproduce.

The coherence of genealogical analysis as a critical practice is therefore informed by two commitments. The first is that social theory is primarily a literature, and tends, when critical, to recognize that its textual practice is constitutive of its contribution. The second is that writing as a form of political action functions within an imaginative geography which pre-organizes the world toward which it is aimed and within which it functions as a critical intervention.

Notes

1. This is a slightly revised version of the first chapter (with the same title) in Michael J. Shapiro, *Reading the Postmodern Polity: Political Theory as Textual Practice* (Minneapolis: University of Minnesota Press, 1992).

2. Michel Foucault's genealogical orientation is, among other things, a reaction against "interpretation," where it is conceived as an attempt to locate the depth lying beneath the surface. This is most dramatically brought out in his approach to discourse, which he produced before he conceived of his approach as genealogical. He asserted that, among other things, the analysis of a discursive formation involves weighing the value of statements, a value that is "not gauged by the presence of a secret content." *The Archeology of Knowledge* A. M. Sheridan Smith trans. (New York: Pantheon, 1972), p. 120.

3. Michel Foucault, "Nietzsche, Genealogy, History," in Donald F. Bouchard ed. *Language, Counter-Memory, Practice*, Donald F. Bouchard and Sherry Simon trans. (Ithaca: Cornell University Press, 1977), p. 139.

4. Ibid., p. 148.

5. Michel Foucault, "The Order of Discourse," in Michael J. Shapiro ed. *Language and Politics* (New York: NYU Press, 1984), p. 127.

6. Michel Foucault, *Politics, Philosophy, Culture: Interviews and Other Writings 1977–1984*. Lawrence D. Kritzman ed. (New York: Routledge, 1988), p. 156.

7. Orvar Lofgren, "Our Friends in Nature: Class and Animal Symbolism," *Ethnos* 50 III–IV (1985), p. 207.

8. Ibid., p. 208.
9. Ibid., p. 210.
10. Ibid.
11. Ibid.
12. Henri Lefebvre, "Reflections on the Politics of Space," *Antipode* 8 (May, 1976), p. 31.
13. Ibid.
14. Arthur Miller, *Timebends: A Life* (New York, Harper & Row, 1987), p. 175.
15. Ibid., pp. 175–76.
16. Ibid., p. 143.
17. Ibid., p. 144.
18. Ibid., p. 236.
19. This quotation is from Stephen Holmes, "Truths for Philosophers Alone?" *Times Literary Supplement* December 1–7, 1989. Holmes' essay is nominally a review of *Leo Strauss: The Rebirth of Classical Political Rationalism*. Thomas Pangle ed. (Chicago: University of Chicago Press, 1989), p. 1320, but it is, rather, a thoroughgoing analysis of the Straussian position on the separation of Philosophy from everyday life and its encouragement of an esoteric, obscure form of prose. As Holmes puts it, in one of his more ironic statements about Strauss's writing, "He apparently thought he was protecting the community by his indigestible prose."
20. For the various positions Habermas has articulated over the years, see his *Knowledge and Human Interests*. Jeremy J. Shapiro trans., (Boston: Beacon Press, 1971) and his more recent *Theory of Communicative Action* Vol. I. Thomas McCarthy trans. (Boston: Beacon Press, 1984), and *The Philosophical Discourse of Modernity*. Frederick Lawrence trans. (Cambridge: MIT Press, 1987).
21. This position is articulated in *The Philosophical Discourse of Modernity*.
22. Pierre Bourdieu, *In Other Words*, Matthew Adamson trans. (Oxford: Polity, 1990), p. 15.
23. This part of Habermas's argument can be found in *The Philosophical Discourse of Modernity*, p. 299ff.
24. For Jacques Derrida's critique of this view that a speaker is wholly present to the meaning of an utterance see, for example, "Signature event context," *Glyph* 1 (1977), 172–197.
25. Stanley Elkin, *The Magic Kingdom* (New York: E.P. Dutton, 1985), p. 66.
26. Ibid.
27. Foucault, "Nietzsche, Genealogy, History," p. 155.
28. Michael J. Shapiro, *Language and Political Understanding: The Politics of Discursive Practices* (New Haven: Yale University Press, 1981), p. 186.
29. Michel Foucault, "Governmentality," *Ideology and Consciousness*, No. 5 (1979), p. 17.
30. Michel Foucault, "Of Other Spaces," Jay Miscowiec trans. *Diacritics* (Spring, 1986), p. 23.
31. See A. J. Gurevitch, *Categories of Medieval Culture* G. L. Campbell trans. (London: Routledge and Kegan Paul, 1985), p. 302.
32. See Donald Lowe, *History of Bourgeois Perception* (Chicago: University of Chicago Press, 1982), p63 ff., for an elaboration of this point.

33. Adam Smith, *The Wealth of Nations.* Vols. I and II. ed. W.B. Todd (Oxford: The Clarendon Press, 1976).
34. Ibid.
35. Foucault, "Governmentality," p. 11.
36. Ibid., p. 17.
37. These distinctions between heterodox positions versus belonging to an unstated doxa belong to Pierre Bourdieu, *Outline of a Theory of Practice.* trans. Richard Nice (Cambridge: Cambridge University Press, 1977), p. 168.
38. Foucault, "Governmentality," p. 11.
39. Ibid., p. 21.
40. Michel Foucault,"War in the Filagree of Peace," *Oxford Literary Review* 4 (Autumn, 1979), pp. 17–18.
41. Maurice Blanchot, *The Space of Literature.* Ann Smock trans. (Lincoln: University of Nebraska Press, 1982), p. 79.
42. Ibid., p. 3.
43. See fn. #4.
44. Nietzsche, *Human all too Human,* # I. 719.
45. Foucault, "Of Other Spaces," p. 27.

12

Representation and the Silences of Politics

Anne Norton

This paper begins to map aspects of the complex economy of words and images, speaking and writing, speaking and silence, that make up—in part—the constitution of politics in linguistic practice. Our practices within this economy, and our understandings of it, are framed by the cultural construction of the practices of speaking and writing. Not only persons, things and events, but practices as well may become symbolic. Speaking and writing are two such practices. Constituted in political theory and popular culture, these practices are cultural constructions that comprehend a range of political meanings. These meanings inform the practices of politics; they provide the structures that determine strategies within a given polity.

Words and Images

Mythic constructions of writing and speech, the practices of conversation, debate, oratory, legislation, legal opinions, books, articles, and reports meet in a common privileging of the word. There is resistance in politics and the academy to the examination of audible, visible, legible signs other than the word.

Images, as has long been recognized, may enable one to say what one lacks words for, and to speak with greater elegance and intensity. In the present polity of the United States, the image has another use. Because the image does not speak in words, it is not to be spoken of. This tacit agreement, this consensual silence, permits people to say in images not only what they could not, but what they would not, say in words.

Consider the employment of the image of Willie Horton in the 1988 presidential campaign of George Bush. Bush would not say "The face of violent, sexual criminality is black." He would not appeal directly, in speech or in writing, to white fears of blacks. Statements of this sort would be immediately challenged, met with reproaches and public outrage, perhaps by Bush himself with private shame. Yet Bush could, and did, make such statements and appeals without reproach and challenge, outrage and refutation, by speaking without words.

The image derives its power from its economy. Concentrated in each image is a dense sediment of reference. Americans who saw the photograph of Willie Horton knew little of the man, yet they read much in the image. They learned, if they listened, that he was a murderer and a sex criminal. Whether they listened or not, they read the text imposed on the silent face. They saw a black man's face, marked by the photographic conventions of the mugshot as a criminal. The photographic image, framed in the context of criminality, called up two centuries of racist reference and reiterated the identification of black men with violence and sexuality.

Where stereotypes are well-established, and the recollected cultural constructions have a long history, a mere gesture—a shuffle or a roll of the eyes—may be enough to call up an entire lexicon of subordination. Perhaps the most striking instance of this is the image of the woman. There is no visible part of the woman's body that has not been made a sign of her subjection. Any picture of a woman, any of a plethora of feminine gestures, citation of any of the numberless portrayals of women in the patriarchal lexicon, carries this dense text of subjecting references with it. Contemporary controversies over the representation of women's bodies—in advertising, in pornography, in anti-abortionists' display of the contents of their wombs—alternately challenge and reiterate the meanings inscribed upon the bodies of women. The debate over the woman's body is the debate over a site of authority.

The image is characteristically conservative in its referential density. It derives its evocative power from the presence of an already established lexicon of image and gestures. The historicity and referential density of the image gives credence to Roland Barthes's initially implausible and apparently partisan contention that mythology is the province of the right.[1] Certainly Barthes's denial of a mythology of the left, with its implicit construction of an unmediated materiality, is implausible. There is, as Eric Hobsbawm has noted, the mythology of banditry, with its subversive discourse on property.[2] There is the mythic Harlem of Langston Hughes, the folk mythology of John Henry, the populist mythology of Vachel Lindsay's poetry, and the persistent populist distrust (one hears a lot of it in Texas) of big business and the power of the rich. The dense fabric of culture with its contradictions, alternatives, variants, affirmations and resistances has a place for a mythology of the left, but that place remains on the margins, in the interstices. The dissidents can—and have—appropriated aspects of the dominant culture to argue, mythically, for its subversion, yet they are hampered in such arguments by the inseparability of these myths from a history and a mythic frame that entails the reaffirmation of their marginality.[3]

Those whom history has advantaged are served by it on several planes. Theyced in their status and possessions, in the conscious exercise of institutional power, and the unconscious enjoyment of a mythic authority. History imbeds acknowledgement of their power in the mythic as well as the institutional structures that govern the subaltern. Literary and imaginary artifacts, like their material and institutional counterparts, bear the marks of their systems of origin. The inequalities that are inscribed in their genealogies inform their use.

The Silence of the Image

The economy of speech and silence in the employment of the image gives it a perverse ambivalence. It is "not only its power but its lack of power that matters."[4] The image speaks, it conveys meaning, yet it lacks a voice. "Statues and dioramas do not move, nor do they scream or whimper."[5] They cannot convey to us the fullness of the experience, the sentiments, the will they represent. The image of Willie Horton speaks stridently to us, but it does not speak, in any sense, for itself. The Barbie doll, the face or lips or hands of a woman pictured in an advertisement or a piece of pornography, speak the texts that have been written upon those bodies. They speak of women, not for them. Women are silent in them.

Yet these images, in their silences, their partiality, convey not only something less but something more. The "inherent inadequacy of the image," its separation from that which is represented, joins the image to others: other images, other people, other contexts, other meanings, other discourses.[6] The partiality of the image is (as the word has it) also its superfluity. The act of representation invests the image with surplus value, if you will; it is its supplement.[7] What is lost is the voice of the represented. What is added are the texts of authority.

It is this economy of meaning that persuades me to refuse Baudrillard's term "simulacrum." These representations are not, as Baudrillard's description of the simulacrum suggests, divested of meaning, unconnected to history. They are continually invested with it. Nor are these representations readily emptied of the meanings they convey. It is difficult indeed to detach the racist meaning from the image of Willie Horton.[8] These images are constantly transformed, as all signs are, but not with the ubiquitous rapidity Baudrillard ascribes to them. On the contrary, it is the persistence of racist meanings in the image when other discursive systems have been transformed that gives the imagery of racism its strategic importance. It is this property which enables people to speak silently, legibly, persistently, for systems of subordination they nominally denounce. Baudrillard's account of the simulacra cannot accommodate this ambivalent economy of speaking and silence, or the political strategies it structures.

The inscription of history upon the image gives a distinctive asymmetry to the imaginary strategies available to the powerful and the subaltern. When the powerful employ images of their own power, these images speak both of and for them; they recall a history of past and present power. Images of the subaltern employed by the powerful recall a converse history. Such images speak of the powerless, but not for them. The asymmetry is still more striking when the subaltern serve as author. Images of the powerful produced by the subaltern continue to affirm the entitlement of the powerful to power. History invests the images with remembered cruelties and excesses perhaps, but also with remembered power and remembered praise. Images of the subaltern invoked by the subaltern will, conversely, protest against any power they claim. They will recall silently, persistently, a history of slights, powerlessness and degradation. History thus tends to deny authority—literary and political—to those who have not had it, and to secure it most tenaciously in the hands of those who have held it longest.

This delineation of the economy of speaking and silence, of authority and subjection, in the language of images might seem to recommend that the subaltern reject imagery altogether. This is, of course, as impossible as any other rejection of language. The subaltern will be spoken of—and will speak—in images whether they wish to or not. The recollection of history in the image ensures, moreover, that they will also speak silently and unwillingly for their continued subjection. Such speech need not, however, be uncontested. A critical language, directed at the language of the image, is necessary for the self-determination of the subaltern and any approach to political equity.

Silence About the Image

The conventions of political discourse have opened writing to dialogue. Written words are challenged, debated, opposed, supported, expanded, responded to as if they were speech. They are read, they are critiqued.

We read the image, but we do not critique it; no response, in words or images, comes back to challenge or oppose it. The image remains a single message, outside debate. Consequently, we have constructed the image as a monologue. The absence of a debate of the image takes two forms. The first maintains that there is the absence of conversation, of debate, in images. The images that figure in political discourse speak only indirectly to one another. Though on a daily basis we employ visual images as forms of communication, the possibility that these forms might be employed, like words, in response to one another—that one might propose alternatives, amend or deny assertions, contradict or refute statements made in the language of images—seems arcane and improbable.

This argument is absurd. Each of us in dressing everyday, for example, manipulates a complex system of signs conveying information on class, gender, occupation, politics. We read these signs in the clothing of others. We can affirm, challenge, or mock these.[9] We possess, therefore, the skill to read and to critique messages carried in visual images. We perform these acts daily, in activities we disingenuously mark as apolitical. We fashion images to carry messages in return. We have the capacity to speak of—and through—signs other than the written and the spoken word.

These capacities are not only employed, but explicitly acknowledged in those spheres and acts we do mark as political. The Supreme Court has acknowledged the wearing as well as the burning of the flag as instances of political speech. The Executive and the Legislature have likewise acknowledged the significance of such acts. Much of contemporary debate over the freedoms of speech and the press has concerned not the written or spoken word, but images: nativity displays at City Hall and in the public schools; the images of women in pornography.

Speech in images, a visual discourse, is thus commonplace in popular culture and in institutional politics. It has been recognized, directly and obliquely, in politics and the academy. Yet both of these venues have been marked by a persistent reluctance to speak of the image. The Willie Horton ad became notorious because the message it conveyed through the visual image was noticed and critiqued. Yet debate over the image, the visual content of the advertisement, was excluded by the common consent of both parties from the public debates of the campaign. Indeed, Dukakis took considerable care to distance himself from charges that the ad was racist.

Political scientists have also been reluctant to recognize language in forms other than the word. While politicians employ it, albeit clumsily, in the staging of appearances and the production of advertising, political scientists commonly refused to use visual discourse consciously or systematically in their work. Perhaps more importantly, the discipline also consistently discouraged the systematic examination of the use of images by others. When political discourse took place in visual images, it made itself invulnerable to critical examination and political analysis. Possession of the faculties necessary to interpret images, and the exercise of these faculties in everyday life, suggest that the absence of a visual discourse and a debate over visual images in politics is the consequence not of lack alone, but of refusal.

It is a refusal with important strategic consequences. Where politics is conducted in words, there are contesting statements, challenges and refutations. The language of the image, inclined by its referential density to speak for the status quo it recalls, goes uncontested.

The Silent Speech of Structure

Structures speak as silently and persistently as the image. A particularly telling instance of the silent and strategic speech of structure can be found in the conventions affording the party which does not control the executive branch a response to the State of the Union Address. As we listen to these speeches, we read the attendant text, written in the structures that frame their presentation. There the authority of the executive and the subordination of the legislature are writ large.

The president's address is presented from a podium on the floor of Congress to an audience of the powerful. The speech is framed by pageantry and applause. The reply is presented off the floor, by a single individual, without pageantry, without applause, without an evident audience. Written in these arrangements is a denigration of the reply. The president speaks as president, the representative of the nation. The one who gives the reply speaks as the representative of a party. The president speaks to the powerful; the one who replies is not heard by them. This suggests that those who watch the reply on television are also denigrated by it, for they are marked by the recurrent dichotomies of the structure as powerless.

The legislature is silenced in this arrangement. The Congress has to hear the president, while the president does not have to hear the representative of the Congress. The party out of office is given a response, but the Congress is not. As Jeffrey Tulis has observed, this arrangement constructs the State of the Union Address as a partisan speech.[10] It also serves to construct Congress as a silent, receptive institution, subordinate to the executive, instructed by him.

When the Congress and the presidency are held by different parties, the message of deference is underlined. While Congress has to hear the president, the president does not have to hear either Congress, speaking in its own voice, or the representative of the majority party. Most importantly, the arrangements affirm the primacy of executive authority. The president gives the speech; others respond to it. The president establishes the terms and topics of debate. The spectacle of the address foregrounds the president and, as Jefferson observed, presents a monarchical text independent of the literary content of the address.[11]

Strategic Speech, Strategic Silences

Some speak silently in structures; others, made to speak within them, may find themselves silenced.

Liberal theories and therapies commonly turn on the neutrality of language. Negotiation is recommended as if all were rendered equal in speech, as if it were an instrument that would serve any hand.[12] Yet those nominally neutral words are inscribed with diverse systems of domination.[13] Hierarchies of class and race, of gender and regional difference, are written into language. Often, they can be heard in speech. Differences of accent and dialect, of idiom and word choice, mark the speaker. Even if one were to speak from behind a veil these would inscribe identity. They will inscribe inequality and impute advantage and disadvantage as well.

Where dialogue reiterates already established identities and hierarchies, equality may be better served by silence. Where speech inscribes inferiority, silence may refute it. Yet the refusal of speech will inevitably be read not as the refusal of subordination, but as a refusal of equality. The mythic construction of speech—as the expression of a self secured from politics in the confines of an open mind and a closed body—reiterates the identification of speech with freedom and equality.

Dialogue, where speech is so constructed, becomes difficult if not impossible to refuse. Refusal is read as the denial of a voice to another, as the denial of another's rights. The demand for dialogue is often, however, coercive in itself. The obligation to participate imposes an obligatory community where none may be desired, giving the lie to the tolerance of difference. Coerced participation in dialogue, coerced speech, is presented as an invitation to self-expression and equality, yet those who are brought into these against their will have already been denied one aspect of their self-determination. They enter subordinate. Those whose inequality is written into language will find themselves doubly subordinated in the process, as well as in their concession to the dialogue. They will be at a disadvantage in this medium, and experience this putative freedom as subjection.

The construction of dialogue as obligatory gives strategic advantage to the majority and the dominant culture, which is thereby enabled to intrude itself into every space. Instances of this can be found in the most quotidian dimensions of popular culture and political discourse. The column "Hers" in the magazine section of the Sunday *New York Times* alternates with "About Men" in an affirmation of equality in symmetry that denies the preference given to men, male activities, and male interests in the remainder of the paper. Whites excluded from black student groups or meetings who charge "reverse discrimination" make the same strategic assumption of symmetry, denying the exclusion of blacks and African-American culture in the dominant culture. The exclusion of whites from African-American groups and activities does not deny them a voice. They are given a voice in every medium, and virtually every venue. Their inclusion, however, denies expression to an African-American voice, which cannot be heard elsewhere.

Context is critical to the economy of expression in another respect as well. The expression of views or the assumption of identities unacceptable to the dominant culture will entail no costs. They may indeed bring advantage with them, as those in positions of power are able to identify individuals possessing traits which certain institutional procedures would prevent them from observing. Freedom of expression is not, however, free for the subaltern or the dissident. The experiences of dissent and agreement in a room where one view is dominant, in a state where people disappear, are likely to differ finally and decisively.[14] In liberal regimes, the woman who makes public her abortion, the man who announces that he's gay, will pay—often heavily, in private as well as public life—for their expressions. So widely recognized (and presumably heavy) are these costs that established scholars will openly cite fears of being marginalized within the discipline as a defense for their erasure of women.

Demands for negotiation may be similarly deceptive. As participation in dialogue may effectively deny to the subaltern the full expression that speech purportedly secures to all, so demands for negotiation may make possible strategies of covert repression. Recourse to negotiation may silence mass movements that speak in action rather than in words. Actions, and the collective speech of signs and chants, songs and gestures, are replaced with a conversation between nominally representative individuals. The replacement of collective action—often disordered, subject to continual changes in organization and tactics—with conventionally governed, highly-structured negotiations deprives insurrectionary movements of one of their principal strategic advantages: the capacity for surprise. The identification and installation of representatives of the mass movement reifies (where it does not establish) hierarchies, and may deprive aspects of the movement of a voice. It reinforces the liberal construction of politics as between individuals rather than collectives. Finally, and most importantly, replacing collectives with individuals entails acquiescence to the construction of systems of representation as transparent and authoritative.

Speaking and Writing

The representational foundations of the American regime manifest an overt privileging of speech, and a covert economy of speaking and writing, speaking and silence. The canonical documents of the regime are cast, for all their writtenness, as instances of speech. The nation is brought forth (so Lincoln speaks of the text) as speech.[15] The Declaration is made, heard, acclaimed. Then it is signed. The Constitution is written, but the text is cast not as if it were written in the past, but as if it were spoken in the present.[16]

The privileging of speech follows from the cultural construction of that act. Speech, as we have been given to understand it, effects and signifies the individual independence and communicative entry into public life central to liberalism. The speech comes directly from the mouth of the speaker.[17] It is immediate; no time, no person, intervenes. Speech is said to be the utterance of an internal will, a will otherwise unknown. It is through this expression of an interior, private will that the individual enters into relations with others. Liberalism, as Derrida observed, sees itself fulfilled in "the self-presence of its speech."

Writing, on the other hand, is cast in theory and practice, in popular culture and the academy, as the medium of external domination. Weber identified writing with the bureaucracy, bureaucracy with the Iron Cage. The phrases he used to contrast the dictates of structure with the disruptive power of charismatic moments reiterated this dichotomy: "It is written . . . but I say unto you." Scripture, for Weber as for Calvin, sets in motion a concatenation of determinations that end in a polity where self-determination is precluded, where all selves are indeed always—and already—determined. Writing is experienced by most people as authority imposed upon them; in religion, in education, in law. They rarely act as authors—or with authority—themselves. Quotidian condemnations of "red tape" and the bureaucracy, of restrictions and regulations, express the experience of these conditions.

Liberalism, for all its privileging of speech, depends on writing as well. Rousseau's democracy fulfills itself in the people assembled: the present citizenry, speaking its mind.[18] Yet behind the speech of the citizenry is the writing of the Legislator. For all its valorized dependence on utterance, on expression in the word, liberalism depends on strategic silences. Locke's construction of consent in practice turns upon a reading of silence. It is in the silence of the people that one reads their consent to the regime.

Reading the Written in Speech

In this context, the economy of the word seems to alternately hold out and withdraw a promise. The founding of the political order in speech promises self-determination and the legitimation of the regime through the immediacy of spoken consent. This speech, the realm of freedom, is replaced by writing—the instrument of rule, the order of authority. Yet writing holds out the hope of reproducing the freedoms promised by speech. The forms of the American regime argue for the presence of consent, of self-determination, despite the rigors of political order, in the preservation of speech in writing.

Writing holds out promises as well. The lie of writing enables constitutional regimes to construct themselves in an ideal, scriptural form that transcends past or present defects.[19] In his speech at the Lincoln Memorial, Martin Luther King, Jr. referred to the Constitution as a promissory note which had yet to be redeemed. In this contemporary instance of what Sacvan Bercovitch termed "the American jeremiad," speech recalled the promises of writing, restoring them to an authoritative place in contemporary political debates. Here too, however, it is speech which serves to realize the promise of self-determination.

This promise is challenged by the reading of writing in speech. Where speech is constructed as the medium of self-determination, writing as the medium of an imposed authority, the recognition of speech as written threatens to erase the possibility of self-determination entirely. The spectre of the Iron Cage haunts liberals who read the texts of Gadamer, Foucault, Canetti, Ricoeur and Derrida.[20]

When these writers read writing in speech, they raise the possibility that "the words speak for themselves" in a sense quite different from the liberal understanding of speech. The transparency of meaning and intention, the coincidence of utterance and will that the phrase evokes, is answered by an echo, reflecting and opposing it. The words speak not for the speaker but for themselves. They have authority over the one who utters them. One who experiences, desires, feels pain, and then casts these—in thought or utterance—into words casts an inchoate sensation into an already defined form. It is through these words that the sensation is understood. The words author not only our utterances of ourselves, but our interior understanding of our experience, sentiments, and desires. Writing is present and active, therefore, not merely in speech but prior to speech, in thought. Rather than merely supplying the self with a means of utterance, words mediate the self's understanding of itself. They are constitutive of private, as well as public, identity. As thought is cast into words and uttered in speech, the already alienated sentiments of the speaking subject are further removed. As these words are heard by others, they escape the speaker's authority. They will be invested with meaning and effects foreign to the speaker's intention. They become part of a public discourse in which he is bound with others. If the subject writes, or these spoken words are recorded (represented) in writing, they are alienated not only from the speaker but from those who heard them spoken—who, in hearing them, invested them with meaning and effects. They are alienated from the context in which they were spoken. They are made to transcend their time and place. Translation and interpretation—by readers, ethnographers, political analysts—impel successive moments of alienation and transcendence. At each remove, the speech is alienated from the speaker. At each remove, the speaker is bound within a larger communicative community. At each remove, the speech, acquiring additional meaning and effects, extends its own significance and authority, and the significance and authority of the speaker. Power and subjection, community and alienation, are inextricably linked within this process, for each is the condition of the other. The ambivalence of this process is lost in the construction of speaking as freedom, writing as domination. Yet despite the conspicuous interplay of speaking and writing in the mythology of American constitution, acceptance of this rigid dichotomy and a determined inattention to the linguistic turn in philosophy continue to dominate liberal theory.[21]

Liberal theorists fear seeing the written in speech. If one sees speech as written, one sees the text as veil.[22] Meaning and will lose the shared transparency they were ascribed. If we cannot see clearly through the words to the will, consent is compromised. If words speak not simply for the speaker but for themselves, if our sentiments are written for us—in us—before we speak, then the words we hear are not simply the speech of the subject, but the speech of subjection.

In reading the silent texts of speech we discover the silences of the speaker. Those who initially appeared as the authors of their words now reveal themselves as authored by them: constituted in language. The words which once appeared as the means for a singular and pristine interiority to impose itself on the external, political world now reveal themselves as the medium through which the external world imposes itself—before speech, before thought—on those who live in language.[23]

Liberals—and romantic existentialists—identified self-expression and self-discovery with liberation. Their enterprise was predicated on the notion of an autonomous self, an independent will, which the individual could discover within. Freud's writings revealed the impossibility of such an enterprise. The self was necessarily constituted as such in a cultural framework; it was dependent upon, and followed from, a political order.[24] Nevertheless, successful efforts to assimilate psychology to the demands of liberalism identified the ego with the self and mandated the restraint of passion (now, the id) and the avoidance of external tyranny (now, the superego) in a long-familiar economy. Psychoanalysis became "the talking cure," and Freud another partisan of the discovery of the self and the reconciliation of the world through speech.

Freud could be assimilated, bowdlerized. Lacan was more difficult. The referential and structural density of Lacan's elegant prose ensured that it would avoid the dangers of too facile a reading. Lacan reaffirmed the priority of the political order. In this he followed Nietzsche's recognition that "we are all philologists now," conscious of ourselves as being in language. The self at the core of the self, the will, was neither autonomous nor singular. It lacked integrity, it lacked boundaries.[25] It was created under the authority of language.

In speaking of words, we come to speak of that which speaks silently in speech. Reading what is written in speech reveals covert and unacknowledged, unvoiced, structures of governance and constitution. Hegel ascribed determinative power to those constitutive categories in which we find ourselves. Prior to consciousness, they were nevertheless the occasion for it; prior to the self, they were nevertheless the means for its realization. Gadamer's account of our being in language likewise affirms the value of established categories: the virtue, in his words, of prejudice. Althusser's account of hailing, or "interpellation," on the other hand, is concerned entirely with the coercive effects of these constructions. Foucault's revelatory readings of those cultural constructions we took to be most natural—reason, sexuality, and the shape of knowledge—are likewise recognitions of this silent coercion.

Those who recognized, with Hegel and Gadamer, Nietzsche and Lacan, our deep indebtedness to established categories and conditions saw the enterprise of self-determination and self-discovery as simultaneously individual and collective, uniting public and private constitution in the recognition of a common genealogy. Those who looked, like Althusser and Foucault, for deliverance from coercive structures found them in the very constitution of the self. The recognition of subjection written into the speaking subject recasts, indeed replaces, the liberal struggle for liberation. The recognition of the self, no longer an apolitical and ahistorical enterprise, becomes an activity of political comprehension. For those who would remake themselves, the task becomes, in Foucault's words, not to discover, but to refuse who we are.

Reading the silent texts of speech entailed a revision of the assumption of the pristine interiority of the will on which liberalism was based. It revealed the presence of domination within the self, and the subjection of the will to language. The recognition of the subjection of all people to language brought with it notice of the presence of an aspect of being outside language. It is here, of course, that words fail. The exploration of such a subject can merely be alluded to in the confines of this paper. It remains inarticulate in psychoanalysis.

Silence about being outside of language, if such there is, is necessary and inescapable. Silence about being in language, on the contrary, is silence of our own volition. The silence of the will and experience of the subjected in speech is preserved by the silence about the authority of language. The recognition that the political order inscribes itself upon our thoughts before we speak, even before we think—that in speech we are always, already, part of the political order—extends the reach of political thought, and reveals new fields of political action and analysis. The repeated dismissal of those who recognized the constitutive power of language as apolitical is therefore inappropriate, if not disingenuous.[26] It is a silence with strategic implications.

Silence concerning the authority of language over the constitution of the self, the realization and expression of the will, permits liberal regimes to maintain the myth of the word, particularly the spoken word, as a neutral instrument for the utterance and realization of the individual will. It enables liberal regimes to maintain established hierarchies by predicating the achievement of equality and the establishment and maintenance of cultural difference on involvement in practices that obstruct or preclude these ends.

Those who read the silent texts of speech recognized not consent, but a more subtle coercion. Reading these texts enabled them to speak of that which was silent in speech, and in doing so to begin to speak for those who had been silenced as well. Speaking of the silent texts of speech made it possible to give voice to those formerly denied it. There were those liminal to the nation, whose images signified traits assigned them, who spoke not for themselves but for those who employed them as signs. There were those who saw politics in practices previously identified as apolitical: in popular culture, folklore, high art, religion, sexuality and domestic life. It was the capacity of symbolic politics, of semiotics and poststructuralist analysis to give voice to the silenced that commended these methods to students of race, class, and gender. There were also silenced subjects: the authority of language; the constitutive power of representation; the speech of the image; the determinative power of conceptual and linguistic as well as political and economic structures. These subjects, and with them diverse political strategies already in use, were articulated by those who heard what was said in images, and read what was written in speech.

In "The Meaning of Ethical Neutrality," Weber argued that social scientists should keep silent their political partisanship. In view of the fact that certain value-questions "which are of decisive political significance are permanently banned from university discussion, it seems to me to be only in accord with the dignity of a representative of science to be silent as well about such value-problems as he is allowed to treat."[27] Speech, Weber recognized, served established powers and conventions. Silence serves these as well. The refusal, in politics and the academy, to speak of that which speaks silently in speech, wordlessly in the image, runs counter to the vocations, coupled in our discipline, of politics and science. Those who would not keep silence have kept instead to their vocations. In doing so they give to the discipline a new authority.

Notes

1. Roland Barthes, *Mythologies* (New York: Farrar, Strauss, Giroux, 1972).
2. Eric Hobsbawm, *Bandits* (New York: Pantheon 1969).
3. Maurice Agulhon, in *Marianne Into Combat: Republican Imagery and Symbolism in France* (Cambridge: Cambridge University Press, 1981), provides some interesting instances of the power of images and forms to retain conservative associations even after their appropriation by revolutionaries. Agulhon's examples argue that French revolutionary republicans were undermined by their adoption of religious forms and imagery. These forms and images, though made to speak for the secular, were inscribed with religious references. They silently recalled, and covertly maintained, the authority of the Church.

4. E. H. Gombrich, "The Edge of Delusion," a review of David Freedberg's *The Power of Images*, *New York Review of Books*, February 15, 1990, p. 6.

5. Gombrich, p. 6.

6. On separation see Jacques Lacan, *Ecrits* (New York: W.W. Norton, 1977) and Norton, *Reflections on Political Identity* (Baltimore, Md.: Johns Hopkins University Press, 1988).

7. Jacques Derrida, *Of Grammatology*, trans. Gayatri Chakravorty Spivak, (Baltimore, Md.: Johns Hopkins University Press, 1976), p. 145.

8. Doubly difficult. It is difficult, given the terms of debate we presently employ—the rules of the game—to detach that message analytically and show it for what it is. It is no less difficult to divest that image of that meaning, to use it in a way which will not convey the racist constructions attached to it.

9. Consider traditional feminine dress. Women who adopted the dress of men—or like Amelia Bloomer, modified it—challenged the limits written in dress. Women, like Madonna, and other women who exaggerated elements of traditional feminine dress, mocked the traditional identities it had once affirmed.

10. As he also observes, this was not always the case. The first State of the Union Address was debated for a week after its delivery and Congress delivered a reply to the executive. See Jeffrey K. Tulis, *The Rhetorical Presidency* (Princeton, N.J.: Princeton University Press, 1987), pp. 55–59. Jefferson's attentiveness to the monarchical text written in the spectacle of Presidential speeches is particularly noteworthy.

11. Tulis, pp. 55–59.

12. For examples of such assumptions see Bruce Ackerman, *Social Justice and the Liberal State* (New Haven, Conn.: Yale University Press, 1980).

13. A variety of inscriptive strategies have been articulated by scholars of race and gender. Denigration has been deconstructed etymologically. The erasure of women has been read in mankind, and the (nominally ungendered) "he."

14. Aspects and instances of this discrepant silencing have been examined by the practitioners of quite diverse methods. Elizabeth Noelle-Neumann's *Spiral of Silence* (Chicago: University of Chicago Press, 1984) and Michel Foucault's account of the regulation of sexuality through the selective liberation of speech and writing about sexual practice are exemplary. Foucault, however, understands the theoretical implications of this effect and articulates its constitutive power in the empirical realm with a force and precision that Noelle-Neumann's method does not permit her to achieve.

15. In the Gettysburg Address. "Fourscore and seven years ago, our fathers brought forth upon this continent a new nation . . ."

16. In the Preamble, "We the People of the United States of America . . . do ordain and establish this Constitution." The recognition of the ambivalent textuality of the Constitution has produced a diverse and illuminating literature in public law and constitutional studies. Among those accounts that speak to the point I raise here are William Harris, "Bonding Word and Polity," *American Political Science Review*, Winter 1982; and my article "Transubstantiation: the Dialectic of Constitutional Authority," *University of Chicago Law Review*, Spring 1988. Akhil Reed Amar questions the textuality of the Constitution from another perspective in "Our Forgotten

Constitution," *Yale Law Review*, December 1987. Sotirios Barber and Sanford Levinson have written widely and well on this and related questions.

17. The evident embodiment of speech may be the decisive element in establishing its primacy in liberalism. Self-preservation for all liberals, assembly for Rousseau, the establishment of original property and the possession of rights for Locke, all link liberalism to the privileging of embodiment.

18. Rousseau's works contain an extraordinarily complex and interesting economy of speech and writing. Derrida supplies an account of Rousseau and writing in *Of Grammatology*. Look, too, to Rousseau's analysis of writing in *On the Origin of Languages* (New York: F. Ungar Pub. Co., 1967). In distinguishing the phonetic alphabet from ideograms and hieroglyphics, Rousseau notes its connection to a particular political economy: one of trade and representation. The need to represent the sounds of other languages is said to produce the phonetic alphabet. This alphabet is manifestly deconstructive; it breaks down the representational media of speech for analysis. It also casts speech into writing. The connection between the spoken and the written in ideograms and hieroglyphs is more arbitrary and less intimate than in the phonetic alphabet.

19. Norton, "Transubstantiation."

20. The bulk of these criticisms have been directed toward Derrida and Foucault. This insight into the determinative power of language is not, of course, peculiar to them. An interesting, somewhat eccentric, argument for the priority of writing over—and in—speech can be found in Elias Canetti, *Crowds and Power* (New York: Viking Press, 1962). The argument for the presence of writing in speech is present as well in Ricoeur's excellent essay "The Model of the Text" (in Paul Rabinow and William Sullivan, eds., *Interpretive Social Science: A Reader* (Berkeley: University of California Press, 1979); in Hans Georg Gadamer, *Philosophical Hermeneutics*, trans. David Linge (Berkeley, Ca.: University of California Press, 1976); and in Lacan, *Ecrits*.

21. Richard Flathman is a notable exception, and conscious of himself as such. See *Toward a Theory of Liberalism* (Ithaca, N.Y.: Cornell University Press, 1989).

22. The text may be usefully understood as that "veil of ignorance" that intervenes between the mythic subject of Rawls's account and the world to be made. It appears neutral, yet it imposes features on the subject.

23. Is there anywhere else? Gadamer, for one, thinks not. He has stated explicitly that it is in language that we are, in language that we have our being.

24. See Freud, *Group Psychology and the Analysis of the Ego*, trans. James Strachey (New York: W.W. Norton, 1959), p. 5.

25. It lacked. It was only because of lack that it existed at all.

26. This has been reiterated in academic works and the popular press. The charge, commonly directed at Derrida, Foucault, and Baudrillard, also embraces Nietzsche, whose early recognition of our constitution and consequent admonition "we are all philologists now" instructed hermeneuticists and poststructuralists. He was, those so inclined declare, not a philosopher but a poet.

27. Max Weber, "The Meaning of Ethical Neutrality," in *Methodology of the Social Sciences*, trans. Edward Shils and Henry Finch (New York: The Free Press, 1949), p. 8.

Afterword

Murray Edelman

The papers in this volume resourcefully explore the capacity of language and symbols to create, alter, confuse, and illuminate the worlds we experience. That they are written by distinguished scholars with disparate concerns, on diverse subjects, and with different methodologies makes their convergence on that pivotal theme all the more impressive.

These unusual contributions furnish a strong stimulus to further investigations of the crucial roles language and symbols play in political maneuver. The twentieth century has witnessed an exciting revolution in our understanding of language, but the most searching insights have come from students of philosophy and of linguistics who have rarely drawn upon politics as a source of understanding or examined the political applications of their findings. Those applications are wide-ranging and important, and these essays offer a tantalizing set of perspectives on language and symbolism as themselves paramount forms of political action and as key influences on all other political action as well.

The central focus in such explorations is upon the generation of meaning. A paramount theme of twentieth century language philosophy, including these papers, is the ubiquity of the sources of meaning, which are certainly not limited to written and spoken language. Everything that human beings experience engenders meanings. They are all texts: mothering; professional practices and discourse; movies; public spaces and institutions; ceremonies; the expenditure and acquisition of money; inequalities in benefits and sacrifices; bureaucratic behaviors and processes; what is *not* said, as well as what is said, in election campaigns, zoos—the settings in which actions take place.

The meanings that emanate from these and other human experiences may change with situations as well as with different individuals, and they are often ambiguous. They flow from a potpourri of catalysts of which the principal ingredients are their textual content, their context, and, above all, the knowledge, social position, fears, hopes, and ideologies of the people who experience them. The significance for human beings of their environments and experiences is highly variable, and much of the value of these papers lies in their analyses of the occasions for the variations. The mandate of an election, the fairness of a wage, the social import of a movie, the threat or promise of an administrative regulation change as people's lives do. What individuals know, anticipate, dread, and believe are likely to shift from time to time. These mental processes are themselves shaped by symbols, even while they evoke and influence the symbols. There is frequent flux in the realities the mind creates and therefore in the worlds human beings experience.

In the last analysis, meanings inhere in minds, not in objects or actions. Though they cannot be idiosyncratic if there is to be communication, cooperation, and conflict among human beings, they reflect the variations, as well as the similarities, in social situations and therefore in people's emotional and cognitive behaviors.

It is precisely this psychological flux, this potentiality for re-creating worlds and meanings, that students of symbolism find intriguing; and the more we learn about it, the more mysterious, as well as the more wonderful and enlightening, it becomes. It is one of the great enigmas, but it is also a practical instrument for leading and misleading others, for inciting people to action and for reassuring them into quiescence, for justifying things as they are and for winning support for a changed social order. In short, it is the fundamental agent of politics.

It is also what makes us human. If the world in which we live were really fixed in its constitution and every item and action in it were constant and clear in its meaning, there would be little use for creative minds. The rewards for doing things correctly and the penalties for doing them wrong would soon be learned and remain valid, as animals learn how and where to forage for food. We would live in a Skinnerian world in which only conditioning would be required for survival.

Because realities and meanings vary and are ambiguous, we can be inventive, and art and science become necessary. Works of art show us new perspectives, unrecognized realities, and stimulating possibilities. In re-creating the world, the artist helps us realize our own potentialities and sometimes inhibits them—as the papers in this collection that deal with cinema, writing, symbol creation, myths, and rituals suggest.

Science develops from ambiguity and change in a rather different way. It focuses upon the unknown and helps us learn to know it, but always tentatively and provisionally, so that what scientists think they know at any time will predictably be altered or replaced with something else at later times and in new circumstances—partly because we learn and partly because minds become different instruments as they function in different milieus. In this sense, science is more nearly the history of error than the history of truth, but always error that serves useful functions and will serve them differently in the future. The truths and the errors in these papers constitute an impressive body of knowledge about the place of language and symbolism in politics, and they will generate still more striking truths and errors in the future. This never-ending process is possible only because human beings constantly create and alter their worlds through the symbols these papers analyze.

Symbols similarly change and periodically transform the meanings of social relationships, of engineering achievements, of work and leisure time, and of everything else that distinguishes human beings from other forms of life.

The Focus Upon Politics

The focus in this volume is upon politics, but that is hardly a constriction in scope because everything we encounter has political ramifications. Interpretations of anything that holds people's interest are likely to influence how valued resources are distributed, and are therefore likely to conflict with one another to serve different clienteles.

Negotiation of the meanings of language and other symbols is the paramount political dynamic because it constructs the political scene for officials, elites, victims, and every segment of the public. That scene is primarily a subjective one, shaped by ideologies, by beliefs, knowledge, and fantasies, and by economic interests—all of which determine which aspects of the world are noticed and what they are taken to mean.

It is tempting to reduce that frequently-shifting, often reconstructed phenomenon, negotiated among groups with diverse concerns, to verifiable facts or to a process driven by rational choices. To believe in a social world of objective events and political claims rooted in logic is reassuring. The comfort it offers is doubtless directly proportional to the evidence the news constantly provides that political actions are often illogical and frequently misguided or disastrous. The essays in this volume dwell upon the roles in politics of myth, ritual, and dubious political beliefs and decisions. In exploring the nonrational bases of politics, the authors replace reassurance with honest observation and insightful interpretation.

That approach is bound to carry disturbing implications about our most deeply cherished political institutions, processes, and policies. Dubious and ambiguous language and symbols create authority and also construct rationalizations for courses of action, inequalities, severe deprivations, lavish benefits, and occasional changes in all of these. Those constructions also create social stability because they justify things as they are.

The kinds of research this volume presents unsettle these foundations of the political status quo and so are subversive, a contribution that runs counter to mainstream political science, which too often identifies with power and explains it in ways that justify it.

In my judgment the challenge of these studies to the conventional wisdom, though invaluable, is not their chief contribution. It is even more impressive that in both subtle and explicit ways they explore the integral links of politics to art and literature, to fantasy, to economics, to reason and its abandonment, and to other human activities. Politics no longer appears as one among many interests, but rather as an expression of all that human beings care about, shaped by those concerns and also influencing them in a process that never ends. To read these papers is to realize that we are learning a great deal about just how those elusive links construct a whole social transaction that is, in some important senses at least, systematic, though often not apparent without careful analysis.

These papers persuade me to reassess some of the conclusions in my own work and to abandon some of them, and they will have that provocative effect on many others as well. They also remind me that serious inquiry is itself a potent form of political action.

For these reasons and for some personal ones as well I am profoundly grateful to the contributors, to the scholars who served as commentators and critics of these studies, and especially to Richard Merelman, who organized and edited the project.

About the Contributors

Robert R. Alford is Distinguished Professor of Sociology at the Graduate Center of the City University of New York. He is coauthor (with Roger Friedland) of *Powers of Theory: Capitalism, the State and Democracy* (1985), and author of *Health Care Politics: Ideological and Interest Group Barriers to Reform* (1975), *Bureaucracy and Participation: Political Cultures in Four Wisconsin Cities* (1969) and *Party and Society* (1963). His research interests include comparative politics and political economy, social theory, and the sociology of culture.

Lance Bennett teaches political science at the University of Washington, and is the author of numerous books and articles on public opinion, the news media and political communication. His recent works include *News: The Politics of Illusion* (2nd ed. Longman, 1988) and *The Governing Crisis: Media, Money and Marketing in American Elections* (St. Martin's, 1992).

Kristin Bumiller is Assistant Professor of Political Science and Women and Gender Studies at Amherst College. Her publications include *The Civil Rights Society: The Social Construction of Victims* (1988). She teaches in the areas of feminist theory, sexuality and violence.

Murray Edelman is Professor Emeritus of Political Science at the University of Wisconsin–Madison. He has published a considerable number of books and articles on political language and symbolism, including *The Symbolic Uses of Politics* (1964) and *Constructing the Political Spectacle* (1988).

Martha Albertson Fineman is the Maurice T. Moore Professor of Law at Columbia University in the City of New York. She is a 1975 graduate of the University of Chicago Law School. In 1984 she developed the Feminism and Legal Theory Project at the University of Wisconsin Law School. The project is now located at Columbia Law School and is devoted to fostering interdisciplinary feminist work on law and legal institutions. Professor Fineman is co-editor and contributor for *At the Boundaries of Law: Feminism and Legal Theory*, (Routledge Chapman and Hall, 1990), and author of *The Illusion of Equality: The Rhetoric and Reality of Divorce Reform*, (University of Chicago Press, 1991).

Benjamin Ginsberg is the David Bernstein Professor of Political Science at the Johns Hopkins University and Director of the Johns Hopkins Center for the Study of American Politics. He is the author of a number of books, including *Politics by Other Means*, *The Captive Public*, and *The Consequences* *of Consent*. His most recent book, *The Fatal Embrace: Jews and the State*, is being published by the University of Chicago Press later this year.

Marjorie Randon Hershey is Professor of Political Science at Indiana University specializing in political parties, interest groups, and the media. She is the author of two books on political campaigns and a number of articles in journals including the *American Journal of Political Science*, the *Journal of Politics*, and the *Public Opinion Quarterly*.

Michael Lipsky has written many books and articles on the intersection of politics and public policy, including *Protest in City Politics* (1970), *Commission Politics: The Processing of Racial Crisis in America* (with David J. Olson) (1977), *Street Level Bureaucracy* (1980), and a forthcoming volume on nonprofit organizations, government and the welfare state, written in collaboration with Steven Rathgeb Smith. He is at present on leave from his position as Professor of Political Science at M.I.T. to work for the Ford Foundation in New York.

Richard M. Merelman is Professor of Political Science at the University of Wisconsin, Madison. His principal interest in recent years has been culture and politics in industrialized societies. He published *Partial Visions: Culture and Politics in Britain, Canada, and the United States* in 1991 (University of Wisconsin Press). He is currently engaged in a study of race and cultural politics in the United States.

Anne Norton is Professor of Political Science, University of Texas at Austin. She is author of *Alternative Americas: A Reading of Antebellum Political Culture* (1986) and *Reflections on Political Identity* (1988).

David J. Olson is Professor of Political Science at the University of Washington. He is the author of numerous articles on state and local politics and several books. His most recent research has focused on public enterprise and his articles on subnational politics have appeared as chapters in edited volumes and in journals on state and city politics.

James Scott teaches political science at Yale University and is the author of *Domination and the Arts of Resistance* (1991), *Weapons of the Weak* (1985), and *The Moral Economy of the Peasant* (1976). He is currently trying to understand the relation between the modern state and people who "move around" (e.g. gypsies, hill peoples in Southeast Asia, Berbers, Bedouin, vagrants, pastoralists). He also raises sheep.

Michael J. Shapiro is Professor of Political Science at the University of Hawaii. His publications include the edited volume *Language and Politics* (1984); *Language and Political Understanding: The Politics of Discursive Practices* (1981); *International/Intertextual Relations: Postmodern Readings of World Politics* (1989, edited with James Der Derian); *The Politics of Representation* (1988); and *Reading the Postmodern Polity* (1992).

About the Book

From the "telerhetoric" of 30-second "sound bites" that deliver campaign slogans to the legal rhetoric that shapes our notions of social roles and values, or the official rhetoric of bureaucracies that legitimizes social problems, our perceptions of political reality are determined by the language and symbolism of the institutions of our culture. In the words of Murray Edelman, we view politics as "a series of pictures in the mind, placed there by television news, newspapers, magazines, and discussions."

In *Language, Symbolism, and Politics*, leading political scientists, lawyers, and philosophers explore some of the multiple roles that symbolism and language play in political life. Edelman's ideas inspire discussions of political organization, political symbolism, elections, public policy, political culture, and political philosophy. But these essays also extend Edelman's work to encompass contemporary efforts in structuralism, deconstruction, textual analysis, post-structuralism, critical theory, and neo-Marxism. That so many important political topics can be tied together with the help of Edelman's analysis of language and symbolism is not only a tribute to his work but also ample testimony to the central place of language and symbolism in politics.